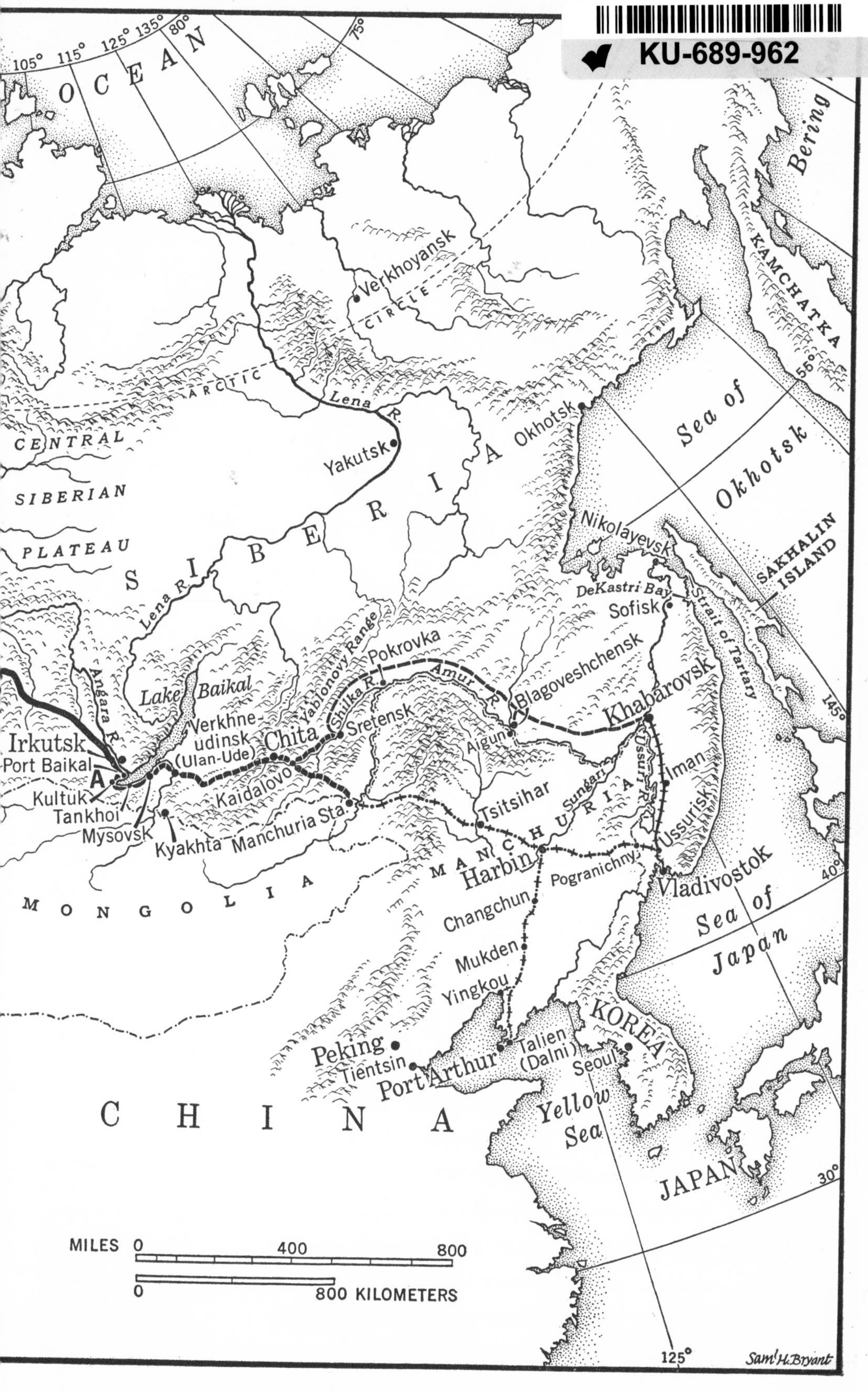
105°
115°
125°
135°
80°
75°
OCEAN
Bering
KAMCHATKA
Verkhoyansk
ARCTIC CIRCLE
55°
Lena R.
Sea of Okhotsk
Okhotsk
CENTRAL SIBERIAN PLATEAU
Yakutsk
SIBERIA
Nikolayevsk
SAKHALIN ISLAND
DeKastri Bay
Sofisk
Strait of Tartary
Lena R.
Yablonovy Range
Pokrovka
Blagoveshchensk
Angara R.
Shilka R.
Amur R.
Khabarovsk
145°
Lake Baikal
Verkhne-udinsk (Ulan-Ude)
Chita
Sretensk
Aigun
Irkutsk
Port Baikal
A
Kultuk
Tankhoi
Mysovsk
Kaidalovo
Kyakhta
Manchuria Sta.
Tsitsihar
Sungari
Ussuri R.
Iman
Ussurisk
MANCHURIA
Harbin
Pogranichny
Vladivostok
40°
MONGOLIA
Changchun
Mukden
Yingkou
Sea of Japan
KOREA
Peking
Tientsin
Port Arthur
Talien (Dalni)
Seoul
CHINA
Yellow Sea
JAPAN
30°
MILES 0 400 800
0 800 KILOMETERS
125°
Saml. H. Bryant

To the Great Ocean

Siberia and the Trans-Siberian Railway

To the Great Ocean

SIBERIA AND THE TRANS-SIBERIAN RAILWAY

---

by Harmon Tupper

with photographs

LONDON
SECKER & WARBURG

Grateful acknowledgment is made to the following for permission to reprint copyrighted material:

Hurst and Blackett, Ltd., THROUGH SIBERIA, AN EMPIRE IN THE MAKING by R. L. Wright and Bassett Digby, Copyright 1913. Reprinted by permission of Hutchinson & Co., Ltd.
The Macmillan Company, New York, THE RUSSIAN REVOLUTION 1917–1921 by William Henry Chamberlin, Copyright © 1957. Reprinted by permission of The Macmillan Company.
The New York Times, © 1961, 1962, 1964, by The New York Times Company. Reprinted by permission.
G. P. Putnam's Sons, TIME EXPOSURE by William Henry Jackson, Copyright 1940. Reprinted by permission of Putnam's & Coward-McCann.
Abraham Yarmolinsky, THE MEMOIRS OF COUNT WITTE edited by Abraham Yarmolinsky, Copyright 1921. Reprinted by permission of the author.

First published in England 1965 by
Martin Secker & Warburg Ltd.
14 Carlisle Street, Soho Square, W.1

PRINTED IN THE UNITED STATES OF AMERICA

To
my wife Elsie

With the iron road awakening the echoes of the vast tracks of solemn forest where, three centuries ago, the Tunguz and Buriat might only note the cries of animals scarcely wilder than themselves; and bridging rivers where, till yesterday, the fisherman's birchbark canoe alone glided through the solitary reaches, Siberia will be, indeed, conquered, and, with a steel yoke about her neck, compelled to yield her all: of grain and cattle, furs, fish, and timber; porphyry and gold; coal, lead, and mercury; silver, copper, and iron — all the wealth she has, under guard of eternal snow and ice, so long held in trust for future centuries.

— ARCHIBALD R. COLQUHOUN:
Overland to China (1900)

Contents

List of Illustrations

List of Maps

maps by Samuel Bryant

To the Great Ocean

Siberia and the Trans-Siberian Railway

CHAPTER I

Introduction to Siberia

> We are now launched into the greatest piece of solid earth, if I understand anything of the surface of the globe, that is to be found in any part of the world . . .
> — DANIEL DEFOE: *The Life and Adventures of Robinson Crusoe*

THE Trans-Siberian remains today as a far-reaching monument in steel, wood, and stone to Man's triumph over Nature despite handicaps and adversities without parallel in the construction of any other railway. It is also a monument to mark the transformation of an industrially backward country and the end of an era perhaps as multicolored and bizarre as any the world has known from the time of Peter the Great, whose gorgeous grandees, as Macaulay drily remarked in his famous phrase, "came to the court balls dropping pearls and vermin."

Thousands of miles of track have been laid on almost every continent since Russian engineers completely spanned Siberia, but the Trans-Siberian still ranks as the longest continuous railway on earth. Geographically, it extends from the Ural Mountains, a low, wooded range that divides European Russia from Asia, to the Sea of Japan, where it terminates at Vladivostok, nearly six thousand miles southeast of Moscow.

Once lyricized in the Russian press as "the fairest jewel in the crown of the Tsars," and belittled by various Britons and Americans as "rusty streaks of iron through the vastness of nothing to the extremities of nowhere," the Trans-Siberian crosses the broadest plains, the largest forests, and four of the longest rivers in either hemisphere. To the right and left lie inestimable treasures in iron ore, precious metals, diamonds, oil, hydroelectric power, timber, furs, and enough coal to last the Soviet Union for hundreds of years.

Spirit away the railway, and access to this fabulous wealth is confined to aircraft with inherently limited cargo capacity, to slow river vessels of relatively small tonnage, and to motor vehicles whose sole transcontinental highway is no more than a narrow road little changed since the eighteenth century. One may safely say that the Trans-Siberian, structurally the weakest of long lines and with but a single eastbound and a single westbound track over much of its course, is the most indispensable of all railways today.

While traveling along this artery a few summers ago, the writer lost all count of flatcars laden with great pine logs, structural steel and prefabricated concrete building sections, heavy machine tools, electrical equipment, army vehicles, and shiny new bulldozers and tractors, trucks, and compact automobiles. Coal and grain gondolas, boxcars, and tank and refrigerator cars rumbled by in ponderous processions headed by steam, electric, Diesel, or Diesel-electric locomotives. Frequently, one passed long strings of open boxcars jammed with baggy-jacketed soldiers, most of whom looked as rugged as the "Young Pioneers" and workers in the coaches of the writer's train, the Number 4 Moscow-Vladivostok Express. From the windows, one caught glimpses of the single transcontinental highway: in summer, a dusty, potholed strip reminiscent of stagecoach days in the American West. Knowing that this primitive road is Siberia's only other lifeline by land, one can understand why the railway is worth billions to the Soviet Union, a fact dramatized by the presence of countless civilian track-guards and by the military sentries who stand with bayoneted rifles at each end of every major bridge from the Urals to the eastern seas.

The name Siberia is missing from modern maps because it is no longer used as an all-embracing term for the political divisions of the region, but it remains the popular designation of the Asian land mass eastward from the Urals and north of Soviet Central Asia, Kazakhstan, China, Outer Mongolia, and Korea. The eastern shores lie along the Sea of Japan, the Strait of Tartary, the Sea of Okhotsk, Bering Sea, and Bering Strait. We shall sometimes use the more convenient term "Pacific" for these waters.

In a straight line varied by curves and gradients in mountainous country, the railway parallels the treeless wastes of the arctic tundra to the north and the plains, semideserts, and mountains to the south. Its route in western and central Siberia roughly follows the fifty-fifth degree of latitude and passes through territory traversed since the sixteenth century by fur hunters, traders, Cossack freebooters, religious dissenters, gold and silver prospectors, and hosts of convicts, political exiles, and free peasant settlers. It crosses rich farming and cattle-raising regions, penetrates an enormous expanse of virgin forest, and loops round the world's deepest lake, the only freshwater home of seals whose ancestors presumably inhabited the Arctic Ocean untold millennia ago. It then climbs to heights where the skies are fair for more than three hundred and forty days a year, and the air as bracing as a sharp, dry wine. Descending to an area swarming with insects that torture humans and animals, it progresses into former pockets of pestilence where smallpox, cholera, leprosy, syphilis, typhus, typhoid, tuberculosis, goiter, ophthalmia, and alcoholism were the common scourges of the native population. Not very far from the eastern coast, the line turns abruptly southward and proceeds to Vladivostok through the haunts of Manchurian tigers, largest and most dangerous of Asiatic carnivores except for brown bears.

Even in these days when ultrasonic aircraft seem to shrink the linear dimensions of our planet, Siberia's immensity is still spectacular. Its area — almost five million square miles — has been graphically defined by George Kennan, the nineteenth-century American telegrapher turned Siberian explorer and distinguished authority on penal conditions under the Tsars.

"If it were possible to move entire countries from one part of the world to another," he wrote in his classic two-volume work first published in 1891, *Siberia and the Exile System,* "you could take the whole United States of America from Maine to California and from Lake Superior to the Gulf of Mexico, and set it down in the middle of Siberia, without touching anywhere the boundaries of the latter territory. You could then take Alaska and all the States of Europe, with the single exception of Russia, and fit them into the remaining margin like the pieces of a dissected map; and after having thus accommodated all of the United States, including Alaska, and all of Europe, except Russia, you would still have more than 300,000 square miles of Siberian territory to spare . . ."

To convey some idea of the distance, in terms of time, from far eastern Siberia to European Russia before the construction of the Trans-Siberian, a historian cites as an example the six Kamchatka virgins whom the Empress Elizabeth Petrovna had invited, many months in advance and together with other exotic inhabitants of her realm, to visit her at St. Petersburg. Escorted by an Imperial officer, these chaste eighteenth-century maidens set out for the court from their volcanic, fog-wrapped peninsular home opposite Alaska's southernmost tip. Shortly before they reached the town of Irkutsk, the trading and administrative center of eastern Siberia, each gave birth to a child fathered by the military chaperon. He was replaced by a supposedly more trustworthy guardian; nevertheless, by the time the young mothers reached St. Petersburg — nearly nine thousand miles from Kamchatka — their firstborn had half brothers and sisters.*

These complaisant Kamchadals had originally begun their journey on a path blazed by Russian and Cossack explorers who established *ostrogi,* or stockaded outposts resembling those of early pioneers in America, for the collection of fur tribute from native tribes. At Irkutsk, this route joined the "Trakt," the crude highway that wandered westward to the mother country.

During the eighteenth century, the trail across Siberia had

* George Kennan takes an affable view of the Kamchadals, whom he describes as "a quiet, inoffensive, hospitable tribe of semibarbarians, remarkable only for honesty, general amiability, and comical reverence for legally constituted authority. . . . They will suffer and endure any amount of abuse and ill-treatment, without any apparent desire for revenge, and with the greatest good-nature and elasticity of spirit. They are as faithful and forgiving as a dog. If you treat them well, your slightest wish will be their law . . ."

According to Henry Lansdell, an English cleric who crossed Siberia in 1879, the Kamchadals carry on a regular trade with lemmings, the circumpolar rodents who have immortalized themselves by their suicidal migrations. These little creatures cache away grain and roots much prized by the Kamchadals, and cover them with poisonous plants against the depredations of other animals. The Kamchadals then carefully remove the plants and extract the stores for their own consumption. With a greater degree of enlightened self-interest than of compassion for the lemmings which might otherwise starve to death, the Kamchadals refill the caches with caviar or fish scraps and replace the poisonous covers. Apparently, the lemmings are satisfied with this barter between beast and man, for they continue to gather grain and roots and to thrive on the substitutions.

been widened to twenty-one feet by exiles and free settlers under government supervisors. Posting stations — two-room log cabins identified by the Imperial escutcheon above a gateway and by two black-and-white-striped pillars at the door — were established at anywhere between ten- and twenty-mile intervals for change of horses and drivers. In George Kennan's time, travelers paid the equivalent of about three and a half cents a mile for hire of a driver and the customary troika, or team of three thick-coated Siberian horses.

Abroad, the Trakt was known as the Great Siberian Post Road, a flattering misnomer in the opinion of foreigners who ventured upon it. As late as 1894, the ordinary traveler's progress was so slow that he could more quickly reach St. Petersburg from the Pacific by sailing eastward from Vladivostok to the American West coast, crossing to New York by rail, embarking for Germany, and entraining there for the Russian capital.

Then, as now, the Trakt in spring was a wallow of mud so gluey that some post-station coachmen refused to drive vehicles whose wheels did not fit the ruts, in many places upwards of twenty inches deep. In summer, wheels sank to the hubs in thick, gritty dust that held horses to a floundering walk. In winter, ice and hard-packed snow gave far greater speed to sledges, but storm-felled trees and skids into gullies frequently immobilized wayfarers for hours. When sleigh runners smashed to bits against snow-covered obstructions, a wait of a day or more for repairs was inevitable in some wretched village, where, as one Englishman observed, the houses looked like dismasted ships "rolling and tumbling about in a high sea, some with their sterns high up out of the water, others with their bows buried in the waves. This phenomenon is caused by the depression of the ground in spring, when the snow melts, and when their foundations being very insecure, the houses fall about in all directions." (The same may be said, with somewhat less exaggeration, of log cabins seen along the Trans-Siberian today.)

Once again on their way after a mishap, travelers often found the road blocked by hundreds of one-horse sledges loaded with hide-bound boxes of tea and all roped together to form a single file perhaps a mile long. The law required teamsters to pull aside, but since they usually curled up on their loads at night and fell fast asleep, the caravan stuck to the middle of the Trakt and forced other vehicles to detour round it. "This so exasperated our driver," George Kennan relates with relish, "that he would give every horse and every sleeping teamster in the whole caravan a slashing cut with his long rawhide whip, shouting, in almost untranslatable Russian, 'Wake up!' (Whack.) 'Get a move on you!' (Whack.) 'What are you doing in the middle of the road there?' (Whack.) 'Akh! You ungodly Tartar pagans!' (Whack.) 'GO TO SLEEP IN THE MIDDLE OF THE NIGHT, WILL YOU?' (Whack, whack.)"

In all seasons, travelers lived in constant danger of attack from runaway convicts and exiles turned *brodyagi,* or roaming tramps who lay in wait between post stations to rob them of money, passports, and clothing, sometimes with the connivance of post drivers. To prevent testimony against them later, they clubbed unwary victims to death, cut their throats, or garroted them with a length of gut or twine. At forest encampments following a breakdown, a fire had to be kept burning brightly at night, and a keen watch maintained for bears, which have their own clever ways. "It is a fact well known," declared the noted nineteenth-century English explorer Thomas Witlam Atkinson, "that a bear will not attack a man . . . sleeping by a fire, but will first go into the water, saturate his fur, then return, put out the fire, and devour his victim at his leisure."

Wolves, however, were not quite the peril pictured by romantic artists if, that is, one believes Lionel F. Gowing, who assured the traveler that it was really unnecessary to take along a supply of babies and throw one out now and then to distract the pack, for "the Siberian wolf is a cowardly animal . . . [and] an attack on a post-sledge is utterly unknown in Siberia." As Gowing covered five thousand Siberian miles in such a sledge, he may have spoken with authority, but in the opinion of Vladimir V. Vladimirov, a knowing Russian hunter of our time, famished wolves will indeed set upon a defenseless person in a sleigh. (Alexandre Dumas, who traveled through central Russia in 1858, wrote that they had attacked so many villages in the area that the government offered a bounty of $2.50 for each wolf tail brought in.* After acquiring half a million tails at a cost of $1,250,000, suspicious officials discovered that an enterprising Moscow concern had bought up whole wolf skins for practically nothing, and from them made bogus tails with which to defraud the Treasury.)

Throughout the empire, the most common conveyances in winter were sledges and sleighs, and tarantasses and telegas in summer. The tarantass resembled a large, shallow basket,

---

* It is exceedingly difficult to relate the Russian ruble accurately to the American dollar or the English pound sterling for specific years between 1850 and 1900. We have therefore adopted the practice of most American and British travelers in the empire by figuring the ruble at fifty cents or slightly more than two shillings in the latter part of the past century, when the average exchange rate of the pound was $4.87.

As a rule, fractional linear and other measures have been reduced or increased to the nearest round number, as 99 for 99.4 and 100 for 99.6. These decimals often result from conversion of Russian or metric units to those of English-speaking countries. A table of equivalents appears in Appendix E.

Two yamshchiki, *or drivers on the Siberian post road*

about seven feet long by five feet wide and big enough for two adults, that rested on springy wooden poles attached to the axletrees of four wheels. There was a perch in front for the *yamshchik*, or driver, but no bench for the passengers, who dovetailed their baggage into the concave bottom, covered it with straw, blankets, and sheepskin robes, and rode either on their backs or with knees squeezed up in a way to mitigate the bone-shaking, joint-wrenching jolts. "Had I been rolled down hill in a hogshead," remarked Thomas W. Knox, one of the first Americans to cross Siberia, "I think my sensations would have been little worse."

The one-horse telega — a smaller, cruder version of the tarantass but similarly equipped with a leather hood and a front curtain for weather protection — was essentially a

Passenger sledges and posthouse of the 1890s

farm wagon, and still exists in Siberia today. If tarantasses were available, the acutely uncomfortable telega was pressed into service only for the transportation of extra baggage. The proselytizing Reverend Dr. Henry Lansdell, for example, carried bundles of religious tracts and Holy Scriptures — in Russian, Polish, German, French, Hebrew, Tartar, and Mongolian — of which he distributed 55,812 copies in the course of his three-and-a-half-month expedition from the Urals to Vladivostok in 1879.

Since travelers journeyed by night as well as by day, drowsy, vodka-sodden *yamshchiki* brought many tarantasses and telegas to grief in the ruts and potholes of the opaque and unpredictable Trakt. Severed harness ropes could be mended if the driver were sober enough to make a splice, and broken shafts could be replaced with birch saplings. But if an axle snapped or wore away from lack of grease, passengers could only pray that their driver would find his way to a village or post station and spend their money for another axle rather than for a bottle. East of Irkutsk, ironwork was so scarce that breakdown victims had no choice but to abandon their tarantass and buy another that had survived the long trek across Siberia. Regardless of condition, owners rarely sold one for anything less than its $100 to $150 value when new.

Merchants, fur and tea traders, prospectors, government functionaries with their families, and once in a while an adventurous Briton or American, a German commercial agent, or a French tutor or chef bound for some millionaire's household in Irkutsk, "the Paris of Siberia" — these were typical travelers who braved the myriad perils, delays, and wracking discomforts of the Trakt in the second half of the last century. The government posting system added vexations and ordeals from which only Crown couriers, Imperial mail postilions, and high officials escaped.* Regulations forbade a speed greater than eight miles an hour between stations, but drivers often refused to maintain even this pace unless they were tipped in advance with "drink money." Anyone who hired a post-station tarantass instead of buying his own at the beginning of the journey was required to surrender it at the next stop. This meant that all the paraphernalia of "traveling *sibirski*" — baggage, provisions, blankets, robes, teapots,

* "Before the establishment of telegraphic communication between China and Russia," says Kennan, "imperial couriers, carrying important despatches from Peking, often made the distance between Irkutsk and St. Petersburg — 3618 miles — in sixteen days, with two hundred and twelve changes of horses and drivers. In order to accomplish this feat they had to eat, drink, and sleep in their sleighs and make an average speed-rate of ten miles an hour for nearly four hundred consecutive hours."

hatchets, ropes — had to be unpacked and reloaded on another tarantass every two hours or so.

Government rules bound the station proprietor, called the postmaster, to keep a certain number of horses in reserve for couriers and the Imperial mail, but this he seldom did if importunate travelers bribed him well. What with harnesses to be repaired and wheels to be removed and greased, however, tarantasses frequently failed to get off before the Crown drivers arrived in a cloud of dust or a spattering hail of mud. In this event, the postmaster hastily unhitched the civilians' horses, harnessed them to the government equipage, and rolled his eyes mournfully heavenward, muttering that such was God's will. It was also God's will that the bribes remained in his pocket.

The chagrined travelers sometimes waited two or three days before they could resume their journey, for a spate of couriers, important officials, and persons who merely looked important might stream in and requisition every horse. Dr. Lansdell was not one to allow a mere postmaster to halt the spreading of the Scriptural Word. "I was told of the potency," the Anglican clergyman says with some complacency, "of wearing arms and insignia of office, and of the difference it makes at the post-stations in getting horses. . . . Accordingly, I so far profited by this information as to put on certain splendid array which I possessed . . . and . . . I obtained the horses."

The average station house contained living quarters for the postmaster and his family, and a travelers' common room, about twenty feet long by eighteen feet wide, the two sections being heated by a huge brick oven in the dividing wall. Illumination at night was provided by a lamp or a candle, and, in daytime, by whatever light that filtered through the small, dirty, double-paned windows, both kept tightly sealed even in warm-weather spells. Furniture comprised a battered table, a couple of straight-backed chairs, and a wooden bench or two; a samovar for tea-making occupied one corner, and on the greasy, whitewashed walls hung an icon of the Virgin or of the Savior, a few engravings from illustrated papers, and lurid oleograph portraits of the Tsar and the Tsarina.

Firstcomers preempted chairs, table, and benches in the misplaced hope that these might give them some security against rats and shoals of cockroaches. Later arrivals, who stamped in at all hours of the night, slept on the uncarpeted, worm-eaten floor, caked with mud and littered with straw, paper scraps, fishbones, and, as one foreigner noted with distaste in 1892, "other abominations." Sanitary arrangements were indescribable, and washing facilities seldom existed, not that traveling Russians would have used the latter in cold weather, for they believed that soap and water sensitized the skin and increased the danger of frostbite.

Stationmasters posted a bill of fare as regulations demanded. It gave the prices of beefsteaks, cutlets, sausages, and such, but these were as unavailable as the cucumbers and fresh greens listed on winter menus in Soviet hotels today. If travelers neglected to bring their own white bread, tinned meats, leaf tea, sugar, and pots of jam, they subsisted on the postmaster's meager store of clammy black bread, salted fish, inferior brick tea, and eggs in a state described as "fossil" by a British traveler of the nineties.

It was no hardship for lower-class Russian women to remain unwashed for days at a time, but one sympathizes with the aristocratic ladies who traveled from St. Petersburg or Moscow to join their husbands in Irkutsk or in towns farther east. "The prettiest looked hideous in the early morning hours, with tangled hair, disordered dress, and pale, pasty faces,

Engraving of an old Russian inn

while their diamond rings only served to show off the blackness of their hands and nails," comments Harry de Windt, a Fellow of the Royal Geographical Society.*

Postmasters were required to keep a "Black Book" in the common room for the registration of complaints. Theoretically, these would be noted by a touring inspector, who would report the delinquencies of stationmasters and drivers. But inspection was perfunctory, and accusations went unheeded unless they came from couriers, custodians of the mail, or officers and dignitaries of impressive rank. More often than not, proprietors kept the Black Book locked up and professed loss of the key when wrathful civilians demanded it. Hence, little was done to improve these medieval conditions.

The rigors of post travel were aggravated, except in winter, by Siberia's waterways. During the spring thaw, these were choked with swirling ice floes that made navigation impossible; shortly thereafter, they became swollen carriers of uprooted trees, dead branches, and other debris that imperiled ferries and bridges. When the latter washed away, traffic halted until peasants rebuilt the span or contrived a raft. Bridges in some places remained neglected until they sagged with rot. Such decrepit structures were the delight of spirited *yamshchiki*, who regarded them more as personal challenges than as deathtraps. With wild whoops and curses, the drivers urged their steeds to a furious gallop on the bridge approach and raced over the timbers as though pursued by the horsemen of the Apocalypse. "It is the only way, masters," one coachman assured his terrified passengers upon reaching the

* De Windt once investigated the feasibility of boring a railway tunnel under Bering Strait between Siberia and Alaska, a distance of fifty-two miles.

other side just before the span collapsed. "Go fast enough and the bridge will not have time to fall under you."

Wider rivers were crossed on various types of primitive ferries that could carry only a few vehicles at a time. Now and then, a *yamshchik,* in a frenzied dash to obtain a place ahead of others waiting on the bank and thus qualify for additional drink money from passengers, overshot the deck and had to be fished out with his charges from a watery tangle of ropes and kicking horses. If travelers arrived during the embarkation of tea caravans, to which the government granted precedence at ferry crossings if not on the Trakt, they might be halted for a day or more for the transport of three or four hundred carts unless they heavily bribed the ferryman, or, like the persuasive Englishman S. S. Hill who crossed Siberia to Kamchatka in the late eighteen-forties, convinced the Charon that

Krasnoyarsk ferry on the Yenisei

the tea in their provisions entitled them to caravan priority. In late summer, when rains swelled broad expanses like the Ob and the Irtysh and kept all boats shorebound, they might be delayed for weeks until the rivers froze. In such cases, they camped out, endured a posthouse, or obtained quarters through the aid of a local police chief, who had the power to requisition rooms in private dwellings.

Most Siberian ferries consisted of flat-bottomed rafts or barges moored to a long chain or cable anchored in midstream. When the helm was put over, the force of the current swept the craft in a pendulum swing to the opposite bank. This limited maneuverability made it a frightening target for ice cakes and trees. Unless the crew stood at constant alert with stout fending poles, the ferry could be struck so hard that horses lost footing and tumbled with tarantasses or telegas over the side, seldom to be seen again alive.

During the ice-free period of barely five months, travelers could avoid hundreds of miles on the Trakt by boarding paddle-wheel steamboats that towed freight and convict barges via the Irtysh, Ob, and tributary rivers from Tyumen, one of Siberia's main western gateways, to Tomsk, an important mercantile, distributing, and gold-smelting center to the east. Reasonably comfortable accommodations in first class for the 1450-mile voyage cost only $7.50, with good three-course dinners at twenty-five cents each. Otherwise, the boat line left much to be desired. For lack of an adequate number of buoys and beacons, steamers grounded on sandbanks, where they sometimes remained stuck for half a day until hauled or poled off by the crew. In slack water, some undredged channels were so shallow that vessels might be stranded for a week or two until rains helped to float them. Fouled towing lines, impenetrable fogs, and the frequent need to take on wood fuel delayed them for hours on end. Quite often, abnormally severe frost set in before the season's official close in October and locked steamers in ice. Such an event was a heaven-sent blessing to neighboring peasants who charged exorbitantly to transport the marooned to the nearest posting station.

In far eastern Siberia, where much of the Trakt was impassible in spring and summer except to horsemen and pack animals, water communications were maintained by the Shilka and Amur rivers. Travelers bound for Pacific regions embarked at Sretensk, an overgrown village on the Shilka, for a voyage of about fourteen hundred miles to Khabarovsk, where they transferred to a stern-wheeler and steamed up the Ussuri River toward Vladivostok to the south, or continued on the Amur River in a northeasterly direction to the present Nikolayevsk-na-Amure (hereafter referred to simply as Nikolayevsk), a commercial port near the mouth of the Amur.

Since the Shilka-Amur watercourse was erratically inconstant in level and flowed over more than a hundred and twenty shoals that shifted with each flood, barges towed by tugs grounded with frustrating regularity. Sometimes, passengers were put ashore and had to trudge to a point along the bank for reembarkation when deck hands freed the craft in an operation that might take days instead of hours. In one instance recorded by William O. Greener, a British writer who voyaged down the rivers in the summer of 1901, a barge stranded in midstream without means for removing passengers. The temperature in the humanity-packed steel hull soared to a hundred and forty-eight degrees, with the result that an average of four babies a day perished, and even toughened gypsies died of heat stroke.

Altogether, Siberia's archaic transportation system effectively hamstrung the tsarist regime in its sporadic, half-hearted attempts to develop industry and commerce in the country during most of the nineteenth century. The cost of importing heavy machinery to eastern regions was prohibitive, and consequently even gold and silver mines — collectively the territory's most valuable known assets next to fur-bearing animals — were worked by such antiquated and wasteful methods that some proprietors, excluding the Tsar, whose private "Cabinet" mines could draw on convict labor without limit, made more money from the sale of food, clothing, and tobacco to their miners than from the diggings themselves.

Skilled factory workers were practically impossible to obtain; scarce enough in Russia, they preferred their hard estate there to what they pictured as an infinitely harder one in Siberia, in their minds a frightening wilderness inhabited only by savages and deported criminals. Native tribesmen were wedded to hunting, fishing, and pastoral pursuits, and were generally too uncivilized to be worth training. Free settlers had long since followed a firmly rooted life in agriculture, cattle-raising, homecrafts, or petty shopkeeping. The hiring of exiles was hedged by innumerable governmental restrictions.

Merchants and producers in central and eastern Siberia traded with Russia at their peril. Goods and commodities were in many instances a year in transit, and, if not lost or stolen en route, frequently arrived in damaged or deteriorated condition. Except in the western area, payments for Siberian products were so slow that even fairly well capitalized entrepreneurs managed to survive solely because of personal, long-term credits from a handful of venturesome German or

English firms, together with Siberian branches of Russian monopolies.

Apparently, the foreign houses dealt honestly with the distant "Sibiryaki," but the St. Petersburg and Moscow cartels clearly engaged in robbery by barter. When purchasing, they credited furs, hides, and other exports at the cheap Siberian prices, then liquidated the credit with shipments of alcoholic beverages, sugar, inferior tobacco, and shoddy metal and cotton goods — all bought at bargain levels in Russia and elsewhere, but sold to merchants in the Siberian interior at tremendous markups to cover losses in transit, fictitious financing costs, and profits ranging from 135 to 500 per cent. Their captive customers were helpless; they could not threaten to expand their trade with foreign concerns at the expense of Russian interests, for the latter would then incite the Tsar to eliminate competition entirely. Private monopoly was in fact so powerful that the citizens of Irkutsk, for many years the capital of the country, were forbidden to buy meat except from certain butchers designated by a coalition of three Russian wholesalers.

Consistent with its indifference to such practices, the government made no appreciable effort to control pernicious traders in the vast northern and eastern forests, where sable, ermine, and other precious-fur animals abounded. These traders, as viciously unscrupulous as sixteenth-century Spanish conquistadors in the New World, set up vodka stills in violation of the law, and befuddled native hunters and trappers into surrendering an entire season's catch for practically nothing. The victims gradually realized they were being cheated, yet they demanded nothing but more vodka to which they easily became addicted. In many cases after the traders' departure, native men, women, and children drank to such stupefaction that they let fires go out, and froze to death.* Before long, entire settlements of skillful hunters were exterminated by the vodka, syphilis, and tuberculosis brought by the white traffickers, the same who bitterly complained that English coastal traders paid tribesmen unfairly high prices for furs.

This was Siberia in the nineteenth century, a dormant colossus all but forgotten and forsaken by Alexander I during his conflict with Napoleon and his subsequent preoccupation with European affairs; by Nicholas I, who ignored it until the closing years of his reign; and by Alexander II, who saw little future for the East and sold Alaska to the United States for two cents an acre. It is perhaps one of the rarest paradoxes in Russian history that Siberia's illimitable potential was first recognized, not by the exalted hierarchy that stood to profit most from the country's development, but by a jolly, forty-three-year-old American gold-dust broker with an appreciative eye for the ladies, Perry McDonough Collins. Before his entry on the scene, however, it is important to have some brief idea of the three centuries of Siberian history that preceded him.

---

* The Yukaghirs in northeastern Siberia, an easygoing lot who viewed body lice as a sign of good health, were especially punctilious in seeing that even babies received their share when liquor was passed around.

CHAPTER II

The Early Empire-Builders

> Is this not the place for the legendary hero of Russian fable, here where there is plenty of room for him to spread himself and move about freely?
>
> — NICHOLAS V. GOGOL: *Dead Souls*

IN 1574, three years before Sir Francis Drake began his circumnavigation of the globe and at a time when Western monarchs and merchant princes were equipping expeditions to exploit the riches of the Orient and of the Americas, Ivan the Terrible invested the Stroganov brothers with the right to extend their enterprises into the domain of Tartar rulers beyond the Urals. The Stroganovs, inheritors of a fantastic fortune accumulated in eastern Russia from salt works, mines, furs, and mercantile activities, had first to subdue the Tartars. The Tsar had provided no military aid, and so the brothers enlisted the services of an outlawed Cossack band led by Yermak Timofeyevich, a Russian whose piracies on the Volga had obliged Ivan to put a heavy price on his head.

By most accounts, Yermak struck out for the Tartar realm in 1581 with a small force believed to have numbered about eight hundred men, including three priests and a runaway monk. These horseless freebooters built a fleet of rafts and boats, and followed streams to the Tura River, entrance to the kingdom of the warlike Khan Kuchum, a potentate who claimed descent from Genghis Khan and called himself Tsar of Sibir, though he controlled only a comparatively small area along the Ob and Irtysh rivers. At the Tura, Yermak easily won the first skirmishes with one of Kuchum's vassals, whose men were armed with bows and arrows, lances, and swords, and fled in terror from the invaders' muskets and harquebuses. Yermak then advanced to the Tobol River, where he routed the Khan's war minister. Kuchum rallied his forces and strengthened the earthen ramparts and wooden palisades of his capital, known as Isker or Sibir and not far from the

Yermak Timofeyevich, conqueror of "Sibir"

present city of Tobolsk. Late in October 1581, the Cossacks stormed the citadel.* In hand-to-hand fighting, they forced Kuchum to bolt with the remnants of his army and retreat to the south.

Yermak informed the Stroganovs of his victory and dispatched envoys to Moscow, where they presented the Tsar with a treasure in magnificent furs and figuratively laid Kuchum's realm at his feet. Ivan pardoned them and their comrades in Siberia for past crimes, assured them of reinforcements, and rewarded Yermak with a gilded silver drinking cup, a massive breastplate of armor, and, as a supreme token of esteem, a fur mantle that had draped the royal shoulders.

On a stormy night in August 1584, Yermak's enjoyment of these gifts was cut short by Khan Kuchum's warriors who fell upon him and his small reconnaissance party while they slept on an island in the Irtysh. According to tradition, Yermak tried to swim to safety but was drowned by the weight of the armor from the Tsar. Only five months before, Ivan himself had died of a stroke or possibly mercurial poisoning, unaware that Yermak, the notorious brigand who had overrun a trackless wilderness without the help of maps, compass, horses, or a sizable army, had opened the way to a territory that was to be the richest ever won in Russian history.†

---

* Dates given in this book are according to the Western (Gregorian) calendar unless followed by the words (Old Style). A brief description of the Gregorian and Julian calendars will be found in Appendix E.

† A dispatch from Moscow published in the *New York Times* of March 22, 1964, reported that Ivan's remains had been transferred in 1963 from his sarcophagus in the Kremlin to laboratories of the Soviet Academy of Sciences. Chemical analysis established the presence of an overdose of mercury in his organs. Since the Tsar is believed to have been ill "with a painful, unexplained affliction that made his body swell to abnormal proportions," he may have been treated with mercury ointments, but the possibility of foul play had not been ruled out by the investigators. "The scientists also discovered," the article continues, "that the Czar's arms were not folded on his chest, as is the custom in Russian Orthodox burials. His right

Although the leaderless Cossacks were forced to retreat from Siberia under renewed Tartar attacks, Yermak had destroyed the cohesion of the enemy's power. The advance resumed with the support of Boris Godunov and subsequent rulers, and continued in a northeasterly direction where the natives were scattered and weak. Born rivermen, the adventurers improvised boats and barges of wood and hides, shouldered them over portages, floated them in shallows by damming the stream with sails (often of reindeer hides), and availed themselves of Siberia's remarkable hydrographic system that allowed them to descend north-flowing rivers and to follow more or less latitudinal tributaries toward other major waterways beyond. By 1633, they had established blockhouses at strategic points as far east as the present Yakutsk, on the Lena River more than twenty-three hundred miles from the Urals as the crow flies, and much longer by the circuitous water route. At each of these forts, a small garrison collected fur tribute from the natives on behalf of the Tsar and of the voivodes, the military commanders of an area or a district.

The value of this fur has been dramatized by Professor Robert J. Kerner in his *The Urge to the Sea,* an exhaustive study (published in 1942) of the role of rivers, portages, and furs in Russia's eastward expansion. "Estimates of the income of the state from Siberian furs in the middle of the seventeenth century range from about 7 to about 30 per cent (or approximately from 125,000 to 600,000 rubles) of the total revenue of the state. . . . What value was represented by the

arm was raised, as if in a gesture of defense. . . . Several theories [were] considered by the scientists to explain this. One was violence at the moment of death. Another was that the arm may have been frozen in that position during the ruler's last days. Until now . . . it has been assumed that Ivan died of a stroke while playing checkers with a member of his court." An inscription in the sarcophagus gave March 19 as the date of his death, rather than the previously accepted March 18 (Old Style).

ruble of that time is to be noted from the fact that two black fox pelts in 1623 brought 110 rubles. With these 110 rubles the owner could buy fifty-five acres of land, erect a good cabin, buy five horses, twenty head of cattle, twenty sheep, several dozen fowl, and still have half his capital left."

Inevitably, traders and adventurers followed close on the heels of the military, and even the voivodes sent out expeditions to bring back not only the precious furs but also the rumored gold and silver of the East. In 1639, thirty years after Henry Hudson's last attempt to find a northeast passage to Asia, a Cossack detachment reached the Sea of Okhotsk along the far eastern coast.

The spanning of Siberia had been completed within fifty-eight years, an accomplishment to be compared with that of the Americans, who required nearly two centuries to gain the Pacific. In 1643, another Cossack, Vasili Poyarkov, led a small force from Yakutsk in search of fabled silver to the south. At the Amur, he found no silver but an apparently fertile land which he visualized as the future granary of eastern Siberia. He descended the river to its mouth, then sailed north along the shore of the Okhotsk sea without navigational instruments, and finally struggled back to Yakutsk in 1646 after enduring almost incredible hardships that cost the lives of most of his company. Three years later, his expedition was followed by that of Yerofei P. Khabarov, a rich Russian fur trader who set out from Yakutsk to exploit the Amur region.

Poyarkov had received a friendly welcome from the indigenous tribes, but like the Spanish and the English in the Western hemisphere, he had plundered and betrayed to an unspeakable degree, with the result that the natives fled at the approach of other Russians in the persons of Khabarov and his bravoes. Discovering their grain stores and finding fish and furred animals in abundance, Khabarov was convinced that the country was ideal for Russian settlement. He returned to Yakutsk, collected more than a hundred and thirty men, and departed again for the Amur, where the natives now took up arms against him. Khabarov destroyed their strongholds, looted and burned villages, and, in one instance out of many, seized 350 horses and cattle, 118 children, and 243 women and girls. (He is said to have admitted that he tortured and burned hostages; he and his successors' barbarity was in fact so long remembered that Amur natives told the scientist and explorer Alexander T. von Middendorf almost two hundred years later that the Russians were devils who roasted children on gridirons formed by the bodies of their parents.)

Khabarov's cruelly oppressed victims appealed for help to their neighbors and nominal masters, the Manchus, who sent slightly more than two thousand men armed with bows and matchlocks to storm the Russian fort along the lower Amur. The assault failed, but Khabarov retreated upriver to avoid further massive attacks. In that summer of 1652, more than a third of his men deserted him. News of his atrocities had reached Tsar Alexis I, who summoned him to Moscow for an accounting. Officialdom was prepared to throw him to the wolves, but Khabarov — a tremendously persuasive personality — spoke with such conviction of the riches he had won for the Crown that he was hailed as an empire-builder, elevated in rank, and awarded the superintendence of a number of Lena villages, from which he never returned to the Amur. As a historian has said, "He had been cruel, acquisitive, and licentious . . . [but] had shown ability and daring, and had worked for the future of his country."

The commanders the Tsar sent to the Amur territory to succeed Khabarov threw away one of the most brilliant opportunities ever offered to the roaming conquerors of the seventeenth century. Far from obeying Alexis's order to treat the natives fairly and to foster peaceful development of the region, the Russian and Cossack troops turned buccaneers on the Amur, pillaged and burned villages, carried off women, and laid waste to the countryside at the slightest resistance to their extortionate demands for food and tribute. "When the Russians first arrived on the Amur," Ernest G. Ravenstein records in his colorful *The Russians on the Amur,* first published in 1861, "the natives cultivated fields and kept cattle. Ten years afterwards these fields had become deserts; and a country, which formerly exported grain, could not even support its own reduced population. There is no doubt that, had these expeditions been carried out upon a more sensible plan, Russia might have enjoyed these resources of the Amur two centuries before our times."

The desperate natives appealed again to the Manchus for protection from their rapacious foes. Since the Russians had extended their holdings and raided deep into the heart of Manchuria — ancestral home of the ruling dynasty in China — the Emperor K'ang Hsi mounted strong offensives against them. A protracted series of sieges and bloody engagements continued until overwhelming Chinese armies finally destroyed the invaders' forts and settlements, drove out marauding outlaws, and forced Sophia, regent over the youth later to rule as Peter the Great, to come to terms. At the Russian stronghold of Nerchinsk, near one of the principal headwaters of the Amur, the Chinese ambassadors strengthened their negotiating position with a huge fleet of armed junks and a force of nine or ten thousand men. Uneasy and inept, Sophia's envoy gave in to practically every Chinese demand and, late in August 1689 (Old Style), signed the Treaty of Nerchinsk, the first ever to be concluded between the Celestial Empire and a Western Power. The pact banned Russian soldiers, settlers, and hunters from Manchuria, and defined the Sino-Siberian frontier. On the west, the new border began at the Argun River and ran to a point about two hundred miles north of the Amur; it then proceeded easterly along the summit of the Stanovoi Range to the Okhotsk seacoast.

Russia was thereby deprived of the vital Amur waterway to the Pacific approaches, so that once again the tide of her expansion veered to the northeast. Near the end of the century, a detachment of Cossacks explored Kamchatka and collected tribute. Subsequent to Bering's voyages of 1728-1741, Russian fur traders ventured into the Aleutians and, in 1784, founded the first Russian colony in North America on Kodiak, an island east of the Alaska Peninsula. Fifteen years later, the Tsar Paul I granted a charter to the Russian-American Company (wholly owned by Russian interests), which was to hold a trading monopoly over Alaska, the Aleutians, and the Kuril island chain between the Japanese Empire and Kamchatka. Russian America, as Alaska and the Aleutians were called, was annexed to the Crown and remained an Imperial colony until Alexander II sold it to the United States in 1867.

After the Treaty of Nerchinsk, the Chinese made annual inspection trips on the middle Amur and its southern tributaries to assure their sovereignty, which they are said to have enforced by beheading trespassers. They neglected to extend their occupation and administration to the northern limits of their frontier, but for a hundred and fifty years and more the region remained clear of Russians except for a few fugitives, occasional adventurers, and several scientific expeditions. In the eighteen-forties, however, changes in the international sit-

Count Muravyev-Amurski

uation prompted St. Petersburg to ponder a shift in its hands-off Eastern policy. England's so-called Opium War against China had not only resulted in the cession of Hong Kong and commercial advantages to Britain, but had also revealed the weakness of the once-vigorous Asiatic empire. Nicholas I feared that Russia's overland trade with Peking would suffer materially from overseas competition, and that the British sought control of the Amur estuary. Accordingly, he appointed the bold and far-seeing Lieutenant-General Nicholas N. Muravyev — a thirty-eight-year-old, relatively unknown veteran of campaigns against Turks and Caucasus tribesmen — governor-general of Eastern Siberia in 1847.

Muravyev's mission was to protect and expand Russian interests in the Far East. He had been keenly interested in the Amur territory well before he assumed office at his capital of Irkutsk, and soon set about to annex it in violation of the Nerchinsk treaty. One of his first moves was to order a naval exploration of the Okhotsk seacoast and the mouth of the Amur while he himself voyaged to Kamchatka, where he chose Petropavlovsk as Russia's great Pacific port of the future. Meanwhile, Gennadius I. Nevelskoi, an ambitious young naval captain who commanded the small exploratory fleet, had discovered that Sakhalin was not the peninsula it was thought to be but an island separated from the mainland by the Strait of Tartary. The discovery was kept secret, for the southern coastal approach to the Amur's mouth would be strategically valuable in speeding Russian war vessels to the defense of the area.

In 1850, Nevelskoi, who shared Muravyev's expansionist views, sailed up the Amur estuary for twenty-eight miles and raised the Imperial standard at a site he named Nikolayevsk in flattering homage to the Tsar. News of this brazen violation of the Nerchinsk treaty roused a conservative St. Petersburg faction into a storm of protest. This clique, led by the Minister of Foreign Affairs, opposed any cause of conflict with China, clamored for the abandonment of a Russian post on Chinese soil, and brought about Muravyev's recall to the capital. The confident viceroy put his case directly to the Tsar, who backed him to the hilt. "Where the Russian flag has once been hoisted," Nicholas intoned, "it must never be lowered."

With the Emperor's consent, Muravyev moved swiftly to obtain other footholds on Chinese soil. A post was set up for the ostensible purpose of trading by the Russian-American Company at Aleksandrovsk, on De Kastri Bay opposite northern Sakhalin and not to be confused with the present town on the same island, while settlements and blockhouses sprang up on Sakhalin itself and on the Manchurian side of the Strait of Tartary. Muravyev commissioned an ironworks in Transbaikalia — the region between Irkutsk and the Amur — to construct the *Argun* (the first steamer to be built in far eastern Siberia), molded Transbaikalian peasants into an effective army, and dispatched increasing numbers of settlers down the Amur. Neither Chinese nor natives lifted a finger to oppose him, for Peking was enmeshed in internal troubles, and the local inhabitants found the Russians under Muravyev easier to deal with than they did the grasping Orientals.

The opportunistic General capitalized on the outbreak of the Crimean War in 1854. That May, he sailed on the *Argun* at the head of a mile-long flotilla of barges and rafts transporting an eight-hundred-man infantry battalion, a Cossack cavalry squadron, a division of mountain artillery, and a great quantity of cattle and stores — all for the announced purpose of "protecting" China but actually to strengthen Russia's own settlements and military installations against attack by the Anglo-French coalition. Although he asked permission from local mandarins to pass through their territory, he did not wait for them to consult Peking. He had nothing to fear, since the Chinese in Manchuria were armed only with bows and arrows, spears, a matchlock here and there, and ineffective cannon that had been exposed to the elements for years.

Never had Siberia known a Russian with energy comparable to Muravyev's. He built fortresses, set up batteries, made maps, investigated Sakhalin's coal resources, and superintended the shipment of troops and artillery for the defense of Petropavlovsk, on the southeastern coast of Kamchatka, against an English and French fleet. Thanks to his precautions, the Petropavlovsk garrison beat off the allied attack, and Amur forces repulsed superior numbers trying to land at De Kastri Bay. Muravyev dispatched expedition after expedi-

Alexander II. The frame, a creation of Carl Fabergé and Victor Aarne, is of silver with green, white, and ruby enamel

tion of troops, immigrants, cattle, and supplies for consolidating his position along the lower Amur. With the end of hostilities in 1856, he obtained from the new emperor Alexander II more money and men for the permanent occupation of the upper and middle reaches of the river's northern bank, where he settled several thousand soldiers and colonists despite the protests of the Chinese, who refused to consider a revision of the Treaty of Nerchinsk boundaries. At his urging, the Amur Company was organized early in 1858 to operate steamers and trading stations throughout the length of the waterway. In the same year, he founded Khabarovsk, at the confluence of the Amur and the Ussuri, and, farther upriver, reinforced the military post that was renamed Blagoveshchensk, later the scene of one of the most atrocious massacres since the Golden Horde had swept across Asia in the thirteenth century.

China offered little or no resistance to Muravyev, for she had been disastrously weakened by the prolonged Taiping Rebellion and by her struggles against the aggressions of England and France. Muravyev took skillful advantage of her difficulties, and intimated war unless she met his territorial demands. In the spring of 1858, the enfeebled Chinese signed the Treaty of Aigun, which surrendered to Russia the territory north of the Amur and, if a line were drawn from Khabarovsk to the Strait of Tartary, all the area north of that.

In celebration of this prize acquisition, an archbishop in Blagoveshchensk laid the first stone for construction of a church in honor of the Annunciation to the Holy Virgin, and Muravyev issued a flamboyant order of the day to his troops. "Comrades! I congratulate you! Our efforts were not in vain, the Amur has become the property of Russia. The Holy Orthodox Church prays for you! Russia is grateful. Long live the Emperor Alexander II! May the newly acquired country prosper under His mighty protection! Hurrah!" When the General returned to Irkutsk, he entered it under a triumphal arch erected to his glory. Congratulatory messages poured in from many parts of Siberia and of Russia, and the greatest conqueror Siberia had known since Yermak received from the Tsar the title of Count Muravyev-Amurski.*

In the following year, China disavowed her envoy who had signed the Aigun treaty, and refused to ratify it. However, she had become embroiled again with the English and French, who finally forced her to her knees. Through the extraordinarily adroit and unscrupulous doubledealing of the twenty-eight-year-old diplomatic genius Nicholas P. Ignatyev, Russia was appointed to mediate during the ensuing negotiations. Ignatyev operated so successfully that he brought about the withdrawal of the allied troops, and convinced the Manchu court that he had saved the dynasty. As reward, he wrung from China the Treaty of Peking in 1860. This agreement reaffirmed the Treaty of Aigun frontiers and also gave Russia an extravagantly fat plum: possession of the entire Manchurian tract eastward from the Ussuri to the seacoast and southward as far as the Korean border, including the site of Vladivostok, already seized by Muravyev's forces for its superb harbor, well sheltered and ice-free for a longer period than any other haven on the Siberian littoral.

---

* Peter Kropotkin, the celebrated revolutionist and exile in Siberia, pays high tribute to Muravyev in his *Memoirs of a Revolutionist* (1899). "He was very intelligent, very active, extremely amiable, and desirous to work for the good of the country. Like all men of action of the government school, he was a despot at the bottom of his heart; but he held advanced opinions, and a democratic republic would not have quite satisfied him. . . . He had gathered around him a number of young officials, quite honest, and many of them animated by the same excellent intentions as himself. In his own study, the young officers . . . discussed the chances of creating the United States of Siberia, federated across the Pacific Ocean with the United States of America."

Muravyev suffered from a bad liver, and, perhaps realizing that his mission had been accomplished, resigned his governor-generalship in 1861. (By happy coincidence, it has been said, Alexander accepted the resignation on the same day he freed the serfs, a step the liberal-minded viceroy had long favored.) Within only fourteen years, Count Muravyev-Amurski had brought about the defeat of superior British and French forces, won control of the priceless Amur River route, and aggrandized the empire by roughly four hundred thousand square miles, an area larger than Texas and New Mexico combined, and only a little less than twice the size of France.

To the indefatigable Muravyev also belongs the distinction of being the first Russian proponent of a railway in Siberia, short though the route was. He had hoped to develop Nikolayevsk as the Amur's chief commercial port. But he found it obstructed by sandbanks and other navigational hazards to deep-draft merchant vessels; Aleksandrovsk, on De Kastri Bay, proved to be far more advantageously situated. After a survey in 1857, he cut a rough road between Aleksandrovsk and Sofisk, on the Amur some forty miles to the west, then proposed that St. Petersburg grant a ninety-nine-year concession for a railway to be built by a private company with a million dollars in capital. This concern would be given the right to borrow five thousand workers employed by the state and to take title to nearly a quarter of a million acres on both sides of the track. In 1858, Muravyev optimistically assured the Grand Duke Constantine, brother to the Tsar, that construction would soon begin. But he was mistaken: in the words of a future high official of the Trans-Siberian, "the idea of building a railway so far away was too novel for the central administration to support."

Meanwhile, news of Russia's expansion in the Far East had spread throughout the world and reached the ears of an imaginative if shadowy individual identified by St. Petersburg only as "an English engineer named Dull." In 1857, he asked Minister of Ways of Communication Constantine V. Chevkin for permission to build a tramway from Nizhni Novgorod (now Gorki) through Kazan and Perm to the Urals, and thence by "the most commodious way" to the Amur and the Pacific. On the rather mystical assumption that four million wild horses still roamed Siberia, the engineer suggested that a number be trained to haul the trams until such time as the government could afford to replace them with steam engines. As compensation for construction of the line, whose commercial and strategic value Dull strongly emphasized, he asked the government to guarantee him four per cent interest, plus two per cent for each of the provinces traversed, on the capital of $20,000,000 he was prepared to raise. He estimated that revenues from the tramway would amount to fourteen and a half per cent of the amount invested, and that shareholders would receive a dividend of ten per cent on their money.

Chevkin was scarcely enthusiastic about this proposal. Unable to bring himself to refer to Dull's untamed "horsepower," he pointed out to his colleagues that the Englishman seemed to know very little about Siberia and that his conclusions on financial returns were highly problematical. To Dull, he said merely that the enterprise "did not seem easily realizable because of climatic conditions." In 1860, the persevering engineer repeated his offer only to be turned down again.*

* The author unhappily confesses that neither he nor the innumerable Russian, British, and American historical, railway, and engineering societies and institutions he has consulted can give the first name and professional background of the elusive Mr. Dull. He seems to have vanished from all known records, but was evidently a visionary not without a prac-

Some years later, a former governor of Tomsk named Suprunenko suggested a horse tramway from Tyumen to Irkutsk and, possibly aware of Chevkin's official reply to Dull, advanced a startling solution for the weather problem. To protect the line from snowdrifts, he said, why not build an uninterrupted wooden gallery between the two cities? Not surprisingly, this proposal met the same fate as Dull's, for the Communication Minister had reason to doubt the practicality of building a surface tunnel that would run along for nearly nineteen hundred miles.

In 1858, three Englishmen the Russians identified only as Morison (also Morrisson), Sleigh, and Horn offered to construct a steam railway from Nizhni Novgorod to the Strait of Tartary in order, they said, "to facilitate relations between Europe, China, India, and America." They waived financial guarantees, but asked that land be given them for the right of way, passenger stations, and shore installations at two ports on the Strait. In return for this grant and a ninety-year concession for private operation of the line, the entrepreneurs bound themselves to organize a company with $25,000,000 in capital assets, to conduct preliminary surveys of the route within twelve months at the firm's expense, and to complete the railway six years after the start of construction.

Although Chevkin suspected that Morison, Sleigh, and Horn knew next to nothing about Siberia, he submitted their scheme to Alexander, warning him that the Britons would be in a position to monopolize Siberian trade through control of the railway. He also told the Tsar that investigation had revealed Morison to be a banker of doubtful trustworthiness, Sleigh a bankrupt, and Horn a lawyer, in the opinion of the

tical turn of mind, for it cannot be denied that Siberian horses gave off no fire-setting sparks, foraged for their own fuel, and would not blow up.

Russian ruling class a profession infested with dangerous revolutionists. Alexander needed to hear no more, and rejected the offer without another thought.

If Morison, Sleigh, and Horn were somewhat unsavory characters, the same could never be said of the enterprising Perry McDonough Collins, the first American to cross the entire breadth of Siberia, the first foreigner to propose a Siberian steam railway, and undoubtedly the first businessman to reap a fortune legitimately from an international telegraph line that never clicked out a message.

CHAPTER III

Yankee with a Vision

> Will not enterprise spring to its feet and enter this new seat of Asiatic commerce; covering the North Pacific with our ships, rivaling the famed shores of Southern India and the islands of the sea? Let us grasp this commerce, and not imitate Venice in her heedless apathy to the relations of Marco.
>
> — PERRY McDONOUGH COLLINS: *Lecture Before the Traveler's Club and Other Societies* (1865)

A FEW weeks before the first railway train rolled across the Mississippi River from Rock Island, Illinois, to Davenport, Iowa, in April 1856, President Franklin Pierce, Secretary of State William L. Marcy, and Russian Chargé d'Affaires Edward de Stoeckl conferred in Washington with a middle-aged San Franciscan who looked like a prosperous businessman and spoke with the fervor of a latter-day Columbus. With a flow of oratory enriched by quotations from the Book of Job and references to Herodotus, Genghis Khan, and Marco Polo, this eloquent visitor to the capital conveyed to his listeners a dazzling vision of the riches of Siberia. He was Perry McDonough Collins, in the light of later tributes from such distinguished personages as William H. Seward, His Imperial Highness the Grand Duke Constantine, and Count Muravyev-

Perry McDonough Collins

Amurski, an honest, persuasive, and immensely likable self-made man.

Collins was born at Hyde Park, New York, in 1813, and, like that community's more famous son, came from a good family. He studied law in New York City, then went to New Orleans, where he worked for a steamship company. During the gold rush of the forty-niners, he voyaged to San Francisco and established a partnership with the brother-in-law of Ulysses S. Grant as a banker and gold-dust broker. This business could have hardly consumed Collins's interest, for shortly after mid-century we find him deep in the study of Siberia, to which his inquiring and imaginative mind had been drawn by

Ferdinand von Wrangel's narrative of an expedition through northern Siberia in the eighteen-twenties. "Reflecting on the vast extent of the country, its mighty rivers, its stately and boundless forests, its immense mineral wealth," Collins writes in his lively, observant, and thoroughly engaging book, *A Voyage Down the Amoor,* "I was struck with the magnitude of its natural resources, and with its possible value to the commerce of the world, if it could only obtain an easy outlet to the ocean. . . . I had already fixed in my own mind upon the river Amoor as the destined channel by which American commercial enterprise was to penetrate the obscure depths of Northern Asia, and open a new world to trade and civilization, when news arrived in 1855 that the Russians had taken possession of the Amoor country, and formed a settlement at the mouth of the river."

Collins hastened to Washington for accurate information. "To have gone to the mouth of the river myself, as I was strongly inclined to do, would have required me to charter a vessel for the express purpose, and this I was scarcely able to afford. And besides, on arriving there, a private adventurer, without credentials, I could have no assurance of being permitted to ascend the river or explore the country." In Washington, he must have received this assurance from De Stoeckl. Secretary Marcy, perhaps as favorably impressed by Collins's evident lack of interest in government aid as by his dollar-bright vision of a Siberian El Dorado for Yankee traders, appointed him "Commercial Agent of the United States at the Amoor River" on March 24, 1856.

Armed with credentials and letters of introduction, Collins sailed from New York and arrived on May 19 at St. Petersburg, where he found that Governor-General Muravyev, to whom he had been referred, was taking the cure at Marienbad. During his absence, Collins assiduously cultivated influential dignitaries, and by his geniality and infectious enthusiasm soon won their good will. In August, he was cordially received by the invigorated Muravyev, who promised him every facility for exploring the Amur to determine its suitability for steamboat navigation.

Since Muravyev advised him to defer his Siberian trip until he could travel more quickly by sleigh, Collins proceeded to Moscow, where he witnessed "the superb ceremonial" of Alexander the Second's coronation in September. In the next three months, he gathered information about Russia's overland trade with China, and "continually practised myself in the Russian language, wandering daily about the streets, markets, bazaars, and shops of the city, taking my meals at the native eating-houses, many of them sufficiently curious places, drinking great quantities of tea in the tea-houses, and visiting theatres, gardens, and all kind of places where I could acquire the tongue and study the habits of the people."

On December 3, the impatient American and a companion he identifies only as "Mr. Peyton, a countryman and friend," departed by sleigh for distant Irkutsk. In their possession was a document signed and sealed by Muravyev himself, which they found magically effective in procuring horses and speeding their journey. Collins records that he carried "six-shooters," together with the supplies and equipment of the experienced Siberian traveler of means: vodka, tea, sugar, salt, spices, hams, sausages, biscuits, cups and eating utensils, a mattress, two pillows, furs, sheepskin coats, a splendid buffalo robe Peyton had brought from America, ropes, nails, and a quantity of "Persian powder" to exterminate posthouse vermin. Against the biting frost that ranged from ten degrees above to fifty below zero, the Americans deposited a teaspoonful of red pepper inside their socks. "In fact, we had determined to make the journey a frolic," the ebullient Collins remarks, "intending to have a good time of it, or at least the best possible under the circumstances; we therefore took every thing as we found it, mended it if we could, grumbled at nothing, kept as warm as possible, and paid the yamscheks liberally for fast driving."

This cheerful approach to the rugged ordeals of Siberian posting was put to severe trial: horses plunged through thin river ice, runners shivered to bits against hidden obstructions, harness ropes broke, drivers lost their way while exploring ostensible shortcuts, or fell asleep and stuck fast in snowdrifts. One night, the travelers dove headlong into a deep chasm. On being tugged back to the road with Collins and Peyton still tightly wedged inside the sleigh, the excited horses took off downhill at full gallop, leaving the slow-witted *yamshchik* behind. "We thought of divesting ourselves of our furs and trying to get from the door to the box to see if we could not recover the reins," Collins relates with the calm of hindsight, "but the speed was so great, and the motion of the sleigh bounding from one side of the road to the other, was so violent, that we concluded not to make the attempt." They told themselves that downhill must surely be followed by uphill, where the slowed team could be brought under control; instead, they collided in the dark with a hit-and-run driver from the opposite direction. "In an instant there was a crash and a stop, as if the whole sleigh had been torn to atoms, yet we found ourselves occupying our accustomed places, and no bones broken, though pretty thoroughly shaken up." One of the horses had been killed, the shafts were shattered, and the front end stove in. With the arrival of the missing driver, whom Collins and Peyton awaited "calmly and *very coolly,*" repairs got underway; starved and half-frozen, the party finally limped into the nearest post station. (Collins observes that *yamshchiki* customarily stripped off the hide of a dead horse and cut the smoking carcass into quarters. "At the next stopping place, the flesh afforded good steaks or soup, while the hide would be exchanged for a bottle or two of *vodka*.")

Despite accidents and delays common to winter traveling, Collins and Peyton made reasonably fast time, as the former notes in statistical detail. They reached Irkutsk on January 7, 1857, "within a few hours of thirty-five days since leaving Moscow, a distance of 3,545 miles; having slept out of our sleigh only three whole nights. . . . We changed horses 210 times, and drove over 700 on the journey, with some 200 drivers, and twenty-five postilions. The actual time employed in the journey, including ordinary delay, was about twenty-eight days and nights, averaging, therefore, a speed of 126 miles every twenty-four hours, or five miles and a fraction per hour." (As a passing reflection on the march of progress, today's fastest express between Moscow and Irkutsk averages less than thirty-four miles an hour.)

The first Americans to set foot in Irkutsk since the obscure, penniless Connecticut adventurer John Ledyard had hitch-hiked to it in the seventeen-eighties, Collins and Peyton were lionized to a fare-thee-well. "The hospitality of the principal citizens was unbounded," says Collins delightedly, "the people kind and civil, society agreeable, ladies handsome, wine good, and dinners excellent — what could a traveller ask more? We had hot baths, sleigh rides, pic-nics, ice-hills, suppers, routs, balls, and sleigh-promenades, to refresh and divert us." *

* Ice hills are still to be seen in Russian and Siberian communities. They are wooden slides, twenty-five or more feet high, over which water is poured to form ice. From a platform at the top, men, women, and children coast

Irkutsk: Official residence of the governor-general as photographed in 1895

The crowning gala during their stay was a stag banquet given for Muravyev, just returned from St. Petersburg. In the Governor-General's mansion — an imposing, porticoed building that oddly resembles a side view of the White House in Washington — Muravyev welcomed the Americans "as the pioneers to the Amoor, embracing us in the true Russian style, giving us a friendly hug, and kissing us at the same time." In the course of the festivities enlivened by a military band and all sorts of wine, Collins responded to a standing toast proposed by Muravyev to America and Russia with a lengthy speech that resounded with references to "an epoch in

down the slope on small sleds to a smoothed, fenced-off track extending for several hundred feet. The hills have lost popularity to ski slides since the development of skiing as a major winter sport in the Soviet Union.

history," "peace and good will," and "enlightened, sagacious, and far-seeing policy." He fails to say if these familiar allusions were translated as he went along, but tells us that he "was cheered by the guests, and the band struck up a lively Russian march." When champagne flowed again after dessert, Muravyev drank to the health of the two visitors. Altogether, the affair was without doubt the most sincere and heartwarming official tribute ever accorded Americans in eastern Siberia to the present day.

Collins and Peyton departed early on the morning of February 3 for Kyakhta, a town on the Russian side of the Mongolian frontier southeast of Irkutsk and the chief center, at that time, of Russo-Chinese trade. Fabulous fortunes were made there by Russian merchants who bartered woolens, cotton goods, furs, and hides for tea and silk. Two days later, the travelers were sumptuously put up in the house of one of these millionaires. In company with their host's wife, daughter, and a handsome widow, they explored the nearby Chinese town of Mai-mai-ch'eng (now Altan Bulag) across the border, where the ladies shopped for porcelain jars, lacquered boxes, fans, Tibetan musk, Cashmere shawls, rubies, pearls, opals, and other "little Celestial notions." A Chinese merchant entertained the visitors at dinner, after which they were invited to inspect the kitchen. "A glance was sufficient. The ladies silently retreated the instant they reached the threshold," Collins says with evident shock, "and we followed them with little delay. The walls of the kitchen were covered with paintings, as large as life, of the most grossly obscene character."

On the eve of their departure for Irkutsk, Collins and Peyton were lavishly wined and dined by local merchants, officers, and civil functionaries in the merchants' clubhouse, where the mayor hailed them "as the pioneers of American commerce, and the heralds of steamboats on the Amoor." Collins drank so many toasts — to the Emperor, Muravyev, and the President of the United States, among others — that he "began to fear that I should really run over before the dinner closed." This he did in volubility, for he made not one but three speeches, each of which brought down the house, though again the Russians may not have understood a word he said. Peyton, apparently a shy man, shook his head firmly when Collins asked him to rise and say a few words; in extenuation of his own verbosity, Collins explains that it "let off a little of the champagne."

Dinner over, the exhilarated Russians honored their overseas guests with a startling ceremony that is still observed occasionally in Siberia and Russia. ". . . I noticed a pretty dense circle encompassing Peyton," Collins narrates, "and in an instant he was seized by half-a-dozen stout, jolly merchants, and tossed up in the direction of the ceiling. Fortunately it was not a very low one, or else he must have gone through to the roof. Down he came, however, into the hands of his tormentors, who sent him up again, if any thing, higher than ever, the most uproarious mirth and laughter prevailing. My companion was not a small man, or a light one, but he was no more than a feather in the hands of these portly Siberians. This sport is called in Russian *podkeedovate*, or tossing-up, and is considered a mark of great respect. General Mouravieff told me, after our return, that he had had *podkeedovate* performed upon him in the same room. During the performance, I stood half-aghast, looking at the figure Peyton was cutting, a man six feet high and well proportioned, going up and down like a trap-ball, his coat-tail flying sky-high, and his face as red as a brick."

Collins's turn came as he drained his umptieth glass of

champagne. "Being much lighter than Peyton, and handled after him by these stout, and now very jovial and mellow fellows, I have a distinct recollection of touching the ceiling. . . . Having taken Peyton's guage [*sic*] with regard to weight, they did not take into consideration my lightness, and I came near going through the top of the house. Up I went and down I came, only to go up again, until my friends were satisfied that if I was not drunk before, my head would certainly swim now. However, I was able to stand when I came to my feet, which was more than I calculated upon when tossing between the floor and ceiling."

Early the next morning, the sleepless and presumably disheveled Americans departed for Irkutsk. After three weeks of "balls, suppers, parties, sleigh-rides, dinners, and theatricals in profusion," Muravyev gave them a farewell banquet on March 7. Peyton returned to the United States via Moscow; shortly thereafter, Collins set out with "Captain Gourieff, a good English scholar," on the final leg of his journey to the Amur, which he apostrophizes in one of his typical purple patches. ". . . Upon this generous river shall float navies, richer and more powerful than those of Tarshish; mines shall be found upon its shore richer than those of Ophir, and the timbers of its forests more precious than the *Almugim* [*sic*] of Scripture; a mighty nation shall rise upon its banks and within its valleys, and at its mouth shall arise a vast city, wherein shall congregate the merchant princes of the earth, seeking the trade of millions of people."

Collins intended to sail down the Ingoda, Shilka, and Amur rivers to test their navigability to and from the Pacific. But they were still icebound when he reached Chita, capital of the Transbaikal territory and about five hundred miles east of Irkutsk via the post road. In the weeks of waiting for the spring thaw, he made the most of his opportunities to learn about the region. With transient officers and acquaintances from Irkutsk, he hunted goat on the highlands and wild geese on the plains. Major-General Michael S. Korsakov, governor of the territory and described by Collins as one of the most handsome men he had ever seen, invited him daily to dinner, and took him on shooting expeditions into mountain gorges, where the sportsmen tried unsuccessfully to bag antelope bounding away from the whoops and horns of Cossack beaters. Mindful of his mission as a prospector for trade, he visited villages around Chita and conferred with leading merchants; all agreed that steam navigation on the Amur and its headwaters would bring enormous prosperity to eastern Siberia and good profits to American business interests.

Early in April, Collins and "Gourieff" braved savage winds, forty-below frost, and a treacherous mountain track "like the worst mule trail in California" to see the convict-worked silver mines of the Nerchinsk district and the extensive gold deposits near the Onon River, along whose banks lies the reputed birthplace of Genghis Khan. Not far from the Mongolian border, Collins studied the economy of Cossack settlements, and was appalled by the squalid living conditions of the frontiersmen, so different from those in the American West. ". . . Whole families for two or three generations . . . [are] packed in pairs and fours, and in sixes, around the room. You walk in, and the mistress of the house gets up and strikes a light, frequently of splinters of wood, and there you see the family lying heads and tails, arms and legs, odds and evens, dressed, half dressed, and not dressed at all, snoring, sleeping, groaning, coughing, stewing, squirming, and sweating. That they don't all die of fevers, is a strong proof of the salubrity of the climate and the robust constitution of the people."

When the river ice broke up in May, Collins joyfully embarked on a flat-bottomed, partly roofed wooden barge for the descent of the Ingoda River to the Shilka. His companion now was a "Captain Fulyhelm," of the Imperial Russian Navy. At the old silver- and gold-mining town of Shilka, Collins boarded another barge in company with Fulyhelm, the latter's servant, and five Cossacks who comprised the crew. When shallow or tortuous sections of the river were encountered at dusk, the voyagers tied up for the night and camped ashore. But with a bright moon and full water, they sailed on, as Collins remarks in one of his more lyrical moments, "while nought disturbed the profound stillness of nature but the mournful notes of the cuckoo, or the hooting of some amorous owl calling to his mate."

At 10 A.M. on Thursday, June 4, 1857, he precisely records, he set foot on a little point of land near the junction of the Argun and Shilka rivers, where the mighty Amur begins; a few minutes later, he bathed in its chilly waters. His exultation knew no bounds. "I had not been the first to discover this river, neither was I the first white man, like De Soto on the bank of the Mississippi," he exclaims, "but I was the first live Yankee who had seen it, and, as the road had been a pretty long one, and some of it rather hard to travel, I felt, I must admit, a little proud of the American people, inasmuch as I had perseveringly set my face towards it two years since, and had never, for a moment, turned my back upon it, and had confidently looked, with hope and faith, as well as works, to the day when I should stand at the head of the Amoor."

Without native pilots or navigational aids other than a steering oar, two side oars, sundry poles, and a small square sail on their seven-foot-wide barge, the voyagers found themselves largely at the mercy of the uncharted, deceitful Amur, called "Black Dragon River" by the Chinese. Time and again they grounded on sandbars, to be freed only by the herculean Cossacks, who plunged over the side and hauled the craft off. They were often blown ashore by gales, or immobilized for hours by fog, rain squalls, and contrary winds; on some days, they progressed for no more than eight to eighteen miles. Though he was alternately drenched, chilled, and baked (his thermometer readings dropped to the low fifties at night and soared into the upper seventies in late afternoon), Collins seldom lost his high spirits. On one trying occasion, when the barge whirled uncontrollably down a narrow, sinuous passage, he reassured Fulyhelm with the simple philosophy of Mississippi flatboatmen, "If the current is sufficient to suck you in, it will be found strong enough to puke you out."

In the intervals of fine weather and easy sailing, he saw much to corroborate his belief in the Amur valley's potential riches for international trade. He comments admiringly on the majestic cliffs streaked with iron, the shore well-timbered with pine and, somewhat farther downriver, deciduous trees, and meadows carpeted with shoulder-high grass. He notes the profusion of antelope, elk, reindeer, ducks, and geese; at night, he likens the Amur nightingale to the mockingbird of the American South, and the great flapping cranes to "evil spirits from the Dead Sea shore." While camping along the bank, he finds rich black soil in one locality, and seams of coal in another. Wild apple trees with eighteen-inch diameters, grapevines, strawberry beds, patches of asparagus and peas — these excite his eye to a degree equaled only by the sight of "monster" sturgeon in the river itself.* As for steamboat navigation, he concludes that all would go well if channel depths were measured and marked.

Collins derived unforgettable visual pleasure from his encounters with the picturesque Manchu officials who tried to make him turn back, and with the pretty native girls he and Fulyhelm sought to cultivate while they bartered blue cotton cloth for fresh caviar, chickens, dried fish, beans, corn, and round cakes of white bread. At various times, a Manchu chief inspector, distinguished by a cap sprouting a peacock feather, two black squirrel tails, and a white ball, rowed out to the barge, and, with sawing motions of hand against throat, indicated that Collins and his companions would lose their heads if they continued farther downstream. But with the exception of one brief scuffle in which Fulyhelm's indignant servant laid about the inspector's retinue with a pole, the "white-balls" meekly accepted vodka, tea, preserves, and biscuits, politely shook hands, and departed with their satellites.

When the foreigners landed at a village, the Manchus sometimes drove off the natives themselves with shouts and sticks. This unexpected tactic annoyed Collins and Fulyhelm, for they wanted to get on good terms with the girls, whose "color was red, to be sure; yet the color of the peach-bloom was in their cheeks, and they were very sprightly, and well formed." The Cossacks, too, had reason to resent "white-ball"

* Nineteen years before Collins's Amur voyage, George Mifflin Dallas, American minister to Russia from 1837 to 1839, attended a dinner given by Prince Yusupov in St. Petersburg. "Among other varieties of the table was a fish which had been brought from a distance of more than two thousand versts [1326 miles]," the envoy recorded in his diary. "I observed two waiters carrying a porcelain dish about nine feet long and two wide, and being seated next to my hostess, I inquired what the monster could be; it was more than two yards in length, was of delicate flavour, and tasted to me like salmon; its name I forget." The "monster" was probably sturgeon. Some are eight to twelve feet long and live for three hundred years.

Goldi women and child in their best attire

interference, since they carried on a profitable trade with native children, who knew coins only as ornaments and eagerly exchanged the silver Collins had given them for the Cossacks' larger coppers worth four times less.

In the lower reaches of the Amur, the susceptible American was attracted by the summer costume of the Goldi women. "Their whole wardrobe consisted of a single garment of fish-skin," he says with perhaps avuncular objectivity, "which was not too long or too full to impede the free movement of their limbs, nor yet so closely fitting or transparent as to reveal nature unadorned; but yet one could see, as they stood gracefully in their boats, resting upon their oars, that they were not destitute of either shape or form; and one of them in particular had a well-developed bust, though yet young —

Goldi shaman and assistant

Pipe-smoking Goldi belle

perhaps fifteen or sixteen. . . . The young girls, dressed in these new, shining fish-skin *robes*, trimmed off with shells, beads, and trinkets, laughing and frolicking along these wild shores, are doubtless quite as attractive to the young men around them as are their crinolined sisters of Broadway or Pennsylvania Avenue to the youth of New York or Washington."

The irrepressible Collins so openly admired the beautiful teeth of a tribesman's wife in one village that her scowling, jealous husband roughly called her away. Moments later, Fulyhelm saw the woman with head bloodied and spouse belaboring her with a heavy stick. The Captain drew his revolver and stopped the beating, but let the husband go, for "he did not think our party quite strong enough to set up a reform society for the amelioration of woman in these parts . . ." Collins adds contritely, "Out of compassion to woman, I admired no more teeth while among this tribe on the shores of the Amoor — at least, not while in the presence of the men."

On July 10, 1857 — fifty-two days and some twenty-two hundred miles from his departure point near Chita — Collins landed wearily at the port of Nikolayevsk, where five American trading schooners and barks were moored — "an unexpected and agreeable surprise to me to find the stars and stripes floating from the masts of so large an American fleet in these, until recently, unknown waters." After a restorative sleep assisted by a pill of opium from his medicine kit, he called on the Russian rear admiral in charge of the region, and learned to his chagrin that he had missed sight of the *Lena* "puffing and blowing like a true Mississippi craft" on her first ascent of the Amur. This iron steamer had been built in Philadelphia for the Russian government and shipped disassembled on a sailing vessel to Nikolayevsk. With the *Amur*, she was a forerunner of other steamers delivered to the eastern Siberian seaboard from shipyards in Philadelphia, Boston, and San Francisco.

Collins must have been deeply disappointed to find no response from St. Petersburg regarding a remarkable project he had submitted to Korsakov at Chita. While waiting for the rivers to clear, he had sent the Governor a letter in which he advanced the first proposal in Russian annals for a Siberian steam railway: a line to run from Chita, picked by him as the uppermost head of future cargo-ship navigation in eastern Siberia, to Irkutsk by way of Kyakhta. "The Amoor," he stated, "must become in the hands of Russia a very important country, through which a great trade will flow, opening Siberia to the commerce of the world. What is necessary then is to assist nature a little, and, by building this road, make the heart of Siberia easily accessible to commerce, so that her products can be quickly and readily exchanged or transported to the ocean by way of this railroad and the Amoor, where a ready market can be found. With steam upon the Amoor, and this railroad constructed, aside from commercial views, the road would be highly valuable to Russia in the development and protection of her possessions on the Pacific coast, both in Asia and America [that is, Alaska]."

To finance his "Amoor Railroad Company," Collins proposed to sell to the public four hundred thousand shares of stock at one hundred rubles ($50) per share, payable on terms of ten per cent down and five annual installments of eighteen kopecks on each ruble (or a total of $45). The Russian government would grant land for the right of way, stone and wood for construction, and iron rails for which it would receive stock as compensation. By guaranteeing seven per cent of the railway's estimated cost of $20,000,000, the government would possess the right to purchase it at any time, payment to be completed within twenty years. Collins calculated that twenty thousand men would be needed for construction, and suggested that they be obtained from Chinese or other labor contractors if such a large force could not be recruited in Siberia or Russia. As an example of his business astuteness, Article Ten in his supplementary memorandum to Korsakov stipulated that the company would have the right to work mineral deposits found on its land, or, if this prerogative were withheld, to receive equal acreage elsewhere. Collins pressed for ratification of a contract as early as possible in 1858, and asked for a favorable reply from St. Petersburg by the time he would reach Nikolayevsk.

At Chita, Korsakov had acknowledged Collins's letter with

an alacrity unusual in officials of the day. Assuring the American that he recognized "all the advantages that must result from such an enterprise in the Trans-Baïkal province under my administration if your proposition might be realized by our government," he wrote that he was reporting on the subject by special courier to Muravyev in Irkutsk. (Collins fails to explain why he did not write directly to the Governor-General.) Muravyev then also wrote to Collins, saying that he had forwarded the proposal to St. Petersburg. "I sincerely wish," he confided, "our government may give its consent to an enterprise in which I take the most lively interest, and in which I wish you all possible success." In his covering report to Communication Minister Chevkin, he described Collins as an "earnest and prudent man," and strongly emphasized the importance of the "Amoor Railroad" to the state.

Collins replied to Muravyev's heartening letter by reiterating that "the road must reach Irkutsk, from whence would be distributed the whole trade and enterprise of Siberia, making Irkutsk a great city, as it is justly entitled to be — the centre and capital not only of Eastern Siberia but of Northern Asia — from whence in a very few years after the completion of this enterprise, a commerce of fifty millions of rubles would flow annually." Then, perhaps resigned to the fact that the notorious sluggishness and timidity of the Russian bureaucracy might doom his project, he interpolated a rather affecting passage in which he said that "even if we find it cannot be accomplished through our efforts, we shall have the remembrance (satisfactory to ourselves) of having known the wants of the country only a little in advance of the times."

Collins heard nothing more about his plan during his four-week sojourn at Nikolayevsk before sailing home on an American bark to San Francisco. Chevkin — reactionary, quarrelsome, and getting on in years — deprecated the proposal, complaining that Collins had not defined the terrain to be crossed, the construction methods he would use, and the financial organization of the railroad company. Chevkin doubted that the American could raise $20,000,000 by public subscription, and questioned the availability of enough food in Transbaikalia for twenty thousand laborers over a period of several years.

The so-called Siberian Committee, in existence at that time for study of major questions on Siberian affairs, voted with Chevkin against the project. However, the Committeemen directed Muravyev to avoid details and to tell Collins only "in the most polite and flattering terms that the government had found his undertaking premature." Tsarist Russia thus dismissed and forgot the "Proposition to construct a railroad from Chetah to Irkutsk, by 'The Amoor Railroad Company,'" a bold enterprise that might have exploited Siberia's prodigious resources long before their actual development in our century, and might have also extended American influence into Siberia through the quickened expansion of Russo-American trade by way of the Amur and the railway to Kyakhta and Irkutsk.

And what became of Collins, the possibly self-seeking promoter or, more likely, the dedicated champion of commerce and improved communications? Although he refers to it only once in his *A Voyage Down the Amoor,* he had another string to his bow. With the failures of Cyrus W. Field's Atlantic cable in 1857 and 1858, Collins interested influential Americans, Russians, and Britons in a round-the-world overland telegraph to link Europe and the Russian empire with the United States by means of a line from Nikolayevsk to the American transcontinental system via Bering Strait, Alaska, and British

Columbia. In 1861, he obtained a useful letter from the venerable and esteemed inventor of telegraphy, Samuel F. B. Morse, who testified to the feasibility of the venture. A year later, he served for two and a half months as American vice consul at St. Petersburg, conferred frequently with the Grand Duke Constantine, Foreign Minister Alexander M. Gorchakov, and the Minister of Posts and Telegraphs, and received the honor of presentation to Tsar Alexander himself. Finally, on May 23, 1863, he obtained a thirty-three-year Imperial concession to build and operate the telegraph from Nikolayevsk to Bering Strait and southernmost Alaska, the Russians agreeing to extend the line from Irkutsk to Nikolayevsk at their own expense. Less than a year later, the British granted him permission to continue through British Columbia, then a colony separate from the Dominion of Canada, so that connection could be made with the American transcontinental system.

Collins had already secured the backing of the Western Union Telegraph Company, whose executives could hardly fail to be impressed by his estimate of revenue from a capital investment of $10,000,000. Two wires transmitting a thousand messages every twenty-four hours at $25 each would gross more than $9,000,000 a year; if volume were reduced to only two hundred and fifty messages daily, the company would still take in at least $2,280,000. The mellifluous Collins also won support from senators, representatives, and Secretary of State Seward, who said of him that "the country could not have a more enlightened, assiduous, and faithful representative." Largely at the urging of Seward (to whom the Civil War had emphasized the need for rapid communications with England and the Continent), Congress passed an act that granted Collins, among other things, land for the right of way and the assistance of a Navy vessel in laying a cable across Bering Strait. Lincoln signed the measure on July 1, 1864, and said in a presidential message, "The unbroken harmony between the United States and the Emperor of Russia is receiving a new support from an enterprise designed to carry telegraphic lines across the continent of Asia, through his dominions, and so to connect us with all Europe by a new channel of intercourse." Collins was somewhat less restrained. In a full-blown talk to the Traveler's Club and other societies in New York, he declared that the line would unite America and Europe "in the gentle bans [*sic*] of iron fillets, while Old Mother Asia stands bridesmaid to the distant couple. The Czar of Russia, however, guarantees the union, and Great Britain sanctions the contract — so that we have the presence of an array of high contracting parties, whose faith is not to be impeached; nor will there be lack of guests, for the whole world is asked to the nuptials."

Collins transferred his franchises to Western Union, which formed a subsidiary known as the "Collins' Overland Telegraph, Western Union Extension Via Behring Strait." Survey and construction work began in British Columbia and in Siberia in 1865. (Twenty-year-old George Kennan, the future authority on the Siberian exile system, was one of the telegraphers who landed at Kamchatka that summer.) Some $3,000,000 had been spent up to the latter part of July 1866, when the Atlantic cable was successfully laid and so doomed the exposed and vulnerable pole-strung wires of the forty-seven-hundred-mile Extension. Told to sell tools and unused supplies worth $15,000 to $20,000, Quartermaster Kennan and his colleagues disposed of the lot to Siberian natives for a total of $150. "We put the price of telegraph wires down until that luxury was within the reach of the poorest Korak family," Kennan relates. "We glutted the market with pickaxes and long-handled shovels, which we assured the natives would be useful in burying their dead, and threw in a lot of frozen cucumber pickles and other antiscorbutics which we warranted to fortify the health of the living. We sold glass insulators by the hundred as patent American teacups, and brackets by the thousand as prepared American kindling-wood. We offered soap and candles as premiums to anybody who would buy our salt pork and dried apples, and taught the natives how to make cooling drinks and hot biscuits, in order to create a demand for our redundant lime-juice and baking-powder. We directed all our energies to the creation of artificial wants in that previously happy and contented community, and flooded the whole adjacent country with articles that were of no more use to the poor natives than ice-boats and mouse-traps would be to the Tuaregs of the Saharan desert. In short, we dispensed the blessings of civilisation with a free hand." In British Columbia, Indians used abandoned wire to make bridges over gorges and rivers; on completing a span, the braves ordered their squaws to do a potlatch dance at its midpoint before venturing upon it themselves.

If Western Union lost money from this unlucky venture, Collins did not. For his franchises and rights, he had received from the telegraph company $100,000 in cash, paid-up stock amounting to another $100,000, and the privilege to subscribe to additional shares with a face value of still another $100,000. In 1876, he took up residence in the St. Denis Hotel, at Broadway and Eleventh Street, in New York, where he lived as a bachelor until his death on January 18, 1900, at the august age of eighty-seven. Some idea of how shrewdly he invested his fortune may be gained from the fact that his heiress, a favorite niece who died in 1917, bequested according to his wishes a total of more than $1,679,000 to New York University, Columbia University, and the Presbyterian Hospital.

Surely, Perry McDonough Collins must have read every scrap of news about construction of the Trans-Siberian during the last decade of his lifetime. And if he knew of the tremendous difficulties that beset Russian engineers building the line, we may venture to guess that, but for his old age, this remarkable American would have been in Siberia to give them a hand, "intending," as he had written some thirty years before, "to have a good time of it, or at least the best possible under the circumstances . . ."

CHAPTER IV

"It Is Time, It Is High Time!"

> Things move slowly and without system, with much talk and little organization, so why worry? Russia has much of the Orient. On a hillside in China is a tombstone which says: "He came here to hurry the East. He rests in peace." Russia can't be hurried.
>
> — JUNIUS B. WOOD: *Incredible Siberia*

ON June 21, 1887, all London was in a ferment of excitement over the fiftieth anniversary of Queen Victoria's accession to the throne. Early in the afternoon, hundreds of thousands of hearts beat faster as the royal Jubilee procession — the Queen in a handsomely gilded landau — passed through Piccadilly, Waterloo Place, and Parliament Street on the way to thanksgiving services at Westminster Abbey, where the freshly dusted effigies of Britain's illustrious dead awaited the sovereign and her entourage: the kings of Denmark, Belgium, Greece, and Saxony, five crown princes, and an exotic assortment of other personages such as the Maharaja of Indore, the Grand Duke Sergius of Russia, and Queen Kapiolani of Hawaii.

In view of the obligation of newspapers to report every Jubilee event in profuse detail, it is not surprising that the London *Times* buried a dispatch from a St. Petersburg correspondent in a back page of the June 25 edition. This read, in part: "A very important decision in Russian railway construction has just been come to regarding a scheme which has often been ridiculed as utterly incapable of present realization. The great 'through Siberian Railway' right away [*sic*] to the Pacific is to be commenced at last. . . . The prolongation of the railway now in progress through Ekaterinburg and Tiumen will shortly be met by several other lines, laid across the Siberian plains from the port of Vladivostok. . . . Part of the line is, if possible, to be commenced next spring, and it is estimated that the whole may be completed in about five years. Direct communication will then be established between St. Petersburg and Russia's Pacific ports."

Seasoned readers of *The Times* could only be expected to regard this news as typical Russian vaporing. For close to thirty years since Perry Collins had submitted his "Amoor Railroad" proposal to Governor Korsakov in 1857, the pros and cons of railway extensions into Siberia had been inconclusively debated by state ministers, provincial governors, engineers and geographers, industrialists, merchants, and town fathers from both sides of the Urals who periodically swarmed into the capital to urge a route that would benefit their community. Successive governors-general in Siberia insisted in one annual report after another on the urgent economic and strategic necessity to join their provinces with Russia by rail, but procrastinating St. Petersburg avoided a decision by saying that such a costly venture should be put off until a thorough study of Siberia's commercial and industrial potentialities had been made.

In the mid–eighteen-seventies, a special government commission reported favorably on the suggestion of a certain Anosov to connect Vladivostok with the Amur basin; then, southern Russia suffered a disastrous famine that combined with a sharp drop in export prices and the value of the ruble to kill Anosov's project. A war with Turkey in 1877-1878 severely strained the Treasury, thereby ending consideration of an appeal by Eastern Siberia's Governor-General Dmitri G. Anuchin for a railway from Yekaterinburg* to Tyumen and from Tomsk to Irkutsk. The Old Guard in Irkutsk — Anuchin's own capital — grumpily disapproved. "We like better to travel by tarantass," they said to a foreign visitor. "One leaves when one likes, stops where one likes, and at post stations of one's choice. With trains, you must board them at a fixed hour and ride in a carriage full of strange and unpleasant people; you are transported like a trunk, and you haven't the right to stop the train when you please."

A pertinacious champion of the Siberian railway during this period was Communication Minister Constantine N. Posyet. In 1875, he declared in a memorable report — the first official document to advocate an ultimate trunk line from Russia to the Far East — that Siberia had ceased to be "a desolate and terrible country inhabited by convicts," and that its rich resources must be developed with the aid of a through railway. If Russia could not afford at that time to spend an estimated $125,000,000 for a line from the Volga to the Amur, he said, at least one should be built between Moscow and Irkutsk.

Alexander II was not greatly concerned about Siberia's welfare, but he and his ministers approved Posyet's recom-

---

* Now Sverdlovsk, the industrial city where Nicholas II, last of the Tsars, and his family were executed in 1918 at Bolshevist order, and over which the American U-2 pilot Francis G. Powers was downed in 1960.

Tyumen, Siberia's oldest community founded by the Russians, was the important western terminus of river vessels from Tomsk and Omsk, and was also the largest forwarding station for convicts and exiles until the completion of the Trans-Siberian. Today, it continues to flourish as a transshipment port for timber and grain.

Alexander III

mendation in principle and agreed to a railway from Perm southeastward to Yekaterinburg; this was completed in 1878 despite the Turkish war, and was later (in 1885) extended to Tyumen. For four years, the Treasury's penury prohibited further construction, but in 1882 finances improved enough for Posyet to reopen the matter with the Committee of Ministers, now subject to Alexander III, who had ascended the throne after the assassination of his father by bomb-throwing revolutionists in March 1881. Following much discussion, two years of technical and economic studies of various proposed routes, and another year of ministerial deliberation, Posyet was at last authorized to begin construction in the spring of

1886 of a single-track line from the terminus of the East Russian system near Samara (today's Kuibyshev) northeastward to Zlatoust, a metal-working city as famous in Russia for its cutlery as Toledo, in Spain, had been for sword blades.

Meanwhile, the rest of the world had been smiling scornfully at every mention of Russia's tentative moves toward the creation of an iron road of unprecedented length across the "forbidding wastes" of Siberia. Foreign journalists delighted in calling the project a Slavic pipe dream as fantastic as the novels of Jules Verne. The British, with natural disaffection for any nation that might balk their own imperialistic designs, were particularly disparaging, and, in the words of a furious St. Petersburg senior official, "searched for a thousand details to discredit the enterprise in the eyes of Europe." Belittlement of Russia's railway plans became such an obsession among Britons that Her Majesty's military attaché at St. Petersburg publicly rebuked them in a semi-official London journal. "British energy," he admonished, "should be directed to obtaining orders for the iron rails, rather than cavilling and carping at a railway extension."

Alexander III — a huge, muscular man who liked to unbend horseshoes and to form pokers into knots with his bare hands — took far greater interest in Siberia than had his father. He saw in the railway a means to draw wealth from his eastern domain, stimulate emigration from overcrowded or famine-prone agricultural lands in the mother country, and strengthen the nation's position in the Orient. But, like Posyet, even the Autocrat of All the Russias found himself confronted by the timidity, hair-splitting, and shilly-shallying of the ministerial hierarchy whose prolonged conferences and investigations had resulted in the authorization of a few baby steps toward the East.

In 1885 and 1886, however, St. Petersburg received alarming reports from Count Alexis P. Ignatyev, governor-general of Irkutsk Province and brother of the crafty Nicholas Ignatyev who had finessed the land-grabbing Treaty of Peking from China in 1860. The Count warned that Peking appeared to be reorganizing the army and that large numbers of Chinese were infiltrating Transbaikalia. Russia must prepare for all eventualities and be in a position to move troops more quickly from the homeland. As the first step, he proposed a railway between Irkutsk and Tomsk, a major mid-Siberian city with river communications to the terminus of the Perm-Yekaterinburg track at Tyumen. Aside from its military value, he added, such a line would be indispensable in activating Siberian commerce and industry.

Disturbed by these revelations and exasperated by his feet-dragging ministers, Alexander wrote on the margin of Ignatyev's latest dispatch: "How many times have I read such reports from the governors-general of Siberia! I must own with grief and shame that up to the present the Government has done scarcely anything to meet the needs of this rich but forsaken country. It is time, it is high time!"

Their Excellencies took the hint and set up a fact-finding commission with the greatest alacrity. Comprising the ministers of Communication, Finance, and other key officials, this commission heard testimony from Baron Andrew N. Korff, governor-general of the Amur territory. Korff, who had submitted a report similar to Ignatyev's, reiterated their appeals for action and pressed for a railway from the eastern shore of Baikal to Sretensk, approximately six hundred and sixty post-road miles to the east. Sretensk was the uppermost river port for steamer navigation on the Shilka-Amur waterway to the coast.

Every member of the commission but Finance Minister Ivan A. Vyshnegradski tumbled over himself to endorse the Ignatyev-Korff proposals. When asked by Posyet to allocate funds for preliminary topographical surveys in Transbaikalia, Vyshnegradski — a cautious standpatter who guarded the Treasury as if it were his own personal property — declared flatly that Russia could not afford them. He seldom found it hard to prove his points, since he had a phenomenal memory for facts and figures. "On one occasion in my presence," a colleague recalled, "he read a page of logarithms and then repeated it all without making so much as a single mistake."

Alexander dissolved this commission and appointed another to reconsider the proposals. When it convened in June 1887, Ignatyev and Korff presented such convincing new arguments that even Vyshnegradski grudgingly conceded that the Tomsk-Sretensk surveys should be begun at once. The commission then took up the strategic needs of Vladivostok, since 1872 Russia's main naval and military base in the Far East. This bastion was cut off from the interior but for a primitive road and largely unnavigable streams up to the Ussuri River about halfway to Khabarovsk, on the Amur to the north. Alexander was at one with Ignatyev and Korff in warning of the seaport's perilous isolation, and so the commission authorized engineering studies of the terrain between Vladivostok and the Ussuri. Summarized, the June decisions foretokened, for the time being, the transportation of troops by water and rail from Russia to Tyumen, whence they would proceed on steamers and barges in summer or sledges in winter to Tomsk. There, they would entrain for Irkutsk, cross Lake Baikal, and entrain again for Sretensk, where shipping would carry them down the Shilka, Amur, and Ussuri rivers to the railhead of the line leading to Vladivostok. The eastern river

Military caravan on the Amur

routes presented no problem in winter, since there were shoreland post stations not far from the frozen mid-river track for private travelers and military caravans of sledges drawn by shaggy Bactrian camels.

The commission next discussed the unpleasant subject of construction costs. With wary regard for the parsimony of Treasury Watchdog Vyshnegradski, the members decided that utmost economy could be achieved only by adopting building standards well below those in Russia and the West. There must be no more than a single track of lightweight rails laid on fewer, shorter ties (or sleepers) and a narrower, more thinly ballasted roadbed. Russian engineers would ignore the "red-tape precautions" of their Western contemporaries, and avoid tunneling and hill-cutting if this work merely reduced

Steel bridge over the Ob River

acute curves and gradients for greater safety. Timber would substitute for stone or steel in spans over streams, while steam ferries would take the place of long, costly metal bridges across the Irtysh, Ob, and other wide rivers, on which tracks would be laid in winter. Stations were to be modest wooden affairs without freight platforms except in cities and important towns. According to the Communication Ministry's forecasts, these specifications, cheeseparing though they were, would allow for the passage of three daily freight and passenger trains in each direction during peacetime, and seven each way during hostilities. The speed of passenger and freight trains was not to exceed thirteen miles an hour and nine miles an hour respectively.

Alexander approved this program with the marginal notation: "All this is perfectly sensible. I hope that the Ministry [of Ways of Communication] will prove that it can build quickly and cheaply." As one of his eminent ministers, Sergius Witte, was subsequently to write when in safe retirement abroad, "Neither in the Imperial family nor among the nobility was there anyone who better appreciated the value of a ruble or a kopeck than Emperor Alexander III." Witte adds that this exceptionally tightfisted monarch, whose recreations seem to have been limited to poker-twisting and playing the bassoon at family concerts, set a notoriously poor table and habitually wore garments until his valet could no longer mend them.

It was in this period that *The Times*'s St. Petersburg correspondent wrote his dispatch, which may be counted among the notably premature announcements of the nineteenth century. To be sure, exploratory surveys were begun. In September 1887, Nicholas P. Mezheninov, appointed chief engineer of the Tomsk-to-Irkutsk section, set out on horseback from Tomsk, accompanied by three work crews, each comprising four subordinate engineers, a local guide, two Cossacks, and twelve soldiers. The Communication Ministry had enjoined him to hurry. In consequence, his survey was anything but thorough, as may be deduced from the fact that he staked out more than a thousand miles of unfamiliar swamps, forests, and mountains within only nine months. Haste also characterized the expedition of Chief Engineer Alexander O. Ursati in the Vladivostok region. By the summer of 1889, another chief engineer, Orest P. Vyazemski, had completed the hurried tracing of a route from Irkutsk to Sretensk.

In October 1887, Governor-General Korff submitted further warning evidence that the Vladivostok, or South Ussuri, line should be started at the earliest possible moment. He had learned that China was indeed reorganizing her army to bring it to effective combat readiness. She had also improved communications by building a telegraph line and river steamers (future gunboats?) in Manchuria, from which an attack could be mounted against Vladivostok. In addition, she stood to gain commercial prosperity from stepped-up trade with Britain and Canada by means of an active Anglo-Canadian mercantile fleet and the recently completed transcontinental Canadian Pacific Railway. Then, too, there was the possibility that Ferdinand de Lesseps might succeed in his attempt to open a shipping canal through Panama, in which event Sino-American commerce would increase. With a strong army, numerous war vessels, and an enriched economy, the Chinese might very well ally themselves with Powers jealous of Russia and attack Siberia to recover the territory Peking had surrendered in 1858 and 1860. Their first objective, Korff pointed out, would obviously be the seizure of isolated Vladivostok.

Posyet made the most of these dismaying disclosures to back up his appeal for $2,000,000 toward the purchase of materials and rolling stock for an immediate start on the South Ussuri line. But Vyshnegradski — described by Witte as lacking "that breadth of imagination which is so necessary in transacting business on a large scale" — countered with an adamant *nyet*. The Treasury, he asserted, was barely able to afford railway and port improvements in Russia itself! He had had trouble enough in raising an internal loan that spring, he said, so that it would be futile to seek outside funds from the then uneasy European money market. As this argument appeared to be unshakable, Their Excellencies threw in the sponge and added their veto to that of the Finance Minister.

In November 1888, the undiscouraged Posyet asked again

for authorization to begin the South Ussuri line. In addition, he sought to extend the track, in the west, from Zlatoust to Chelyabinsk. But before these projects were discussed by the Committee of Ministers, the sixty-nine-year-old Posyet was forced to resign because public opinion had held him responsible for a train wreck in which the royal family had been gravely endangered that October. He was succeeded in April 1889, by Adolf Ya. von Hubbenet, his former associate in the Ministry.

In the late eighteen-eighties and early nineties, various enterprising individuals beset the Communication Ministry with Siberian railway schemes. A certain Hartmann vainly offered to build from Tomsk to Irkutsk and from Lake Baikal to Sretensk for an annual subsidy of $2,000,000 over a concessionary period of eighty-one years. General Michael N. Annenkov, constructor of the Trans-Caspian Railway from the Caspian Sea to Samarkand, contributed a memorandum in which he wrote that he himself could complete the Trans-Siberian in six years for less than $30,200 per mile; the Ministry replied tartly that there was sheer absurdity in establishing a fixed mileage cost over terrain the General knew nothing about.

A really attractive proposition came from the representative of a private French company that guaranteed to float a $150,000,000 loan, keep the funds in the Russian Treasury, and draw on them solely for payment of completed sections, the whole to be finished in eight years. In return, the company asked for no more than the surveys on hand and an honorarium of less than $2263 per mile. St. Petersburg declined this enticing bid with a rather wistful reply that it had arrived too late for consideration. The decision had been reached to build the Trans-Siberian under government auspices.

Communication Minister von Hubbenet was as zealous as his former chief in championing the railway. In June 1889, he repeated Posyet's request to link Zlatoust with Chelyabinsk, but this was denied owing to the opposition of Vyshnegradski. Von Hubbenet made another attempt in the next year, asking for approval of the link and the South Ussuri line. This time, Their Excellencies vetoed the latter but cautiously sanctioned construction for a mere forty miles to Miass, sixty miles short of Chelyabinsk. However, the tide had begun to turn under the influence of that inverse Cato, Governor-General Korff, who insisted more vehemently than ever on the importance of the South Ussuri section. English engineers, he reported, were working on plans with China to build a railway in southern Manchuria and to carry it northward to a point only ninety miles from Vladivostok. Thoroughly aroused by this new danger and his ministers' continued support of the obstructive Vyshnegradski, Alexander laid down the law in an annotation on Korff's report: "It is essential to proceed at once with the construction of this line."

The Tsar was influenced by other factors besides the presumptive Anglo-Chinese threat. His commercial advisers sang siren songs of burgeoning transpacific trade with America, a nation "cherishing sincere sympathy for Russia," according to the director of the Department of Trade and Manufactories, who blandly ignored the then-current ill-feeling generated in the United States by Alexander's repressive measures against the Jews. Commerce between Europe and Asia, he said, would flourish as never before because of cheaper rail rates, the saving of Suez Canal tolls, and rapid turnover brought about by a reduction in delivery time from weeks to days. Consumers would benefit from lower prices concomitant with the railway's competition against the Kyakhta caravan monopoly. "As the line shortens the distance from European Russia to the east of Asia," another official predicted in rosy summation, "in a like measure will the power of Russia increase in the East."

These alluring prospects and the Emperor's demand for action forced Vyshnegradski to temporize. In a report submitted in the latter part of 1890, he advanced the view that construction should be gradual and in proportion to economic growth in western and central Siberia. He saw no merit in the South Ussuri line, which he considered of little military value to Vladivostok unless it were connected with the Russian network, and he doubted if Peking would put through a railway to the vicinity of the base. At most, he said in substance, let us concentrate on building easterly from Tomsk, already connected with central Russia by navigable rivers and the western rail system.

Von Hubbenet caustically replied that everyone from the Tsar down to local officials in the Far East supported the South Ussuri line, and that its construction must not be delayed just for the benefit of western and central Siberian communities. But since these also should be aided, he said, let us proceed with the entire transcontinental system, starting simultaneously at its extremities, Vladivostok and Miass. He estimated the cost of this 4950-mile undertaking at $181,250,000, or an average of $36,616 per mile. He then repeated his request to commence work in the South Ussuri area, and asked permission to survey northward to Khabarovsk on the Amur while tracking between Miass and Chelyabinsk and surveying the terrain from Chelyabinsk to Tomsk.

On February 24, 1891 — almost twenty-two years after the driving of the golden spikes that marked the completion of America's first transcontinental railway, and a bit more than five years since Canadian Pacific engineers had spanned the Dominion — the Committee of Ministers convened in one of its most momentous meetings. We might wish that the pioneering Collins, Count Muravyev-Amurski, the English engineer Dull, and even the raffish trio of Morison, Sleigh, and Horn had been there.

Overriding Vyshnegradski at last, Their Excellencies announced their firm intention to join Vladivostok with Khabarovsk, then proceed westward from there and eastward from the Urals until the tracks met. In his customary role, Vyshnegradski warned that if Russia proclaimed to the world her intention to build such a fantastically long railway and to spend from $150,000,000 to $200,000,000 on it, then the value of the ruble would probably tumble to ruinously low levels. The public, already aware of Russia's straitened resources, would be quick to realize that she would be forced to seek a large loan, and that years might elapse before the railway's revenues would even begin to defray construction costs. Speculators would seize on this long-term financial burden as a means to destroy the last vestige of confidence in the ruble, with the result that the purchasing power of the currency would be disastrously reduced. But the Committeemen were now thoroughly convinced by the accumulation of military and economic evidence that the Trans-Siberian must be got on with immediately, and so they approved all of Von Hubbenet's proposals. Thus, after more than a third of a century of wars, famine, state impoverishment, and factional deadlocks, one of the most ambitious projects ever undertaken by Man was on the way to fulfillment.

The Tsar was of course delighted. "Not content with having given precious tokens of his interest in the great work," a state secretary was to write later, "Alexander III wished solemnly to underline its importance." To this end, the Emperor suggested to the ministerial committee that he issue a proclamation to the Russian Senate (an assembly bearing no relation in powers or functions to that of republics), directing the Heir Apparent, the Grand Duke Nicholas, to inaugurate construction of the transcontinental railway at Vladivostok upon his arrival there after a tour of Greece, Egypt, India, Indo-China, and Japan. Their Excellencies replied that they thought the Emperor should go further and release the news in the form of an Imperial decree, which would carry a great deal more weight to the skeptical world. Alexander approved this thoughtfully constructive recommendation and, on March 29, 1891, addressed the following rescript to his son:

YOUR IMPERIAL HIGHNESS!

Having given the order to begin the construction of a continuous railroad line across the whole of Siberia, destined to unite the Siberian lands, so rich in natural endowments, with the railway network of the interior, I entrust You to proclaim My will on this matter upon Your return to the Russian land after Your inspection of the foreign countries of the East. Furthermore, I charge You with the duty of laying the foundation stone, in Vladivostok, of the Ussuri section of the Great Siberian Railway, which is to be built at State expense and under direction of the Government.

Your significant role in the commencement of this truly national task which I have undertaken will give fresh evidence of My sincere desire to facilitate communications between Siberia and the other parts of the Empire and thus will demonstrate to this region, which is so dear to My heart, My very keen interest in its peaceful prosperity.

Beseeching the Lord's blessing upon the long journey through Russia which lies ahead of You,

I remain Your sincerely affectionate ALEXANDER

On May 23, His Imperial Highness the Tsarevich Nicholas — a short, spare, narrow-shouldered young man just turned twenty-three — disembarked from the belted cruiser *Pamyat Azova* at Vladivostok. He was pale and nervous, for he had barely escaped assassination a short time before in Japan. A fanatical police agent had wounded him with a saber and undoubtedly would have killed him if Prince George of Greece, Nicholas's cousin, had not deflected the second lunge with a stout walking stick.

Vladivostok was a slatternly town of muddy, unpaved streets, open sewers, grim military barracks and warehouses, unpainted wooden houses, and hundreds of mud-plastered straw huts of the Chinese and Korean settlers who comprised about a third of the port's fourteen thousand inhabitants. Nicholas could hardly have regarded this dismal scene with aesthetic pleasure, but he fulfilled his princely duties with a gracious spirit perhaps buoyed by an emotionally affectionate letter from his "dear darling Mama." During his visit, he opened construction of a drydock named for him, and laid the first stone of a monument to Admiral Nevelskoi, founder of Nikolayevsk on the lower Amur some forty years before. (The completion of this illustrious naval hero's memorial was delayed for six years, conceivably because Vladivostok lacked stonecutters capable of incising the pedestal with Nicholas the First's glorious but lengthy declaration to the effect that the Russian flag, once hoisted, must never be lowered.)

Nicholas II in old Russian court dress

On May 31, the Grand Duke, as representative of "the Most August Founder of the Great Siberian Railway," inaugurated construction of "the Noble Work." At the conclusion of open-air religious rites swept by harsh Siberian winds, he grasped a ceremonial shovel, filled a wheelbarrow with clayey soil, and emptied it upon an embankment of the future Ussuri line. A short time later, this royal navvy doubled as a mason and laid the first stone of the passenger station. On the same day, Alexander's decree to him was published in St. Petersburg "in order that all the true subjects of the Tsar," so goes the official account, "might join in their hearts in the memorable and historical solemnity performed by the wish of the Emperor in the distant borderland of the Empire."

In view of later events, it is significant that an image of St. Nicholas the Miracle-Worker was placed where the Tsarevich had officiated at the station site. For of all men engaged in monumental undertakings, few ever stood in greater need of supernatural aid than the builders of the Trans-Siberian Railway.

CHAPTER V

Enter Sergius Witte

> It will not be an exaggeration to say that the vast enterprise of constructing the great Siberian Railway was carried out owing to my efforts, supported, of course first by Emperor Alexander III, and then by Emperor Nicholas II.
>
> — *The Memoirs of Count Witte*

THE question of the construction of the Great Siberian Railway," records a tsarist historian, ". . . was now settled, representing the most important event of the century, not only in our country, but in the whole world." The Heir Apparent had broken ground at Vladivostok; in western Siberia, engineers were building the sixty-mile link between Miass and Chelyabinsk while surveyors traced a course eastbound from Chelyabinsk to Omsk. But the Committee of Ministers, lacking dynamic leadership, beset by financial worries, and for the most part ignorant of Siberia, had yet to agree on a master construction plan.

Nearly three months after the Vladivostok ceremonies, Von Hubbenet recommended that the transcontinental route be divided into six geographical sectors: the WEST SIBERIAN from Chelyabinsk to the Ob River; the MID-SIBERIAN from the Ob to Irkutsk and Lake Baikal; the CIRCUMBAIKAL round the

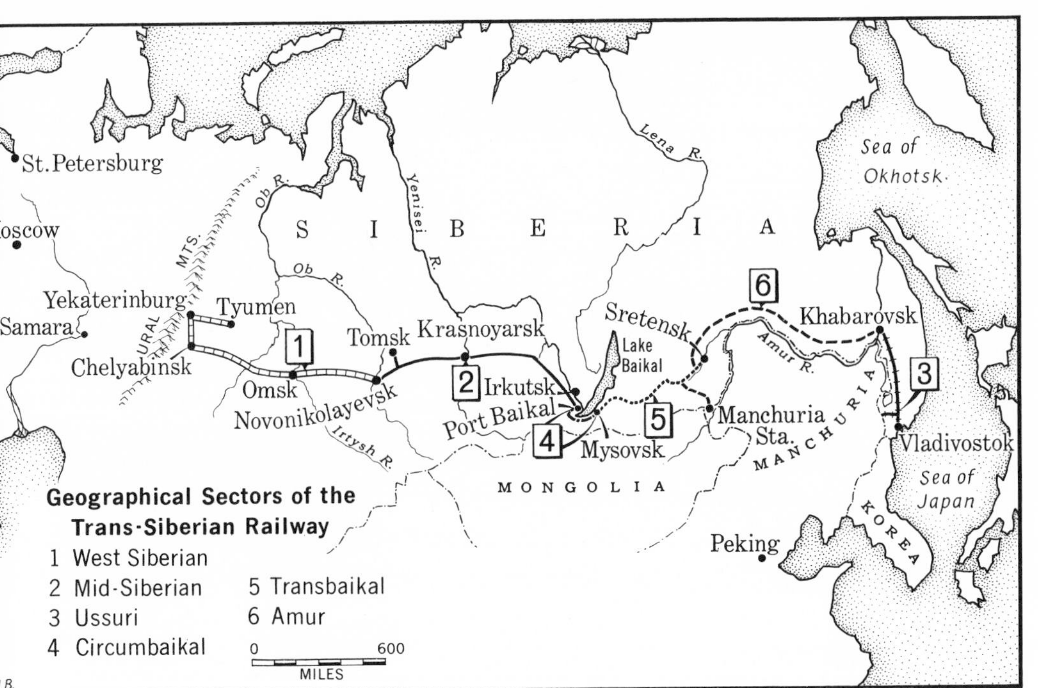

lake; the Transbaikal onward to Sretensk; the Amur from Sretensk to Khabarovsk; and the Ussuri from Vladivostok to Khabarovsk. He also presented a tentative timetable that set the end of 1903 as the opening date for traffic on uninterrupted tracks from the Urals to the Pacific. His estimated cost of about $175,000,000 was lower, by more than $6,000,000, than the amount he had quoted in 1890.

When asked for his opinion on this reduced figure, Finance Minister Vyshnegradski replied evasively that he could not foretell costs without detailed information on construction problems in Siberia, but that his colleague's estimate still seemed very high. He then referred the question to an "extraordinary commission" headed by Count Dmitri M. Solski, in whose hands it remained until early in 1892, when Von Hubbenet was succeeded by Sergius Yulyevich Witte, a remarkably resourceful, hard-working, and ambitious forty-two-year-old railwayman, without whose adroit and contriving mind the Trans-Siberian might have ended forlornly as a few hundred miles of rusted and weed-choked rails.

Born of a cultured family in the Georgian city of Tiflis (now Tbilisi), in 1849, Witte graduated from the New Russian University, in Odessa, and entered the service of the Odessa State Railway. He rose rapidly from the ranks to become Traffic Supervisor, a post in which he distinguished himself during the Turkish war of 1877-1878 by transporting large numbers of troops despite inadequate rolling stock. Further promotions culminated in his appointment as Communication Minister in February 1892. He held this post until August, when Alexander named him Finance Minister to replace Vyshnegradski, invalided by a stroke earlier in the year.

Professor Theodore H. Von Laue has graphically described the new Minister in his *Sergei Witte and the Industrialization of Russia* (1963). "He was what in Germany would be called a *Sitzriese,* a man with a massive head, a long and heavy torso, and weak, oddly short legs. At closer range he appeared more harmonious and dignified. An official photograph, taken sometime before 1900, shows him dressed in a simple dark broadcloth suit — not in court uniform — in the prime of his life. He wore a well-trimmed beard in the style fashionable during the reign of Alexander III, and his hair, smooth and still full, was combed back from a prominent, unruffled forehead. His face had the serious expression of a man used to handling hard facts and able to master them. It betrayed both the arrogance and the humility of greatness, and the determination of a man who never spared himself. By his own testimony, he had worked sixteen hours a day ever since he was a student."

Witte could not have taken over at a more opportune moment. Russia was still staggering from the effects of calami-

Sergius Yulyevich Witte

tous crop failures in the central and eastern provinces. Famine had reached such appalling proportions that Vyshnegradski had been forced to spend millions of rubles for the relief of starving peasants, whose desperate straits moved private citizens in America to contribute shiploads of wheat and flour to the stricken areas. A fervid supporter of the Siberian railway,

Witte turned the catastrophe to its advantage. With the argument that work must be found for the destitute, he persuaded the Committeemen in May 1892 to authorize construction between Chelyabinsk and Omsk. Their Excellencies agreed also to continue to the Ob but no farther, for the unconvertible Vyshnegradski had drummed into their heads that each extension should be undertaken only when government means permitted.

Witte bided his time until he had stepped into the ailing Finance Minister's shoes. Although the Treasury was so bare that he was obliged to postpone a government payday until he could print several million paper rubles, one of his first acts was to create an elaborate program to win over doubting ministers and assure the swift completion of the Trans-Siberian. Siberia's economy, he stated, must be developed by means of the railway, improved waterways, expanded metallurgical plants, and more efficient mining and agricultural enterprises. To obtain manpower, he urged the encouragement of emigration from the disaster regions, where too many peasants had struggled for years to survive on too little cultivable land. He pictured the tremendous gains to be derived from the Trans-Siberian, even though it might not earn profits overnight. It was an undertaking of supreme national importance, he emphasized, and its construction from the Urals to the Pacific should not be postponed for purely financial considerations. Aside from the inestimable economic benefits that would accrue to Siberia over the long term, Russia herself would enlarge her revenues by using the superior speed of the Trans-Siberian to cut into the East-West seaborne trade of Britain and other maritime nations. The proximity of China to the overland rails would mean a vast increase in the sale of Russian textiles and metal wares to that immense reservoir of consumers; in addition, Chinese products would cost less in Russia because of cheaper freight rates than those of ships and caravans. The Trans-Siberian would also transport tons of Siberian grain, timber, hides, butter, and minerals to bolster the mother country's internal and export trade. Finally, the railway would facilitate the victualing and coaling of the Pacific fleet, and assure amicable relations between Russia and the Orient and the United States.

The railwayman-turned-finance-minister proposed that each of the West Siberian and Mid-Siberian sectors be divided into two parts to hasten construction: Section One of the West Siberian to extend from Chelyabinsk to Omsk, and Section Two from Omsk to the Ob; in the Mid-Siberian, the first section would lie between the Ob and Krasnoyarsk, on the Yenisei, while the second would continue on to Irkutsk. Separate crews would start work simultaneously at the beginning of each of these sections, men and supplies to be transported mainly by steamers and barges as soon as the rivers opened.

Witte discarded Von Hubbenet's timetable and assigned construction to three chronological periods: the West Siberian, Mid-Siberian, and South Ussuri lines, together with a branch from Chelyabinsk north to Yekaterinburg, to be commenced in the first period and completed between 1894 and 1900; the North Ussuri and Transbaikal in the second; and the Circumbaikal loop and the long Amur extension in the third. The Finance Minister considered it premature to give starting dates for the sections in the last two periods because construction problems and costs had yet to be determined. He proposed an expenditure of $75,000,000 during the primary stage, including $7,000,000 for colonization, river improvement, and auxiliary projects, plus $4,250,000 for the stone and iron bridges he regarded as more practical than the steam ferries originally suggested for the Irtysh, Ob, Yenisei, and other wide rivers.

With the possible exception of his bold, realistic, and far-reaching program for the stimulation of the Siberian and Russian economy, there was little else in his proposals that might not have occurred to almost any capable and experienced railway administrator. But few other officials in Russia possessed his skill in financial legerdemain. However much the Soviets today may echo Lenin's condemnation of Witte* — a forthright economic imperialist and a sincere believer in autocracy — they owe him an everlasting debt, since he was as fully responsible for the completion of the Trans-Siberian as the thousands of engineers and laborers who built it.

Witte was well aware that the Committee of Ministers, regardless of the entrancing future he painted, might still balk at the expenditure of so much for the railway. He therefore devised an ingenious scheme by which he made use of forgotten notes issued by the Imperial Bank during the Turkish war fourteen years before. Then he juggled the accounts of the Bank and of the Treasury in such artful fashion as to produce a credit of $46,350,000. The balance of $28,650,000 he raised by levying on the "ordinary and extraordinary expense" budget, and by securing a loan from French and other sources.

In the following years, Witte cured the nation's financial ills

* Lenin bitterly attacked Witte in a 1902 issue of his revolutionist publication *Iskra* [*The Spark*]. ". . . The conjurer . . . assures us that he is not deceiving us, that there is no deficit, and that his liabilities are less than his assets. . . . While you [Witte] laud the 'cultural role' of the railways, you modestly refrain from mentioning the purely Russian and very uncultured custom of *plundering the Treasury* when railways are built (to say nothing of the shameful exploitation of the workers and the starving peasants by railway contractors!). . . . You are merely demonstrating to the people that they should get rid of those who squander their assets, and do so as quickly as possible."

so effectively that they never seriously jeopardized construction of the Trans-Siberian. He restored confidence in the buffeted ruble by establishing a gold standard and accumulating substantial reserves, thereby ending speculation and luring large blocks of foreign capital to Russia. On the one hand, he lowered duties on imported heavy machinery and agricultural implements, and, on the other, he raised tariff barriers against articles that domestic manufacturers might be expected to produce themselves. Industries revived and flourished with the aid of subsidies, concessions, and sizable government orders. Coal production doubled, while the output of oil and pig iron tripled.

To reduce the excesses of peasants and artisans who often got so drunk on holidays and special family occasions that they could not work the next day, Witte introduced a state liquor monopoly at Alexander's request. It largely failed in purpose and swelled jails with moonshiners and bootleggers who had neglected to pay off enforcement officers. But the Treasury made money hand over fist. For example, within a year after the law took effect, six hundred and eleven liquor shops in the Moscow province alone sold more than eight million gallons, or something in excess of three and a quarter gallons per annum for every man, woman, and child in the region; from sales totaling nearly $15,800,000, the Treasury cleared no less than $11,740,000.*

* George Kennan defined Russia's two great institutions as "the church and the grog-shop." Even in far eastern Siberia, a quart of the best vodka cost only a dollar in the eighteen-nineties, while a cheap grade — described by the American photographer William Henry Jackson as "not bad" — could be bought for about thirty-three cents.

In her *Recipes of All Nations* (1935), Countess Morphy says that vodka "was formerly made from rye, but the staple raw materials now used are potatoes and maize, and green rye malt instead of barley malt is used to effect saccharification. . . . It is drunk in very small glasses and should never be sipped, but drunk down in one gulp. . . . In Russia, there was a

If members of the Solski commission could have foreseen the rich fruits of Witte's policies when they convened in December 1892, they might perhaps have honored him with a jubilant "tossing-up" such as Collins and Peyton had experienced in Kyakhta thirty-six years before. Instead, they argued at length over his novel financial stratagem. No one was so ingenuous as to object to the juggling of accounts, but there was considerable dissension as to *how* they should be juggled. The commission finally adopted Witte's method as the most deft, and endorsed the rest of his program. Possibly warmed by that comfortable, money-in-the-bank feeling, the members also approved a resurvey of the Tomsk-to-Irkutsk route Engineer Mezheninov had raced over in 1887-1888, and allotted $3,850,000 for the 150-mile branch from Chelyabinsk to Yekaterinburg.

Somewhat belatedly, Alexander expressed the opinion that the Trans-Siberian represented such a grandiose undertaking that it should be placed under the supervision of a special group comprising the chief ministers. The Solski commission therefore formed a "Committee of the Trans-Siberian" (hereafter to be called the Trans-Siberian Committee or the Committee) for the coordination and direction of all matters pertaining to the railway and ancillary Siberian enterprises. This Committee, whose creation was heralded in an Imperial decree of December 22, 1892, assumed sweeping powers. Subject to the Tsar's sanction, it had the right to allocate funds, fix expenses, expropriate land, timber, and buildings, requisition convict and military labor, establish a separate railway police force, select routes, and determine where and when construc-

custom of forming letters with rows of these small glasses, writing the name of a man's lady-love on the table. Each little glass was filled with vodka and if he loved her truly he was supposed to finish all the glasses which formed the letters of her name — often with dire results."

tion should begin. Although the Communication Ministry was entrusted with the engineering and construction of the line, all major decisions rested with the Committee. It was, in short, The Works.

At Witte's suggestion, Alexander appointed the Tsarevich Nicholas president of this powerful conclave. He did so with some reluctance, remarking that the Heir Apparent, then twenty-four years old, was "a mere boy." However, he never regretted his decision, for Nicholas lent constant support to the railway and to the advancement of Siberia, whose inhabitants had won his esteem by their rapturous welcome during his journey from Vladivostok back to Russia in the summer of 1891. Every town he passed through had raised triumphal arches in his honor, greeted him with bread, salt, and its holiest icons, and entertained him with military reviews, concerts, and gala balls.

Membership of the Committee included almost every important figure in government circles. Besides His Imperial Highness the Tsarevich and a vice president in the person of a former finance minister named Abaza, there were the ministers of the Interior, State Domains, Finance, Communication, War, and the Navy, together with the State Controller, two of Alexander's favorite aides-de-camp, and Anatoli N. Kulomzin, an able, conscientious bureaucrat charged with the administration of the Committee's business. Delegated to assist as needed were the ministers of Justice, Foreign Affairs, and the Imperial Household, as well as the governors-general in Siberia. Seldom, if ever, in Russian history had any peacetime project been accorded the services of such an impressive congeries of bemedaled and beribboned noblemen, satraps, and functionaries in the highest stratum of civil service.

The awesome Committee first assembled on February 22,

Anatoli N. Kulomzin, administrator of the Trans-Siberian Committee's business

1893. Nicholas delivered a brief but ingratiating speech that befitted this prince of whom Witte was later to write, "I never in my life met anyone who had nicer manners." "In opening the first meeting of the Trans-Siberian Committee," the young president said, "I view with profound emotion the grandeur of the task before us. But love of my country and an ardent desire to contribute to its welfare have induced me to accept the commission from my beloved Father. I am convinced that you are animated by the same feelings, and that our joint efforts will bring us to the desired end." The meeting was then given over largely to procedural matters and discussion of the Committee's powers and responsibilities.

During Witte's tenure as Communication Minister, he had secured authorization to bypass the rich commercial metropolis of Tomsk and connect it at some indefinite later date with a branch to the main line. Tomsk was rapidly overtaking Irkutsk as Siberia's largest city; it possessed the only Russian university east of the Urals, and, far more cherished by hard drinkers for miles around, a total of more than forty distilleries, breweries, and yeast factories among its two hundred-odd industrial establishments. How could the important citizens of Tomsk — millionaire gold miners and almost a thousand merchants who made at least fifty per cent profit on every transaction by their gouging practices — have been so humiliatingly mistreated? Why should the Ministry, whose original plans placed this self-styled hub of the universe on the trunk line, have changed its mind?

According to Witte, fifty-seven miles of track could be saved by routing the Trans-Siberian south of the city; in addition, the railway would lie closer to mining and agricultural lands in the lower part of the province. But according to communities jealous of Tomsk, surveying engineers visited the most opulent burghers and demanded 100,000 rubles ($50,000) as personal "honorarium" for bringing the tracks directly to the city. Turned down cold, the surveyors reduced their price. "Give us fifty thousand rubles or even forty thousand, and we will be content," they pleaded. But the Tomskians scorned them. "Have we not the most prosperous city in Siberia?" they asked. "Why should we pay you when you will have to bring the line here in any case?" In consequence, the empty-handed surveyors vengefully reported to the Communication Ministry that hills, streams, and bogs on the approach to Tomsk would delay construction and greatly increase costs, whereas a route about sixty miles to the south would not. As soon as the city fathers discovered to their horror that the bypass had been approved, so the story goes, they sought out the surveyors, wept on their shoulders, and begged them to restore the original plan. But it was too late. The surveyors shook their heads and replied that they would lose professional standing if they backed down on their recommendations.

There is probably no truth in this often repeated tale, for the Communication Ministry's engineers laid out routes with economy foremost in view. For instance, the location of most communities had been determined long before by early pioneers who chose sites with a river harbor protected from destructive spring ice floes; if these sites did not coincide with the cheapest location for bridges, the engineers built the spans where the river narrowed or presented other money-saving advantages. A station went up, and from there passengers got to town as best they could.

The Tomskians indeed screamed with anguish when they learned that no date had been set for building the branch suggested by Witte. Their cries of impending ruin reached the ears of the Minister of the Interior, who vainly urged the Committee in February 1893 to authorize an immediate start. The Tomsk municipal council then petitioned Alexander, who took no action beyond approving the suggested route. Thoroughly distraught, the councilmen petitioned him again in 1894. For reasons that shall be seen, they were to wait another year until the spur was begun, and about two and a half more years before it was opened to regular traffic.

With completion of the railway in western and central Siberia, Tomsk lost supremacy despite its branch.. Novonikolayevsk, a miserable settlement on the main line roughly a hundred and twenty miles southwest, soon captured much of the profitable river traffic and eventually became Siberia's largest city — the present Novosibirsk, often referred to by journalists as the Chicago of the Soviet Union. Today, it is a proliferating metropolis with innumerable industrial and commercial enterprises, the biggest opera house in the U.S.S.R., and a rapidly increasing population. Among other products strange to the rough-and-tumble shantytown it once was, Novosibirsk manufactures perfume and toilet water.

CHAPTER VI

The Spanning of the Steppe

Eastward all is black, save for the blinking of a signal light a mile away. That is the road to Siberia, and here is the commencement of the Trans-Siberian Railway.

— ROBERT L. JEFFERSON: *Roughing It in Siberia* (1897)

THREE miles from the old district town of Chelyabinsk — "the Gateway of Siberia" — construction of the eastbound tracks at last got under way on July 19, 1892, almost seventeen months to the day since the ministerial committeemen had pledged themselves to an immediate building start on the through line. During this interval, the Communication Ministry had assigned the surveying and construction of the two divisions of the West Siberian sector — that is, from Chelyabinsk to Omsk and from Omsk to the Ob — to Constantine Ya. Mikhailovski. This uncommonly energetic and accomplished civil engineer had built the much-admired Alexander Bridge across the Volga and was completing the last railway link between Samara and Chelyabinsk.

Mikhailovski soon found himself up to his handlebar mustache in trouble, notwithstanding the fact that the thin, colored line on his survey map followed a nearly straight course across level plains for about nine hundred miles. He was pre-

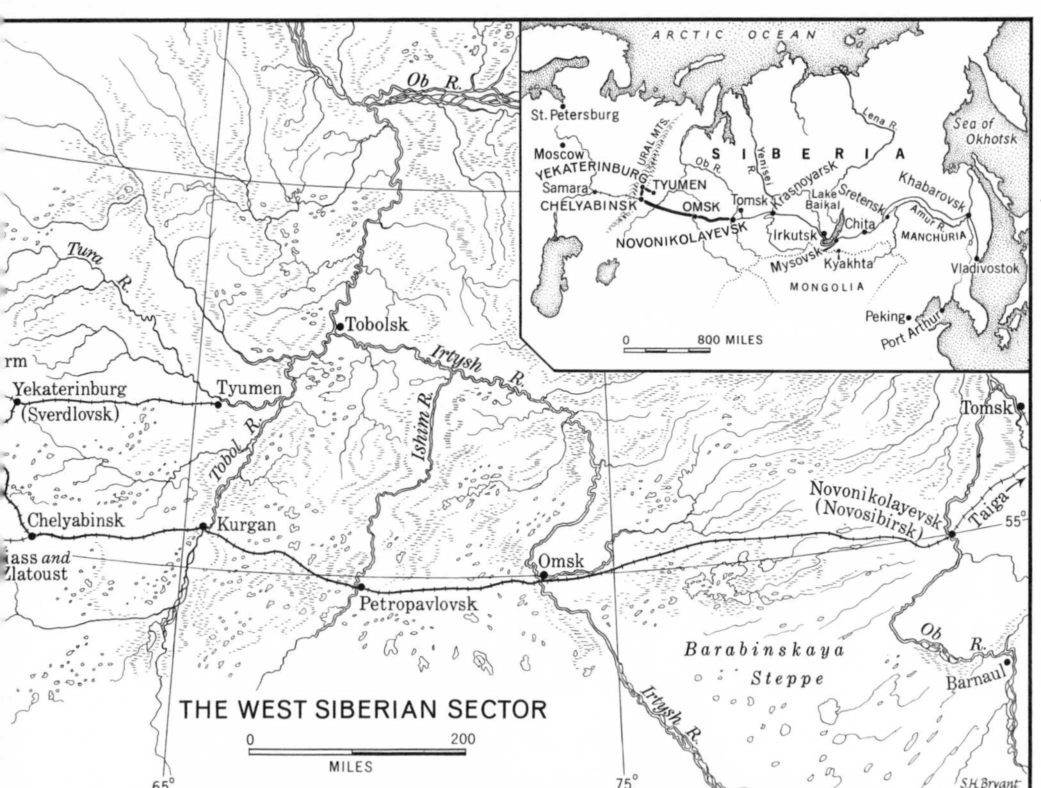

pared for heavy frost that limited the all-out working season to only four months, but he had not anticipated such a crippling shortage of wagons, carts, horses, barges, and steamers. In consequence, his staff had to buy and import them at a heavy cost that must have furrowed brows in the Communication Ministry's gloomy gray headquarters along the Fontanka Canal in St. Petersburg.

Even in the relatively well-populated agricultural districts between Chelyabinsk and Omsk, artisans were hard to come by, for the peasant settlers lacked technical skills. In grazing country, nomadic herdsmen refused to leave their cattle, which they prized so highly that it was their custom to inquire politely after the health of one's beasts rather than that of one's family. Mikhailovski's subordinates were therefore obliged to recruit workers from Russia, Turkey, Persia, and Italy through special labor contractors. In temperate weather,

Constantine Ya. Mikhailovski, constructor of the West Siberian sector

these laborers camped out. In winter — a period given over to bridge and station construction, road clearance, and the accumulation of sledge-drawn supplies (horses could pull on frozen surfaces twice the load of a cart on dirt roads) — they bunked in portable log cabins, boxcars, or crude huts thrown together with railway ties and partly covered by sod. At mealtimes, they extracted a wooden spoon from the inside of one of their boots and scooped chunks of meat from a great iron kettle that served as the communal kitchen. If they fell sick, broke a bone, or got knifed in a brawl, they were treated by a *feldsher,* or surgeon's assistant, unless they were near a city or working on a big stationary project such as a bridge over the Irtysh or the Ob, where qualified doctors were available.

Except for a single forest in the vicinity of Kurgan — a butter-and-grain-distributing town more than seven hundred miles from Mikhailovski's destination at the Ob — the countryside was utterly bare of timber suitable for ties and bridges; such trees as there were consisted of small birches and willows good only for fences and firewood. Consequently, the already overtaxed land and water conveyances had also to transport lumber from such distant points as Ufa, practically three

Construction site in the Mid-Siberian sector: digging earth for embankments

Laying ties in central Siberia

The next step: laying rails

The smoke pouring from the locomotive's stack is a contribution of some Russian retouching artist

hundred miles *west* of Chelyabinsk. Stone for culverts and the piers and abutments of large bridges was conspicuously absent save in the Urals and in quarries along the upper reaches of the Irtysh six hundred miles south of the railway route. To obtain sand for track ballast (sparingly used to save time and labor), teamsters drove as much as fifty miles to and from the nearest deposits.

Mikhailovski had expected to build smithies, brickworks, and limekilns but not to drill artesian wells, least of all in the lake area east of Petropavlovsk, a part-Russian, part-Asiatic city with half a dozen minareted mosques and a large Moslem population that had drifted north on the ancient caravan trails from Bukhara, Samarkand, Tashkent, and Turkestan. The lake water, however, was nauseously brackish, and so wells had to be driven at various station locations. Unluckily, the drillers tapped limy formations that necessitated the importation of purifying filter systems. Meanwhile, carters brought in potable water from wherever they could find it.

Mikhailovski must have thanked his patron saint on September 11, 1894, when the section from Chelyabinsk to the west bank of the Irtysh, opposite Omsk, was opened to traffic.* Despite his difficulties and a climate that limited full-scale operations to a hundred and twenty days annually, he had tracked close to five hundred miles in little more than two years. This was something of an achievement, for he had built with primitive methods and equipment imposed by Russia's backwardness in mechanization and St. Petersburg's pinchpenny program. In the field, logs for ties were tediously handsawn by two-man teams which worked a saw back and forth through a horizontally propped-up tree trunk. A few horsedrawn excavating machines had been imported from the United States, but for the most part soil for earthworks was extracted with picks and shovels, then carried in barrows, often wheelless, along a plank. Some shovels were fitted with an iron scoop or a blade, while others were entirely of

* Although Mikhailovski was responsible for construction throughout his sector, he entrusted much of it to aides, since he could not be everywhere on such a long stretch. But he frequently left his headquarters at Chelyabinsk to inspect work in progress and issue orders. His conveyance, a converted first-class car called a *Fonar*, or "Lantern," because of its glassed-in front end, was equipped with sensitive measuring and other instruments, and was pushed by a locomotive that drew several staff cars behind. Mikhailovski's eighteen-year-old daughter Eugenia and her close friend Vera V. Pokrovskaya, who was later to marry the engineer-contractor in charge of the western section of the Circumbaikal loop, often accompanied him on these trips. There were no stops for delightful pastoral picnics along the way, however, for (as the former Miss Pokrovskaya told the author) Mikhailovski was "a steady worker and a strict disciplinarian."

wood and lacked even a strip of tin on the digging edge. Since the subsoil was frozen until midsummer, laborers worked only the thawed upper stratum, leaving shallow craters all along the right of way. A large wooden bole with a stick driven into it served as sledgehammer. Supporting wooden piles for trestles and bridges were pounded home in the most painfully clumsy fashion by a big boulder hauled up with rope and pulley to the peak of a tall tripod, then released to strike the piling.

Foreign laymen visiting Siberia marveled that the Russians laid track frequently at the rate of two and a half miles a day under ideal summer conditions. Certain critical British experts, however, pointed out that the light rails, barely forty-nine pounds to the yard on flat stretches, could be handled faster than the much heavier metal then standard in Europe, Britain, and North America. They noted that ballast was meager where it appeared at all, that ties were spaced wider apart than sound practice dictated, and that spikes and bolts were used with unadvisable parsimony. Turning their attention to the broad excavations on either side of the track, they observed that these collected water and, as one Scotsman remarked, became in warm weather "the spacious nurseries of mosquitoes and other objectionable forms of insect life." Every one of these foreign professionals was convinced that the railway would be unsafe.

Shortly after Mikhailovski's crews reached the Irtysh, a large company of masons, ironworkers, and unskilled laborers settled in during the winter of 1894-1895 to build a span nearly half a mile long across the Irtysh to Omsk, a city memorable for its prison, long since demolished. There Fedor Dostoyevski, the former engineering student who searingly described this "house of the dead" in his book of the same

Robert L. Jefferson

name, served for four years at hard labor in the mid-nineteenth century.

Some hide-clad herdsmen from the Kirgiz Steppe (where a wife cost four sheep fewer than did a good cow) may have regarded Omsk with wide-eyed enchantment when they arrived for the early-winter fair. More sophisticated visitors detested the place: in summer, they sweltered in temperatures that soared into the high nineties; in winter, they were numbed by cold that touched forty-two below. In all seasons, winds swept through the unpaved streets — treeless because of the barren, saline soil — and raised storms of acrid dust or piled snowdrifts high against the dismal houses and buildings, almost all of which were wooden. Although a magnificent, multidomed cathedral was rising above a cornerstone laid in the presence of the Tsarevich Nicholas himself in 1891, the city's medical institutions for a civilian population of more than thirty thousand comprised exactly one lunatic asylum, one lying-in hospital, and one municipal hospital with only twenty-five beds.

The importance of Omsk as an administrative, military, trading, and shipping center was belied by its atrocious inns. According to Robert L. Jefferson, a jovial English traveler of the eighteen-nineties who put up with three companions at "a low, mean-looking wooden house which a dilapidated signboard announced to be the 'Grand Hotel Moscow,' " this ramshackle caravanserai was constructed of logs laid one on top of another, with moss and hay stuffed into cracks against the bone-chilling winds.

"A delectable hotel this," Jefferson cheerfully observes in his book, *Roughing It in Siberia,* "but in nowise worse than the majority of such places throughout the whole of Siberia. . . . The proprietor of the hotel received us with the glare of avarice in his grey eyes. We bargained with him at length for merely the favour of a shelter; for that was all we could expect. He gave us a room for the outrageous charge of four roubles (eight shillings and sixpence), and that was thirty per cent. below his original demand. A lovely room it was too! Two rickety, broken-backed chairs, a small square table, and a truckle bed, on which reposed a suspicious-looking mattress, formed its sole furniture. The floor was carpetless save for a canvas strip by the door. The usual domestic utensils were absent; there was not even a washstand. . . . We did not mind the blackbeetles so much as the animals which dropped from the ceiling in order to disturb our slumbers. I think we were all pretty hardened members, but the vermin of that room rather got the best of us."

The narrator describes the experiment of another traveler who sought to protect himself by taking along his own bedstead, four saucers, and a can of kerosene. Placing the bed legs into the saucers and filling the latter with the coal oil, he thought that the bugs would be "asphixiated." "But," says our Englishman, ". . . these things of life, with a sagacity which one would hardly credit in so small an insect, would make a detour by getting up the wall, on to the ceiling, and then, having accurately poised, drop down upon the victim . . ." *

* Robert Louis Jefferson was a leading light in the Society of Cyclists and had bicycled from London to Constantinople in 1894. On April 20 of the following year, he set out from Kensington Oval in an attempt to break all records by riding to Moscow and back within fifty days. He tells us that his machine was an Imperial Rover and that he had equipped himself with nuts, bolts, ball bearings, a revolver, "a mackintosh cape, leggings, maps, check-book, cyclometer, a plentiful supply of Bovril, a box of Homocea, a can of White's Electrine Oil, and one or two handkerchiefs . . ." He averaged about a hundred miles a day, often on "bad and greasy" roads in heavy rain, thunderstorms, and headwinds, and "accomplished the journey from London, 2120 miles, in twenty-three days one hour." Russian cyclists gave him an enthusiastic welcome, toasted him with champagne, and pinned a gold brooch on his jacket.

Jefferson departed on May 16 and "pulled up at Kensington Oval twenty-three hours fifty-four minutes inside time," he narrates in his book, *Awheel to Moscow and Back.* "My cyclometer showed the distance as 4281 miles, and this had been accomplished in forty-nine days six minutes, constituting absolutely the longest consecutive ride ever done in a given time. . . . I lost two stone weight [twenty-eight pounds], two-and-a-half inches around the chest, and four-and-a-half inches around the stomach. . . . It will be readily granted that black bread, sour milk, and *vodki,* however toothsome they might be, are certainly not fattening. The reception I received at the hands of my brother wheelmen was deeply gratifying. Naturally there were one or two carping critics, who could see no good purpose in the ride — but let that pass. There was not a man who had the true interests of British sport at heart who was not pleased to see me back, and pleased that I had accomplished the task I had set myself. And as for myself — well, I can say no more than that I'm glad I've done it."

In the very early spring of 1897, he traveled with two other Englishmen and an American named Thomas Gaskell on the Trans-Siberian as far as Krasnoyarsk, and thence to the Minusinsk mining district south of that city. "With the exception, probably, of the Captain Wiggins' expedition, we

Much better off than their counterparts in central and eastern Siberia, the merchants and boatline operators of Omsk regarded the approach of the Trans-Siberian with deep misgivings. For years, they had been isolated from competition and had made fortunes from ruthless profiteering. In monopolistic concert, they paid little for grain, meat, hides, and other regional products which they sold at steep markups in the mother country, then gouged the public for imported hardware and merchandise. The railway, these Omskians feared, would open the area to Russian competitors who might bring in tons of goods at cheap freight rates and undersell the local cartel.

The shipping interests were equally worried. They had fattened for decades on inordinate transportation tariffs on the Tura, Tobol, and Irtysh river route from Tyumen. Shallows and obstructions were so common along this winding course of a thousand miles and more that the shipowners refused to guarantee delivery dates for freight, which was handled with minimal regard for damage or loss. Even the Imperial post was distributed haphazardly: on approaching tiny settlements where stops were seldom made, a deck hand on the moving steamer waved a red flag as the signal for a boatman to leave shore and fish from the muddy waters a corked glass bottle containing the mail.

Since the shipline magnates charged three to four times more than did their equivalents on the Volga, the mere mention of the Trans-Siberian was enough to plunge them into Slavic melancholy. The railway did indeed reduce their swollen profits and those of the merchants, but Omsk was

constituted, I think, the first English party to enter Siberia in order to inquire into the commercial resources of that vast country." Whatever his avowed purpose, he returned to England with material for his highly amusing *Roughing It in Siberia,* published in the year of his journey.

spared the stagnation of communities not connected with the Trans-Siberian. By 1899, the value of the city's industrial output had increased by nearly sixty per cent; its population soared from some thirty-seven thousand to more than fifty thousand in the period of 1897-1899 alone.

Mikhailovski's problems in the Chelyabinsk-to-Omsk section did not prevent him from beginning construction on the second leg — a distance of three hundred and eighty-four miles from Omsk to the Ob — in May 1893 (the same month and year in which the New York Central's immortal "999" locomotive rocketed the Empire State Express at a record-breaking one hundred and twelve and a half miles an hour over a straight and level course between Batavia and Buffalo, New York). Eastbound from Omsk, the route ran through the approximate center of the inhospitable Barabinskaya Steppe, a vast expanse of greenish plains dotted with shallow lakes and ponds, where coarse reeds and sedge grass concealed swamps, peat bogs, and here and there patches of firm ground. While the workers labored through this watery wilderness, clouds of gnats and mosquitoes tortured them almost beyond endurance until they were issued netting that at least protected their heads. For all of one summer, the men hacked through jungles of nettles eight feet tall; chopped down groves of birch, willow, and aspen; dug canals to drain marshes and divert underground springs; built dikes and sank trestle pilings into beds of slime; and brought from the rear untold tons of fill for a solid track foundation. Finally, on August 31, 1895 — twenty-seven months after their departure from Omsk — the crews reached their goal at the Ob, one of Siberia's longest rivers. Less than two months later, the entire division was opened to uninterrupted traffic except at the Irtysh, where the bridge was not completed until the end of March 1896.

In spite of the complications that had beset him, Mikhailovski built the West Siberian at a saving in excess of $622,300 below the original estimate. For this he was warmly commended by Anatoli Kulomzin, the Trans-Siberian Committee's administrator and an official historian of its activities, who acclaims his "remarkable experience in railway construction." To the present writer, Soviet experts at the Institute of Railway Transport Engineers, in Leningrad, declared without a moment's hesitation that the greatest civil engineer in tsarist Russia was Constantine Yaklovlevich Mikhailovski.

As they went along, Mikhailovski and his colleagues on other sections of the Trans-Siberian put up wooden bridges over small rivers and streams intersecting the route. These spans were narrow, single-track affairs that averaged a mere hundred feet in length and could be quickly assembled to avoid delay in the passage of work trains to the far side. At the Irtysh, Ob, Yenisei, and other wide watercourses where a stone-piered metal bridge was obligatory, engineers and laborers crossed to the opposite bank by boat or sledge and continued to clear the path ahead while a small army of carpenters, masons, and ironworkers stayed behind to build the structure.

Most of the steel bridges of the early Trans-Siberian are still in use today. They are solid, no-nonsense-about-them, single-track overpasses of more or less look-alike appearance, comprising from one to eight main spans, each averaging about three hundred and fifty feet in length. In many cases, their frame rises in the middle to a hump, from which derives the engineering term of "hog-backed" for this genre. Supporting the girders are massive stone piers, each with a thick buttress that slants outward at a deflective angle against the grinding spring ice floes.

For nearly seventy years, these piers have withstood the impact of inestimable tons of ice that perennially crunch downriver without letup for three or four weeks at speeds varying from four to six miles an hour. In the Yenisei, pressure reaches such gargantuan proportions that it propels ice packs, sometimes rising as much as thirty feet above the surface, at speeds of up to twenty miles per hour. According to Henry Seebohm, the noted British ornithologist who studied the Yenisei's annual dissolution in the course of his bird-watching expeditions, "Some idea of what this pressure must have been may be realised by the fact that a part of the river a thousand miles long, beginning with a width of two miles, and ending with a width of six miles, covered over with three feet of ice, upon which was lying six feet of snow, was broken up at the rate of a hundred miles a day."

Depending on technical factors familiar to civil engineers but perhaps unnecessary to go into here, the stone piers were built within either caissons or cofferdams. Completed piers and abutments were then connected with wooden falsework — temporary scaffolding that supported sections of the permanent structure until they could be riveted together and made self-sustaining. In some instances, workers prefabricated the spans in temporary riverside shops that could be disassembled and transported to the next bridge site; the spans were then pulled with steam tackle over rollers on previously prepared falsework between piers.

For the riveters and semiskilled laborers who, like the stonemasons, stayed on the job in winter as well as in summer, bridgemaking was an extremely hazardous occupation. Structural gangs perched a hundred or so feet above the frozen river, bolting and riveting without protective hoarding against the subzero temperatures.

"This extreme cold," a civil engineer named Lodian wrote in the American journal *Railway and Locomotive Engineering* after completing a year-long inspection of the Trans-Siberian near the turn of the century, "caused the death of a number of bridge mechanics: they would allow their body temperature to run down more than they were aware, with the result that some of them would make a slip or find they could not get their numbed fingers to grasp a support in time, and down they would go, and, unless providentially caught by a fellow-worker or their fall obstructed by something during the tumble, would go through to the granite-like frozen river below, being instantly killed. So accustomed are the Russians to this that they look to it as a matter of course. Thus, they calculate at least one death to every million rubls [*sic*] spent on a big bridge. So, if a great bridge has cost four millions, four men have dropped to death therefrom from climatic exposure. This is the official calculation. Privately, the deaths average three or four per million rubls spent, but that would be too much for official reports to acknowledge." These reports omitted mention of the practice of crooked paymasters who, according to other non-Russian authorities, kept the names of dead men on the rolls and collected their wages, amounting to twenty-five to thirty dollars a month for an ironworker.

Most of the masons were Italians, as Lodian discovered to his surprise. "They executed the stone work of most every bridge on the Trans-Siberian," he told his readers. "Working hard, they made but 100 rubls per month (say, $50). They agreed pretty well with the severe climate, but missed the good, pure cheap wine of their own country, which was a sore trial to them, and the Russian gin (fodka) they wisely avoided."

One can only imagine what these Italians related to their

families when they returned home. Did they say that there were enormous elephants in Siberia, for how else could one account for the ten-foot-long, crescent-curved ivory tusks one saw on traders' sledges from the north? * Did the Italians speak fearfully of the ghosts of brigands who left Hell on the coldest winter nights and fired shots along the railway tracks, though in truth these supernatural visitors were only rail bolts snapping apart in the glacial air? Did they heap scorn on the mad, extravagant Russians who christened the piers of the Yenisei bridge by showering gold and silver coins on wet cement and covering forever the small fortune with a granite topping block?

Cast steel for this great bridge — well over half a mile long — was transported from the Urals; cement came from St. Petersburg; and steel bearings from Warsaw, in then Russian-controlled Poland, nearly thirty-five hundred miles from the Yenisei by the present rail route via Chelyabinsk. These long distances would not have mattered much if the first freight trains on Siberian tracks had moved with anything like the speed prevalent in western countries. But since many seg-

* These tusks were taken from the refrigerated carcasses of hairy mammoths — patriarchs of the genus *Elephas* and second only to African imperial elephants as the largest land animals ever hunted by Man — which had lain imperishably preserved in frozen arctic crevasses and riverbanks for several hundred thousand years. Nils A. E. Nordenskjöld, the first Arctic explorer to navigate the entire northeast passage across the top of the world, says in *The Voyage of the Vega . . .* (1882) that early Russian settlers in Siberia called mammoth bones "Noah's wood," and that the tusks of probably more than twenty thousand mammoths had been collected since the conquest of the country. He adds that the Chinese at Kyakhta believed the ivory "to be tusks of the giant rat *tien-shu,* which is only found in the cold regions along the coast of the Polar Sea, avoids the light, and lives in dark holes in the interior of the earth. Its flesh is said to be cooling and wholesome. Some Chinese literati considered that the discovery of these immense earth rats might even explain the origin of earthquakes."

Another source says that tusks sold at the Yakutsk fair for about seventy-five cents a pound and weighed as much as two hundred and fifty pounds. The ivory is whiter than that of elephants today.

Mariinsk: a street typical of Siberian towns in tsarist times

ments of the line had not passed the constructors' rather casual safety tests, prudent crews poked along at barely more than walking pace. "Accidents to the first trains to run over new sections have been numerous," Robert Jefferson records. "On one new piece of road between Marinsk and Atchinsk [Mariinsk and Achinsk] the first engine to travel over the road disappeared bodily through the ballast into a small river below, necessitating a delay of several months for repairs . . ."

Before bridges went up, completed sections of the railway were opened to "provisional" traffic, which meant that passengers rode in fourth-class cars attached to work or supply trains, and got across rivers as best they could. In winter, they walked across frozen streams, the train following behind on tracks held in place by a method the Russians considered highly orthodox. "Naturally it was impossible to nail the ties to the ice,"

Jefferson observes, "but the Russian engineer had obviated this difficulty by freezing them on, and kept them frozen on by continual douches of water which was brought in buckets from a hole in the ice. . . . How deep the [Chulym] river was we did not know; and whether the ice was thick enough to bear the several hundreds of tons of locomotive and fifteen heavy carriages was another problem. Anyway, we were all glad when . . . the conductor came up and requested us to descend and walk to the other side — cheerfully remarking that if the train went through only he, his fellow-conductors, and the engine-drivers would be drowned." After noting that the river was twice as broad as the Thames at London Bridge, the Englishman relates that "the engine snorted, puffed, snorted again, puffed three or four times and got up way slowly, drew to the shelving bank and laboriously descended on to the ice. There was a distinct crunch as it did so, and another crunch when the first car rolled on; but gradually the whole train descended, and, at a pace not exceeding five miles an hour, moved across the frozen surface. As it passed us we felt the ice quiver, and heard innumerable cracks, like the reports of pistols in the distance; but the train got across the centre safely, spurted when near the bank, climbed up, and was on *terra firma* again."

For traversing broader rivers such as the Ob — where the seven-span, million-dollar bridge was not completed until April 1897 because the wooden falsework had burned down — local sledge-drivers stood by to give travelers an exhilarating ride. Jefferson recounts his experience with the mingled feelings of Mr. Pickwick. "Down a little road past the station at a mad gallop; swish! round the corner, and out over a level plateau. We banged against tree stumps which stuck out through the snow, cannoned against fence corners protecting some agricultural property, until, with a whirl and a clatter, we dashed down a short slope and were out on the river. . . . The whole surface was one jumbled mass of broken ice, which seemed as if at the very moment of its breaking, it had been arrested by King Frost and frozen solid. Great lumps, ten to fifteen feet high and four to five feet in thickness, towered above us . . . and through this wilderness of congealation [*sic*], a narrow road had been formed for the passage of vehicles. Over this road we galloped at a terrific pace, bumping and scrunching, whirling and swishing, the drosky clattering from side to side, now on one runner, now on the other, and all our traps jerking about like peas in a frying-pan, while we, poor unfortunate mortals, hung on by one hand, and with the other hand endeavoured to smother the mouth in order to warm the air for the lungs. . . . With a whoop and halloo, we scuttled over a narrow stretch where the water oozed and spirted [*sic*] between a crack; then up the bank at a mad scramble, to disappear in a miniature forest, to whirl around at a breakneck speed on the edge of an embankment, and to clatter into the station yard at Ob with smoking horses, excited driver, and bruised bodies we, but pleased nevertheless."

In summer, unfordable streams were crossed mainly on pendulum ferries, ranging in type from dinky rafts to the pride of the Yenisei, a majestic catamaran that accommodated twenty vehicles and horses with ease. Impressive as this craft was in size, it was dependent on the current to swing it from one bank to the other, and, in the opinion of some travelers, compared unfavorably with the Ob's "mechanical" ferry, on which three circling ponies turned an arrangement of wooden cogs and axles that rotated two splashing paddle wheels.

Upon completion of each metal bridge, it was subjected to a series of tests. As the first step, enginemen were required to drive four locomotives with four loaded freight cars halfway across the span and, barring its collapse, to remain there for two hours while structural bend was measured. The crews were then directed to cross the bridge at a low speed that was gradually increased in subsequent runs until it reached a maximum safety limit of fifteen miles an hour. As far as can be determined, no bridges failed these tests. Even the critical Lodian took off his peaked cap to them, "one of the best features on the Trans-Siberian — all being examples of lightness and strength combined."

Everyone working on a major span looked forward with the keenest relish to the blessing ceremonies conducted by priests of the Orthodox Church just before the first flag-decked official train crossed the span. These rites provided the excuse for a glorious celebration in which all the participants consumed vodka until they became, in the words of the disapproving Lodian, " 'half-tracks over.' " "I have seen a number of these bridge-festival drunken orgies," he says, "but, being a temperance man, was never affected thereby. The last one — in central Siberia — was a warning. Soon after the dinner, all the company were drunk and lying under the tables or about the floors, with the exception of the writer; so I locked the company in and sent for the sledge. But the driver himself was drunk, and took up beside him a companion equally drunk. The horses — three abreast — flew like a whirlwind to get home to their feed and snug stalls, but unfortunately the *isvoschik* and his 'pard' began quarreling, then fighting for the reins. With horses going at breakneck speed in the pitch-black night, fighting for the reins does not inspire confidence in a passenger, so at the next sudden lug-up I was out in an instant, the sledge vanished in the darkness, and I walked the remaining three verstas [two miles] to quarters."

Despite the acknowledged sturdiness of the long bridges and the ecclesiastical benedictions bestowed upon them, it seems evident that Russian travelers and train crews regarded them with something less than unqualified trust. Perhaps for this reason, further spiritual protection was sought by an encased picture of a saint, with flanking oil lamps and a capacious bowl beneath, at each end of the structure, as Lodian noted. When nearing one of these icons, train crews crossed themselves and slowed to five or six miles an hour, while passengers, also crossing themselves, tossed coins into the bowl as advance tokens of gratitude for a safe passage. This they did in summer through opened car windows. In winter, when these were sealed, the faint of heart could only pray that Heaven would watch over them without benefit of a thank offering at that particular moment.

CHAPTER VII

Into the Heart of Siberia

IN the early summer of 1893, a construction party figuratively leapfrogged over Mikhailovski's crews in western Siberia and began work on the Mid-Siberian sector, the longest between the Urals and the headwaters of the Amur. The route led through sparsely inhabited country, hilly or mountainous in the eastern portion, and heavily forested over much of its eleven hundred and thirty-odd miles. Like the West Siberian line, it had been divided into two sections: from the Ob to Krasnoyarsk, on the Yenisei, and from Krasnoyarsk to Irkutsk. The engineer in charge was Nicholas P. Mezheninov — a plumpish railway veteran with a small, pointed gray beard, bushy eyebrows, and thinning hair en brosse — who had hurriedly explored part of the terrain in 1887-1888. He was under instructions to finish the first section by 1896, and then continue to Irkutsk, which he was scheduled to reach in 1900.

Witte's successor as Communication Minister was Alexander V. Krivoshein, an "unscrupulous, self-seeking office-hunter" (in Witte's words). In 1893, Krivoshein sent a high-ranking engineer named Adadurov to inspect the work in progress. Adadurov returned in November and reported that the track to Irkutsk could be completed in 1898 — two years ahead of time. At a subsequent meeting, Their Excellencies

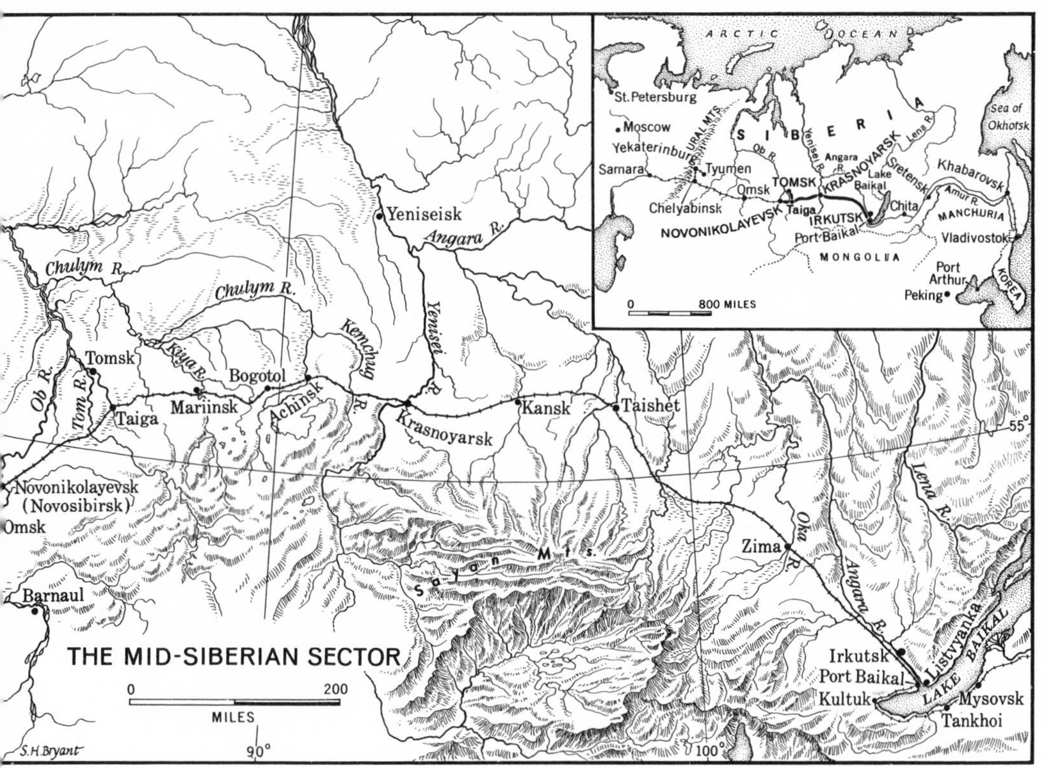

hemmed and hawed over various financial technicalities involved in such a drastically accelerated program, but they finally approved it at the urging of Witte, who reiterated that "the Trans-Siberian will bear full fruit only when it is open to traffic from one end to the other." As finally worked out in May 1894 by the ministries concerned, the new plan called for nothing less than the connection of Russia and Vladivostok with combined rail and water communications by 1899, at the latest.

Meanwhile, Mezheninov was inching through forbidding virgin forest, the Siberian taiga. "Dark and almost impenetrable," wrote the Swedish explorer Jonas J. Stadling at the turn of the century, "it covers a marshy lowland extending more than 4500 miles from east to west, and from 1000 to 1500 miles from south to north. In this endless monotony there is no change, no variety. You may travel hundreds and thousands of miles without seeing a human habitation, or any living thing other than wild animals or perhaps some stray Tungus or Ostiak.* Only by means of the great rivers and their tributaries may civilized man penetrate this gigantic wilderness, whose inmost depths have never been trodden by the foot of any human being, for even the natives keep near the rivers."

Mezheninov's task would have been less difficult if he could have followed the post road from the Ob to Tomsk and beyond. But with the bypassing of Tomsk, he had to hack out

---

* The Tungus (now called Evenki) were notorious as the filthiest of Siberian tribes, but even they could endure vermin for only so long. As part of an annual housecleaning, they dug up ants' nests and brought them into their huts; the ants killed off the vermin, then conveniently perished during the first severe frost.

Captain John Dundas Cochrane, the British naval officer who journeyed by foot across Siberia to Kamchatka and back in the early eighteen-twenties, was astounded at the appetites of the Tungus. "I have seen three of these gluttons," he relates in his *Narrative of a Pedestrian Journey Through Russia and Siberian Tartary,* "consume a rein-deer at one meal; nor are they nice as to the choice of parts; nothing being lost, not even the contents of the bowels, which, with the aid of fat and blood, are converted into black puddings."

In his *My Flight from Siberia,* Leon Trotsky noted that the lazy but ingenious Ostyaks — short, husky, large-headed, and almost as dirty as the Tungus — snare ducks by stretching a net across a river down which they fly at night. When a covey strikes, the waiting hunters pull a line that drops the net and traps its catch. Rather than kill the birds with a stick, the Ostyaks bite off the head, for "teeth make a better job of it." These primitives, who revere bears and swear their most solemn oaths over a bear skull, apologize to the animal for killing it. "Do not blame *me* for your death," the Ostyak may say to the bear, "since it is not I but the Russian maker of my gun who is responsible." The redoubtable traveler Thomas Atkinson observed in 1860 that this reverence was expressed somewhat differently by the Goldi tribe in far eastern Siberia. "The bear is held in great veneration by these people," he declares, "who bestow much care upon him; his dwelling is kept clean, and he is well fed; in short, it may be said that he leads the life of a gentleman, living in luxury, and receiving every attention. Unfortunately for Bruin, he finds out to his cost that a selfish motive has produced all this attention, and procured for him the delicious fruits with which his palate has been pampered. Notwithstanding the endearing epithets of son and brother, he is at last removed from his room, paraded about with marked consideration, and then barbarously murdered in the presence of all his friends; and what is still worse, they finish by showing themselves cannibals, and feast on the body of him whom they constantly addressed as their nearest relative."

Nicholas P. Mezheninov, engineer in charge of the Mid-Siberian sector

a new path — two hundred and fifty feet in width to reduce the hazard of conflagrations fired by locomotive sparks — through this northern jungle of pine, larch, spruce, and birch, so dense in places that sunlight never reached the debris of centuries on the ground. Nature guarded her wild, primeval domain with defenses so diversified, so stubborn and frustrating that one marvels that Mezheninov crept along at all.

Instead of thawing in late May, as in western Siberia, the taiga's surface itself remained frozen to flinty hardness until mid-July, thereby slowing the clearance and grading of the right of way. When Nature relaxed her glacial grip, she transformed the soil into a boundless swamp in which workers wal-

Sod-hut winter quarters of the convicts

lowed in muck two feet deep while they piled logs side by side for a makeshift road. No sooner were drainage canals dug than the shallow-rooted conifers along the clearing lost their hold and crashed in jumbles of trunks and branches that imperiled lives and cost precious days to remove. More time was lost in probes of the soggy subsoil to find solid footing for bridges and trestles. Stone for the purpose had to be transported from quarries sometimes a hundred miles away. Ironically, the one potentially useful material Nature had provided in astronomical abundance — timber — was neither strong nor durable. Even temporary bridge construction could not proceed until hard wood was brought from stands seventy-five to three hundred miles distant.

Interior of the hut at night

Long, hard winters with sixty-below cold spells allowed Mezheninov barely three months of good weather. He was in a worse spot than Mikhailovski in other respects. Fewer Russian contractors could be induced to venture so deeply into the Siberian wilderness. Until the completion of the West Siberian line, all supplies were shipped from Russia and the Urals via the circuitous river route to construction camps; frequently, orders were wrongly filled, while consignments of spikes and other vital materials arrived only after harassing delays. Supply chiefs had to search far afield for carts and horses. Local manpower was practically impossible to obtain in this thinly populated territory that averaged one inhabitant per square mile. Still shorthanded in 1894 despite thousands of workers transported from Russia, Mezheninov requisitioned approximately fifteen hundred convicts from a prison near Irkutsk to fell trees and build earthworks and wooden bridges.

To the relief of Mezheninov's hard-pressed engineers, even incorrigible criminals turned out to be exemplary workers, thanks to what was probably the first incentive plan in Siberia. As reward for good behavior, the Ministry of Justice decreed that eight months' railway labor counted as a year off a sentence. For instance, a man with four years still to serve was eligible for freedom after two years and eight months; in addition, he received a daily wage of twelve and a half cents, which in those days went a long way toward the purchase of such luxuries as tobacco and sugar, or vodka sold sub rosa by vènal guards. Political and other noncriminal exiles were granted *two* years off for each year on the railway. According to an 1899 Justice study, this unprecedented magnanimity paid off handsomely: exiles and convicts worked hard and, except for fifteen who went over the hill, committed no crimes during their railway service.

When Mezheninov's crews emerged from the worst of the taiga, they made remarkably rapid progress in fair weather. But to avoid the expense of tunnels and cuttings Mezheninov was obliged to follow a meandering course to surmount elevations that blocked the path. Wide declivities often necessitated earthworks of abnormal length across them; one of these embankments cost $45,000, or as much as a hundred-and-seventy-five-foot steel bridge.

In the vicinity of the present Novo-Chernorechenski — some eighty miles west of Krasnoyarsk — rails were laid at the foot of a precipitous hill that was less firm than it looked, as laborers instantly realized while fleeing for their lives from the avalanche of sand that wiped out several days' work in a matter of moments. Along a stretch of the Kemchug River, an apparently identical formation turned out to be of impermeable flintstone; rather than blast a costly cut through it, one of Mezheninov's rare contractors — a man with the reassuring name of O. K. Sidorov — diverted the stream and built the roadbed on the river bottom skirting the hill. While altering the course, men toiled hip-deep in icy water; along the banks, only fast action by their comrades saved a number from perishing in quicksands. Not a soul was lost in the entire operation, if we are to believe an 1899 railway picture album called *The Great Way*. In fact, the author asserts in those rhapsodical terms familiar to readers of modern Soviet publications, the workers actually "sang with happiness," their euphoria being shared, he adds with unblushing omniscience, by even the cart horses.

It will be recalled that no action had been taken on the piteous appeals of the Tomsk city fathers in 1893 and 1894 for immediate construction of a branch to the main line. Alexander and the Committee had approved it, but a rail shortage at that time deferred building. When Russian foundries caught up with demand in 1895, Their Excellencies authorized Mezheninov to put some of his 29,300 men to work on a spur from Taiga station to Tomsk.

Taiga had been appropriately named, for it stood in the midst of the sepulchral forest that had given Mezheninov a bitterly hard time in 1893-1894. The distance to Tomsk was only fifty-four miles, but these were so swampy and thickly wooded that the crews required a year to lay rough tracks to the city, and nearly another year and a half to improve them for regular traffic. Although this short line had cost slightly more than $371,200 in excess of the estimate, the Committeemen found solace in the knowledge that Mikhailovski's savings on the West Siberian sector covered this overexpenditure by a comfortable margin.

In the interval, the naval ministry had initiated a project to prove that substantial shipments to the heart of Siberia could be delivered via the Kara Sea — above the Arctic Circle — eastward to the mouth of the Yenisei and thence upriver to the Krasnoyarsk area. Six thousand steel rails were bought in England in 1893 and transferred to a small fleet led by Captain Joseph Wiggins, an English explorer who had made the passage before. In the Yenisei estuary, Wiggins managed to unload most of his cargo on waiting barges despite "an orgy of storms," a Russian historian says. Three of the barges sank, with the result that only sixteen hundred rails reached their destination that October. In the following year, practically all of the sunken rails were recovered and shipped upriver. Together with the ones already received, they were enough to track eleven miles of the Trans-Siberian west of Krasnoyarsk. The overall venture had cost $150,000, which brought the cost per mile to more than $13,600 for the metal alone. Nonetheless, Their Excellencies justified the expedition on the grounds that it had demonstrated the feasibility of navigation in the northern seas with ordinary ships. The railway builders made no further use of the route, however, chiefly because Russian industrialists strenuously opposed the purchase of railway supplies from abroad.

The Communication Ministry undertook the improvement of rivers to expedite transportation of supplies to building sites. Waterways were deepened, widened, and cleared of sunken obstructions with dredgers and explosives, while other navigational hazards were reduced by channel markers and water gauges. Only the turbulent Angara River — to the north and east of Krasnoyarsk — continued to defy the efforts of the Department of Waterways to tame it.

Mezheninov had intended to begin construction of the second division (from Krasnoyarsk to Irkutsk) after the scheduled completion of the first in 1896. Under the accelerated program, however, he ordered another crew to begin work on the eastern leg in the summer of 1894. He had hoped to track in both directions from Krasnoyarsk and Irkutsk, but a belated exploration of the Angara, on which he had depended for transport, revealed that rapids and boulders prohibited barge traffic over much of its course. He had also counted on a foundry northwest of Irkutsk to provide rails and other hardware, but the proprietor went bankrupt. In addition, a couple of Siberian contractors failed to build a cement plant with an advance of $61,000 from the government; pleading insolvency, they shut up shop and never repaid the advance. Two other contractors joined their ranks after collecting preliminary payments totaling more than $74,000 for construction near Irkutsk. Mezheninov therefore abandoned his original plan and continued to work in a single direction toward Irkutsk.

Although there seems to be no firm evidence that the ostensibly bankrupt contractors had defrauded the government, it is still true that Siberians frequently abused the public trust. For example, a government mining official in a town southwest of Krasnoyarsk, Kennan reports, "cooked" accounts and mulcted the Crown of $50,000 a year, which enabled him to maintain a chef and a governess from France and send his soiled linen to Paris by mail to be washed and starched. Only fifty-odd years ago in Irkutsk, a press censor one night received telegraphed newspaper dispatches from Moscow announcing the failure of a big trading concern in Kiev. "Now the censor held some thousands of *roubles'* stock in that company," two journalists narrate in a jointly written book. "With autocratic indignation, he blue-penciled the report as it came in from each newspaper office — and next morning, bright and early, he disposed of every *kopeck*'s interest he held in the sinking ship of commerce, to his unsuspecting neighbors, before the bad tidings had had time to get far by word of mouth . . ."

In Krasnoyarsk, a nineteenth-century tea merchant insured his caravan shipments from China, then entered into a deal with thieves, who hijacked the caravans and secretly delivered their loads to him. As soon as his distant and unsuspecting insurers in Russia paid off, the merchant quietly sold the tea. "By such methods as these," Jefferson records, "this particular tea-trader grew up in affluence. . . . The exercise of his capital was so great that in a few years of his trading he had been able to crush all formidable opposition, and could not only supply all markets of Siberia and European Russia at a cheaper rate than any other trader, but he was able to purchase from the Chinese grower a class of tea which could not be rivalled." Local officials evidently caught on to his swindle but looked the other way, for who cared about the losses of money-grubbing Moscow and St. Petersburg underwriters as long as this fellow Siberian supplied the best tea at sensible, rock-bottom prices? *

---

* While wintering in Moscow, a rascally Tomskian with good connections sold the state residence of the city's governor to a rich English lord in search of a home. First (William O. Greener relates), the Tomskian told the governor that the distinguished foreigner was unable to find accommodations befitting his rank and that it would be a gracious act to allow him temporary use of a wing in the gubernatorial mansion until something turned up. Taken in by the assurance that his guest would pay well for the privilege, the governor agreed. The Siberian then sold the building to the lord, who was given to understand that the present tenant would stay on

Typical curves in eastern sections of the Great Siberian Railway

In order to track the mountainous second section with all speed, Mezheninov's engineers risked train safety by reducing ballast, narrowing the base of embankments, and increasing the acuteness of curves and gradients. This construction was as economical as it was quick, but nevertheless expenses soared. An unexpectedly large number of bridges had to be built; on one stretch of only forty-four miles eighty-two were required. A crop failure in the Krasnoyarsk and Kansk districts tripled the price of oats, raised that of rye flour by almost five

---

in another wing only until *he* found somewhere else to live. As the weeks passed with Russian and Briton bowing politely to each other but neither showing the slightest intention to leave, each began to wonder how to get rid of the other. By the time they came to a showdown, the Tomskian was living high on the hog in Siberia, where he was never brought to book.

hundred per cent, and virtually doubled wages. These and other totally unforeseen expenses skyrocketed Mezheninov's construction costs alone — not counting surveys and rolling stock — to almost $43,632,389, or practically $16,980 per mile more than on the West Siberian line.

But Mezheninov had accomplished what many of his European contemporaries would have judged an almost impossible task. Early in January 1898, the Ob-to-Krasnoyarsk division was opened to regular traffic, and, on August 28, the first official train chuffed triumphantly under the bunting and Imperial flags on welcoming arches at Irkutsk station; regular traffic commenced in the following January. Mezheninov might have given his sharp gray beard a proud little tweak, since he had completed the Mid-Siberian line in five years instead of seven and had fulfilled to the letter the orders of Alexander III, the Tsar of Peace whose son Nicholas was to win the "full fruit" — in Witte's words — of the Trans-Siberian, only to lose it all, together with his throne, his wife and children, and his life.

CHAPTER VIII

Convicts and Exiles

We have parted from our fathers,
From our mothers;
We from all our kin have parted,
We are prisoners;
Pity us, O our fathers!
— "Miloserdnaya," or exiles' begging song

TODAY, it is the proudest boast of old Siberians — who consider themselves stronger, harder working, more self-reliant, and less garrulous than European Russians — that their forebears were exiles. They are understandably vague about the precise nature of ancestral offenses, for these included not only political crimes but also murder, incest, rape, theft, smuggling and illicit distilling, counterfeiting, forgery, cheating at cards, attempted suicide, and army desertion.

Not even George Kennan ventured to estimate how many human beings tsarist regimes had relegated to Siberia. But he states that between 1823, when official counting began, and 1888, nearly 773,000 exiles and voluntary followers passed over the Urals. According to modern researchers, the total from 1800 to the outbreak of the First World War approached a million.

When punishment by exile was first written into tsarist law in the seventeenth century, the Russian criminal code was almost incredibly cruel and barbarous, as Kennan points out in *Siberia and the Exile System*. "Men were impaled on sharp stakes, hanged, and beheaded by the hundred for crimes that would not now be regarded as capital in any civilized country in the world; while lesser offenders were flogged with the *knut* and bastinado, branded with hot irons, mutilated by amputation of one or more of their limbs, deprived of their tongues, and suspended in the air by hooks passed under two of their ribs until they died a lingering and miserable death. When criminals had been thus *knuted*, bastinadoed, branded, or crippled by amputation, Siberian exile was resorted to as a quick and easy method of getting them out of the way; and in this attempt to rid society of criminals who were both morally and physically useless Siberian exile had its origin." *

* George Kennan was one of the most influential journalists of his day and, in the words of Peter Kropotkin, "knew everything worth knowing about Siberia." Of Scotch-Irish ancestry, Kennan was born in Norwalk, Ohio, on February 16, 1845. His mother was related to Samuel F. B. Morse, and his father — a Hamilton College graduate who became a schoolteacher in Norwalk — taught him telegraphy at a very early age. Frail health barred young Kennan from combat in the Civil War, but he served with such distinction as a military telegrapher in Western Union's Cincinnati office that he was appointed a member of the expedition setting out to build the Russo-American telegraph line conceived by Perry McDonough Collins. He arrived at Kamchatka in 1865 and remained in northeastern Siberia for somewhat more than two years, a period he described in his lively and well-written *Tent Life in Siberia*, first published in 1870. After a 5714-mile journey by sledge from the Sea of Okhotsk to Russia, he returned to America and, in 1877, became night manager of the Washington bureau of the Associated Press. Two years later, he married.

In 1885, Richard Watson Gilder, editor of the *Century Magazine*, commissioned Kennan to investigate penal conditions and exile life in Siberia. At St. Petersburg, he received permission to inspect prisons and exile centers because, he surmised, "all my prepossessions were favorable to the Russian Government and unfavorable to the Russian revolutionists." He and George A. Frost, a Boston artist who had been with him in Siberia and also knew Russian, crossed the Urals in the early summer of 1885. For a year the two endured all the hardships of Siberian post travel, and learned from the exiles themselves the shocking iniquities of the Russian penal system. "In my frequent skirmishes with the police, and with suspicious local officials in remote Siberian villages," Kennan wrote, "nothing but the letter which I carried from the Russian Minister of the Interior saved me

Shortly before the eighteenth century, severe mutilation was abolished and replaced by banishment to Siberia for felonious assault, fortune-telling, vagrancy, prizefighting, snuff-taking, setting fires *by accident,* and begging under false pretenses, as when women wrapped a short log in a blanket and solicited alms for their starving "baby," or when men rolled their eyes to sham blindness. In decrees of 1753 and 1754, the Empress Elizabeth Petrovna, Peter the Great's easygoing, pleasure-loving daughter who indulged her passion for finery to the extent of fifteen thousand silk dresses and five thousand pairs of shoes, abrogated the death penalty, for which she sub-

---

from summary arrest and imprisonment, or from a search of my person and baggage which probably would have resulted in my expulsion from the empire under guard and in the loss of all my notes and documentary material." What he saw and heard completely changed his former view that "the nihilists, terrorists, and political malcontents generally, who had so long kept Russia in a state of alarm and apprehension, were unreasonable and wrong-headed fanatics of the anarchistic type . . ."

His subsequent *Century* articles (later issued in book form as *Siberia and the Exile System*) were so thoroughly documented and so expressive of his deep compassion for the exiles that they aroused public opinion in America and Britain. Kennan was quickly recognized as "a great force of civilization and humanity," affirmed Robert Underwood Johnson, Gilder's successor as *Century* editor. "What began as a magazine enterprise soon became, despite the author's personal hardships and continuous perils to his health and safety, a labor of love, a propaganda of freedom."

A *Century* contributor named Anna Laurens Dawes described Kennan as being "of slight physique, somewhat delicate in appearance, — so thin, so white, so dark is he, — but possessed of great powers of endurance, especially in the capacity to bear strain. Lithe and active, his nervous energy is intense, and a considerable muscular development enables him to perform feats . . . apparently quite beyond his strength." He had "a buoyant and sanguine temperament . . . [as well as] the peculiar facility of adaptation to strange peoples . . ."

Kennan's later career was given over to lecturing about Russia, writing on-the-spot news accounts of the Spanish-American and Russo-Japanese wars, and later serving on the staff of the *Outlook,* a popular American magazine of a half-century ago. Besides *Siberia and the Exile System,* he was the author of *Campaigning in Cuba; The Tragedy of Pelée;* and, among other books, a two-volume biography of the railway magnate, Edward H. Harriman. He died at Medina, New York, on May 10, 1924. George F. Kennan, a former American ambassador to the Soviet Union and to Yugoslavia and a well-known author in his own right, is George Kennan's first cousin twice removed.

stituted exile at hard labor. Owing to the need for workers at newly discovered Siberian gold and silver mines owned by the Imperial family, punishment by exile was broadened by Catherine the Great to cover a host of additional crimes, such as usury, debt, incorrigible drunkenness and wife-beating, felling

A Siberian criminal convict of the nineteenth century

trees without a permit, and habitual idleness and failure to provide family support. Exiles were herded on foot to Siberia and died by the thousands for lack of food and shelter. Prisoners' records were often so confused by bungling clerks that confirmed criminals convicted of capital felonies were released as colonists in western Siberia, while harmless peasants guilty perhaps only of impertinence to a police officer, were listed on muster sheets as murderers and confined to the grim eastern mines for years.

In 1817, the shocking conditions in "the cesspool of the Tsars," as the civilized world called Siberia, had aroused highly placed Russian reformers during the comparatively liberal reign of Alexander I. Through the efforts of these humanitarians, exiles received proper identification papers and traveled in convoys. *Étapes,* or stockaded rest stations with two or more barracks-like rooms, were built at intervals along the wayside; smaller enclosures, or half-*étapes,* were placed midway between. In 1823, a Bureau of Exile Administration

A Siberian étape

was set up at Tobolsk (later removed to Tyumen), where the outcasts were counted, classified, and sent on their way under military guard to auxiliary bureaus at Tomsk, Krasnoyarsk, and Irkutsk. There they were distributed to prisons and penal settlements, or, if not hard-labor prisoners, to a place of domi-

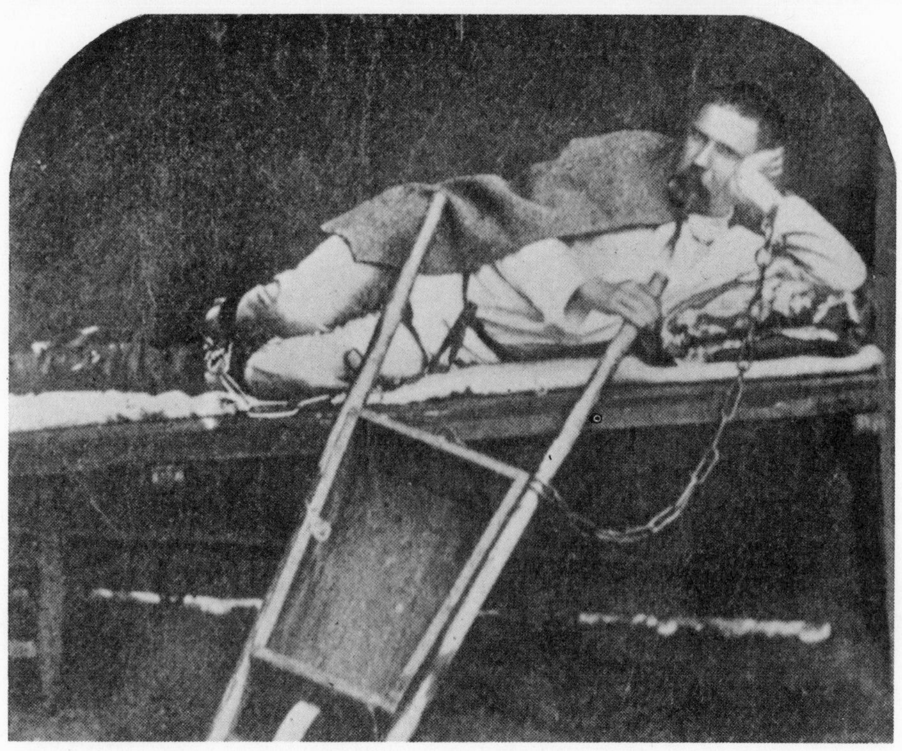

Convict chained to a wheelbarrow, a form of disciplinary punishment authorized by law

cile under police surveillance. At Irkutsk, many convicts and political exiles under hard-labor sentence were forwarded to the infamous gold and silver mines in the desolate Kara and Nerchinsk districts, a rugged two-months' march from Irkutsk and so far removed from central authority that sadistic wardens committed any number of brutalities with impunity.* When the victims could no longer endure the beatings, the boots of guards stamping on their bodies, the scanty and rotted food, the all-pervading vermin and stench, they killed

* The private property of the Crown, the Kara placer gold deposits lay along the small Kara River eighty-four post-road miles northeast of Sretensk. The Nerchinsk silver mines, also owned by the Crown, were scattered over a desolate, mountainous region thousands of square miles in area and known as the Nerchinsk Silver-Mining District. Its southernmost limits bordered on the Manchurian frontier about two hundred miles southeast of the town of Nerchinsk, on the Shilka River.

Executioner with plet

themselves, not infrequently by drinking water in which they had soaked the poisonous heads of matches.

Some prisoners were chained permanently to wheelbarrows, others were left to virtual starvation on water and black bread in so-called "secret cells" furnished with nothing more than an excrement bucket. On Sakhalin island, off Siberian's eastern coast, two "politicals" were flogged for the failure of one to take off his cap to a minor official; at the Omsk prison, the novelist Dostoyevski was thrashed almost to death because he complained of a lump of filth in the soup. Many offenders were stripped to the waist and almost sliced to pieces by a hundred strokes from the *plet,* a three-tailed rawhide lash four feet long. Not even girls were spared this punishment. A colonel who had formerly commanded the Cossack guards told Kennan that a female servant of the criminal class at the Kara gold mines had been caught in "an intrigue" with a convict, the lover of the warden's wife. " 'Enraged by jealousy,' " Kennan quotes the colonel, " 'she made such representations to her husband the warden as to induce him to have the servant-girl flogged. The girl received 150 blows with the stick on her bare body, and then when she went to the *zavéduyushchi* [the governor of the penal establishment] and complained of the cruel treatment to which she had been subjected, she got ninety blows more with the *plet,* — 240 blows in all, — and I stood by and saw those executions carried out.' " *

Until an Imperial decree in 1900 temporarily ended banishment to Siberia, exiles were grouped into four major classes: (1) hard-labor convicts; (2) penal colonists; (3) individuals simply deported without imprisonment or hard labor; and (4) voluntary followers, such as wives and children accompanying exiled husbands and fathers. Those in the first two categories were exiled for life and remained in penal servitude for terms ranging from four to twenty years or longer, after which they could become settlers, depending on behav-

* Vicious as this lash was, it did not compare with the grisly knout, a bundle of leather thongs laced with wire. When swung with full force, the knout could break an inch-thick board or a human spine in a single stroke. Executioners were so skillful in its use that, if bribed beforehand by the victim, they could ease the blows without seeming to do so, an illusion of intimate concern to themselves since they were liable to twenty-five strokes on their own backs for dereliction of duty.

As a more cheerful note, we may repeat an anecdote related by Jakob Staehlin von Storcksburg, a member of the Imperial Academy at St. Petersburg in the eighteenth century. Peter the Great had condemned a man to be flogged, and though his wife Catherine and other members of the court interceded on his behalf, the Tsar refused to rescind the sentence. Catherine and the courtiers then tied a note of petition to the collar of Peter's favorite dog, which ran out to greet his master. Peter read the note and laughed. "Since this is the first time you have petitioned me," he said to his pet, "your wish will be granted."

Sketch of a criminal convict with half-shaved head

ior; they lost all civil and property rights, and their spouses could remarry. Grotesquely shaven lengthwise across one side of the head, these prisoners were fettered with riveted ankle bands linked together by a four-foot-long, five- to eight-pound chain which, for easier walking, was drawn up between the legs to a rope or leather belt round the waist. Violently refractory prisoners were handcuffed as well.

Prior to the mid-nineteenth century, felons were branded on the face with one or more letters to stigmatize their crime. After 1845, the searing irons were replaced by almost as disfiguring but less painful tattooing needles that indelibly scarred forehead or cheek with such symbols as "KAT" for *katorzhnik* (convict) or "B" for *brodyaga* (vagrant). About twenty years later, Alexander II prohibited this defilement; thanks perhaps to some spark of compassion, the authorities

A branded brodyaga

had at no time applied the practice to women prisoners, who were never shorn and seldom fettered.

Exiles of the third class comprised a vast hodgepodge of religious dissenters, peasants outlawed by their village communes for inveterate laziness, alcoholism, or bad conduct in general, and individuals from all ranks in society who were either exiled by a court or by arbitrary order of the Minister of the Interior. These *ssylnye* were not chained or disfigured; they retained some civil rights and could hope to return home when their terms expired. As a rule, they were not imprisoned but were strictly confined to a small district as colonists under the suspicious eyes of the police.

"Politicals" living in Siberian exile

The Interior Ministry's "administrative order" was a lettre de cachet as sinister, capricious, and unappealable as any issued by the French autocracy before the Revolution. In an instance cited by Kennan, a governor took a spite against a local councilor and not only had him banished from the province but also prohibited him from staying in any one place for more than ten days, compelling the victim to spend the rest of his days in aimless wanderings through Siberia. Innocent university students were arrested if seen in company with actual or merely suspected malcontents, and were held in prison without hearing or trial for anywhere from two weeks to two years before being shipped off to Siberia; parents were exiled

Five murderers of their husbands

if their children became revolutionists even though they themselves had never had a disloyal thought. No less a personage than Prince Alexander Kropotkin was taken into custody solely for possession of Emerson's essay "Self-Reliance." It was not uncommon for politicals acquitted by a court to be rearrested and exiled by the apprehensive Ministry on the charge that they were "untrustworthy." No one could demand a trial or a hearing, examine witnesses, obtain a writ of habeas corpus, or communicate with relatives. In short, the Ministry violated every principle of justice with the tacit approval of the Tsars.

The majority of female hard-labor convicts, averaging something between five and eight per cent of the total for both sexes, had been condemned for murder, usually that of their husbands. Contrary to lurid accounts by foreign journalists who had never visited Russia or Siberia, these women did not slave deep in the mines.* Their most strenuous chore even in the notoriously oppressive Nerchinsk district was to break up and sort silver ore in a shed. Others worked in the kitchens, laundries, and primitive hospitals of prisons and hard-labor camps, helped in the fields, or worked as teamsters. "Some of the women who are condemned to the far east," observed Dr. Lansdell, "have the good fortune to be taken as domestic servants by officers, and even favoured civilians, who, in a new country where ordinary servants are not to be had, are allowed for this purpose to take the prisoners, subject to inspection, of course." Those criminal wives who had not done in their husbands were seldom accompanied by the latter, whose reluctance to join them may be explained by the fact that they had to pay their own way, an obligation not affecting exiles' wives, provided that they and their children traveled with the exile convoy and submitted to penal discipline.

All those condemned to Siberia were sent from every part of European Russia first to the exile-forwarding prison in Moscow. From there, they departed for Tyumen in companies of three to four hundred. Until the eighteen-seventies, they and their family followers journeyed by barge and on foot, carts being provided only for the sick, infirm, aged, children under twelve years old, and nobles or certain politicals of consequence. With the extension of the railway, they rode in

* It is odd that foreigners the world over came to associate Siberian exile labor with *salt* mines, for the fact is that relatively few prisoners were assigned to them. Russian sovereigns derived far greater profit from their privately owned gold and silver mine holdings, and, to enrich themselves even more, used convicts and exiles to work them. George Kennan could not find out if the Tsars shared any part of the government's costs, which amounted to about $50 a prisoner per year. From his mines in eastern Siberia alone, says Kennan, Alexander III received approximately thirty-six hundred pounds of pure gold annually, with a value of more than $1,190,000 at the market price of that day.

LEFT: *Nineteenth-century exiles at the "Monument of Tears" that marked the boundary between Europe and Asia*
RIGHT: *Convicts, exiles, and voluntary followers on the march*

window-barred cars under military escort. Prison barges at Tyumen conveyed the exiles to Tomsk by way of the Irtysh, Ob, and tributary rivers. The barges, towed by passenger-and-mail paddle-wheel steamers, transported an average of slightly more than 10,500 exiles during the four-month ice-free season. Typical of these arks was the *Irtysh,* a black iron hull two hundred and forty-five feet long by thirty in beam, surmounted fore and aft by deck houses containing a galley, an infirmary, quarters for convoying troops, and a few cells for politicals. Amidships, a large, zoolike, roofed-over cage of heavy iron wire was partitioned to separate men from women and children. Below this area, dubbed "the chicken coop" by its occupants, a similarly divided deck was lined along the sides and above the keel with sleeping shelves. The *Irtysh* and her sister

Prison barge of 1900

ships could each accommodate eight hundred prisoners, but when human cargo accumulated excessively at the Tyumen forwarding station, several hundred more were jammed in almost to the point of suffocation.

During the seven- to ten-day voyage from Tyumen to Tomsk, the hapless prisoners were roasted in the hold, drenched by rain in the "coop," or chilled to what they called a "gypsy-sweat" shiver by icy blasts in spring and autumn. But they could gamble, exchange coarse pleasantries with peasant girls at landing stages, or fish over the side with willow poles for the salmon, sturgeon, perch, and pike abounding in the rivers. By all accounts, brawls and assaults with intent to kill were rare, even though each barge carried a number of quarrelsome brutes, some as unbalanced as the young man who jauntily confessed to Harry de Windt that he had killed his mother and two sisters because, in his words, "I wanted to try my luck in Siberia — *that's* the place to make your fortune!"

At Tomsk, prisoners destined for eastern regions began their interminable march in convoys of three to five hundred men, women, and children guarded by a handful of soldiers with bayoneted rifles. Their chains clanking dismally, the men wore the government garb that comprised, in summer, trousers and shirt of unbleached linen, strips of linen or flannel as substitutes for stockings, leather or felt ankle-guards to help prevent leg-irons from chafing, and slippers so flimsy that everyone soon went barefoot. The costume was completed by a visorless gray cap, a gray overcoat with one or more yellow, diamond-shaped patches sewn on the back to designate the prisoner's length of sentence, and a belt or rope from which dangled a saucepan and a teakettle. Winter wear included a woolen shirt and trousers, partly cured leather boots stuffed with straw at the top, a sheepskin coat, wool-and-leather mittens, and a cap with earlaps. Women's clothes differed only in respect to a dress, and a kerchief over the head in summer.

"The exiles, although uniformly clad in gray, presented, from an ethnological point of view, an extraordinary diversity of types, having been collected evidently from all parts of the vast empire," Kennan relates. "There were fierce, wild-looking mountaineers from Daghestán and Circassia, condemned to penal servitude for murders of blood-revenge; there were Tatárs from the lower Vólga, who had been sunburned until they were almost as black as negroes; Turks from the Crimea, whose scarlet fezzes contrasted strangely with their gray convict overcoats; crafty-looking Jews from Podólia, going into exile for smuggling; and finally, common peasants in great numbers from all parts of European Russia. The faces of the prisoners generally were not as hard, vicious, and depraved as the faces of criminals in America. Many of them were pleasant and good-humored, some were fairly intelligent, and even

Interior of an étape *in the 1880s*

the worst seemed to me stupid and brutish rather than savage or malignant."

During the high season from May to the first week in October, the exiles waded through the mud or thick grit of the post road from six in the morning to seven in the evening, pausing overnight at *étapes* or half-*étapes*, and stopping every third day for twenty-four hours' rest. In a month, they seldom covered more than three hundred and thirty miles.

On arrival at one of these yellow-sided, red-roofed barracks of logs or rough-hewn planks — often patched-up wrecks thirty to fifty years old — the prisoners were counted outside the palisaded courtyard. At the instant of dismissal, both sexes stampeded to find a place on sleeping platforms, comfortless enough to weary bodies but preferable to the unspeakable floor. A convoy of five hundred might be packed like herrings into dark, damp, and unventilated rooms designed for only a hundred and fifty. These loathsome *kamery* — the same for women and children as for men, who were separated at night from the former — were barren of furnishings save for a brick or iron stove, a large, seldom-covered wooden tub used as a communal night vessel, and sleeping platforms, or *nary*, that consisted of uninterrupted rows of wooden boards set against the walls or down the center about three feet above the floor.

Voluntary and involuntary exiles slept on these splintered and inflexible planks without removing their overcoats, as there were no mattresses, blankets, or pillows. Cockroaches, fleas, lice, and bedbugs swarmed beyond count and, as one prisoner remarked, "just regularly drink blood." The sick, feeble, crippled, or aged who were knocked aside in the scramble for resting places on the *nary* camped on room or corridor floors unless they had the kopecks with which to buy space seized by firstcomers. During the twenty-four-hour stopovers, stated an official 1880 report to the Tsar, "the male prisoners and the families that voluntarily accompany them . . . spend the greater part of the day together, and the scenes of debauchery to be witnessed here cannot possibly be described. All the shame and all the conscience that a criminal has left are here lost completely. Here go to ruin also the families of the criminals, irrespective of age or sex."

Political prisoners fared immeasurably better in isolated cells, each with a bedstead, a crude wooden bench, and possibly a table. The government granted them this comparative luxury because they were not common criminals; but like lepers, they were cut off from all contact with everyone else in the convoy for fear that they might infect others with iconoclastic ideas.

The trek's hardships fell most heavily on the sick and old, who languished without medical care except at the largest *étapes*, of which there were fewer than six in the thousand miles between Tomsk and Irkutsk; in between, the sum of a convoy officer's medicinal stores came to a few jugs of castor oil and a little quinine. The chief of prison administration himself admitted these evils in a report to the Interior ministry. "All prisoners taken sick on the road between Achinsk and Irkutsk, up to the year 1885, have been treated at . . . three *étapes* — not, however, in the army lazarets, but in the common cells of the *étape* buildings. There they have been kept, not only without separation according to age, sex, or nature of disease, but without any of the conveniences and appliances that a lazaret should have. In the cells set apart for sick exiles there were neither nurses, nor hospital linen, nor beds, nor bedding, nor even dishes for food." Children and adults died in a profusion that may almost be likened to the quantities of crushed vermin that bloodied *kamery* floors and walls. Pneumonia, dysentery, diphtheria, scarlet fever, smallpox, syphilis, scurvy, typhoid, and typhus fever took heaviest toll, typhus accounting for an average of one third of all sickness and death in the *étapes* between Tomsk and Irkutsk.

When Eastern Siberia's Governor-General Anuchin documented the state of affairs for the Tsar in 1882, Alexander III annotated the report with one of his marginal comments. "I have read this with great interest, and I am more than troubled by this melancholy but just description of the Government's forgetfulness of a country so rich and so necessary to Russia," he wrote characteristically. "It is inexcusable, and even criminal, to allow such a state of affairs in Siberia to continue." Although hundreds of thousands of rubles were appropriated for the amelioration of the exiles' tragic straits, the loss of life continued without appreciable abatement.

"The 'lamentable condition' of the Siberian *étapes*," Kennan concludes, "seems to me to be mainly attributable to corrupt and incapable administration, and to the inherent defects of a bureaucratic system of government. For these very *étapes*, bad as they are, an immense amount of money has been appropriated; but the greater part of it has been divided between fraudulent contractors and corrupt Government officials. An inspector of exile transportation, who had excellent opportunity to know the facts, told me that it was hardly an exaggeration to say that if all the money that had been appropriated for the construction and maintenance of these 'tumble-down buildings' could now be gathered together, it would be enough to pay for the erection of a line of solid silver *étapes* along the whole route from Tomsk to the city of Irkutsk."

Exiles on the march foraged for themselves with a government allowance of five cents a day for each man and woman in the convoy except nobles and politicals, who received two and a half cents more. From peasants who catered to the trade of the Neschastnye, or "Unfortunates," the exiles bought black bread, fish pies, boiled meat, hard-cooked eggs, and the thin beer called kvass. At *étapes*, soup was usually obtainable for a price from the guards, who also sold hot water for a penny a kettleful to those who could afford the additional luxury of brick tea, a mixture of tea stems and inferior leaves held together by a gum and resembling an oversized plug of tobacco.

Those who had blown in their dole on lice races* or on

* "A common method of gambling among criminal convicts in Siberian *étapes*," says Kennan, "is to spread down an overcoat or a dirty linen foot-wrapper on the floor of the *kámera*, and guess at the number of fleas that will jump upon it within a certain length of time. Every convict, of course, backs his guess with a wager. Another method, equally common, is to draw two concentric circles on one of the sleeping-platforms, put a number of lice simultaneously within the inner circle, and then give all the money that has been wagered on the event to the convict whose louse first crawls across the line of the outer circle. Exiles on the road are not supposed to

vodka (sometimes smuggled into *étapes* by peasants who poured the liquor into raw cattle entrails, then wound the latter round their torso and thighs for concealment) were in the van of marchers who wailed the funereal "Miloserdnaya," or exiles' begging song, when approaching villagers, ordinarily generous in times of plenty. In times of famine, when foodstuffs were ransom-priced, mortality among the Unfortunates from malnutrition and scurvy rose directly in proportion to the degree of want throughout the land.

Since hard-labor convicts possessed no rights or legitimate means of protection against penal functionaries — the common enemies hated so venomously that escaped prisoners had been known to dig up the bodies of recently deceased officials and pound stakes into their hearts — they organized an artel, a cross between a union and a cooperative. They elected a leader, bound themselves to strict, unwritten laws, and contributed to a mutual welfare fund. When a member was sentenced to flogging, the artel drew from this nest egg and bribed the flagellator to lash with only simulated severity. It hired telegas from peasants when convoy vehicles lacked space for sick or exhausted brethren. It created the post of artel storekeeper, from whom exiles could buy tea and sugar, and, with the connivance of suborned guards, vodka and other intoxicants. It planned escapes, or prohibited them if this worked to the advantage of the whole group. Convoy officers were called to stringent account by their superiors if any prisoner got away, and so they made a deal with the artel chief. In return for his guarantee to ban flight for a specified length of time, prisoners were allowed to shed their onerous legshackles, which they hammered into elliptical shape and

have playing-cards, but facilities for gambling in the manner above described are never lacking."

slipped off over the heel. If anyone in the clan defied the interdiction, the artel was honor-bound to bring him back. As punishment, the recaptured absconder was either thrashed by his comrades or forced by them to march with a heavy sack of earth on his back.

Paradoxically, the penal code of these self-reliant jailbirds was harsher than the government's in some respects. Members could commit every imaginable crime but two: if they disobeyed the organization or betrayed its secrets, they were sentenced to death. In numerous instances, fugitives from the artel's vengeance paid the penalty years later and far from the place of judgment, for loyal partners in crime kept their oath to the cabal though collectively guilty of almost every iniquity. Once they spotted a traitor, who might have been freed long before and had kept out of sight in some remote settlement, that traitor was as good as dead.

The artel also enforced agreements, however unfair they might be to one of the contracting parties. In every convoy, there were always some alcoholic, dim-witted deportees — banished to Siberia simply as colonists without hard-labor or imprisonment — who would sell their souls for a few rubles and a bottle of vodka. Offering these as payment, a convict condemned to the mines for a maximum term would cozen one of these dolts into an exchange of identity — name, papers, and clothing — the victim being assured that he would be freed as soon as he revealed his real name at the mines. The artel convened, ratified the pact, then adjured the colonist and, somewhat superfluously, the convict to abide by it. At subsequent roll calls, each answered to the other's name without challenge from the guards, who could not have cared less about the features of several hundred look-alike ruffians. In 1885, the government ended this fraud by affixing the exile's photograph to his documents. Before that, however, countless scoundrels, called *varnaki,* had been released as colonists while their dupes, whose only offense lay in an unquenchable thirst for vodka, slaved underground for years on end. Mining settlement governors desperately needed workers to meet the Imperial demand for greater production, and hence paid no attention to the assertions of weeping riffraff that they were not the convicts Such-and-such on muster sheets.

Few exiles were so foolish as to attempt escape during Siberia's killing winters. But when they heard the mating call of the cuckoo in spring, many hard-labor felons in particular acted on an irresistible urge for freedom unless flight were under artel taboo. Workers in outdoor gangs found it fairly easy to make a getaway in the forests while guards dozed off from the aftereffects of vodka or from a sleepless night at cards. Pounding off their leg-irons and turning westward toward Mother Russia, they followed hieroglyphic guidemarks left on trees and village outbuildings by other vagrant *brodyagi* in what they called "General Cuckoo's Army." *

---

* One of the most familiar songs in the Soviet Union today is "Holy Baikal," with verses from "Thoughts of a Fugitive on Baikal," written years ago by a D. P. Davydov. The words, sung to a sad, slow melody, would win no poetry prize in Russia. Marshall S. Shatz, a young American scholar specializing in Russian revolutionary movements of the last century, has made the best of them in a fresh English verse translation that appears for the first time in this book:

Holy Baikal — glorious sea,
An old fish barrel — my glorious ship.
Ho, North Wind, stir the waves for me,
And hasten a brave lad's trip.

Heavy chains I dragged for many a day,
Through the hills of Akatui I went.
An old friend helped me run away,
I came to life with freedom's scent.

Shilka, Nerchinsk, I've been everywhere,
The mountain police didn't catch me,

Nicknamed "the hunchbacks" by reason of the shoulder-slung tramp's sack that gave them a misshapen appearance, the fugitives subsisted on berries, mushrooms, and edible roots until they came to a hamlet, where it was the nightly custom of householders to leave scraps of bread and meat and perhaps a jug of milk on a windowsill rather than to incur the anger of a constant flow of runaways, who retaliated for withheld food by setting inhospitable homes afire. Under pain of death, artel law barred theft of crockery containing the handouts. Horses were also let alone, for every well-informed *brodyaga* knew the peasantry's punishment for rustling: a lingering and excruciating death when the captors released two springy, bent-down birch trees, the tops of which were tied, one to the culprit's hands and the other to his feet. In the Mariinsk district east of Tomsk, Kennan remarks, it was the practice of the countrymen to throw a horse thief to earth, force ground glass into his eyes, and leave him with the words, "Ah, you *varnak!* You won't find your way to us again."

Varnaki were the most vicious of all *brodyagi.* The scourges of the post road, they plundered freight caravans and pounced on solitary travelers who had stopped to rest their horses. After robbing them of food, clothing, and, most prized of all, the money and passport that provided the surest means of reaching Russia without detection, these brigands bludgeoned,

---

In the forests the gluttonous beast kept his lair,
No rifleman's bullet could scratch me.

By dark and by broad daylight I fled,
Near the towns I glanced left and right,
The peasant women would give me bread,
The lads kept my pipe alight.

Holy Baikal — glorious sea,
A kaftan in holes — my glorious sail.
Ho, North Wind, stir the waves for me,
Peals of thunder portend a gale.

strangled, or stabbed their victims to death to prevent later testimony against themselves. In February 1886, an organized band of *varnaki* terrorized the citizens of Tomsk by riding through the streets at night and robbing pedestrians after catching them with hurled grappling hooks. In eastern Siberia, the desperadoes became such a widespread menace that the government offered the native Buryats a bounty of a dollar and a half for each *varnak* brought in dead or alive. This handsome reward transformed the ordinarily friendly Buryats into implacable manhunters. "If you shoot a squirrel," they said, "you get only its skin, but if you shoot a *varnak,* you get money and his clothing, too."

Foreigners studying Russian prison statistics were amazed by the phenomenally long lives of exiles. According to a British Foreign Office report, none suspected that these patriarchs "existed only in official lists of the Siberian authorities, who prolonged the lives of thousands of exiles on paper in order to put the money received from the Government for their support into their own pockets." By not recording the dead or missing, wardens continued to draw the prisoners' clothing and rations. These they sold at bargain prices to shady dealers, who then resold the garments and food at tremendous markups to equally shady government purchasing agents. Obviously, official morals had changed little since the time of Peter the Great, who proposed to hang everyone who stole as much as would buy a rope. The procurator-general replied that if the Tsar did this, there would be no officials left. "We all steal," he added with breezy candor, "the only difference is that some of us steal larger amounts and more openly than others." Peter, a writer of the time reported, "taking his meaning, began to relax likewise and permitted things to remain as they were."

Since it was extremely difficult to escape from Siberia's heartland within a single spring and summer, General Cuckoo's followers faced two alternatives when September night-frosts foreboded winter. They could either risk death from wild animals, starvation, or glacial cold in the forest, or they could turn themselves in at an *étape* or police post as distant as possible from the place of escape.* The second course was frequently adopted in spite of the forty *plet* strokes that awaited them. Even as a hard-labor convict with a long sentence writhed under the lash, he had excellent reason to congratulate himself. He had not only spent a pleasantly idle summer holiday in the company of congenial fellow runaways met along the way but had also benefited from an inspiriting change in his penal status. When interrogated by officers, the *brodyaga* had pretended loss of memory. Asked his name, he replied that he was "Ivan Don't-Remember" or "Peter Know-Nothing." He was therefore classified as an unidentifiable vagrant and sentenced to a flogging and only four years at hard labor. If he behaved himself until his term was up, he could count on release as a colonist, free again to take to crime when profitable opportunity appeared.

These "amnesic" *brodyagi* became so numerous throughout Siberia in the latter part of the nineteenth century that the government summarily packed off all those apprehended to the coal mines of Sakhalin, that wet, foggy Sea of Okhotsk island convicts called "Hell on Earth." But even in this natural

* *Brodyagi* could not hope to be harbored by sympathetic peasants, for none dared to hide them and risk a long term in the mines. . . . "During the spring thaw when the snow commences to melt," the explorer Stadling tells us, "a large number of corpses of 'unknown persons' are found in the forests in the vicinity to villages and cities. These 'unknown persons' are either escaped convicts who have perished from exposure, or else persons who have been murdered; and these finds of corpses are so common that they are called by the people 'podsnieshniks,' or 'snow-flowers.' "

bastille, confirmed runaways tried to disprove the old saying of Siberian turnkeys: "The Tsar's cow pasture is so large you can't get out of it." From the prisons at what is now Oktyabrski (a port about halfway up the island's western shore), "the runaway must first walk 200 miles along the coast, and this through a country where he can get no provisions," Dr. Lansdell says in his *Through Siberia* (1882). "He dare not show himself to the natives, since there is a price on his head, and they receive 6*s*. [then about $1.46] for taking him to the police, dead or alive; and even if he should succeed in crossing the six miles of ice to the continent, he is often compelled to give himself up to get food. Thus, out of 100 who were reported to have run away the winter before my journey, 32 were caught by the Gilyaks, and one case of cannibalism was said to have taken place among the starving fugitives."

Other escapers made rafts and put to sea in the foolhardy and seldom realized hope of rescue by American whalers or sealers. Women prisoners — about five per cent of the total and almost all murderesses — rarely tried to escape, but they had their moments of freedom. ". . . The female prisoners were allowed clandestinely to go on board the ships whilst coaling," says Lansdell, "and were expected, on their return, to share with the warders their licentious gains."

With a few exceptions, the frightful conditions in *étapes* were duplicated in prisons. "[The Krasnoyarsk compound] contained 2000 persons, although intended for only 600," reported a St. Petersburg newspaper in 1887. "The prisoners have no laundry, and therefore they either wash their underclothing in their cells, or wear it for three or four weeks without washing. In the water-closets it is actually necessary to fight for a place, since for every such place there are a hundred or more prisoners."

Except at the mines, where meals were somewhat more substantial, the daily food ration consisted of sour, gluey black bread, a few ounces of boiled meat scraps more suitable for soap-making, cooked barley or oats, and a drink of kvass morning and evening. Now and then salted fish, potatoes, and the thinnest of cabbage soup varied this fare. Fresh greens were unheard of; it is a wonder that the incidence of scurvy rose not much above the nineteen per cent reported by six major Siberian prisons in 1888.

In the miasmic hospitals of the Tyumen and Tomsk forwarding prisons two years before, the death rate amounted to thirty-four and twenty-three per cent respectively, as compared to a mortality of a little less than four per cent in French penitentiaries, barely one and a half per cent in English, and two per cent in American. At the Achinsk prison, the hospital doors were locked after 4 P.M., and the sick were left to care for themselves. "No matter what may happen between that time and eight o'clock on the following morning," a Tomsk newspaper disclosed in 1888, "medical help cannot be had. The doctor's time is so occupied with private practice, and work in the city hospital, that he comes to the prison only once a day for an hour or two . . ."

If prisons lacked medical facilities, sick and diseased inmates were sent to the nearest town with a hospital, one of which was described in a magazine article published in St. Petersburg in 1889. "Most of the sick lie on the floors, for want of cots, and lie so closely together that there is barely room to enter the *kamery*. They all complained . . . of the terrible cold . . . from which they were freezing without any means of covering themselves or getting warm. . . . In one small separate cell lay two syphilitic patients — a man and a woman together, as there was no ward for women suffering

George Kennan in Cossack dress

from that disease — and on a pile of rags under a table in one corner of that same cell lay, cowering and getting behind each other, like puppies or kittens, two little children under three years of age belonging to the woman. The *ispravnik* [police chief] explained that he had tried to make some other disposition of the children, in order to save them from infection; but that none of the inhabitants of the town would take them."

Using official statistics for the years from 1879 through 1884, Kennan estimated that slightly less than one per cent of all exiles were politicals. Of these, about three quarters comprised "administratives" whom the Ministry of the Interior considered untrustworthy and had banished for a few years without hard labor or forced colonization. The remaining had been judged guilty of grave offenses against the Crown, the penalty for which was loss of all civil rights, permanent exile, and usually a long term of penal servitude. Some of these "state criminals" had spread seditious propaganda or conspired to overthrow the autocracy by armed rebellion; others were embittered fanatics who turned in desperation to bombing, assassination, train-wrecking, and robbery as a means toward the intimidation and ultimate destruction of the ruling class. Among these terrorists were two refined, well-educated young women and an escaped convict who had secretly dug a tunnel at night to the vault of a government subtreasury and made off with $750,000 in rubles, which they intended to devote to The Cause. But before they could put this huge involuntary subsidy to work, all three were arrested. The convict ungallantly turned state's evidence and revealed the hiding place of the stolen bonanza; the elder of the distaff amateur burglars — a schoolteacher — was condemned in 1880 to the Kara mines as originator of the plot, while her confederate was sentenced to forced colonization under perpetual police surveillance at Krasnoyarsk.

Short-term administratives generally returned to Russia without deleterious effects from their experience, but many under heavier sentence died in Siberia, some in the sod-covered yurts of Yakut savages who slept with their livestock and ate putrid fish and deer meat by preference. Bureaucratic imbecilities knew no bounds. An exiled druggist, for example, was banished to an arctic settlement shown on maps as thirty-two hundred miles north of Irkutsk; when he and his escort arrived after months of hardships, they found only a ghost town that had been abandoned more than fifty years before. At Verkhoyansk, where the temperature in January and February averages fifty-three degrees below zero, the chief of police received orders from St. Petersburg to intensify his vigil over the terrorist Vladimir Zenzinov, who might be planning to escape and wreck the train on which "the sacred person of the August Emperor" was about to depart from the capital for a holiday in the Crimea. Aside from the absurdity of keeping sharper eye on a man who would have literally needed wings to intercept the Tsar in time, the orders were sent with such casual disregard for distances that they failed to reach Verkhoyansk until nearly two months after His Majesty's safe arrival in southern Russia.

Under a code approved by Alexander III in 1882, administrative exiles were forbidden to teach or lecture; work in a library, bookshop, printing plant, photographic studio, teahouse, or tavern; attend scientific meetings, participate in theatrical performances, or appear in court except on their own behalf or that of immediate relatives. Nor could they practice medicine, surgery, pharmacy, or midwifery without permission from the Minister of the Interior, whose approval was also needed before they could attend educational institutions or take jobs as museum curators or state employees. They could not leave the limits of their town or village without a pass from the police who, according to an exile's letter published in a Moscow journal, "enter our quarters repeatedly every day . . . go through all our rooms . . . compel our landlords and our neighbors to watch our movements and report upon them . . ." Letters were heavily censored, and sometimes destroyed or withheld indefinitely by police chiefs, many of whom were common malefactors sent to Siberia and taken into government service under assumed names at the expiration of their terms.

Where regulations were strictly observed, administratives with professions were reduced to manual labor to eke out their subsistence dole of three dollars a month from the exile administration. A number, as we have seen, were recruited to work on the Trans-Siberian. In small communes, they seldom found employment other than in the cultivation of potatoes, turnips, and cabbages *if* the free settlers granted them a small patch within the village boundary. (Baron Andrew Rosen, condemned to hard labor in eastern Siberia in the eighteen-twenties, would have undoubtedly made a good thing out of cucumbers after serving his term; so green was his thumb that he raised sixty thousand in the prison garden and salted them down in brandy casks.) Administratives in town made a bare living as self-taught tailors, cap-makers, cobblers, and such.

In areas controlled by sympathetic officials who winked at infractions of the rules, educated exiles earned small sums by tutoring in private homes, giving music or French lessons to the wives of officials and prosperous citizens, or lecturing on the sciences and humanities in their culture-starved community. Absentee landowners were allowed to hire exiles expert in farm and cattle-raising management to supervise their properties, sometimes paying them as much as $3000 a year, with carriage, horses, and other perquisites thrown in. A number of professional men with a flair for business opened shops after they had acquired a little capital from the sale of their own hand-carved wooden figurines or of their wives' embroideries to the families of rich miners and merchants. Once they had attained a reasonable degree of economic security, they applied their trained, inquiring minds to the study of the region's flora and fauna, prehistoric inhabitants, archeological curiosities, climate, geological structure, or native languages. The fruits of their research, which they were eventually permitted to pass on to learned societies in Russia, contributed immeasurably to the sum of knowledge that had hitherto been acquired in dribs and drabs from military expeditions and comparatively few Russian or foreign scientists.

The custom of allowing wives and children to accompany convicts to Siberia was well-meant but abortive. "Such wives and children are supported — or at least aided to exist — by the Government, with the hope that they will ultimately exert a beneficial domestic influence over their criminal husbands and fathers; but the results rarely justify official anticipations," Kennan writes. "The women and girls in a great majority of cases go to the bad in the penal settlements, even if they have come uncorrupted through two or three hundred overcrowded *étapes* and forwarding prisons." The wives of administratives, however, were generally of the better class, and maintained their respectability. On arriving at their husband's place of exile, they quite often eased the family's straitened circumstances by selling needlework of their own making, or by hiring out as servants, dressmakers, nurses, or music and language teachers in private households. Among the most celebrated of these voluntary exiles was the lovely young Princess Maria Volkonskaya, who followed her husband to eastern Siberia after the unsuccessful insurrection against Nicholas I in 1825, the year of her marriage. At the insistence of her sister-in-law, a clavichord was loaded on Maria's covered sledge to give her the solace of music in barbarous Siberia. (Now in the Irkutsk Museum of Regional History, her instrument stands near an exhibit of some charming tobacco-pipe covers embroidered for Prince Sergius Trubetskoi by his wife Catherine, another voluntary exile as celebrated as Maria for her exemplary loyalty and courage.)

Although some firebrands of both sexes longed to return to their revolutionary activities in the homeland, most exiles banished for life or extended terms came to accept their fate with resignation and eventually with even a certain contentment. Indeed, many preferred to stay in Siberia rather than to uproot themselves and their children and return to European Russia under the occasional Imperial amnesties.

Since exiles shared a common bond in their hardships, they developed a strong sense of mutual loyalty that now and then created difficulties for free settlers with clean police records. In Krasnoyarsk, for instance, one Russian merchant found it so hard to do business with the inhabitants, predominantly exiles, that he decided to become one of them. Folding up shop, he journeyed all the way to St. Petersburg, where he committed a crime and was sentenced to a term in the Aleksandrovski Prison between Krasnoyarsk and Irkutsk. He served his time, then opened for business again in Krasnoyarsk. According to the visitor who chronicled these events in 1897, the ex-convict, though apparently inclined to do things the hard way, thenceforth got along famously.

CHAPTER IX

Setbacks and Advances

IN the spring of 1891, it will be remembered, the young Tsarevich Nicholas had opened construction of the Great Siberian Railway at Vladivostok, the city that sprawled in an amphitheater of hills overlooking the Golden Horn, Siberia's only harbor ice-free for all but three and a half months a year. Here the projected Ussuri line began.

At the end of 1892, Alexander Ursati — original surveyor of the Ussuri route — was replaced as chief engineer by Orest P. Vyazemski, whose tribulations in opening this back door of Siberia must have added to his white hairs. Owing to such grossly handicapping factors as unforeseen natural phenomena, devastating epidemics, convict cutthroats, intractable soldiers, worthless contractors, and Chinese coolies whose abhorrence of rain almost equaled their terror of Manchurian tigers stalking the forests, Vyazemski was to struggle for five years before regularly scheduled trains shuttled between Vladivostok and Khabarovsk. Yet the distance was only four hundred and seventy-five miles, not even one fourth the length of trackage laid in the West Siberian and Mid-Siberian sectors within scarcely more than six years.

Far eastern Siberia's lack of skilled hands and heavy industries meant that ironworkers, masons, and carpenters, as well as locomotives, rolling stock, and practically every item essen-

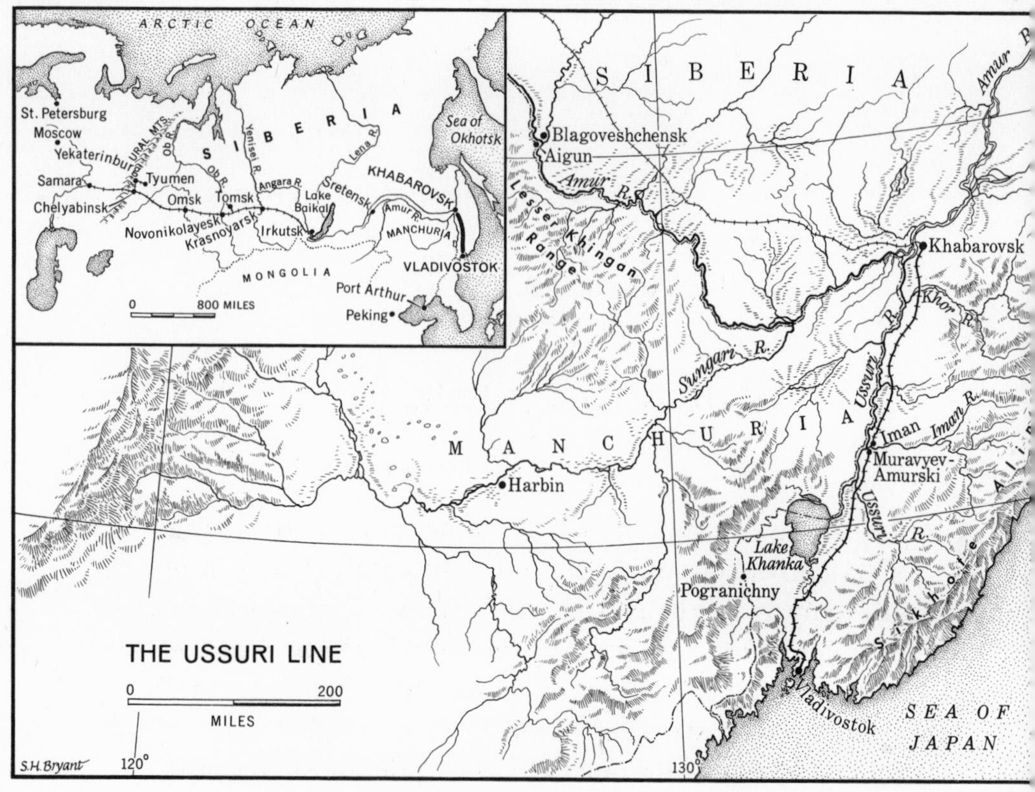

tial to railway and bridge construction had to be transported by ship from Russia. In the best of weather, the voyage required about forty days by the fastest merchantmen from the Black Sea port of Odessa. It was impossible to obtain common laborers in sufficient quantity. Cossacks were eliminated as workers, for they guarded the frontier against smugglers and Manchurian outlaws who kidnaped children and strung the butchered parents up by the heels.* Chinese settlers in the up-

* The Cossacks, whose name derives from a Tartar or Turkish word meaning "frontiersman" or "free laborer," are believed to be of mixed Russian, Ukrainian, and Tartar blood. They settled on the borders of Russia's southern steppes, where they farmed, hunted, bred cattle, traded, and fought off Tartar raiders. Noted for their independence, they ruled themselves through an elected chieftain and shifted their allegiance as they pleased, at times supporting Russia against her enemies, or violently rebelling against the Tsars. In return for land and money allowances, they obligated themselves to Russian military service, compulsory for all Cossack males over eighteen years old, and formed a lightly armed cavalry and frontier guard. In eastern Siberia, a male Cossack child qualified for half

Orest P. Vyazemski, builder of the Ussuri line

per Ussuri valley refused to abandon their profitable cultivation of ginseng, prized as "the first of all plants" by Orientals who believed that it dispelled evil spirits, restored sexual vigor to dotards, healed wounds, and cured migraine, digestive disorders, and advanced tuberculosis. Demand for this magical

---

the allowance from birth to fifth year, and for the full amount thereafter. For this reason, a Cossack woman with several sons was considered rich. Since daughters were ineligible for the government bounty, first pregnancies in particular aroused the liveliest speculation: Would a son be born to give the mother a footing on Easy Street, or would she produce a daughter not worth a kopeck?

For years the Cossacks served as the Emperor's security police and suppressors of revolutionary mobs, which they dispersed in their customary way with whips and sabers. They were strongly against the Bolshevist takeover in 1917, and joined the counterrevolutionary White Russians. The Soviets consequently stripped them of their privileges, but in 1936 reinstated the Cossack cavalry, which fought valiantly against the Germans in the Second World War.

Goldi village along the Amur; the fish are frozen sturgeon

herb was so great that Chinese dealers had been known to pay from $10 to $13 for a single ounce, and up to $1450 for one living root.

As for the North Ussuri's pigtailed Goldi — a sartorially practical tribe which changed from fishskins in summer to dogskins in winter — these hunters and fishermen were too primitive to be of any use to the Russians; the same was true of the Amur Gilyaks who, if handed a chunk of soap, chewed it to a lather and pronounced it quite to their taste.*

* Unlike the Cossacks, the yellow-skinned, polygamous Gilyaks held daughters in such uncommon esteem that few devoted fathers would sell one for less than a sledge, eight to ten dogs, and two cases of spirits from a prospective husband. Apparently, this marriage settlement was not beyond the means of suitors, for Dr. Lansdell remarks that "among these interesting people there are no unmarried ladies," the ladies being pipe-smoking Gilyak girls not yet in their teens. Strangers did well to decline

Goldi men and a boy

One attempt to relieve the manpower scarcity produced twenty-six hundred exiles in the region and fifteen hundred hard-labor prisoners from Sakhalin. For a while, the convicts enjoyed the change and gave no trouble. Six months had barely passed, however, before the residents of Vladivostok trembled for their lives and property as the worst criminals eluded camp guards at night and slipped into town, where they murdered and robbed at will. Public indignation finally boiled over when one convict killed a visiting young French naval officer in broad daylight. Prominent citizens held a protest meeting

Gilyak hospitality, since overnight guests were occasionally killed in the belief that the spirit of the departed would protect the household; the more amiable the guest, the more prized he was as guardian ghost.

The Reverend Dr. Henry Lansdell in Gilyak costume

and wrathfully demanded the immediate ouster of the Sakhalin *varnaki*. The harassed railway administration complied by returning the most dangerous long-termers to the island. Vladivostok breathed easily again when the homicide rate in that port of fourteen thousand inhabitants fell to only one or two a week, the normal number everyone took for granted.

In another move to overcome the shortage of brawn, Vyazemski's staff commandeered several thousand soldiers and put them to pick-and-shovel toil with the exiles and remaining prisoners. His Imperial Majesty's troops considered menial labor alongside the "jailbirds" a shocking insult to their uniform. In sullen mood, they carried out a slow-down strike, dawdling or stopping work entirely when overseers' backs were turned. Their recalcitrance was condoned by sympathetic officers, and hiring bosses were forced to conclude a deal by which Chinese labor contractors would bring fifteen thousand coolies by sea from North China every spring, and ship them back just before the Golden Horn froze over in December.

At first, this seemed an ideal arrangement, eliminating as it did the expense of feeding and housing the migratory horde during slack winter months. But there was a catch. Upsetting all traditions, the Chinese turned out to be highly unsatisfactory laborers, though they were rehired each spring for lack of anything better. Almost unbelievably, they had to be taught how to use shovels and wheelbarrows. Their health suffered from temperature changes, and they refused to work during rain. At the slightest hint of a tiger in the vicinity, they stampeded in squealing hysteria and huddled in camp until driven out by the labor contractors' musclemen who also served as interpreters.*

For want of competent contractors, the administration op-

* One can sympathize with the coolies, for the Manchurian tigers roaming the Ussuri region attacked humans when under the stress of long hunger. These "great lords of the woods whose progress is as silent as the moon's," in the words of the fearful Chinese, sometimes measured as much as ten and a half feet from nose to the *base* of the tail, and weighed nearly eight hundred pounds. According to a traveling British journalist with a possibly overheated imagination, desperately ravenous beasts devoured corpses in graves; between Vladivostok and Korea, he claimed, their wholesale depredations in village cemeteries necessitated armed watchmen who stood guard at night in protective little huts. In the Ussuri area, up to a hundred and fifty tigers were shot or poisoned annually; their bones, blood, heart, liver, claws, and whiskers were bought by the Chinese, who ground the dried ingredients to a powder for consumption to induce courage. Today, the killing of tigers is prohibited in far eastern Siberia, though they may be taken alive for zoos and circuses. Professional teams go after two- or three-year-old cubs individually weighing about a hundred and eighty pounds. When dogs bring the tiger to bay, the hunters pin it down with forked poles until legs and jaw can be tied. "The most difficult thing," says Prokopy Bogachov, a contemporary Soviet tiger-hunter with a dramatic sense of the obvious, "is to get your first grip on it."

Camp of convict workers on the Ussuri line

timistically farmed out roadbed and embankment work to an assortment of petty Siberian merchants, retired officers, and superannuated civil servants who blithely agreed to supply labor and equipment for the jobs assigned them. These amateur entrepreneurs lacked experience and capital if not a hearty relish for cheating the government. Scarcely had they pocketed substantial cash advances than they fell back on the engineers for tools, wheelbarrows, provisions, and fodder, the cost of which they promised to pay when reimbursed for completed construction. But despite shovels, barrows, and other articles the engineers imported from Russia especially for them, about half of these would-be contractors abandoned their projects. It appears that no effort was ever made by the Communication Ministry to recover the advances or to prosecute the defectors.

Vyazemski cleared a path through dense forests choked with undergrowth and vines; built access roads; drained broad swamps and ponds; and blasted cuttings through basalt outcroppings. Bitter winds and subzero cold limited earthwork construction to only a few months a year. The engineer had expected this but was totally unprepared for the perversities of the Siberian warm-weather season. Deluges of rain bogged down horses, carts, and men in black muck. When the Ussuri in spate rose thirty-five feet above normal level — an annual but unreported event that caught the constructors by surprise — the flood submerged the paralleling rails and forced Vyazemski to re-lay them on higher ground. Ordinarily averaging six feet in depth, the Iman River swelled over an area three miles wide and necessitated the costly and time-consuming construction of an earthen levee along the left bank.

To add to these calamities, week-long drizzles (from which the coolies scurried for shelter as though from a cloudburst) created a noxious humidity that fostered disease. *Sibirskaya yazva,* or Siberian anthrax — a virulent infection marked by fiery carbuncles — decimated draft horses, while clouds of mosquitoes spread fever that incapacitated workers and contributed further to construction delays.

In December 1894 — three and a half years after the Tsarevich had set royal foot to ceremonial shovel — Vyazemski's crews reached the end of the South Ussuri section at Muravyev-Amurski (near the present town of Iman), two hundred and fifty miles north of Vladivostok. They pressed on into the North Ussuri, not stopping to erect an 840-foot bridge over the Iman or an even longer one across the Khor, for St. Petersburg had still to decide if these should be of wood or of steel. Their Excellencies had discussed the question in June 1895, but reserved decision until a special commission returned from an inspection of the Ussuri works. When this group revealed that $221,000 could be saved with wooden bridges, Prince Michael I. Khilkov — Krivoshein's elegantly goateed successor as Communication Minister — argued that safety and other factors justified the additional cost of metal. But Their Excellencies failed to reach a decision. A year later, the Tsar finally threw his support to Khilkov, and, in a hardly surprising volte-face after *He* had spoken, the Committeemen not only voted for steel spans across the Iman and Khor but also granted the Minister an additional $326,700 for others of the same type.

Except for a forty-mile stretch from Khabarovsk southward, Vyazemski had built the two Ussuri sections from south to north, leaving behind crews to bridge intersecting rivers. With the last span up, he was finally able to open the entire line to regular traffic in November 1897, a few weeks after the first official train steamed with flying flags from Khabarovsk to

Prince Michael I. Khilkov

Vladivostok in two days, at an average speed of ten miles an hour. (By 1914, this pace had been increased to fifteen miles an hour; nowadays, the fastest Soviet express on the Khabarovsk-Vladivostok run averages hardly more than thirty-one miles an hour.) Actual construction costs had soared to $19,962,512, or a bit in excess of $42,026 per mile and almost $11,200 a mile more than in the West Siberian and Mid-Siberian sectors combined. But to the gratification of the line's persistent champions, Vyazemski had linked Vladivostok with the transcontinental rail and water arteries of the empire, thereby strengthening Russia's hold over her far eastern domain.

Alexander N. Pushechnikov, engineer in charge in Transbaikalia

In the late summer of 1898, only four sectors of the Trans-Siberian remained to be completed. They comprised (1) a short extension from Irkutsk to Lake Baikal; (2) the Circum-baikal link round the lake's southern rim to the hamlet of Mysovsk (also known as Mysovaya) on the eastern shore; (3) the Transbaikal section from Mysovsk to Sretensk; and (4) the long Amur line from Sretensk through the Shilka and Amur valleys to Khabarovsk. Taken together, these divisions extended for some twenty-one hundred miles across rough, thinly inhabited country, a large part of which was to give a young-

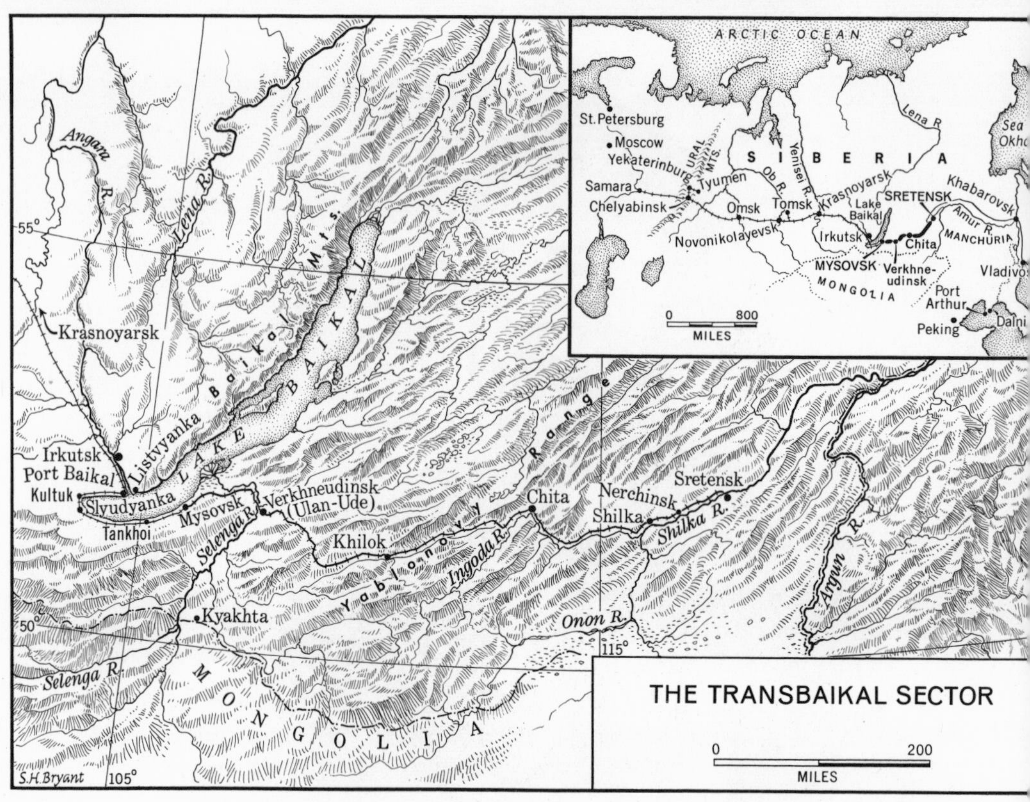

ish chief engineer named Alexander N. Pushechnikov a battle he must have remembered for the rest of his days.

The Mid-Siberian track was to terminate on the Angara River's southern bank, opposite Irkutsk, and so the Communication Ministry proposed to connect it with the city by means of a pontoon railway bridge and to continue for about forty miles to the port of Listvyanka on the western shore of Lake Baikal. Their Excellencies approved the project and, in May 1895, voted somewhat more than $1,108,000 for the Irkutsk-to-Baikal extension along the northern bank on which both Irkutsk and Listvyanka lay. But in the following winter, further surveys indicated that the *southern* bank all the way to the lake presented fewer construction difficulties. In addition, engineers discovered that the floating bridge would require expensive extra features and shore installations to cope with the

Angara's swift current and sharp fluctuations in level. And, like the existing pontoon span for vehicles and pedestrians, it would have to be dismantled and hauled out twice annually, prior to floodwater and to winter freeze. Apparently, the Committeemen never criticized the Communication Ministry for drawing up such ill-conceived plans, nor did Their Excellencies seem disturbed by their own careless rubber-stamp of the program. When Prince Khilkov stated that the route on the southern bank would be easier, shorter, and hardly more expensive than that on the northern, they vetoed the bridge project, asked no further questions, and authorized him to proceed with construction, even though Irkutsk station would be on one side of the river and Irkutsk itself on the other.

When the engineers under Pushechnikov set to work in the summer of 1896, they were disconcerted by the steepness of the Angara's banks and the headlong race of its current. Where they had expected to build on easy slopes, they were

Approach to the partly dismantled pontoon bridge across the Angara at Irkutsk in the winter of 1895-1896

forced to blast out precipitous rock to create a shelf for the roadbed, and where there was earth instead of rock, retaining walls had to be piled up against the seven-feet-a-second sweep of the Angara along its banks. Close to fifty ravines and tributary streams falling into this formidable river required as many wooden bridges. Fighting for every other inch, the engineers did not reach Lake Baikal until the end of 1897; thereafter, the makeshift track needed so many improvements that Pushechnikov could not open it to regular traffic until midsummer in 1900, practically four years to the day since construction had begun.

When Their Excellencies found that this branch of only forty-two miles had cost more than $1,554,000 — several hundred thousand dollars above Khilkov's estimate and roughly $300,000 more than the Tomsk spur that was longer by sixteen miles (including an extension of about four miles to the port north of the city) — they directed a standing watchdog commission to determine the reason for such an inordinate outlay. The commission's findings followed a pattern that had become cheerlessly familiar: the terrain had been surveyed too hurriedly and technical problems had been unforeseen. Khilkov, who had ordered the surveyors to work in the winter of 1895-1896, again escaped censure, for who else but God could have known that exceptionally heavy snow would blanket the frozen Angara's banks so deeply that no surveyor on earth could have accurately determined their contours or the full force of the current?

Meanwhile, construction of the 687-mile Transbaikal line from Mysovsk to Sretensk had begun in 1895 also under Pushechnikov's direction. From Mysovsk (now called Babushkin in honor of an Irkutsk revolutionist of 1905), the route follows the lake in a northerly direction for perhaps twenty miles, then turns east into the Selenga River delta, and, reaching Ulan-Ude, continues through the Uda River valley. Approximately four hundred miles east of Mysovsk, the railway climbs the Yablonovy Range, from which it descends to Chita, in tsarist times the capital of the Transbaikal territory.

(Not many years after completion of the Mysovsk-Sretensk line, a deep cutting in the Yablonovy mountains was roofed over for two hundred and eighty feet to protect the track from rockfalls. This "tunnel" was the first east of the Urals. It was also remarkable for the inscription in Russian that read TO THE GREAT OCEAN — the Pacific goal of nineteenth-century tsarist expansion since Nevelskoi had raised the Imperial banner at Nikolayevsk in 1850 — over the western entrance, and TO THE ATLANTIC OCEAN over the eastern. Railway tunnels were so utterly foreign to Russians that women passengers shrieked with terror when their train plunged into the sudden blackout of the Yablonovy tube, and men were seen to emerge into daylight with blanched faces.)

While Pushechnikov's track-gangs advanced eastward, rolling stock and matériel were transported from Vladivostok by rail and river to Sretensk. There, a labor force shipped from Russia began construction toward Chita, two hundred and forty miles southwest. Like their colleagues in other sectors, the Transbaikal engineers were gravely handicapped by the scarcity of experienced contractors. None existed in the territory, and all but four entrepreneurs in Russia refused to risk losses from an undertaking in a remote area unknown to them even by name. Day laborers to fill out the ranks of the imported Russians were practically unobtainable. Most of the Buryat natives avoided heavy toil as obdurately as they did the use of water for ablutions, which their Lamaist priests forbade as an abhorrent defilement of the body. In the Uda valley, the

A church of the Raskolniki, or Old Believers

pious, puritanical Old Believers would have no part of the satanic railway.*

The governor of Transbaikalia helped to save the day with seventeen hundred convicts from the mines and more than twenty-five hundred exiles. Though granted the dispensation that credited eight months' railway service as a year off their term, the convict group remained unimpressed by this indulgence and loafed at every opportunity despite punishment. In desperation, the administration devised a bonus plan by which each man was paid for whatever work he performed in addition to a fixed daily quota. Thenceforth, the felons put their backs to the job as if their lives depended on its swift completion. Since reasonably steady workers could count on a reward reaching up to twenty-five cents a day to spend on such cherished luxuries as tobacco, sugar, and contraband vodka, these wretchedly deprived devils considered themselves so well off that only inveterate runaways slipped away at the tempting call of General Cuckoo.

The ridges of Transbaikalia obliged Pushechnikov's engineers to follow the winding and steep-banked Ingoda and Shilka rivers. In many places, they found no room for the roadbed and, like their fellow workers along the Angara, had to blast shelvings into cliffs. Although the temperature at Chita, for example, averaged twelve below from the end of November to the beginning of March, crews worked through-

* These Raskolniki, or "Dissenters" popularly known as Old Believers, were descendants of seventeenth-century schismatic sectarians who protested against liturgical reforms of the Patriarch Nikon and the Europeanizing of Russia. Mercilessly persecuted as heretics, many settled over the years as forced or voluntary colonists in Siberia, where they exemplified industry, thrift, and religious fervor. They shunned tobacco, alcohol, and, in some instances, tea as well. Splinter offshoots of the cult included members who habitually looked upward with mouth wide open to receive spiritual manna from on high; observers of silence who refused to utter a syllable even under torture; flagellants who subdued the flesh; and men who castrated themselves, so they said, "for the sake of the Kingdom of Heaven."

out the winter, for the region's unique climate was characterized by clear, sunny, and virtually windless days. But around Verkhneudinsk (as Ulan-Ude was then called), Chita, and the northern stretches of the route, Nature confronted the invaders with one of her most redoubtable weapons. This was permafrost, or permanently frozen subsoil from which picks bounced as if made of rubber.* Not a single tie could be laid until this "arctic stone" had been blown to bits with dynamite or, to save its cost, patiently thawed out by innumerable wood fires.

Workers who did not also blow themselves to bits could thank Heaven rather than prudence for their continued existence. The convict miners had brought along the frighteningly casual habits Kennan had observed at Nerchinsk a decade before. On entering the mine, he had noted with some horror, they stuffed their sheepskin coats with "dynamite cartridges about as big as cannon firecrackers . . . in such a manner as to leave the long white fuses hanging out," then descended the shaft on worn, icy ladders while the fuses swayed alarmingly close to the naked candle in their free hand. After he and his artist-companion Frost had emerged from the foul under-

* This curious phenomenon is found in about one fifth of the world's land area, almost half of the Soviet Union, much of Alaska, and more than a third of Canada. It involves two layers of the earth's outer crust. The surface or "active" stratum thaws in spring to varying depths — a maximum of a few feet at some locations but usually enough for the growth of crops during the brief summer — while the lower, permafrost mass remains frozen continuously. Owing to a combination of temperature differences and hydrographic forces too complex to go into here, embankments and the walls of cuttings on the new route literally melted away after thaw. In winter, the expansion of ground moisture as it froze created hummocks that heaved up the track, then subsided in warm months and either submerged the rails in water-filled hollows or left them arched in air. Similarly, the pilings of timber bridges and trestles were thrust upward to unequal levels, where some remained while others sank back in distorted positions. Whenever remedial operations such as soil-drainage and pile-anchorage proved ineffectual, the engineers had to alter the railway's course regardless of expense.

ground passages and entered a shed, Kennan related, "The convict who had accompanied us through the mine blew out his tallow candle, and without taking the trouble completely to extinguish the wick laid it, still all aglow, in a small wooden box, which contained among other things a dynamite cartridge big enough to blow the whole tool-house into the air. I did not regard myself as naturally timorous or nervous, but when the convict shut down the lid of that box over the long glowing wick of a tallow candle and a dynamite cartridge with fuse attached, I had business out-of-doors."

Transbaikalia in winter becomes extremely dry, with all but large rivers frozen solid to the bottom. Laborers had to chop out and melt vast quantities of ice for themselves, horses, and locomotive boilers. (Later on, water was obtained for stations and maintenance shops by drilling to unfrozen depths and warming suction and delivery pipes in covered galleries heated by steam or hot air.) Although the workers won a victory over Nature in this instance, she revenged herself some months later by unloosing a cruel and ironic prodigy of destruction. To the living beings she had unsuccessfully denied water in winter she suddenly released without warning a deluge such as had never been known in eastern Siberia during Russian occupation.

In July 1897, mountain torrents and extraordinarily heavy downpours flooded the whole river system from the eastern shore of Lake Baikal to Sretensk and beyond. Rampaging waters demolished embankments and retaining walls and overturned locomotives and other rolling stock. Entire settlements were obliterated at uncounted loss of life. More than two hundred and thirty miles of track were damaged in the Ingoda and Shilka valleys. Near Sretensk, the Shilka undermined a mountain flank and released a landslide that buried newly laid track under tons of earth. Fifteen bridges vanished without trace, while two others were wrecked irreparably. West of Verkhne-udinsk, the surging Selenga River swept away great piles of lumber stored on its banks for pier caissons of a future steel bridge.

In St. Petersburg, Tsar Nicholas II, who had succeeded to the throne after the death of his father in 1894, and the ministerial hierarchy dispatched an investigating commission to the scene.* This commission estimated damage to the railway alone at somewhere around $3,000,000, but absolved Pushechnikov from blame. "The authorities," Kulomzin records in his *Le Transsibérien* (1904), "had no way of foreseeing a flood of this extent because they lacked scientific data on the region's waterways and had to base their work on the statements of the oldest inhabitants." In some areas, rivers had risen twenty feet above the highest level anyone could remember.

Reconstruction began that autumn and limped along despite further setbacks. Two of the Russian contracting firms summarily pulled out, claiming ruinous financial losses. In

* Alexander the Third's death at only forty-nine is believed to have been brought on by his heroic self-sacrifice after an accident near Borki, twenty-seven miles south of Kharkov, in the Ukraine. On October 29, 1888, the train in which he and his family were riding jumped the track and rolled down the embankment, killing twenty-one persons and injuring thirty-seven. "At the moment of the catastrophe," Witte says in his memoirs, "the Emperor with his family was in the dining-car. This car being completely smashed, its entire roof fell on him, yet owing to his great strength he supported it with his back, thus saving everyone in the dining-car from injury." But in so doing, he suffered a rupture that led to the internal complications from which he eventually died at Yalta, in the same room, it is said, Franklin D. Roosevelt used fifty-one years later during the wartime conference with Stalin.

After investigating the accident as director of the Southwestern Railway, Witte put the blame on a train inspector and Communication Minister Posyet, who was responsible for the scheduled speed of the Imperial trains. "As a result, both the Minister and the Inspector were soon afterwards compelled to tender their resignations," writes Witte, who bore no love for Posyet. ". . . The Emperor parted with them without any ill-feeling. They were forced to resign because public opinion was incensed by the Borki catastrophe."

the next summer after the flood, extreme drought withered crops and drastically reduced food supplies. Even worse, an epidemic of Siberian anthrax killed off horses and spread among the men; many of those who had not yet caught the infection fled the camps and never returned.

Nonetheless, Pushechnikov succeeded — partly by miracle and partly by his engineers' drive — in opening the Transbaikal line to provisional traffic in January 1900, and to regular traffic five months later. In St. Petersburg, the Committee could have hardly been in a mood to celebrate the event, for there was a whopping bill to pay. Construction and rolling-stock costs alone amounted to more than $39,283,300, or actually $57,181 per mile, the highest up to that time.

The Great Siberian Railway so long in the minds of Tsars, ministers, and foreign dreamers was now complete from Chelyabinsk to Sretensk save for the Circumbaikal section, that relatively short but mountain-blocked link round the lake's southern shore. Eastbound train passengers in 1900 embarked at Baikal, reentrained at Mysovsk, and, upon arrival at Sretensk, boarded rivercraft for the voyage to Khabarovsk, where they proceeded by rail to Vladivostok. In winter, they sledged across the lake and down the frozen rivers.

It had been the innocent opinion of the Communication Ministry, in 1893, that an unbroken flow of traffic could be maintained in winter on tracks laid over Baikal's frozen surface, in just the way certain rivers in Russia had been crossed. But, as everyone living along its shores could have told the Ministry, Baikal was supremely different. In fact, this great if little known lake was and still is the most eccentric and unpredictable body of fresh water on the face of the earth. It was also to put Communication Minister Khilkov through the most difficult test in his career.

CHAPTER X

The Paris of Siberia

And so we were in Irkutsk, four thousand miles east of Moscow, further east, indeed, than Mandalay: a thriving, jostling, gay city — "the Paris of Siberia" you call it when you want to please.
— JOHN FOSTER FRASER: *The Real Siberia* (1902)

PRINCE KHILKOV was nicknamed "The American" by his friends because he had spent some years in the United States, where he had knocked around on his own after a youthful disagreement with his parents over the liberation of the serfs in 1861. Unassuming and easy-mannered, he called himself "a working man, you know — a sort of blacksmith," alluding no doubt to his early days as a mechanic in Philadelphia. The St. Petersburg patrician, who spoke English with an American accent, told a British visitor that he never worried and invariably put his job as Communication Minister out of mind when at home. "Now, an American can't play golf without thinking about business," he added. "The Americans are a fine go-ahead people, the most go-ahead in the world, but if they would just think there was something else besides business, why I guess they'd get some real value out of life."

If Khilkov had possessed that Yankee single-mindedness he

criticized, he might not have given the premature order to open the Trans-Siberian's Krasnoyarsk-to-Irkutsk section to traffic in August 1898. A daily train left Moscow for Krasnoyarsk — an eight-day journey, barring accidents — but beyond Krasnoyarsk the railway was "a muddle of travel," as an Englishman named Arnot Reid crisply put it. The three weekly trains from Krasnoyarsk to Irkutsk operated without timetables, and no stationmaster could say when they would arrive or depart. After ferrying across the as yet unbridged Yenisei, government functionaries, army officers, merchants, commercial agents, and other travelers crowded into decrepit sleeping cars with berths for only half their number. At the bridgeless Oka River, Reid and his fellow passengers waited for three hours in a snowstorm before the ferry departed for the opposite bank. However, "there were at many stations outside markets of stalls kept by the country people," Reid remarks, "and there one could get excellent cold roast chickens, partridges, blackcock, and other game. . . . With these and other such supplies, and with French brandy and Crimean claret — to be had at every buffet — we fed very well." But the journey lasted for more than four days and nights, in the course of which the train averaged less than seven miles an hour on the bumpy, unsettled track. Travelers made almost the same time in horse-drawn sleighs.

Nowadays, one thinks of railways as running into the center of town, but the Trans-Siberian bypassed most communities along the way by anywhere from one to fourteen miles. This inconvenience particularly annoyed Robert Jefferson. "Unwilling to take the bread out of the mouths of the horse-breeding populace of Siberia all at once," the Englishman observes wryly, "it would seem that the Russian Government has purposely fixed the stations of the Siberian railroad as far away from the towns as possible, in order to give the great army of drosky-drivers a chance. . . . What the idea is in calling a station Omsk, when Omsk is two miles away, yet remains to be explained. Nobody that I have asked has been able to give me a satisfactory answer. Whether they expect the town to grow out towards the station, or whether it is out of sheer and simple cussedness, I do not know; I fancy it is the latter." Siberians on closer terms with foreigners, however, expressed their unshakable conviction that surveyors had vindictively altered the route because townsfolk, like the haughty Tomskians, had turned deaf ears to their demands for money.

For the technical reasons given in the previous chapter, even Irkutsk was isolated from the railway. In ice-free months, pedestrians and vehicles crossed the Angara to and from the station on a pontoon bridge which had superseded a swing ferry and which itself was not replaced until 1936 by a steel and concrete span. In winter, after the floating roadway had been dismantled and towed ashore, traffic flowed back and forth on the ice. It was heavy, heterogeneous traffic. Irkutsk was not only eastern Siberia's most important administrative, transportation, and commercial center, but was also a magnet to throngs of gold miners, fur traders, tea merchants, Chinese gold smugglers,* exiles and ex-convicts, footpads, prostitutes, and occasional foreign travelers eager to see the remote

---

* "In side streets are greasy, blue-bloused Chinamen, ostensibly dealers in tea," the English journalist John Foster Fraser wrote after visting Irkutsk in 1901. "Though never a cake of tea enters their stores, they grow rich. . . . Even Chinamen die. And a dead Chinaman must sleep his long sleep in his native land. So his good brother Chinamen in Irkutsk embalm him, and put him in a box, and burn candles over him, and send him away to rest with his fathers. Peeping through a keyhole at an embalming operation not long ago, the Irkutsk police saw gold dust blown through a tube up the nostrils into the empty skull. So they discovered why the Chinese were so anxious to give the soul of their dead brother peace by burial at home. His head was to serve as carrier of gold till he reached the Flowery Land, and then the dust was to be extracted."

John Foster Fraser

city with its "civilized savages" so luridly described by certain British and French journalists of the day.

Situated on a tongue of land at the confluence of the Irkut and Angara rivers, Irkutsk was founded in 1661, nine years after the erection of a Cossack fort on a nearby island. In 1698, the first trading caravans set out for China, and thenceforth the settlement grew rapidly as a transit hub for goods converging from all points of the compass. East Siberian gold discoveries in the first half of the nineteenth century added to its prosperity.

Prior to the midsummer of 1879, this raw "Wild East" town comprised a shabby conglomeration of one- or two-storied, unpainted wooden houses and log huts. Here and there, a stone

Irkutsk: old wooden houses

building rose in solitary grandeur, but even they were mostly destroyed in the Great Irkutsk Fire that broke out on a mild, sunny day in July 1879. Dr. Lansdell was an eyewitness to the disaster. No one, he noted, took command. "Many were drunk," and few of the fire engines worked because "the pipes had become dry and useless . . . The arrangements, too, for bringing water were of the clumsiest description. A river was flowing on either side of the city, but the firemen had no means of conducting the water by hose, but carried it in large barrels on wheels."

Within twenty-four hours, three quarters of the town had burned to the ground — ten churches, chapels, and synagogues, the customhouse, and more than thirty-six hundred other buildings — for an aggregate loss of nearly $15,000,000.

Of the thirty-four thousand inhabitants, upwards of twenty thousand were left homeless. "The people's demeanour, however," says Lansdell with little appreciation of the tough, devil-may-care fiber of Siberians, "was in strange contrast with their pitiable condition; for many, having saved their samovars, were drinking afternoon tea, and on all sides were joking and laughing at their comical situation." Two men were arrested as incendiaries, for people knew from the tragic experiences of other towns that vengeful citizens and *brodyagi* "let loose the red cock" by setting houses on fire. But Lansdell was told that the holocaust had probably started in an accidentally ignited hayloft.

Local officials took immediate steps to prevent a repetition of the catastrophe. The latest thing in fire engines — a bright-red machine that "shone like looking-glass" — was acquired from an English firm. New fire towers with a booming alarm bell and a lookout for round-the-clock watchmen were erected at key points.* In the station house, firemen, horses, and equipment were kept in constant readiness, and carters of barreled water to well-to-do residents were made liable to severe punishment if they failed to leave their rounds and rush to the scene of a fire. Construction of wooden houses in the center of town was proscribed by law, though those still standing were allowed to remain. In consequence, the new Irkutsk became a patchwork of repaired shacks chockablock with just-completed brick or stone structures.

Despite the gradual passing of the most repellent eyesores,

* These towers have long since disappeared. But in Irkutsk there are no street fire-alarm boxes. "We do not need them," an official firmly assured this writer. "We just dial 'Zero One' on the phone, give the fire's location, and it is soon put out." As Irkutsk has relatively few private telephones, an inhabitant whose house catches fire may have to run quite a distance before dialing the two digits, if he happens to remember them in his excitement.

Irkutsk: The Drama Theater

Irkutsk presented "an untidy, unfinished appearance . . . a strange mixture of squalor and grandeur," the disapproving Harry de Windt reported in the early nineties. Every street, not omitting the Bolshaya (the equivalent of Main or High Street), was unpaved and pitted with chuckholes. In spring, vehicles churned thawing ruts into quagmires of mud that dried in summer to ankle-deep dust so thick that it fairly darkened the sky on windy days. Affluent citizens thought nothing of contributing $150,000 toward construction of the rose and buff Drama Theater that is still one of the show places of Irkutsk, and paying two permanent companies $36,000 a year to perform in it. But these same patrons refused to spend a kopeck on what they considered the lunatic extravagance of street-surfacing that would be blanketed with snow and ice for more than half the year.

"The sidewalks are boards put on trestles over open sewers," the British author William Greener observed in 1901, "and here and there planks are broken or missing . . ." There were no water works; except for those who had barreled water delivered to their door, the citizens still drew buckets from the swift and unpolluted Angara as generations had done before them. In the eighteen-sixties, the telegraph line from St. Petersburg and Moscow had reached the city, but, at the time of Greener's visit, the public was so poorly served that nonofficial telegrams sometimes took six weeks to pass between Irkutsk and European Russia unless sent "urgent" at triple the ordinary rate.

By 1891, a private company had installed telephones in government offices, homes of leading citizens, and a few big business houses. A few years later, electric lights supplanted the flickering oil lamps along the Bolshaya and one or two other avenues. Elsewhere, darkness shrouded the streets save where

Wooden sidewalks in Irkutsk

an occasional lantern glowed from a post. These murky purlieus provided a hunting ground for *varnaki* who lay in wait for solitary pedestrians. "Garroting is the usual device of the footpad," Greener said. "With a short stick and a noose of twine he approaches his victim stealthily from the rear, slips the cord over his head, and strangles the man, woman, or child, who is unable to utter a cry; then he strips from the body everything likely to lead to his identification, and decamps." The unarmed were in barely less danger during daytime blizzards, for it was the custom of criminals to cruise close to the sidewalk in a sledge, lasso a lone pedestrian, and drag him at a gallop up a back alley, where he could be robbed of valuables, passport, and clothing at leisure. If the *varnak* were by some off-chance pursued, he cut the lasso, lashed his horses, and vanished under cover of the storm.

"The police here seem to amount to nothing at all, and to be of the most corrupt order," comments Michael Myers Shoemaker, an American travel writer who journeyed to Irkutsk a year after Greener. "A gentleman of the town tells me that he was robbed here some weeks since, and upon reporting it to the police was told that if he desired the matter investigated he must pay fifteen roubles [$7.50] to begin with, and much more to follow. There is an average of a murder a day every year, and last fall the assassinations amounted to two hundred and forty in one month."

If any inhabitants witnessed a crime in the making, they rarely intervened because it was not "*sibirski*" to mix into what was clearly someone else's affair. However, they took precautions to protect themselves and their property. The rich hired watchmen to patrol the neighborhood at night with metal clappers or a noisy wooden rattle whirled at every few paces to warn off burglars and thieves. Ordinary householders adopted a do-it-yourself means to the same end: by firing a shot from a window or doorway before retiring, they served notice on lurking malefactors that lives and belongings would be defended to the death. (One wonders why the homeowners assumed that this warning would also scare off larcenous prowlers entering the area long after the shot was fired; sometimes, one cannot explain the Siberians any more than one can the Irish.)

Fearful burghers also unchained savage watchdogs, as the vade mecum of British travelers — *Bradshaw's Through Routes to the Chief Cities of the World* — warned in 1913. "The police are few, escaped convicts and ticket-of-leave criminals many. In Irkutsk . . . the stranger should not walk after dark; if a carriage cannot be got, as is often the case, the only way is to tramp noisily along the planked walk; be careful in making crossings, and do not stop, or the immense mongrel mastiffs, turned loose into the streets as guards will attack. [To walk] . . . in the middle of the road is to court attack from the garrotters with which Siberian towns abound."

The criminal element found it well worth while to risk the slight chance of arrest, for the pickings were substantial. At the close of the summer working season at the gold diggings north and east of Irkutsk, the city was the mecca of several thousand miners, each with a bankroll of $250 or more. On holiday, they indulged in the common forms of debauchery until thugs, cardsharps, swindlers, or trollops took their last kopeck, whereupon they plodded back to their native villages or worked at odd jobs until the goldfields reopened in spring.

While in the chips, some of these carousers released their fantasies of wealth and self-importance in dramatically droll ways. Dr. Lansdell tells us that, for example, one miner bought bottles of champagne, not to drink but to set up in a row and shatter with stones. "To indulge his aristocratic tread," says Lansdell, another vainglorious fellow purchased a length of printed cotton, laid it across each puddle he came to, then walked on it like a rather self-centered Walter Raleigh. A third, wishing to convey that he was too superior a personage to be drawn by a mere horse, unhitched one from a hired telega and yoked in its place a team of stony-broke companions he paid to pull him around town. All in all, the miners with money were like gluttonous bears stuffing themselves with honey.

Mine managers also flocked into Irkutsk and engaged in prodigious drinking and card playing.* On entering restaurants, they followed respectful custom by doffing their caps to the Tsar's portrait on the wall, then joined the crowd of garrison officers, fur traders, tea barons from Kyakhta, and local bigwigs dressed in the badly fitting black suits and dirty highboots that identified middle-class adult males throughout Siberia.

"There were the fat little doctor of the 27th regiment," recalls Richardson L. Wright, co-author with Bassett Digby of *Through Siberia, an Empire in the Making* and later the longtime editor of the American magazine *House and Garden*, "who would ever and anon wobble unsteadily over to the orchestra and get the pretty girl with the rose in her hair to let

* Siberians were passionately fond of cards, "the solace of the whole of Russia," as Gogol said. One of the most popular games was vint, a form of auction bridge in which players could win or lose large sums. Jefferson describes a host of his who "related quite frankly, and with a smile on his face" that he had parted with $100,000 in three nights. At another time, a vint player haled a card partner into court for calling him a fool — an illegal offense — when he needlessly trumped a trick. "I took the trick with my queen," the defendant explained to the judge who was also a vint devotee, "and instead of throwing away, my partner here played the king." "The fool!" snapped the judge. "Case dismissed."

him bang the drum at noisy crescendos in the marches; and the major who drank two bottles of maraschino, and then watered the fern on his table with half a pint of kummel, rather than leave what he could not manage to the waiters; and others who did not behave so well." In the plushier restaurants, there was a small stage that might be graced by swarthy Polish singers of comic verses, a Prussian with performing cats, and, as Wright witheringly appraises them, "a score of maidens in a minimum of skirt and a maximum of smile [who] go through fatuous double-shuffles and fancy dances executed with a degree of incompetency that would leave a Bowery 'amateur night' audience dumb with scorn." Intermissions were given over to card playing or betting on anything that came to mind.

The single distinction that separated most gold-mine owners from the rank and file was vastly greater wealth. These star-blessed peasants, ex-convicts, and freed exiles began as hired diggers and washers before they turned to small-scale prospecting and struck bonanzas that made them rich within a few years. They deserved their luck, for it took courage to venture into the inhospitable taiga and pan for gold with a helper who must be constantly watched if the prospector were to return alive with his precious metal. A few invested in trading, distilling, ironworking, and mercantile enterprises and built individual fortunes occasionally amounting to as much as $20,000,000, with the purchasing power in the second half of the past century of $80,000,000 to $100,000,000 today. They kept French chefs and hired French tutors for their wives and governesses for their children, but they themselves often remained as ignorant and uncouth as any muzhik in the poorer quarters, where shopkeepers identified their business to the illiterate by means of shingles with gaudy illustrations instead

Irkutsk: the Museum of Regional History

of words: sugar loaves and packages of tea for a grocery; hammers and saws for a hardware store; bread loaves and crescent rolls for a bakery; and boots and women's slippers for a shoemaker's shop.

Like their fabulously rich contemporaries in America, the gold-mining parvenus spent fortunes on their homes, some of which were as elaborate as the Butin mansion Kennan visited in the distant town of Nerchinsk. "Going into it," he says, ". . . was like going into Aladdin's palace from an East-Siberian *étape;* and as I entered the splendid ball-room, and caught the full-length reflection of my figure in the largest mirror in the world,* I felt like rubbing my eyes to make sure

* "This huge pier glass," Kennan adds in a footnote, "was bought by Mr. Bútin at the Paris Exposition in 1878, and was then said to be the largest mirror in existence. It was taken half around the world by sea to the East-Siberian port of Nikoláievsk, and was thence transported up the rivers Amúr and Shílka to Nérchinsk in a barge made expressly for the purpose. . . ."

that I was awake. One does not expect to find in the wilds of Eastern Siberia, nearly 5000 miles from St. Petersburg, a superb private residence with hardwood marquetry floors, silken curtains, hangings of delicate tapestry, stained-glass windows, splendid chandeliers, soft Oriental rugs, white-and-gold furniture upholstered with satin, old Flemish paintings, marble statues, family portraits from the skilful brush of Makófski, and an extensive conservatory filled with palms, lemon-trees, and rare orchids from the tropics. . . . The ball-room, which was the largest room in the house, was about sixty-five feet in length by forty-five in width, and over it, in a large semicircular gallery reached by a grand stairway, there was an orchestrion, as big as a church organ, which played sixty or seventy airs and furnished music for the entertainments. . . . The library, which was another spacious apartment, was filled with well-selected books, newspapers, and magazines, in three

Irkutsk: mansion built by the rich merchant Vtorov in 1897; now a "Pioneer Palace"

or four languages, and contained also a large collection of Siberian minerals and ores."

From the revelations of foreign guests we learn that a few unreconstructed masters of these mansions slept in their clothes from long habit in the wilds and preferred a couch to a bed. One millionaire mentioned by De Windt favored a three-chair arrangement. Another escorted a French caller through his home and pointed to a superb bed — a collector's item with ebony frame, plush hangings, and Gobelin tapestry. "This is my bed," he said. "But I sleep *under* it, you know. It is too good to use."(We may interpolate here that De Windt, an Englishman and a brother-in-law of Sir Charles Brooke, the second Rajah of Sarawak, stayed sometimes for several weeks in Siberian cities and was cordially entertained, for he had taken pains to secure letters of introduction at St. Petersburg.)

For all their flamboyant ostentation (exemplified further by still another Irkutsk host who used a large gold nugget as an ashtray and boasted to De Windt that he lost $1500 in annual interest by doing so), these self-made Croesuses gave a great deal of money to public relief societies, poorhouses, hospitals, asylums, and schools. The mercantile and shipping magnate Alexander M. Sibiryakov provided a large part of the funds for Siberia's first university, opened at Tomsk in 1888; other benefactors donated $2,000,000 for its scholarships. Kyakhtan tea merchants contributed more than $730,000 for a cathedral in their town. "The altar alone, of solid gold, silver, and platinum," De Windt assures us, "cost 30,000*l.* [$146,100], while the principal doors of the building are of solid silver, and weigh 200 lbs." In Krasnoyarsk, a gold-mine proprietor gave $250,000 for the rebuilding of the Cathedral of the Nativity after its vault collapsed.

Although many of these Siberians were abysmally ignorant,

there were a few startling exceptions, notably Gennadius V. Yudin, a cultivated Krasnoyarsk distiller whom the United States' Library of Congress can thank for a magnificent collection of some eighty thousand rare books shipped from the heart of Siberia to Washington, where they formed the nucleus of the Library's Slavic section.

Yudin was born in western Siberia in 1840. Though his parents were fairly well-off, he began work at thirteen as a clerk in a liquor excise office; ten years later, he had saved $300, with which he started his own liquor business in a village not very far from Krasnoyarsk. Within six more years, this capital had grown to $12,500, a sure sign that the young Yudin had relieved quite a drought in the neighborhood. He and his wife took off on a tour of the Near East, and in subsequent years traveled extensively in Siberia, Russia, and Europe. In 1881, he built a distillery in Krasnoyarsk and settled down to the prime love of his life, his collection of Russian and Siberian bibliography, history, literature, archeology, ethnology, and fine arts.

"Studies in my library, which occupies a special two-story building," he wrote in 1903, "provide for me a needed rest from worldly squabbles and a delight which is hard to express." But by that time, this dynamic bibliophile — whose photograph shows him to have been a big, vital man with a high forehead, penetrating eyes, and a patriarchal beard — had been deeply shaken by the loss of two sons and a subsequent decline in health. "With the sole idea of establishing closer relations between the two nations," he wrote to the Congressional Librarian, he sold his collection, valued at a little more than $114,000, to the United States for only $40,000, such a reduction from the actual worth of the volumes that the Library described them to the public as a gift. The Rus-

The bibliophile Gennadius V. Yudin

sian government cleared the Trans-Siberian and Russian tracks to give right of way to the five hundred packing cases containing the books, which reached Washington in April 1907. Five years later, Yudin died of a stroke at the age of seventy-two. But during those five years, this virtually self-taught old man began to collect books again because he could not bear to be without them.

From the accounts left us by De Windt, Jefferson, the American photographer William Henry Jackson, and other foreign travelers in the empire of the eighteen-nineties, prosperous male Siberians took immense pleasure in private dinners, all more or less alike. At about 9 P.M., guests assembled in a front room (which might be embellished with the framed motto in

Russian: "He who does not drain his glass is slighting the lady of the house"), where there were card tables and a long buffet laden with bottles, perhaps a brimful bowl of punch,* and platters of appetizers, cheese, and bread.

"You sit around and take a hand at cards or form one in a dice party," says Jefferson, describing an evening he spent in the home of a Tomskian gold miner. "Ten minutes elapse, the host comes round, pats each one of his guests on the shoulder, and at the same time flicks his third finger against his neck. This is the Siberian invitation for a drink. The crowd collects around the table, each takes a glass filled with vodki, or with some one or other of the many mysterious compounds which go under the name of Siberian liqueurs, tosses it off, makes a grimace, sometimes the sign of the cross, gulps down a bit of bread and sardine, and wanders back to the card-table."

Drinking and gambling continued until midnight, when the host moved his jaws convulsively to signal in Siberian fashion that dinner was waiting in an adjoining room, to which the party proceeded. Some hosts set a poor table consisting of a few diminutive chickens and cutlets, but others provided a feast: fish and meat soups; suckling pig and vegetables; pies filled with eggs, rice, and cabbage, or various kinds of fish; hot sturgeon and game; ices and pastry. But whatever the food, there was always a seemingly bottomless reservoir of wines and liquors, for innumerable toasts had to be drunk.

"It reminded me of the scene between the celebrated Mr. Jorrocks and his huntsman who, when they had exhausted all other toasts, drank the healths of all the hounds separately,"

* De Windt gives the recipe for Siberian punch as follows: Three bottles of champagne, half a bottle of brandy, four glasses of vodka, four of curaçao, two bottles of soda water, four tablespoons of sugar, a sliced apple, and grated nutmeg. Stir together, then *"set on fire."*

Harry de Windt garbed for northeastern Siberia

De Windt wrote after a dinner at the home of a Kyakhtan merchant. "When our friends had exhausted the Czar, the Russian army, the navy, the Queen of England, and all reigning potentates, including the Emperor of China, they fell back on themselves. I must have drunk at least three bottles of port that night, to say nothing of vodka. . . . We then adjourned to the drawing-room, where all sang and shouted at the top of their voices, regardless of time or tune, till past 4 A.M. . . . It was broad daylight when we separated, English bottled stout being handed round as a finale to the entertainment."

At the conclusion of his host's party, Jefferson found it "necessary again to observe Siberian customs, this being . . . to declare that it is the finest food you have eaten in all your life, that you have never tasted such vodki, and that, as long as you live, you will remember the hospitality you have received. Mine host hurries to help you into your shouba [shuba, a fur coat]; but you must on no account let him do that, as it would imply that you have not had enough to eat to make you strong enough for that particular office. You gently ward him off and laugh idiotically; he insists, and *you* insist, until ultimately you manage to get into your furs, shake hands again, cross yourself before the ikon on the wall, bundle down the steps into the yard, where dogs snarl around your legs, open the big gate, and emerge into the street."

Some wives of the rich undertook good works for orphans, foundlings,* needy families, and missionary societies. De Windt took a condemnatory view of the others. "The ladies of Irkoutsk," he declared, "are for the most part lazy, indolent creatures, with no ideas beyond immoral intrigues, dress (on which they spend thousands), and Zola's novels, which, translated into Russian, have an enormous sale in the towns of Siberia. The greater part of the day is spent in sleeping and smoking cigarettes, for in winter they seldom retire to rest till five or six in the morning. Though most of their houses boast a

* Foundling hospitals received all unwanted infants whether abandoned or brought in by indigent parents, who were not required to contribute to the child's support. If, however, a sum of money was left for a boy's maintenance, he became eligible for future officer rank in the army; otherwise, he was brought up to be a common soldier. Girls were put to manual work; their earnings went partly to the hospital and partly to provide a marriage dowry, to which was added anything given by their parents. Murray's *Handbook for Travellers in Russia, Poland, and Finland* — like *Bradshaw* a bible to British and American visitors — speaks of these foundling homes as "a vast breeding-cage," and adds with perhaps unjustified severity that "if the institution is to be viewed in the light of a charity, it is charity upon a very questionable principle."

grand piano, the instrument is solely kept for ornament, and seldom opened."

The women wore clothes imported from Paris, but aroused in some foreign acquaintances the suspicion that they were none too clean. During the high social season in winter, they appeared at first meeting to live in a gay Ouida-world of balls and masquerades. "After the theater," says the photographer Jackson, who visited Irkutsk briefly in 1895 and, among other activities, attended a performance of *King Henry VIII* done in French by a Russian company, "we were taken to a bal masqué at the Merchants Club, where our younger members . . . danced their heels off with fascinating ladies in dominoes and extreme décolletages. And I, despite my skating excesses of the previous afternoon, found myself out on the floor with the others until the music stopped at 3 A.M." But from the narratives of visitors who made protracted stays in Irkutsk, Krasnoyarsk, or Tomsk, most of the galas were stereotyped, provincial affairs attended by the same familiar crowd: the governor, the mayor, army officers, administrative officials, and rich civilians, together with a sprinkling of upper-class political exiles, all with respective wives and grown sons and daughters in tow.

None of the women needed to bother about household shopping, for a head servant assumed this chore. In summer, they attended band concerts in the park if they had not retreated with husband and children to a cool summer house in the country. At Tomsk, river parties were extremely popular. "A large steamer is chartered by a number of the townspeople — some two hundred odd, as a rule," De Windt observes. "There is no distinction as to class. The richest merchant in Tomsk hobnobs with the poorest tradesman, who has scraped up enough money to join the expedition. Higher prices, however,

Tomsk boat landing

are charged for private cabins, and here the millionaires entertain their friends, while their less wealthy neighbours make merry on deck in the open air. The latter are, perhaps, not so much to be pitied, as the cabins, constructed to hold two, frequently accommodate ten, and the atmosphere, on a hot day, would asphyxiate a salamander. Heat begets thirst, and drink is plentiful. In the saloons are large bars, where champagne, claret, beer, and liqueurs flow freely and without intermission throughout the day; while on deck the supply of kvas and vodka is inexhaustible. A brass band accompanies the vessel, which leaves about midday, steams half-speed down stream for a given number of hours, and then — steams back again. In addition to unlimited zakouski, such as salted, raw, or pickled fish, caviare, cheese, etc., a substantial meal is served at four o'clock in the saloon, which lasts till about 7 P.M. Dancing and other amusements then fill in the time till midnight, when (all being well) home is reached."

In clear winter weather, the ladies sometimes joined their husbands at sleigh races on packed snow, or took their youngsters to an ice-hill slide or the public skating rink, where people glided around, as Jackson had, "to the waltz music of a lively brass band." Holidays in good weather were exhilarating occasions, for the wives bundled up in their costliest furs and coursed up and down the Bolshaya in highly polished sleighs harnessed to thoroughbreds "as fine as those of any private carriages in London," observed Julius M. Price, an *Illustrated London News* artist who traveled in Siberia in 1890-1891. The fashionables of Irkutsk were denied the pleasure of attracting further attention to themselves with a profusion of bells attached to the yoke, for the city fathers prohibited bells on all vehicles inside the municipal limits. This rule could be a mixed blessing, since bells reduced the danger of collisions in foul weather.

After they had shown themselves off enough to stoke the fires of envy in the hearts of rivals, the ladies departed to the homes of cronies, where they drank tea and gossiped about absent friends. In Irkutsk, the subject of discussion might have been the exiled Baroness Podorski who, De Windt relates, "had done five years at the mines for murdering her niece, a rich heiress, by slow poison at Moscow, and was now living on the proceeds as a queen of society at Irkoutsk." The titled murderess had become an even livelier topic for clacking tongues when she went to live with a Cossack officer.

De Windt claims that Siberian women were "rather superstitiously inclined." Having attended a ball in Tomsk, he called on his host and hostess on the following day. Since they were out, he was received by their eighteen-year-old daughter, who had been educated in Paris and called herself "Mademoiselle Hélène." "I was shown . . . into that young lady's boudoir, a perfumed little nest, with rose-tinted walls, Turkish embroideries, Persian rugs, palms, low luxurious couches, and a piano. The pretty child, for she was little more, was lying lazily at full length on a sofa, smoking a papiroska. A table at her elbow was littered with flowers, photographs, and yellow-backed French novels . . . During my visit . . . a thunderstorm burst over Tomsk, and at the first clap of thunder my hostess became suddenly silent and preoccupied. Attributing this to alarm, I essayed to reassure her. 'Oh, I am not frightened,' she said, after a long pause. 'I was merely trying to recall the names and features of six bald-headed acquaintances. It averts the lightning.' "

CHAPTER XI

Old Man Baikal

When the Great Siberian Railway was only a tentative tracing on the Communication Ministry's maps, Their Excellencies planned to skirt the southern rim of Lake Baikal and connect Irkutsk with Mysovsk, on the eastern shore of this long, crescent-shaped expanse. But in 1890, the surveys of Engineer Vyazemski, future constructor of the Ussuri line in the Far East, revealed a terrain almost hopelessly obstructed by mountain ridges and river gorges. With the tremendous amount of special construction that would be required — high viaducts and embankments, bridges, cuttings, and a tunnel more than two miles long — Vyazemski estimated the cost of the Circumbaikal loop at a minimum of $12,500,000, or roughly $64,430 per mile.

Their Excellencies, accustomed to a reasonable $30,000 a mile for railways in European Russia, promptly shelved Vyazemski's survey on the assumption that a less expensive route could be found. But they took no further action until 1893, when they postponed the project indefinitely and decided to transport train passengers and freight from shore to shore on steam ferries to be built for the purpose. These would be much cheaper than the extremely problematical rail link, said Communication Minister Krivoshein, who added that whole trains

Lake Baikal: Cape Burkhai

could be hauled on tracks across Baikal's frozen surface in winter, motive power to be supplied by what he called "a system of electric or steam traction." The Committeemen approved, though they knew next to nothing about the strange perversities of the lake, barely a hundred miles north of Outer Mongolia.

The world's deepest body of fresh water, Baikal occupies a crevasse three hundred and ninety-five miles long, fifty miles at its broadest, and more than a mile in maximum depth. Its 12,162-square-mile area would blanket Belgium and leave something to spare. At least three hundred and thirty-six rivers and mountain streams pour into it, yet it is drained solely by the Angara, one of the few watercourses born not as an infantile brook but as a robust river: a half-mile-wide flood discharging 60,600 cubic feet per second, more than a quarter of Niagara's volume.

Siberian mothers still tell their children the ancient legend of Starik Baikal — "Old Man Baikal." This white-bearded tyrant lived in the lake with three hundred and thirty-six sons and one daughter, the lovely Angara, imprisoned by her father because she refused to marry the small Irkut River. While her brothers dutifully brought water from the mountains to Baikal, the restless Angara yearned for the River Yenisei, described to her by water birds from the north as an entrancing young giant. One night, she tore loose from her bonds and fled to Yenisei. Baikal awoke at the rush of her waters and, in a rage, hurled a tremendous cliff to halt her. Angara escaped, but a peak of the missile marked the point of her departure. Called Shaman Rock, it rose about seven feet above water; below the surface, it broadened extensively and partially braked the outgoing current. It still does, but the top of Shaman Rock has been all but submerged.*

Soviet scientists do not rule out the risk that exceptionally heavy temblors might actually dislodge Baikal's "cork" and release enough of the total water volume — estimated at 5513 cubic miles — to annihilate Irkutsk. The region's worst upheaval in recorded history occurred on the evening of December 30, 1861, when the inhabitants of the Gypsy Steppe on the eastern shore were startled by an underground rumble that sounded like an approaching storm. Suddenly the earth shook, cabin floors rocked, and samovars and Christmas cakes fell from tables. Church bells rang of themselves, and doors swung open or shut of their own accord. Terrified settlers and natives fled from their homes and huddled in the freezing out-

* The water level has been slowly rising since 1959, when the Angara Dam and a 660,000-kilowatt hydroelectric station were completed near Irkutsk. About three hundred miles to the northeast, as the crow flies, the turbines of the Bratsk Dam (scheduled for completion in 1965) will have a combined rated capacity of 4,500,000 kilowatts — 330,000 more than that of America's two most powerful installations together, the Grand Coulee, in Washington State, and the Niagara Power Project of the Power Authority of the State of New York.

doors while the ground continued to shift beneath them for the rest of the night. Morning brought a lull, but at noon a new quake transformed the steppe into an utterly unfamiliar landscape of hummocks, gaping fissures, and muddy geysers that spouted up through wells, popping out their wooden frames like corks from bottles. Baikal's waters rushed over the adjacent region, inundating villages throughout a 190-square-mile area. No less than thirteen hundred persons and five thousand head of cattle perished in the disaster. Irkutsk would probably have been laid waste but for the fact that Baikal's "cork" held, and retarded the devastating force of the seismic tide.

Millions of years have passed since the formation of the Baikal abyss, but the bed still shifts restlessly, lifting here and sinking there. Two to five tremors occur annually; they are usually mild, but Irkutsk officials, however much they may yearn to erect tall buildings in emulation of Moscow, cautiously limit structures to five stories. ("My father lives in a low wooden house put up before the Glorious October Revolution," a militantly progressive Irkutsk female guide said plaintively to the author, "and we can't persuade him to move into our modern apartment. He says his old wreck gives with the quakes, and swears he'll survive to dig us out if we get a really bad one.")

Surrounding the limpid turquoise water — so transparent that a dropped coin can be followed with the eye for a hundred and thirty feet down — somber gray cliffs of granite, marble, and basalt rise to forested, snow-tipped mountains, some towering for more than a mile above the lake. In summer, the bracing air, unmistakably alpine though Baikal lies less than fifteen hundred feet above sea level, is sweetened by the scent of pine, fir, and larch trees. Some teeter on crags so steep that they seem suspended rather than rooted, an illusion said to have terrified superstitious seventeenth-century Cossack explorers who feared that the Devil might release the trees and crush the invaders.

Baikal's shores are sparsely dotted with small ports like Listvyanka, a village with a tiny shipyard, a few warehouses, and a picturesque jumble of wooden cottages. Some of the last are unexpectedly gay with jigsaw window frames painted in vivid reds, yellows, or blues; others are drab log cabins strikingly similar to those in the American pioneer West, but all are brightened in summer by garden patches bursting with enormous sunflowers. The square-faced, flat-nosed Buryats of the region are descendants of nomadic Mongols who migrated north after the Middle Ages. They were among the filthiest humans, so verminous that tsarist army conscriptors seldom drafted them for fear of catching typhus and other dangerous infections. In recent times, the Buryats yielded to steam baths and health propaganda, and they are now regarded as the most intelligent, industrious, and trustworthy natives in eastern Siberia, where they number about a quarter of a million.

Baikal teems with seventeen hundred different kinds of flora and fauna, a large number of which are found nowhere else in either hemisphere. It is unquestionably the world's foremost museum of living fossils, the only known home of certain relict but healthy and vigorous mollusks, bristled worms, snails, and small shrimp that miraculously survive from prehistory. Emerald-green sponges — some shaped like coral branches, others as round as softballs — look as if they had been plucked from tropical waters, yet they are endemic to Baikal. Long ago, Buryat women discovered that there was nothing like these chlorophyll-rich sponges for shining up pots and pans.

Most grotesque of the lake's creatures is the *golomyanka*, a transparent little fish with eyes protruding from a preposterous head that occupies a third of its three- to eight-inch-long body, a great part of which is fat. They produce live young instead of eggs, and seldom rise voluntarily from a fifteen-hundred-foot depth. When some do, storms cast them ashore, where the fat melts and leaves barely more than the skeleton after twenty-four-hour exposure. Though inedible, these "lamp fish" are still prized by the more primitive northern natives, who gather them as fast as they can after a storm and burn the fat for lighting, or swallow it in the belief that it relieves rheumatism. Russian chemists say that the fat is rich in vitamin D, but question its medicinal powers.

How do scientists account for the flourishing of these primeval organisms, many of which are extinct elsewhere? As far as can be determined, the lake has always contained a remarkably large amount of oxygen, no sulphur, and very little salt. These optimum conditions, the experts believe, do not exist in quite the same balance in other parts of the world.

Appropriately named Bai-kul, or "Rich Lake," by the early Mongols, Baikal abounds in food fishes, notably grayling, turbot, and a whitefish known colloquially as *omul* and scientifically as *Coregonus autumnalis migratorius Georgi*, which originated there. More than six and a half millon pounds of this foot-long *omul* are caught annually by net-fishermen; Siberians eat it salted or smoked, but prefer not to cook the raw fish until it has ripened to a fairly high odor.

Baikal is also the home of seals, though the nearest salt water lies more than nine hundred miles away. Some scientists believe that the ancestors of these mammals swam eastward from the Caspian Sea when many more rivers and lakes covered Asia. But the Arctic theory is more widely accepted. At some remote time, the first seals entered the Yenisei River mouth and, generation after generation, progressed upstream to the Angara and to Baikal, gradually adapting to fresh water as they went along.

These *nerpy* frolic in the lake's northern reaches in herds estimated at 25,000 to 30,000 head. Native hunters sneak upon them Eskimo-fashion behind sleds camouflaged with white cloth to blend with the snow, and shoot an average of two thousand a year. The seal fat is used in Siberian soap works, and the pelts provide clothing and boots for the hunters; fur strips sewn on their skis speed forward movement and resist backward slide. Bear, elk, moose, deer, foxes, wolves, lynx, mountain sheep, and now and then a stray Manchurian tiger are found in Baikal's surrounding forests and mountain heights, with abundant ducks, geese, and other game birds on the lake itself.

Oddly enough in a country celebrated for the costliest of fine sables, the most lucrative animal commercially is the common squirrel, in high demand for coats and mittens, and still thriving in vast numbers despite wholesale slaughter for scores of years. Almost as prolific are the descendants of a small muskrat colony imported from the United States in 1927. The magnificent Barguzin crown sables, famous for their very dark and luxuriant fur, were rescued from extinction in 1913, when the government clamped down with hunting restrictions.

In June and July, the lake presents an expansive vista of blue serenity, and seems incapable of harm. In a brief but tender mood, its waters blossom alongshore with flowering aquatic plants that float decoratively on the rising or falling tide, for this inland sea reacts to lunar pull. In August, the hottest month, the surface temperature averages forty-six degrees and, beginning a few hundred feet down, remains constant at about thirty-seven degrees. This immense cold mass lends the area its alpine character, and accounts for the edelweiss and other flora one would expect to see in the Swiss Alps.

Frequently, summer air in contact with Baikal's chill surface creates fogbanks as impenetrable as the worst of those along the Newfoundland Banks, and sometimes halts lake traffic for a fortnight. In early September, spectacular hurricanes roar in at eighty miles an hour. ". . . It is only upon the Baikal in the autumn," Lansdell wrote, "that a man learns to pray from his heart." Off and on through December, gales whip up sixteen-foot waves characterized by a violent choppiness that capsizes even the most skillful boatmen. Bodies of the drowned are never lost in the lake's depths, but are eventually cast ashore by the turbulent seas.

Despite its own frigidity and exposure to subfreezing atmosphere in late autumn, Baikal's surface does not congeal until the end of December in the north and the early part of January in the south. Climatologists attribute this phenomenon to the slowness with which large water masses change in temperature; frost is further retarded by the wave-churning winds. But when these vanish and midwinter becomes so cold that spoken words freeze in the air — such is the belief of venerable Buryats, who surely never read Plutarch's quotation from Antiphanes or the Paul Bunyan legends to the same effect — ice reaches a thickness of three to six feet.

Uncounted vehicles, horses, and the two-humped Bactrian camels of tea caravans have fallen victim to the most startling of Old Man Baikal's peculiarities. With only a warning boom like distant thunder, a crack will streak like lightning through the ice and leave a water-filled fissure up to six feet wide and from six to eighteen miles long. Scientists ascribe these potentially fatal traps to variations in air pressure and wind movement that act together like a gigantic ax splitting the ice. But nobody knows where or when the ax will strike.

Among time-capsule memorabilia that have plummeted to the bottom are an eighteenth-century Cossack sledge topheavy with natives' fur tribute to the Tsar, a nineteenth-century Imperial mail sleigh laden with twenty thousand gold rubles, and a twentieth-century locomotive. If any of these had plunged to Baikal's greatest depth, they would have reached bottom at 5315 feet. "That's what our echo-soundings give us so far," Nicholas P. Ladeichikov told this writer in the stark white building of the Baikal Limnological Institute, established at Listvyanka by the Academy of Sciences in 1928. "We are still exploring, and may find an even deeper spot. You know, Baikal is quite a tank," the scientist added. "If not another drop of water entered and the Angara continued to flow out at its present rate, the lake would take more than five hundred years to run dry."

After the decision to substitute steam ferries for the Circumbaikal loop, Communication Minister Krivoshein's successor Prince Khilkov won over Their Excellencies to his opinion that the first should be a large icebreaker capable of transporting an entire train and all its passengers across the lake in winter as well as in summer. Since the Russians knew little about the design and berthing of such an unconventional leviathan, they sent an engineer to study the icebreakers of the "go-ahead" Americans on the Great Lakes. In 1895, this engineer recommended construction of a wooden train-ferry like the *Sainte Marie* that plied the Straits of Mackinac between Lakes Michigan and Huron. Khilkov convinced his colleagues that a steel hull would be more practical, and was granted $1,500,000 for the vessel, landing slips, and repair shops. Of the dozen shipbuilders who submitted bids, the English firm of Sir W. G. Armstrong, Mitchell and Company, Ltd., offered such a low one that Their Excellencies sacrificed the Russian companies on the altar of economy, and signed a contract with Armstrong on December 30, 1895. Within six months, Armstrong's Walker Shipyard, at Newcastle upon Tyne, built the ferry from the keel up, painted and stamped every part with an identifying letter and number, then dismantled the whole and shipped it in sections to Russia for reassembly at Listvyanka. Machinery, boilers, and other equipment followed in December of the same year, 1896.

Whereas the British had built and delivered the *Baikal,* as the icebreaker was subsequently christened, in twelve months, more than three years elapsed before the Russians managed to put it into service, even with an Armstrong superintendent, a marine engineer, and four foremen on the spot to supervise plating, riveting, caulking, and carpentry. "In the summer of 1897," says Isaac O. Handy, a ruddy-faced Northcountryman in the group, "the chief of the shipbuilding staff . . . left England for Siberia to superintend the carrying out of the work. On his arrival at Lake Baikal, after a long and trying journey, several hundred miles of which had to be done in a tarantass . . . he found practically nothing to commence work upon, as the non-existence of the railway in that district compelled the shipment of material from Krasnoyarsk *via* the Yenisei and Angara rivers, a distance of over 1,000 miles, by barges, and at one point in the latter river the presence of rapids necessitated a portage of several miles, and, as usual in awkward circumstances, the cart preceded the horse, and heavy castings for the machinery began to arrive before

The icebreaking train ferry Baikal

the floors and double-bottom portions of the hull. During 1898, however, matters proceeded in a more satisfactory manner, and a commencement was made with the erection of the vessel, good progress being made with the material at the disposal of the erectors. . . . In spite of the many thousands of parts dealt with, of all weights and sizes, and the way in which they were transported through such a great distance, yet nothing of any importance was lost . . ."

Finally, on July 29, 1899, the *Baikal* was launched at Listvyanka, but without her fifteen boilers (smaller and more numerous than normal because Russian flatcars could accommodate nothing wider than eleven feet or heavier than twenty tons) that had lain at Krasnoyarsk for two years until the great Yenisei bridge was completed. Within six weeks after their arrival, Handy had them ready for service. In the meantime, Russian engineers had constructed slipways at the new port of "Baikal," on the Angara's south bank opposite Listvyanka, and at Mysovsk, on the eastern shore about forty miles distant. This work had involved months of grueling and expensive underwater blasting and the building of extensive breakwaters, together with a pair of jetties, set like the prongs of a slingshot fork, at each landing to lock the *Baikal* in place while railway cars rolled over the train-deck gangway in the bow. In April 1900, the ferry began regular service between the western and eastern ports.

To the Tsar's subjects who watched her sweep majestically across the Holy Sea, the *Baikal* was a stupendous marvel that almost frightened them by her immensity. Two hundred and ninety feet long, fifty-seven in beam, drawing nearly twenty feet of water, and displacing forty-two hundred tons, she was the biggest ship most Siberians had ever seen, and was second only to American prototypes as the largest icebreaking train-ferry afloat. Her hull, belted with inch-thick steel plates and reinforced by a two-foot inner sheathing of timber, was designed to crunch through three to four feet of ice. She could accommodate the coaches of an entire express train, or from twenty-five to twenty-eight fully loaded freight cars, on three pairs of rails parallel with the keel. Above this deck, a towering superstructure contained a luxurious lounge and a buffet; cabins for a hundred and fifty first- and second-class passengers; a special suite for consequential dignitaries; a chapel; quarters for ships' officers and crew; and deck space for six hundred and fifty persons in third class. Twin triple-expansion steam engines and two steel propellers drove the vessel at a maximum speed of thirteen knots in calm water, while a third engine in the bow powered a bronze forescrew, the purpose of which was to weaken the ice by roiling the water beneath. This innovation derived from the *Sainte Marie*, and was regarded with profound skepticism by that British authority on arctic navigation, Captain Joseph Wiggins, who predicted that it would be virtually useless against ice more than a foot thick.

Russian admiration for the *Baikal* was shared, though not without certain reservations, by the first foreign travelers to set eyes on her. Among them, Fraser — the English journalist who, like Jefferson, was a cycling enthusiast and had circled the globe on his "wheel" in the eighteen-nineties — hailed the ship, in 1901, as "one of the most wonderful vessels in the world," a description he rather hastily amended by adding that she was "by no means pretty, and rather like a barn that had slipped afloat." The *Baikal* was undeniably an ungainly, slab-sided hybrid that combined the physical features of a tubby polar icebreaker and a top-heavy excursion boat. In a word, this queen of Old World ferries, for all her gleaming white hull, neat brown trim, and Imperial flags whipping in the wind, was ugly.

However, she was such a romantic ship especially to affianced young couples that many took their marriage vows in her chapel. If a storm blew up, the wedding did not always come off quite as expected because fearful passengers invariably swarmed into the sanctuary to pray. "Irkutsk people," so Wright and Digby tell us, "cherish a story, which they declare to be true, of one of those rough-weather crossings in the dark and crowded chapel saloon with every one, including the officiating priest, very dizzy, and a clamor of disputes going on, that resulted in the wrong young man being married because the bride felt so seasick that she did not open her eyes, and the groom was in a state of collapse, longing for a swift death rather than matrimony."

At Khilkov's request in 1898, the Trans-Siberian Committee voted $400,000 for another icebreaking ferry, smaller than the *Baikal*. No trains would be carried, but she would share in passenger and freight transportation and assure communica-

The Angara

tions if her big sister broke down. That autumn, an order for the future *Angara* was placed with Armstrong, and, in August of the following year, the dismantled steamer arrived at the lake. Except for a heavily reinforced hull, she was conventionally built and much easier than the *Baikal* to assemble and equip. Two hundred feet long and thirty-five feet in beam, she seemed in comparison with the other to be a greyhound beside a Saint Bernard. Her top speed of twelve and a half knots was practically that of her running mate, yet she was propelled by only one screw and a single engine with a third of *Baikal*'s collective horsepower. The *Angara* could accommodate a hundred and fifty passengers and four hundred tons of cargo and fuel. But she lacked the weight and power to batter through thick ice, and was frequently out of commission with boiler trouble. (There had been no time for lining her boilers, as she was immediately commissioned to transport the troops Russia was speeding eastward in the summer of 1900 to profit from the Boxer Rebellion. The British can be proud of Armstrong's materials and workmanship, however, for the old two-stacker is still in service on the lake. The *Baikal* survived until her destruction during the civil war of 1918-1920.)

Both ferries were doomed to failure except in summer's brief fair weather. Storms and fogs held them in port for days, while freight piled up and train passengers were left stranded on both shores. Hydrographers had underestimated the depth of the midwinter ice cover; the *Angara* was unable to make headway through it unless the *Baikal* broke a path for her. This was seldom a successful performance across the lake, as the American Michael Shoemaker observed on the *Angara* in 1902. "The *Baikal* has cleared the passage for more than halfway — about twenty miles — and we find her hard at work. . . . She has backed off about five hundred feet, and, putting on full steam, rushes at the ice before her. There is a crack and roar, with muttered thunderings far down beneath and around us as the ice gives way and great blocks turn their glistening edges upward, and, piling for a moment on either side, close again behind the ship, which finally seems to mount for a third of her length upon the ice, but settles back again, her great weight not having broken through." Wherever the ice was thickest, the repeated onslaughts of the larger ship (which then carried no passengers) consumed so much time and were usually so unavailing that it became standard practice for the *Angara* to disembark passengers on the frozen surface, where a hundred or more sledges waited to shuttle them to the opposite shore.

The frustrated Communication Ministry pondered over these crippled operations, found them irremediable, admitted defeat, and laid up the ferries for the winter months. Then, in February 1904, the Japanese launched a surprise attack against units of the Russian fleet in the Far East, and brought on the Russo-Japanese War. For the Russians, it could have hardly come at a worse time. Khilkov realized that the entire war machine St. Petersburg was rushing across the Urals would bog down at Port Baikal. The steamers were immobilized; there were sufficient sledges for only ordinary traffic; and the quantity of rolling stock east of Baikal was far too inadequate to convey a twentieth-century army. At temporary headquarters in Irkutsk, Khilkov set in motion a brilliantly devised emergency program for the movement of troops and supplies across the lake, together with enough locomotives and railway cars for their transportation to the battleground.

Never in his career had his talents been more severely taxed. Under his direction, a small army of workers toiled through frequent spells of forty-below frost to lay rails on the ice from Port Baikal to the village of Tankhoi, to which tracks of the Transbaikal line had been extended from Mysovsk. Since borings had indicated the frozen layer to be five feet thick, Khilkov was confident that locomotives could proceed at a fairly good rate under their own power. But Old Man Baikal quickly disillusioned him. The first test engine plunged through in a disastrous demonstration of the lake's treachery. Only then did the railwaymen learn that Baikal concealed occasional warm springs that thinned the ice above. Thenceforth, the heavy locomotives had to be stripped down and cautiously towed with ropes, while their dismantled parts followed on prudently spaced-out flatcars.

Most of the twenty-eight miles to Tankhoi had no sooner

been tracked than the ice suddenly split, as if vindictively commanded by Baikal himself, and left a four-foot wide fissure along the completed section for a distance of twelve miles and more, twisting rails and snapping connection bolts in two. To avert a similar catastrophe, round-the-clock shifts fashioned extra-long supplementary ties from the tallest trees and placed them at thirty-foot intervals, thereby distributing weight over larger areas and providing support if another break occurred. This ingenious improvisation worked so well that, twenty days after hostilities had begun, the engines and rolling stock began to arrive at Tankhoi, to which they had been hauled by a force of six hundred men and a thousand horses.

While the track was under construction, Khilkov had developed a comprehensive system for the swift and reasonably safe transfer of the regiments disgorged from troop trains at Port Baikal. His supply staff augmented the sledges already on the lake by scouring the countryside and commandeering three thousand more; each carried four men or their corresponding bulk in baggage and equipment. When this shuttle service became overtaxed by officers and field gear, the rank and file marched across in waves, departing each day at 4 A.M. and reaching Tankhoi by 9 P.M. Emergency shelters were erected every four miles from shore to shore, with a capacious, well-heated shack at the half-point, where troops thawed themselves out and cooked their principal meal of the day. To avert falls into the icy water of crevices, Khilkov detailed gangs to build bridges over new cracks and to designate the exact route with posts, fir trees, lanterns, oil flares, and when blinding snow fell, bells tolled by watchmen in the shelters, which were connected by a telephone line so that warnings of fresh fissures could be quickly transmitted.

As the result of Khilkov's skill in organizing an efficient transportation complex under conditions that could have scarcely been worse, thousands of troops, countless gun batteries, sixty-five locomotives, and nearly twenty-four hundred fully laden railway cars crossed the lake in five weeks and moved on to the front to relieve Russia's hard-pressed far eastern army. Yet it was this same Prince Khilkov whom former Finance Minister Witte, as Premier, later fired from his job, saying that "he was not administrator enough to be equal to his ministerial tasks."

During that great winter push of 1904 to Tankhoi, the *Baikal* and the *Angara* remained as expensive, frost-rimed mementos of Their Excellencies' three chronic failings: inordinate haste, ignorance of Siberia, and passion for economy. Altogether, the abortive icebreaking-ferry venture had cost something like $3,372,000, or more than twice the amount they had reckoned on. But, even as the young Angara had determined to link herself with the river Yenisei, the Trans-Siberian Committee was as firmly resolved to link the fatherland with uninterrupted rails to the Great Ocean. Their Excellencies had put the steamer fiasco behind them and had already begun to circumvent untamable Starik Baikal by way of the once impregnable cliffs and mountain folds that locked him in.

CHAPTER XII

The Manchurian Coup

> If you would understand Russia, and interpret and forecast aright the march of great events, never forget that, for her, eastward the march of empire takes its way; that as the sap rises, as the sparks fly upward, as the tides follow the moon, so Russia goes to the sunrise and the warm water.
>
> — HENRY NORMAN: *All the Russias* (1902)

WE turn back to the years between 1894 and 1899, when an adverse topographical report, an Oriental war, a superbly finessed Russian deal with a Chinese statesman, and several imperialistic power plays combined to alter the route of the Trans-Siberian in the Far East.

After preliminary surveys of the Shilka and Amur valleys in 1893 and 1894, the Communication Ministry gave the Trans-Siberian Committee a particularly dismal summary of conditions along the proposed Amur line from Sretensk to Khabarovsk. Much of the 1200-mile route (slightly north of China's Manchurian provinces) passed through hills and river valleys that would require high embankments, deep cuttings, and at least a hundred and seventeen bridges, not counting a tremendously costly span almost a mile and a half long over the Amur at Khabarovsk. As in Transbaikalia, the region was bedeviled by permafrost, water scarcity in winter, and swollen streams in summer. The existing road to Khabarovsk would be of little value to construction crews, for it frequently dwindled to a mere pack-animal trail that turned into impassable mire during the wet season. To his gloomy report, Prince Khilkov could have added that the entire sector was literally a scurvy one, for his surveyors had come down with precisely that disease, together with fever and other afflictions, while Siberian anthrax decimated the horses.

"In view of these difficulties," Committee Administrator Kulomzin records, "the Government thought in 1895 of giving preference to a line that would reach Vladivostok by passing through Manchuria. A hasty reconnaissance by the Minister of Ways of Communication in the autumn of 1895 showed that . . . the length of the Trans-Siberian would be reduced by 549 kilometers [341 miles], which would appreciably cut the cost of freight transportation."

Kulomzin omits the paramount reason for diverting the railway to Chinese soil. For some years, Russia had been seeking means to dominate Manchuria and its southern neighbor Korea — and, supremely important, to gain possession of one or more of their ice-free ports. Unprepared to invite war by brazen military take-over, Nicholas and his fervent advocates of expansion watchfully bided their time.

Japan, which had emerged from her centuries-old isolation and was competing with both China and Russia for control of the Korean kingdom, took more precipitous action so as to gain her objectives before the Russians completed the Trans-Siberian and ended their almost total dependence on the long sea lane from Odessa for transportation of troops and armaments to the Pacific. Using the first convenient pretext, the Japanese attacked China in the summer of 1894 and, to the surprise of Europe, decisively defeated her. Tokyo exacted peace terms that included payment of a heavy indemnity and cession of the tip of Liaotung Peninsula in Manchuria, with its year-round open harbors of Port Arthur and Talienwan. The ink had scarcely dried on the treaty when Russia, joined by France and Germany (both of which were poised for their own acquisitive ventures in China), "advised" Japan to abandon Liaotung, since her occupation of this strategic foothold would menace their own land-grabbing plans. Rather than risk war with three Powers — each with strong naval forces nearby — Tokyo restored the peninsular area to China in exchange for a further cash indemnity. Finance Minister Witte, well aware that impoverished Peking could not pay up, instantly stepped forth as her financial savior. By pledging Russia's resources as security, he arranged a loan to China through French banking houses, which in return received his promise of aid in their activities in China.

". . . To express their gratitude to our youthful Emperor for all his benefactions to the Chinese Empire," as Witte puts it, China's Empress Dowager sent Li Hung Chang, the septuagenarian First Chancellor who ran the country, as Ambassador Extraordinary to the coronation of Nicholas in the spring of 1896. Witte had learned that England, France, Germany, and Austria had every intention to decoy Li to their capitals prior to his Russian visit. He therefore saw to it that Prince Esper E. Ukhtomski, one of the Tsar's intimates, met the Chinese dictator at Port Said and whisked him by special steamer and train to St. Petersburg, where he was given an honor guard and a reception worthy of any sovereign in Europe. When the tactful moment arrived to exact reward for their help to his country, Witte and Nicholas induced Li to sign a secret agreement, so secret in fact that its complete text was unknown to the world until the Soviets published it in the nineteen-thirties. This "Treaty of Integrity," as the signatories called it, established a Sino-Russian defensive alliance against Japan, guaranteed China's territorial inviolability, and paved the way for the railway shortcut across Manchuria to Vladivostok.

At his first meeting with Witte, Li maintained an air of tremendous self-importance. "My guest and myself sat, while all the members of his retinue as well as my attendants remained standing," Witte recalls. "When we had taken our tea, I inquired of Li Hung Chang whether he did not want to smoke. He emitted a sound not unlike the neighing of a horse. Immediately two Chinamen came running from the adjacent room, one carrying a narghile and the other tobacco. Then began the ceremony of smoking. Li Hung Chang sat quietly inhaling and exhaling the smoke, while his attendants with great awe lighted the narghile, held the pipe, took it out from his mouth and put it back. It was apparent that Li Hung Chang wanted to impress me with all these solemn ceremonies. On my part, I made believe that I did not pay the slightest attention to all these proceedings." *

Subsequently, Li dropped his display of pomp and got down

* Viceroy of the metropolitan province of Chihli, Imperial Tutor, Grand Secretary of State, Superintendent of Trade, and a noble of the first rank, Li quickly discarded ceremony when anyone wounded his amour propre. While in Moscow, he received a state visit from the Emir of Bokhara, who inquired after the health of the Chinese royal family but pointedly showed no solicitude for Li himself. Controlling his anger at this snub, Li questioned the Emir as to his religious faith, saying that he himself was a Confucianist. His guest replied that he was a follower of Mohammed. "When the visit was over," Witte recounts as an amused eyewitness, "Li Hung Chang accompanied his guest to the very carriage in which the Emir had come. When the carriage was already in motion, Li Hung Chang shouted to the interpreter who was with the Emir: 'Please tell the Emir that I forgot to say to him that the Mohammed he spoke about had been in China. There he was found out to be a convict and they chased him out of the country. Then he must have gone to the Emir's people and founded his religion among them.' This sally was so unexpected," Witte concludes, "that the Emir was taken aback and retorted nothing. Having thus re-

to business. He made no objection to a railway across Manchuria, but adamantly refused to accept Witte's proposal that the Russian Treasury either build or own it. In addition, he warned presciently that any advance south of the tracks — if the Russians were considering such a step — might be disastrous for Russia and China. Witte firmly believed that Russian supremacy throughout the empire could be achieved by peaceful rather than warlike measures. He was quick to assure Li that St. Petersburg had no designs whatever on Chinese territory, and that the railway would serve exclusively for mutual defense and economic prosperity. With Li's tacit approval, he then devised a bit of camouflage to disguise Russian ownership of the projected railway and thereby avoid a nationalistic outburst in the interior of China, where, said Li, "the ignorant masses regard every white as an enemy."

In the final agreement, Li Hung Chang granted the Manchurian railway concession, not to the Russian government but to the Russo-Chinese Bank, a private concern created by Witte and financed mainly by the French bankers who had entered into the loan to China. This institution in turn transferred the concession to another Witte brainchild, the Chinese Eastern Railway Company, a corporation capitalized at $2,500,000 divided into a thousand shares, most of which the Russian Treasury immediately cornered. To lend support to the fiction that Peking controlled the enterprise, a distinguished Chinese diplomat was named chairman of the Board of Management. The shareholders, however, elected Russians

taliated for the offence the Emir had done him, Li Hung Chang returned to his reception room in high spirits."

Li relates in his memoirs that when he was Viceroy of Chihli, "a low fellow came into my courtyard and told the banner captain in charge that he intended taking my life. He had a long piece of wire, and said he was going to hang me to my own gateposts. I had to have his head cut off before he would stop talking."

to the directorships and stipulated that the Russian finance minister was to have the last word in determining the railway's route, construction expenditures, and chief engineering and administrative personnel.

Although some details had to be ironed out after the coronation* and Li's departure, Witte had the best of reasons for commending himself for the deal he had masterminded so brilliantly. In return for a loan and a treaty of alliance (the spuriousness of which was to become shockingly apparent within two years of its ratification), China surrendered a strip across all of northern Manchuria for a railway and a telegraph line more than nine hundred miles long; exempted all railway revenues from taxation; waived customs duties on both freight and passengers' baggage in transit between the Sino-Siberian frontier stations; reduced tariffs on Russian exports and imports; and ceded police and administrative powers within the railway zone to the company. When rumors of this wholesale giveaway reached Europe, chancelleries buzzed with talk that Li Hung Chang had been bribed by Witte, a charge the latter denies without noticeable indignation in his memoirs.

The terms of the agreement were to remain in force for eighty years, at the end of which the railway would be turned

* Witte, who came to detest Nicholas as much as he had admired Alexander III, points to the Tsar's callous behavior on Coronation Day. When a half-million celebrants broke through a Cossack cordon and stampeded into Moscow's Khodynka Field for the distribution of royal gifts to the public — enameled metal cups with the Imperial eagle stamped on one side and the date "1896" on the other — not less than five thousand were crushed to death and many more injured. "A few hours after the Khodynka disaster," Witte wrote in his memoirs, "their Majesties attended a concert conducted by the celebrated Safonov. . . . A gorgeous evening party was scheduled for the same day, to be given by the French Ambassador, Marquis de Montebello. We expected that the party would be called off . . . [but] it took place, as if nothing had happened, and the ball was opened by their Majesties dancing a quadrille."

over to China without payment by her. On the other hand, Peking could purchase it after only thirty-six years. But, as Witte admits with unblushing candor, "the terms of the redemption were so burdensome that it was highly improbable that the Chinese Government would ever attempt to effect the redemption. It was calculated that should the Chinese Government wish to redeem the road at the beginning of the 37th year, it would have to pay the corporation, according to the terms of the concession, a sum not less than 700 million rubles [$350,000,000]." We may reasonably assume that Li Hung Chang did not bring this unpleasant fact to his sovereign's attention, for he clearly believed that what the Celestial One did not know would never hurt him. "I remember when I was Governor-General," Li once observed casually to Witte, "ten million people died from the bubonic plague in the province confined to my charge, yet our Emperor knew nothing about it. Why disturb him uselessly?"

When the Chinese Eastern pact was concluded in September 1896, the Trans-Siberian Committeemen happily abandoned the proposed Amur line, for which the surveys alone had cost $418,500, and no doubt consoled themselves for this wasted expenditure with the thought of the inestimable political and economic benefits that would accrue to Russia from the Manchurian railway. Despite Witte's solemn avowal that it would serve solely for defense and commerce, Japan and every Western nation suspected that the Russians meant to use it to establish virtual suzerainty over much of China and, as Prince Ukhtomski later wrote in words that seem rather familiar, to "annex regions which for a long time have sought to join us and have begged to be made our subjects." England, Japan, and the United States were considerably perturbed, but

Inauguration of construction of the Chinese Eastern Railway in eastern Manchuria, August 1897

none ventured to challenge St. Petersburg's "peaceful penetration," which was not the same thing as armed aggression.

Construction of the Chinese Eastern Railway had already begun in 1897, when Russia again capitalized at the expense of her hapless ally. Following Germany's occupation in November of the land around Kiaochow Bay — key to the rich Chinese province of Shantung, across the Yellow Sea from Korea — the Tsar dispatched a flotilla of troops to the Port Arthur area with the announced intention of "protecting" China from further German encroachment. For the same altruistic purpose, Russia demanded that Peking grant her a long lease of Port Arthur and the Talien area, together with permission to build a southern branch of the Chinese Eastern to them. Witte stormed against this thinly veiled violation of the Treaty of Integrity, not for moral reasons but because he feared that it would inflame the Chinese and jeopardize completion of the Manchurian railway, which he believed to be the surest, safest means for winning Russian economic hegemony in China to the virtual exclusion of other Great Powers. When his protests were ignored by the Tsar and the highly influential ministers of War, Navy, and Foreign Affairs, he tried to resign. But he felt that he was needed to promote the empire's financial welfare, and so Nicholas easily persuaded him to negotiate with Peking. The Empress Dowager, who cherished the Treaty of Integrity so dearly that she kept it in a safe in her own bedroom, angrily refused to come to terms. Witte therefore arranged for Li Hung Chang and another exalted official, Chang Ing Huan, to receive valuable "presents" which, according to Witte, amounted to $250,000 and $125,000 respectively. "This was the first time," he remarks, "that I resorted to bribing in my negotiations with Chinamen."

Although urged by Britain and Japan to stand firm, the Empress Dowager weakened under pressure from the suborned Li and Chang, and surrendered in March 1898. As Witte had feared, the leasehold appropriation of Port Arthur and Talien — to say nothing of the imminent incursion of a 600-mile Chinese Eastern branch down the full length of Manchuria's most prosperous and densely inhabited region — infuriated Chinese nationalists. Li was obliged to retire to southern China; Chang was exiled to the interior, where he was strangled to death; and the Chinese ambassador to St. Petersburg was publicly executed on his return to Peking. Violent antiforeigner riots fomented by a fanatical society of patriots, popularly known abroad as Boxers, were secretly approved by the Empress Dowager, who had never borne affection for those she called "the Western devils."

Construction camps along the Chinese Eastern

By 1900, the massacre of innumerable missionaries and Chinese Christians impelled Russia, Japan, and the Western Powers, including the United States, to send expeditionary forces to suppress the uprising and to rescue besieged foreign legations in Peking. When the capital was taken by these temporary allies in August 1900, the Russians disgraced themselves by looting on a grand scale. From Witte's own admission, even high-ranking officers joined in the pillaging, one lieutenant-general making off with treasure that filled ten trunks. During the ransacking of the Imperial palaces from which the court had fled, the Russians seized Chinese state documents; among them by ironical chance was the original text of the Treaty of Integrity, later returned to Peking at

Witte's recommendation. The thousands of troops St. Petersburg had rushed to the Far East — legions more than were needed to crush the Boxer Rebellion — then settled down to the occupation of all Manchuria. They were there ostensibly to maintain law and order during the reconstruction of the Chinese Eastern and its South Manchurian extension. Built under the most appalling handicaps ever encountered by tsarist engineers, both of these lines — together with bridges, stations, warehouses, employees' housing, administration buildings, and rolling stock — had been all but wiped out by Chinese rebels and roving bandits less than a year before their scheduled completion.

CHAPTER XIII

Ballyhoo and Reality

As the various sections of the Trans-Siberian opened to traffic from the Urals to the headwaters of the Amur at Sretensk, the first pioneering foreigners to travel over them almost unanimously agreed that the Russians had done a first-rate job in building a third-rate railway.

To begin with one of the primary prerequisites of safe and comfortable travel by train — the railway tracks. The flimsy steel rails of the Trans-Siberian weighed slightly less than forty-nine pounds to the yard, as compared with seventy to ninety pounds on American main lines between 1890 and 1900, and sixty pounds or so in England and western Europe. Produced by technologically backward Russian foundries, they were so soft that heavy rolling stock strained their elasticity beyond the recovery point, with the result that they sank and soon became bumpy. The ties were cut from green timber, untreated against decay, and, as a rule, too short, thin, and spongy for lasting support. Ballast on straight and level stretches consisted of rarely more than dirt or sand strewn between ties; on curves, the thickness of crushed-stone ballast common in European Russia was reduced by nearly half.

"I have seen the track so destroyed at times by insufficient ballast that the ties and rails are almost submerged in the bed, and the traffic was reduced to three miles an hour over these weak spots," Civil Engineer Lodian reported in *Railway and Locomotive Engineering*. "The ties are supposed to last four or five years, and date-nails have been driven into every tie, as a reminder to the roadmaster when they are laid down; but about half of these sleepers will have to be renewed considerably in advance of the allotted time." Even the happy-go-lucky Jefferson was disquieted, in 1897, by the "badly ballasted track, that caused the heavy Russian cars to oscillate alarmingly, notwithstanding the crawl at which we were proceeding."

The rails' light weight and flimsy footing also caused them to buckle and spread. "On one curve," Greener wrote in his *Greater Russia* after crossing Siberia twice, "it is said that a certain rail is crushed every time the 'express' passes, the buckling of the web of the rail renders it useless, and it has to be replaced by a new one each time, that is, four rails a week. . . . Short trains with a light load like the Siberian Express may be able to average twenty miles an hour; the heavier, ordinary trains do not often exceed twelve miles the hour, whilst the heavy goods trains rumble along like traction engines on a country road."

Another Briton, however, discovered under hair-raising circumstances that there was at least one redeeming feature in the crude tracks. James Young Simpson, who traveled on the new West Siberian and Mid-Siberian sections in 1896, related that coupling irons gave way on an incline; the detached cars rolled backward, awaking the only brakeman. When they came to a halt, the latter told Simpson "that it was more owing to the rough state of the line than to the efficiency of the brake that the runaway portion was so quickly controlled."

Railway experts from abroad found that the Communica-

Landslide!

tion Ministry had ignored, in its haste, the most rudimentary principles of sound engineering practice in mountainous areas. Along a 556-mile eastern stretch of the Mid-Siberian line, for example, the radius of some acute curves was less than eight hundred and forty feet, while the inclination of the most abrupt slopes reached a dangerously steep pitch. Aside from the peril of derailments on sharp bends and of run-aways on downgrades, these aberrations reduced the haul of a single locomotive to only sixteen freight cars instead of a normal thirty-six on the straight and level, with consequent traffic tie-ups unless twice as many engines were employed. The walls of cuttings were so sheer that ponderous freights brought down falls of earth from above, and created seemingly endless delays until the avalanche was tediously shoveled away. Unsodded and insufficiently shored-up embankments crumbled under floods, while roadbeds washed out during torrential rains. Here we may mention a classic example of fraud in the construction of the Trans-Siberian: when engineers investigated the sinking of track to an unprecedented depth of four feet after a warm-weather spell, they discovered that the contractor, instead of building up the roadbed, had simply laid ties and rails on a then-frozen snowdrift and pocketed the advance the Communication Ministry had paid him to do the job properly.

It is manifestly impossible to determine the number of accidents caused by deficient materials, slapdash construction, and minimal safety margins. But there can be little doubt that passengers had frequent occasion to pray for the Lord's protection, though an eminent engineer of undisclosed nationality may have exaggerated when he told a fellow traveler that "after a spring rain, the trains run off the track like squirrels." However, engines broke down on winter wastes, as Jefferson narrates.

"Bang out in the middle of the steppe, miles from anywhere, the train one day brought up suddenly, and stuck there for three hours. . . . None of our Russian passengers ventured to inquire the cause of the train's inertion, neither did the conductor, who periodically passed through the train with a face about as intelligible as a sphinx, volunteer any information on the subject. Gaskell and I, however, descended, walked along the line to the engine, and discovered that the tank had burst and the water was cheerfully washing away the track. The engineer was complacently leaning against the buffers smoking *papiros*, his fireman was asleep in the cab of the tender, nobody else was about, and the whole situation was so truly sublime that, being in the condition to laugh at anything, we both laughed heartily.

"The engine had broken down, that was clear. How were we going to get on? The engineer didn't know, and apparently didn't care. Had anything been done? The engineer *thought* that somebody had walked along the line to the next station, fifteen versts (ten miles) away, and would telegraph for a new engine. Did he know when a new engine would come? He hadn't the slightest idea. To-day or to-morrow? It was possible, one or the other.

"Back in the car we tackled the conductor, and he, too, evinced as much interest in the proceedings as an ordinary sheep does when it goes to the slaughter-stool. The opportunity for a walk, however, was too great, and so, in high spirits, Gaskell and I set off and walked the fifteen versts to the next station. The line ran dead ahead straight across the steppe, and when we had traversed ten versts we looked back and saw the train still standing there, a tiny black mass on the shining metals . . .

"Our energy, however, was rewarded by forestalling the occupants of the train in regard to the buffet arrangements. The stationmaster had prepared quite a decent dinner, and he alone, of those concerned in the matter, seemed to be perturbed at the train's delay. We had a very good time in the selection of the best dishes to be had, and on being assured that there was no possible hope of the train arriving that night, we curled ourselves up on benches and slept the sleep of the well satisfied.

"Next morning the train rolled up, and hungry and cursing passengers descended and raided the buffet like so many wild beasts. The over-bearing spirit of the Russian came to the front in all its intensity. They jostled and pushed each other without a word of apology, but rather with a growl of resentment and aggression. And yet not one of all that crowd had

A representative wooden bridge on the early Trans-Siberian (more smoke from that retoucher)

been able to shake off the laziness inherited from centuries of lazy progenitors and to tramp the ten miles in order to secure a little food and comfort."

Wooden bridges sometimes sagged ominously as though about to collapse into the river below. Since these spans had been denied even the thinnest protective coating, they were highly vulnerable to rot. In addition, permafrost exacted a heavy toll. As United States Consul James W. Davidson observed, "the ground, at first appearance firm and unbroken, almost in a night swallowed up miles of rail . . . brick engine-houses and heavy water-tanks a month after their construction sank into the lower strata of mire."

Although the jerked, jounced, and side-rolled travelers rode in nervous apprehension of disaster at any moment, catastrophic passenger-train wrecks seem to have been rare, principally because cars were relatively light and crews more careful of human than of inanimate freight. As a rule, they proceeded at a sedate pace that prompted De Windt to say, "I know of only one slower railway in the world, that from Jaffa to Jerusalem, where I have seen children leap on and off the car-steps of the train while in motion, and the driver alight, without actually stopping his engine, to gather wild flowers!" Crack-ups were also reduced by the vigilance of guards who lived along the line in log cabins anywhere from two thirds of a mile to two miles apart and signaled with a furled green flag, or a green lantern at night, if the section they patrolled was clear.*

Freight-train wrecks, on the other hand, occurred with spectacular frequency, as foreign writers attest in articles and books, some illustrated with on-the-spot photos of "The Usual Accident on the Great Siberian Railway." Almost invariably, the toppled locomotives and strings of smashed boxcars were victims of their own heavy loads or of careless or handicapped trainmen. The miserable lot of brakemen in particular aroused Lodian's compassion.

"Would it be believed," he wrote, "such a thing as a caboose is unknown in Siberia in connection with a freight train! The

* Although automatic and semiautomatic signals prevail on much of the Trans-Siberian today, a railway guard — usually a woman dressed in a cotton print in summer or bundled up in winter indistinguishably from a man — still extends the furled flag during a train's approach to a station or crossing. She hardly stands "with all the grace and dignity of a Goddess of Liberty," as an American engineer named McCarroll described one of her counterparts in 1897. But she holds herself as motionless as that statue and reminds us that, in the early days of the iron horse in Russia, all railway and military personnel remained at stiff attention while a train passed, for did it not represent the supreme authority of His Imperial Majesty the Tsar?

"The Usual Accident on the Great Siberian Railway"

poor train-hands . . . huddle up in their sheepskins, settle down on their perches, and try to get the best shelter they can from the ice-blasts of 20 to 40 degrees below zero. They can't even get a nap — so cold is it. So they can only yearn for the next station, when they get a chance of rushing in for a warm [-ing] and some hot tea. How can it be expected that train crews can do efficient work under such conditions? Why, it is an effort for some of them to make their half-frozen hands and arms grasp at the brakes . . . What trainmen in America would work under such conditions, with no warm caboose to resort to? The lay public little know the amount of comfort that can be found in a plain, cosy caboose. The American trainman's life is a luxury compared to the nearly dog's existence of the illiterate Siberian train-hand. And what do you suppose the Siberian trainman receives as salary? Twenty-eight rubls [*sic*] ($14) per month! It just enables him to exist."

Passenger trains on just-completed tracks generally consisted of the usual wood-burning locomotive, a tender stacked high with logs, and the third- and fourth-class cars described by the Reverend Dr. Francis E. Clark, the New England Congregational pastor who founded the Christian Endeavor So-

The Reverend Dr. Francis E. Clark

ciety. With his wife and twelve-year-old son, he rode westward from Sretensk five months after the Transbaikal line was opened to provisional traffic in January 1900. The car he occupied contained wooden seats and three tiers of wooden sleeping shelves, each only five feet long. Clark called it the best in the train. "Others, which might be termed fifth-class . . . are simply box-cars, with no seats, and marked on the outside, 'to carry twelve horses or forty-three men.' Into these cars there crowded, helter-skelter, pell-mell, higgledy-piggledy,

Dr. Clark, his wife, and son Harold waiting with other passengers for the ferry Baikal *(Dr. Clark sits left of center with hands clasped)*

Russians and Siberians, Moujiks and Chinamen, Tartars, Buriats and Englishmen, Frenchmen, Germans, and Americans. If there were fifth-class cars, there were plenty of sixth and seventh class people — some in rags, and many in tags, but few in velvet gowns. Old Moujiks, with half a dozen half-naked children, filthy with a grime that has accumulated since their birth, and alive with unmentionable parasites, crowded every car, or, rather, human pigpen, as each car soon becomes. Odors indescribably offensive made the air thick and almost murky. The stench, the dirt, the vermin grew worse the longer the car was inhabited, and one simply resigned himself to the inevitable and lived through each wearisome hour as best he could."

Delays were as numerous as they were protracted. At unbridged rivers, summer passengers had to descend with their baggage and cross on swing ferries to another train on the opposite bank. In winter, a quick transit by sledge across a river saved no time, for all had to wait on the other side until locomotive and cars inched cautiously over a track frozen to the ice, the way being lit at night by great bonfires. Service was entirely suspended for several weeks when the spring ice floes were too dangerous for ferries, and again in the autumn when the freezing surface had not thickened enough for a safe crossing. "Far from being an extra trial," the photographer Jackson says in a delightful account of his Siberian trip, which he describes as the outstanding railway experience of his life, "cold and snow have always been a positive blessing to travelers in Russia."

This was not altogether true in the first few winters before the Communication Ministry got round to planting trees and

Some of Dr. Clark's "fifth-class people"

putting up fences as snow guards. Locomotives could usually charge through fresh drifts of light, flaky snow three or four feet deep, but if they encountered a hardened layer only six inches thick, they bogged down with wheels spinning until the crew cleared the track, a pick-and-shovel operation that might take half an hour or half a day.

Owing to insufficient sidings and mixed-up schedules, expresses were slowed to the crawl of any wallowing freight ahead. Fuel- and water-supply depots were spaced so far apart that much time was lost while undermanned station crews loaded service cars with extra logs and tubs of water from tank spouts too small in diameter for voluminous flow. A normal station wait of perhaps half an hour often dragged on to twice that whenever a stationmaster forgot to prepare papers that should have been ready for the *chef de train* on arrival. At an order from any high official in the neighborhood, a stationmaster would detain a train until it suited His Excellency's

Oyash station, fifty miles northeast of the present Novosibirsk, with water-tower roof in background

Oyash water tower

convenience to board it. The same held true of Lake Baikal steamer captains: Pastor Clark comments irritably on a delay of twenty-two hours due to the late appearance of a Minister of Justice. Such was the power of privilege that the veteran travelogue Burton Holmes had only to flourish a document signed by Prince Khilkov to be ushered immediately into the *Baikal,* though the ferry was only in freight service at the time. Even first-class passengers on Holmes's train were refused passage with him, and had to wait in a squalid lakeside hotel until the *Angara* sailed hours later in the middle of the night. Jefferson comments on the custom of every engine-driver to waste further time by shaking hands at each stop "with the first half-dozen men that happen to be hanging about near, no doubt receiving in return a sort of congratulatory address to the effect that he has got so far safely." On the eve of a revered saint's day, none but a foreigner was surprised when conductors deserted their trains to attend serv-

"Off the line," in Transbaikalia

ices in the chapel that was a glittering icon- and candle-decked feature of every large station.

There were delays brought about by worn-out locomotives, and wooden bridges burned down by stokers who dumped blazing embers on them while shaking out a firebox. There were also inexplicable delays not even the observant Clark could account for. "Our train," he remarks with mingled puzzlement and exasperation, "would draw up at a wood-pile and a log-house. The peasants would scramble out of the train, build their fires, cook their soup, boil their tea, and still the train would wait. There was usually no baggage to be taken on or put off, no passengers to join us, no passing train to wait for. Water would soon be taken, and still we would wait, a half-hour, three-quarters, a full hour. At last, for no particular reason, apparently, the station-master would ring a big dinner-bell. Five minutes later he would ring another. Then, soon after, the guard would blow his whistle, the engineer would respond with the engine whistle, the guard would blow again, the engineer would answer him once more, and, after this exchange of compliments, the train would move leisurely along, only to repeat the process two hours later at the next station."

In the absence of dining cars and station buffets on newly opened sections of the railway, passengers without the foresight to bring provisions subsisted on whatever peasant women sold at wayside stops. In some districts where the inhabitants had barely enough for themselves, such food was meager, as two English ladies discovered on the Transbaikal line in 1900, when they lived for three days and four nights on a diet of milk, tea, and sour, half-baked bread. Not infrequently, Greener charges, army officers bought up everything in sight; on one occasion, a general appropriated forty eggs and seven bottles of milk, leaving nothing but salt fish for mothers on the train with babies to feed.

In the more developed western sections between Chelyabinsk and Irkutsk, however, dining cars and station buffets were making their appearance. Stations serving sizable cities were spacious, handsome stone and brick buildings lighted by electricity. Those in the vicinity of small towns were of wood, with quaint gables in the style of Swiss chalets, but with never enough space in waiting room and buffet, the last the scene of such jostling and uproar that most foreigners hesitated before squeezing through its narrow doors.

A station restaurant like that at Krasnoyarsk might be remarkable for waiters in full evening dress, and for menus in French as well as in Russian. Such a one was that described by the Honorable John W. Bookwalter, a manufacturer of turbine

Achinsk station, west of Krasnoyarsk, in the 1890s

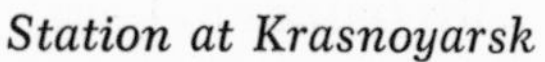

Station at Krasnoyarsk

wheels and an unsuccessful candidate for the governorship of Ohio, who traveled through part of Siberia in 1898. "On entering the dining-room," he wrote to home-town friends, "you will find at one end an immense sideboard literally groaning under a load of newly prepared Russian dishes, always piping hot, and of such a bewildering variety as to range through the whole gamut of human fancy and tastes. You are given a plate, with a knife and fork. Making your own selection, you retire to any of the neatly-spread tables to enjoy your meal at your leisure. . . . The price, too, is a surprise to one accustomed to metropolitan charges. You can get soup, as fine a beefsteak as you ever ate, a splendid roast chicken, whole, done in Russian style, most toothsome and juicy; potatoes and other vegetables, a bottle of beer, splendid and brewed in this country, for one ruble — about fifty cents."

On the other hand, the Swedish explorer Stadling, who traveled at about the same time as the bubbling Bookwalter, found station food to be quite dear: thirty-six cents for a plate of soup, seventy-three cents for cutlets, and fourteen to sixteen cents for a bottle of beer (in terms of purchasing power in the nineties, which was four to five times greater than it is today, the soup, cutlets, and beer would have cost as much as $6.25).

Jefferson was as usual at no loss for bantering words. "In we squeeze, and find ourselves in a long white-washed apartment, heated to a suffocating degree. Down the centre of the apartment runs a long table covered with glasses, plate, and cutlery. Over on one side is a long bar, covered with smaller glasses and large bottles, mostly containing vodki, as well as at least half a hundred dishes of the *hors d'oeuvre* style — sardines, bits of sausage, sprats, caviare, sliced cucumber, pickled mushrooms, artful dabs of cheese, raw radishes, smoked herring, and such like. For the nonce the crowd ignores the long table, equally so a kitchen-like arrangement in the corner where steams a heterogeneous mass of cutlets and 'Russian' beef-steaks, and which is presided over by a couple of marvellously clean-looking men who are rigged out *à la chef*. Vodki is the lodestone of the arrived passengers. Each man gulps down a small glass of the fiery fluid, seizes a piece of fish, or sausage, or cheese, or whatever he may fancy or may be handy, and subsides to the big table, chewing vigorously. Energetic waiters pounce upon him, lay before him a big plate of the universal 'stche,' or cabbage soup, over which our Russian hangs his head and commences ladling away, apparently oblivious to its boiling heat or the feelings of the people around. The tables fill up. Great slabs of brown meat, floating in fat, are distributed with rapidity, and which are with equal rapidity demolished. Manners are delightfully absent. People jostle, growl, and gulp; smoke *papiros* and puff the smoke in each other's faces; or make the most disgusting noises with their mouths. At last, having got through several pounds of meat and fat, and drunk about six to eight glasses of lemon-coloured hot water, which is called tea, per man, the crowd lounges around in contentment, and waits patiently for the bell to announce the probable departure of the train — which may be anything in the region of one hour to four, or while there is a bit of food in the buffet uneaten."

Besides such eating places, there were rough board counters on station platforms where, in normal times, local women sold black bread, eggs, cooked chickens and game, meat pies, fried fish, milk, and kvass.* While government officials and

* A dispatch from Moscow in the *New York Times* of April 9, 1964, states that "An ancient Russian drink known as kvass may soon rival Coca-Cola on the world market if Izvestia has its way. The Government newspaper announced tonight that after nine years of research the Soft Drink Institute

their wives, army and navy officers, merchants and commercial travelers, mineral prospectors, stray foreigners, and other relatively affluent passengers crowded into restaurant or buffet, hoi polloi from third-class cars swept like a voracious Mongol horde upon the outdoor vendors, then rushed to the hot-water tap on every platform to fill kettles for tea-drinking on the train. Aloof from this ravening humanity stood the railway official described by Jefferson as "a red-hatted, despotic-looking individual, who is gazing about with tremendous scorn and indifference, as if this sort of thing was very boring, although ten to one his heart is thumping with pride and excitement; for he is the stationmaster, salary one hundred pounds a-year, princely for him, indeed."

By 1898, traffic volume on the western and central sections of the Chelyabinsk-Irkutsk run had vastly surpassed Their Excellencies' estimates. Whereas only 168,000 metric tons of freight and 106,000 passengers (excluding migrants) had been carried in 1896, the total soared to 336,000 tons and 236,000 passengers in the following year. Despite the construction of thirty-one new sidings and the acquisition of 2230 additional cars and locomotives, the West Siberian line was so overtaxed that 80,000 tons of merchandise and foodstuffs ac-

had developed a competitive commercial method for making kvass, a popular drink of low alcoholic content consisting of malt, rye flour and sugar. . . . The newspaper offered a variety of selling points. 'Kvass invigorates, refreshes and quenches the thirst,' it said. 'It is tasty and aromatic. . . . It has a beneficial effect on the digestive organs and kills harmful bacteria. It regulates the metabolism and the functions of the central nervous system. It promotes oxidation and reduction process in the respiration of living cells. It aids in the normal deposition of calcium in bone tissue and improves the activity of the cardiovascular system.' . . . Izvestia added that the new process would enable four to five kvass-extract factories to supply all the soft-drink bottling plants of the Soviet Union, replacing the primitive wooden barrels on wheels from which kvass is now being dispensed in communal drinking glasses. . . ."

cumulated at depots and shunt points in the winter of 1897-1898. Shipments of grain, animal products, and other perishable commodities spoiled under tarpaulins or sheds during the three and a half months before enough rolling stock could be brought out to move the glut. Worse still, emigrants (of which nearly 277,000 crossed the Urals from Russia in 1896 and 1897) were left stranded at wayside stations for six summer weeks or more until boxcars could be rounded up to transport them to their destinations. James Simpson visited one of their wretched encampments a hundred miles west of Krasnoyarsk, and later was moved to write that "they had much of which to complain. . . . Cholera, typhus and other loathsome enemies of mankind had walked — were walking — at their ease amongst them; 30 per cent had died. . . . Beside them were the railway trenches water-filled, clouds of mosquitoes filled the air. . . . A few branches bent hoopwise, with either end stuck in the ground, and interwoven with yet other leafy branches, formed their rude dwellings. . . . There was borne from some remoter group keeping late vigil one of those soft, weird, minor melodies that are the priceless possession of the Russian folk. And when the dying strains of the song soared to a high-pitched note held by the female voices, while the men prolonged it an octave lower, it seemed like some sad musical interrogation, Why had they left Poltava to die on the Siberian steppe?"

Something had to be done to avert utter chaos. Prince Khilkov himself inspected the line from Chelyabinsk to Lake Baikal and urged an expenditure of $47,500,000 for far-ranging improvements and a vast increase in rolling stock. But Nicholas declared that a decision must be deferred until the whole critical problem had been investigated by a special board, which he then appointed. Under this board, a commission delved, conferred, and estimated costs with such thoroughness that finally, in February 1899, the Tsar was satisfied, and consented to an outlay of somewhat more than $42,385,000 for a corrective program to be carried out over a maximum period of eight years.

To increase the railway's capacity, Khilkov was authorized to build new sidings, warehouses, and wood- and water-supply depots; enlarge existing storage facilities and cramped waiting rooms; augment railway personnel; improve freight-handling installations and equipment at stations and river wharves; and, perhaps most important of all, add 2750 cars to the 3718 units already on hand. The program also called for an increase in the average speed of passenger trains to twenty-three miles an hour (up from thirteen), and of freights from eight to a maximum of fifteen. The Communication Ministry therefore set about to replace wooden bridges with those of stone or steel; put down longer ties and heavier ballast where the need was greatest; and, on abrupt curves and grades in central and eastern Siberia, scrap the light, inferior rails for others of harder steel and sixteen-pounds-to-the-yard greater weight. For the time being, the mainly straight and flat West Siberian track was to be left pretty much as it was.

Then, as now, the gauge of Russian track was five feet, as against four feet, eight and a half inches on Continental, British, and American railways. It has been said that the Russians adopted this greater span to handicap foreign invaders with their own standard-width rolling stock. There is also the rather odd theory that early Russian engineers, sent to study the European system, measured the width of track from the outside rather than the inside of the rail heads, then proceeded to build in the belief that the two gauges were identical. At any rate, the difference of three and a half inches has always meant that the narrower bogies (or wheel trucks) of European through-trains must be changed at the frontiers. Today, the broader Russian bogies are substituted under a twelve-car train in less than an hour, thanks to power jacks, cables that roll bogies out or in, and highly organized changeover crews. Locomotives, with their ponderous wheels and driving-rods, are spared this undignified tinkering with their underpinnings; at the border, Russian engines take over the haul.

With improvements underway, Prince Khilkov laid ambitious plans to put the Trans-Siberian into the luxury-travel big time by means of through expresses to Irkutsk and, later, to Vladivostok and Port Arthur. These would be no ordinary expresses but splendid deluxe trains, some to be owned by the Russians, others by the Compagnie Internationale des Wagons-Lits et des Grands Express Européens, or the International Sleeping Car Company, a Belgian organization similar to the Pullman Company in America. Announcing that the government trains would be called Russian State Expresses to distinguish them from the Sleeping Car Company's "Internationals," the Communication Ministry and the company undertook to convince the world — all too familiar with disparaging newspaper and magazine articles about Russia's "white elephant" — that the Trans-Siberian would provide fast public transportation unparalleled in the Old World for low fares, superb accommodations and food, and a novel assortment of personal services en route.

"When the whole trunk line is completed," Russian promotional brochures proclaimed in four languages, "it will take 10 days to cover the 5,500 miles between Moscow and Vladivostok or Port Arthur, the first class sleeping-car express fare amounting to £12 [about $58] at the present differential

Library section in the dining car of the Russian State Express

tariff. From London or Paris to Shanghai this will take 16 days, and cost £32 instead of the 35 days and £90 required by the present sea route. With the increase of speed of Siberian trains to the European limit, the overland journey between the Atlantic and Pacific will in time be reduced to 10 days." Furthermore, travelers were reminded that seasickness and tropical heat in the Red Sea and the Indian Ocean would be avoided as they rode across Russia and Asia in "an ambulant palace of luxury."

Each State Express was to consist of a locomotive of the latest design; a baggage and service car; a restaurant carriage with a salon, or lounge, at one end containing a piano, easy chairs, writing tables, a library of foreign as well as Russian books and periodicals, and sets of chess and dominoes, together with the benign countenances of the Tsar and the in-

Church car at a wayside stop

Interior of the "ambulatory basilica"

cumbent Communication Minister gazing from framed portraits on the walls; and compartmented, fully carpeted sleeping coaches with occupancy limited to eighteen persons in first class and twenty-four in second. There would also be a "church car," complete with priest, icons, free-standing floor candelabra, and, outside at one end of the roof, a pair of church bells surmounted by the double-barred cross of the Russian Orthodox Church. This "ambulatory basilica," however, never became part of regular express-train equipment, but was dropped off for temporary stopovers at new settlements and railway-employee centers without churches.

In 1900, a typical church car was reproduced in miniature by Michael Perkin, a craftsman in the workshop of Peter Carl Fabergé, the great court jeweler best known for the fabulous gem-studded Easter eggs he created chiefly for Alexander III and Nicholas II. Displayed today in the Kremlin Armory Museum is Perkin's Great Siberian Railway Easter egg, supported by rearing griffins on an alabaster base. Surmounted by the double-headed eagle of the Tsars, it is exquisitely enameled in blue, green, and yellow, and silver-banded with an etched map of Siberia and the route of the Trans-Siberian. Beneath the hollow egg stands a tiny model identified as "the first Siberian train," though it may actually be Perkin's conception of "the Tsar's Special." Driving wheels, double trucks under carriages, and other moving parts were precision-made to work so that, given a few turns with the gold key that has also been miraculously preserved, the gold and platinum locomotive, with a ruby gleaming from its headlight, could actually pull the train. Coupled to the baggage car are a carriage with half the seats reserved for ladies, another car for children, and still another for smokers. The church car, with Russian cross and gold bells on the roof, completes the equipage, in all scarcely

The Great Siberian Railway Easter egg and scale-model train, completed in 1900 by Michael Perkin, a craftsman in the workshop of the great court-jeweler Carl Fabergé

more than a foot long and perhaps five eighths of an inch wide, the whole joined so artfully that it can be folded together and concealed in the egg. How this lovely toy must have captivated Nicholas, who was in many ways a child at heart.

In addition to hygienic, well-equipped toilet rooms, there were to be a bathroom with porcelain tub and needle-shower; a gymnasium with dumbbells, a stationary bicycle, and an " 'exerciser' for those who do not want their body muscles to rest"; a darkroom with measures, trays, fixing baths, and such supplied free to amateur or professional photographers. In first-class sleepers, the compartments, or "coupés," would be limited to two persons, and, in second class, to four, with berths seven feet long. Each car would also feature a communal lounge with an overstuffed sofa, comfortable armchairs, a ta-

A first-class compartment in the Russian State Express

ble for cards and other games, and electric reading lights (power deriving from a steam-driven dynamo in the baggage car). In winter, the vestibuled, double-doored and double-windowed carriages would be individually heated, each coupé to be equipped with adjustable levers for regulating the steam radiators. In summer, passengers would be cooled by electric fans and downdrafts from iceboxes under the roof. These last were not to be confused with the water tanks of live fish for cooking by the chef, who would make no charge for boiling milk, and but a nominal one for roasting wild game which could be purchased at stops along the way.

On every State Express, patrons could rely on a train chief of stationmaster's rank, omniscient conductors, attentive porters, multilingual waiters in evening dress and menus in French as well as in Russian, a barber, and a licensed "dis-

Three of the International Sleeping Car Company's deluxe salon carriages exhibited at the Paris International Exposition in 1900

penser of medicines, competent to treat obstetrical cases." In instances of serious illness, the train chief would telegraph ahead to the nearest section point with a doctor. His services would cost the patient nothing; if hospitalization were necessary, treatment and medicines were also on the house for a specified period. And all this for hardly more than a cent a mile! Even blasé Americans accustomed to the grandeur and pampering services in the Boudoir or Palace cars of Messrs. Mann, Wagner, and Pullman were becoming curious.

Despite the Boxer troubles that curtailed passenger-train service east of Moscow, the Trans-Siberian publicity campaign racketed into high gear at the Paris Universal Exposition of 1900. Thousands of visitors at the Palace of Russian Asia in the Trocadéro gardens thronged round enlarged maps and photographs of mysterious Siberia; a gleaming scale model of the great train-ferrying icebreaker *Baikal;* stuffed seals and polar bears perched precariously on papier-mâché icebergs; reindeer-drawn sledges with fur-clad dummies of Ostyak hunters beside them; and rich, Oriental objets d'art from the private collection of the Emir of Bokhara, that same impolite potentate whose spiritual lord Mohammed, according to the offended Li Hung Chang, had been a convict chased out of China.

But the lodestone of the show was the spectacular prize-winning exhibit of the Sleeping Car Company. To demonstrate that travel by rail across Siberia was anything but "visionary and unworthy of serious consideration" (as a leading Parisian journal had once declared), the enterprising concern put on display four magnificent, fresh-from-the-factory coaches that would ostensibly be assigned to its own Siberian "Internationals." Standing on a track better laid than any in Siberia were two *wagons-restaurants* furnished in both "subdued modern" mahogany and richly ornamented Louis XVI light oak, and two *wagons-salons*, each containing four sleeping compartments with connecting lavatories, a palatial lounge, and a smoking room. In one of the carriages, furniture and décor were of the French Empire period, contrasting dramatically with the adjacent smoking room done up in vivid Chinese style. The lounge of the other car, in which an upright piano with hand-painted panels graced one end, might be said to be a turn-of-the-century version of a Louis XVI drawing room, with walls, chairs, and tables of white-lacquered limewood, a number of large plate-glass mirrors, a ceiling frescoed with diaphanously gowned nymphs and allegorical figures, and, framing the windows, fancifully embroidered valances and drapes. Not displayed at the Exposition but almost as breathlessly described by French publicists was the *fourgon*, a special baggage car with fire- and burglar-proof lockboxes for passengers' jewels and valuable documents; a hairdressing salon in white sycamore; a green sycamore bathroom noteworthy for a tub so ingeniously designed that water could not slosh out despite lurches on sharp curves; and the gymnasium, dignified by the name of "veloroom" because of the peddling machine it contained in addition to dumbbells and other muscle-toning paraphernalia.

As a further draw to jaded travelers in particular, the company invited Exposition visitors to dine (at $1.30 a head) in the stationary *wagons-restaurants* and view from the windows the "Trans-Siberian Panorama of a Journey from Moscow to Peking," a long, train-high strip of canvas said to have been painted by two master scenic-artists of the Paris Opera sent to Siberia especially to soak up local color. While the diners progressed toward nothing but an entrée after the soup, and fruit and coffee after that, they had only to look through the windows to imagine themselves deep in exotic Siberia, for the mechanized canvas, not twenty feet from their eyes, moved at a speed to convey the illusion that the cars themselves were passing by steppes, mountains, virgin forests, onion-domed churches in towns, and station crowds gazing in amazement at the smoke-belching iron monster and its splendid coaches. What with lyrical brochures, railway carriages "equal to the special trains reserved in Western Europe for the sole use of Royalty," and the sensational Moving Panorama, the Russians and the Sleeping Car Company had succeeded in projecting an entrancing image of a journey across Siberia on "the world's unique train."

Despite its ballyhoo, the Sleeping Car Company pursued a cautious policy for several years after it began Siberian operations, and, for reasons that shall be seen, ran nothing so fine as the magnificent carriages at the Exposition. As for the State Express, this much-touted *train de luxe* comprised the familiar wood-burning locomotive, a baggage car, diner, one first-class and two second-class sleepers, and required eight days to complete the journey between Moscow and Irkutsk.

Two of the first foreigners to travel on it were a venturesome thirty-two-year-old spinster, Annette M. B. Meakin, and her white-haired, never-say-die mother, who became the first Englishwomen to cross Siberia by rail and water. They stole out of London "on March 18, 1900, without having explained our immediate purpose to any one outside our immediate circle," Miss Meakin says in her book about the trip. "Our friends were thus spared a great deal of needless anxiety." Although she speaks almost affectionately of the Express as "a kind of 'Liberty Hall,' where you can shut your door and sleep all day if you prefer it, or eat and drink, smoke and play cards if you like that better," other foreigners found their particular train to be inferior to the extra-fare specials in America, Europe, and even in Russia itself. Pastor Clark, who boarded the westbound express at Irkutsk after his harrowing trip in the fourth-class "human pigpens" of the Transbaikal line, described the cars as "rather shabby," while Shoemaker compared them unfavorably with those on the Nicholas Railway between St. Petersburg and Moscow.

To be sure, the compartments were comfortable enough with their ample berths, thick carpeting, and such conveniences as a movable reading lamp, a table, and a pneumatic bell that sometimes brought a waiter, but where were the air-cooling iceboxes, the photographic darkroom, the live-fish tanks, the barber, the combination dispenser of medicines and male-midwife to mothers-to-be? The small lounge in

Annette Meakin and her mother when photographed in Japan after their Siberian journey in 1900. The three white men were Russian officers, and the pigtailed Chinese a servant of one of them; the young man with the cap was unidentified.

the sleepers lived up to its advance billing, but, said Miss Meakin, "card playing went on all the time. . . . If a Russian sits down to a game of cards, nothing but a matter of life and death will induce him to stir from it till it is finished."

Two to a car, the washrooms were shared by both sexes "with consequent delays and embarrassments," as a well-traveled Member of Parliament named Henry Norman decorously put it. Burton Holmes called them crude and ill-kept, and Clark condemned *all* Russian toilet rooms collectively as "a wretched, filthy closet, with a single wash-basin and a very limited supply of water . . . the scarcest and dearest thing throughout Siberia . . ."

As for the proudly advertised bathroom, Clark found only a tub in the baggage car, and thought that the seventy-five-cent charge for its use was out of all proportion to the cost of transportation, which was about $50 per person in first class between Moscow and Irkutsk (quite an increase in the publicized fare of roughly $58 for the much longer run from Moscow to Vladivostok or Port Arthur). In De Windt's experience, the bathtub was used mainly as a receptacle for the storage of ice, vegetables, and meat. Next to it was the gymnasium, an area just big enough for a stationary cycle and another device that looked suspiciously like a crank exerciser of the type then used in British prisons.

Train conductors could usually speak French or German in addition to Russian, but for the most part they were poorly informed about Siberia, as Annette Meakin discovered. "We tried to find out from him whether there was any hotel at Omsk, and what sort of a place it was, but the only information we could extract was that it was warmer at Irkutsk than at Moscow. He knew nothing of Omsk, and could not even tell us when we might expect to arrive till we were within a few hours of the place." However, she was satisfied with the porter, who changed her bed linen twice a week according to regulations. Also according to rule, each change cost her fifty cents, though she had paid a *train de luxe* supplement to her first-class fare.

But De Windt, an experienced and exacting traveler not given to equivocation, denounced the service as "atrocious," an indictment echoed by Dr. Clark. "Our porters on the *train de luxe* never thought of sweeping or dusting the staterooms, and seemed to think it an imposition to be asked to thoroughly make up the berths for day travel, preferring to leave the beds made up by day that they might have less trouble at night. All day long the lazy porters would loll about on their seats in the middle of the car, doing as little as possible, and apparently begrudging that little." Shoemaker relates that his porter made himself obnoxious by spraying the car and Shoemaker himself with perfume from a large atomizer. "His amazement was immense when I objected strongly and promptly opened all the windows at my command. In this I was seconded by a Frenchwoman in the other end of the car, and between us we treated the Russian travellers for five minutes to more fresh air than they have had all winter."

As advance publicity had promised, there were a library and a piano at one end of the dining car, and menus in French. However, the library confined itself only to Russian novels and a few dog-eared French paperbacks left behind by previous passengers. Shoemaker found that the piano was used primarily as a shelf for dirty dishes. Holmes was practically alone among the early travelers in commending the food. "The meals although badly served," he told his devoted audiences in America, "were surprisingly well-cooked and appetizing; good bread, excellent veal, and hearty soups, sometimes frappés, with a clinking cake of ice floating on their chill depths, sometimes seething hot, with a hunk of steaming beef rising from them like a volcanic island." Clark was less enthusiastic, saying that "one must get used to the greasy Siberian soup and to the chunks of tough stewed meat, which may be beef, mutton, or pork, one is never certain which."

Shoemaker comments on the "very stupid waiters who speak nothing save Russian," while Holmes recommends Russian travel as a cure for squeamishness. "For example," the traveloguer wrote after his trip on the *train de luxe,* "napkins are rarely washed; the patrons carelessly throw them down; the waiters pick them up from floor and chair and table, spread them out as flat as possible, spray them as the Chinese washman sprays his washed linen, fold them very carefully, and then put them in presses, so that at next meal-time they may be again produced with neat new creases that deceive those who have never chanced to look behind the scenes. Take plenty of Japanese paper napkins with you when you go to Russia. Take also a big empty bottle, for the little milkmaids are very loath to part with the precious vodka-bottles in which they bring fresh milk to the railway-station."

Greener reports that high-ranking officers and the governmental elite of first class preempted every dining-car table by browbeating the headwaiter to let them in before the scheduled opening hour. After eating, they lingered over tea or champagne and innumerable cigarettes, utterly oblivious to the other passengers waiting for seats. No train official dared to oust the lordly ones, for, Greener remarks, "it was 'impertinent' to be otherwise than servile to those of higher rank." Sometimes waiters were so slow and indifferent that the hungry passengers who had waited for the privileged to depart often sat for almost an hour before their orders were taken. "I thought myself lucky if my meal was served half-an-hour after I had ordered it," a Briton named Dobbie wrote in *Macmillan's Magazine*, "and then it only arrived if I had solicited my man's favour with a rouble. A rouble in fact was the one emollient that made the wheels of our life go round at all, and it had to be repeated in judicious doses." *

How was it that some passengers like Miss Meakin spoke fairly well of the Russian *train de luxe* when others had little good to say of it? The answer is that equipment varied and inspection was lax. Whereas there was only a baggage-car tub in the separate trains taken by Clark and De Windt, Shoemaker discovered in *his* Siberian Express "a fine bathroom in the restaurant car, large and tiled, and with all sorts of sprays, plunges, and douches." Since strict controls were hard to enforce along the several thousand miles from Moscow to Irkutsk and Sretensk, train chiefs and dining-car chefs ran their shops, so to speak, according to their own lights. Some were conscientious and took pride in their jobs, others were lazy and slipshod. Obviously, Miss Meakin and her mother had benefited from the former while Clark, De Windt, and the rest suffered from the shortcomings of the latter.

During the first years of its Siberian operations, the Sleeping Car Company followed wait-and-see tactics and used ordinary first- and second-class carriages in its "International"

* Tips have been officially abolished in the Soviet Union, though they are accepted, at least from foreign tourists, in metropolitan restaurants. The Intourist interpreter who accompanied the writer and his wife on the Trans-Siberian would not hear of our tipping the dining-car waitresses or car attendants. The best way to express gratitude, she said in substance, is to write it in the workers' record books on the train, for "good reports will make them most happy." This we did, in English which the interpreter translated into Russian.

trains that alternated with the State expresses on the Moscow-Irkutsk run. To the hardheaded Franco-Belgians, it made little business sense to tie up highly expensive, ultra-luxurious equipment — identical in every respect to that displayed at the Paris Exposition — when no one could even guess if the Trans-Siberian would attract heavy spenders; and why risk staggering losses if the precious Louis XVI–French Empire palaces ran off the Russians' flimsy track and cracked up beyond repair? The company, for all its glamorous Orient and Riviera expresses, was nonetheless ever-practical, and found no reason to run anything better in Siberia than its regular *wagons-restaurants* and *wagons-lits*. Some foreigners said that they were superior to the Russian deluxe cars; others took the opposite stand, nationalistic prejudices undoubtedly influencing both views. But there was almost unanimous agreement that the food in the *wagons-restaurants* was as bad as that in the government *trains de luxe*. In those earliest years of the present century, the company did not particularly care, for it was losing money from low fares imposed by the Communication Ministry, as well as from predominantly Russian passengers who rode for relatively short distances and shunned first class, the company's main resource for profits. The management therefore continued to mark time until completion of Trans-Siberian improvements and of the Chinese Eastern Railway to Vladivostok and Port Arthur. Then, it would press hard for fare increases, run better *wagons-lits* and *wagons-restaurants*, and concentrate an advertising barrage on rich international travelers seeking pleasure or business in the Far East.

Meanwhile, such was the topsy-turvy world of travel on the Trans-Siberian that, not long after Shoemaker delightedly discovered the bathroom on his train — with its "separate attendant and all the bath-towels you may demand" — the American found himself again faced with less pleasant reality. "We reach Chita at 2 P.M.," he relates, "and have a wretched luncheon at the buffet, bad soup and steak that never was part of any beef. I think it was dog."

CHAPTER XIV

By Rail and Water to the Great Ocean

> If travel to you means simply Paris shops, then do not come here; but if you like travel, if the world is an open book of pleasant reading to you, cross Siberia, — you will never regret it.
>
> — MICHAEL MYERS SHOEMAKER: *The Great Siberian Railway from St. Petersburg to Pekin* (1903)

WHATEVER a journey across Siberia may have lacked in speed and uniform comfort in the late nineties and early nineteen-hundreds, it made up for in color and adventure perhaps unprecedented since the winning of the American West. But to Baedeker, Murray, and other compilers of guidebooks, Siberia remained a hazardous and touristically unrewarding ultima Thule all sensible persons would do well to avoid. Travelers were cautioned to equip themselves with a revolver, heavy woolen underwear, well-lined rubber boots, warm furs, a mosquito veil, a pillow or an air cushion, bed linen, a coverlet or a rug, towels, soap, a portable india-rubber bathtub, and "remedies against insects of a vexatory disposition." To avoid police suspicion as a disseminator of subversive propaganda, one should leave books of a political, social, or historical nature at home and never use anything but unprinted paper for wrapping fragile personal belongings in trunks and handbags. Hotels were almost invariably dear, and became progressively inferior the farther one advanced beyond the Urals; their proprietors spoke only Russian, and charged extra for sheets, pillowcases, towels, and candles. "The traveller must be on his guard against *Thieves*," Baedeker fairly shrieked. In short, he made it clear that if you actually set out for Siberia, you did so in spite of stern warnings and no encouragement from him.

As we know, this premonitory animus failed to scare off intrepid foreigners to whom merely the name Siberia held peculiar and irresistible fascination. When they looked back on their journey, some would have given anything to repeat it. Others, like Pastor Clark who dedicated his book, *A New Way Around an Old World,* "To the Members of the 'Never Again Society' . . . ," were only too glad to leave and never return. But to all these travelers, their Siberian experiences were imperishably locked in memory for the rest of their lives.

In that pre-Soviet period of some sixty years ago, tsarist officials allowed most visiting nationals of the Great Powers a liberty of movement that seems incredible in view of the rigid travel restrictions of the Soviet Union today. Foreigners with the standard six-month Russian passport visa could break their journey wherever they liked and stay for weeks in any community, even in a heavily fortified, security-bound port such as Vladivostok. Unlike modern visitors who are generally confined to cultural centers and "model" thises and thats, they could explore the seamiest slums, dives, and peasants' hovels without the slightest surveillance.

In St. Petersburg, Prince Khilkov rolled out the Communication Ministry's welcome mat for Western journalists, commercial representatives, and venturous tourists who wanted to visit Siberia. Perhaps naively, he hoped their sightseeing would lead them to spread the gospel that another rich new world like Canada and the American West was in the making, with boundless opportunities awaiting outside investors, whom Finance Minister Witte eagerly sought. Khilkov therefore provided invaluable letters of introduction that were open sesames not only to official sanctums but also to prisons, Imperial gold-smelting laboratories, and the homes of provincial governors and prominent citizens. Even for obscure Annette Meakin, who had yet to build her reputation as an outstanding travel writer, lecturer, translator from the Greek, and authority on Goethe and Schiller, he wrote the customary letter, saw to it himself that her railway tickets were in order, and presented her with "a splendid map" of her route, together with the English-language edition of the Ministry's exhaustive and profusely illustrated *Guide to the Great Siberian Railway.* Seldom since the days of that first foreign champion of a Siberian railway, Perry McDonough Collins, had Westerners been more cordially received in the empire.

"The very word Siberia is one to make the blood run chill. It smells of fetters in the snow. You hear the thud of the knout on the shoulders of sickened men. For generations, to whisper Siberia in the ear of a Russian has been to make the cheek blanch. No one ever went there but in chains. The haggard men that ever came back told tales that made listeners breathe hard."

Journalists who returned from Siberia to write sizzling copy like that (lifted with tongs from the writings of Fraser, who described himself as "a vagabond fond of taking things slowly") scorned what they called the "effete" State Express and the Sleeping Car Company's International. In pursuit of color and "the *real* Siberia," they boarded the daily mail train that comprised chiefly third-class cars — grimy, uncushioned, and lit at night by flickering candles, but what could one expect for a fare of $12.60, hardly more than a third of a cent per mile, from Moscow to Irkutsk? This grubby rattler chuffed along at about the same speed as the expresses, but stopped at every fence post, and, depending on accidents, storms, and the crotchets of enginemen and stationmasters, took eleven to fourteen days to complete a one-way journey. Picking up passengers here and dropping them off there, it was the train of the common people, such as Jefferson, the Wright-Digby team, and others have described. Fraser's account is perhaps the most graphic. ". . . The majority were third-class, a higgledy-piggledy community of decent-looking artisans and their wives and hordes of children wandering East to settle, and a fair sprinkling of harum-scarum young fellows, always smoking cigarettes and diving into every buffet and shouting for *pevo* (beer), and making mock attempts to pitch one another out of the window. The mass, however, of my fellow travellers were the moudjiks, shaggy men with big sheepskin hats that gave them a ferocious air, wearing rough-spun cloaks and often with sacking tied around their feet instead of boots. The women were fat and plain, though the colours of their dresses were often startling in brilliancy. Gaudy orange was popular. The lavatory accommodations, even in a first-class car, was limited, and as it was for the joint use of both sexes it was a cause of frequent embarrassments. Ablutions had to be performed singly, and for two hours each morning there was a little crowd of unwashed and semi-dressed men and women standing about the corridor, all smoking cigarettes, women as well as men, and each eyeing their neighbour with side glances of distrust lest there was some underhand move to get possession of the lavatory first. . . .*

"I spent hours among these emigrants and found them interesting. They were horribly dirty, and as they liked to have the windows closed, despite the temperature, the cars reeked with odour. They carried all their worldly possessions with them, some foul sleeping rugs and some bundles of more foul clothing, which was spread out on the hard seats to make them a little less hard. Bread, tea, and melons was the chief food. . . . Besides bread-eating, and scattering half of it on the floor, and munching melons and making a mess with the rind, and splashing the water about when tea-making, there was the constant smoking of cigarettes. . . . The emigrants were happy — there was no doubt about that. Though the faces of the men were heavy and animal, guile was not strong about them. The cars rang with their coarse laughter. . . . [At night] the men lay back loungingly, like weary labourers caught with sleep in the midst of toil. On the seat beside the man, huddled up, with her face hid in her arms, was the wife. Lying on the floor, with a bundle of rags as pillow, were the children. I had to step over a grey-whiskered old man, who was curled up in the gangway — a feeble, tottering creature to emigrate. Close to the door was an old woman, her face hanging forward and hidden, and her long, bare, skinny arms

* Under normal circumstances, Russian and Siberian villagers cleansed themselves with steam baths taken at home or in a communal shed heated by an immense stove. In cities, bathhouses for the lower classes consisted of two large rooms, where the separated sexes paid a few cents per person to scrub and sweat in a murk of almost suffocating steam. In establishments for the more particular who were willing to pay from twenty-five cents to a dollar and a half, there were private units comprising a dressing room and an alcove with bath, from which the patron entered the "Turkish bath" proper, a steam room with several wooden benches arranged near a blazing stove.

drooping over her knees. It was all very pathetic in that dim, uncertain candle flare. There was no sound but the snore of deep-sleeping men and the slow rumble of the moving train."

Almost without exception, these little people of the Tsar showed uninhibited friendliness to the foreigner and, whether or not he understood a word of Russian, fired questions at him like clamorous children consumed by curiosity. "Who are you?" "Where are you from, and where are you going?" "How old are you?" "How many millions of rubles have you got?" "What do you think of our country?" A stranger with some knowledge of the language had only to keep his ears open on the long journey to learn, among other things, that it spelled bad luck to begin a journey on a Monday, that babies are best soothed with opium made from home-grown poppies, and that the coffins of the wicked will float even as they are being lowered into graves water-filled by spring thaw.

Since food and drink were unobtainable on the train, passengers got off at stations to stock up with whatever was available. On their return, frightful altercations broke out when some found their quarters usurped by newcomers. If the conductor merely shrugged shoulders and refused to dislodge the invaders, the more ingenious victims vanished from sight, misleading those in possession to believe it safe to get off for a drink at the next station. The original occupants then rushed back, heaved the enemies' bags and bundles into the corridor, replaced their own, and regained their bunks and dignity.

"The mingling of the sexes in sleeping quarters was at first embarrassing," reported Wright and his fellow journalist Bassett Digby. "At Tcheliabinsk we had captured two bunks, an upper and a lower. The opposite seats were occupied by an old grandmother and a young girl. By day we sat face to face, hardly an arm's reach separating us. But not until the second night did we grow accustomed to this twenty-year-old girl pulling off her boots and generally disrobing, though it was rather annoying when she took a notion to roll a cigarette about midnight and insisted on scattering half the tobacco on the face of the one of us who happened to be asleep on the shelf below. . . . There was still another rather annoying feature to our third class train. Every hour throughout the day and three or four times during the night, the conductor and two assistants raked through the train with a fine-toothed comb, ticket clipping and inspecting. Thirty-one times were our tickets clipped before we reached Omsk. On the twenty-fifth occasion, we begged the conductor to clip them five times and leave us in peace for a day, but he evidently believed in conserving his simple pleasures for a more leisurely enjoyment."

East of Chelyabinsk, in winter, the snow-blanketed expanses of the steppe stretched endlessly, unbroken save by melancholy clumps of birches huddled together as if for warmth, or by a green church dome and thin plumes of chimney smoke from a half-buried village in the distance. Now and then, the eye fell on frozen streams cut by sledge runners, with sometimes a peasant woman or two rinsing laundry in a hole through the ice. Or when the train approached a settlement, one might glimpse, as Jefferson did, "a caravan of patient horses waiting to cross, with white frost hard on their shaggy coats, and icicles from their eyes and nostrils; a sheepskin-clad moujik, with fur hat over eyes and ears, and feet encased in huge felt boots, complacently puffing at a stunted *papiros*." Hamlets were drearily alike: a tiny wooden station, stacks of firewood for locomotives, a single, hard-rutted road with cabins careening within broken fences — the whole calling to mind the forlorn lament throughout the empire, "God is too high and the Tsar too far."

At lower right: wooden bridge and the Siberian post road, or Trakt

In summer, desolate Siberia becomes so marvelously transformed that one feels that Nature must have summoned all her powers to erase her glacial visage from memory. Buttercups and daisies, orange lilies, violets, clover, forget-me-nots, and Queen Anne's lace burst from the soil which, in a peasant saying, "laughs with the harvest when tickled by the hoe." Their boughs no longer heavy with snow, willowy birches stand straight and slim like "the white ladies of the forest" they were called. The plains are vast swaths of green fields over which hooded crows flap and caw, lazily indifferent to the train, while black and white magpies flash past on apparently demented courses. In the middle distances, marsh hawks soar above reedy lakes, and flocks of startled wild ducks and geese on ponds nearer by scud away with a whir of wings one can almost hear. At various points along the line, the Trakt lies only fifty feet away, dusty and potholed today as in former times. Tarantasses have vanished, but horse-drawn telegas

Central Siberian village

and other farm carts are still almost as common as the Trakt's wooden bridges over streams. Villages that appeared so god-forsaken in winter seem to have sprung magically to life, with the bright scarlets and greens of geraniums and the yellow heads of sunflowers in tiny gardens; swallows darting in and out of birdhouses on tall birch poles; and flotillas of ducklings in mudholes, where naked youngsters stop their dabbling to wave frantically at the train.

During runs through the pines and larches of the taiga, passengers on the early Trans-Siberian often caught sight of frightened moose and deer galloping away from the snorting iron horse. Whenever smoke from forest fires darkened the sky, everyone crossed himself and muttered prayers that the train might not become engulfed in the blaze. "Further on we

This contemporary log house along the Trans-Siberian is a close match of an old post station

saw the fire at its fiendish work," Annette Meakin relates. "Blue smoke curled through the forest to our right, and a strong smell of burning permeated the air. Blackened trunks lay smouldering on the ground, and now and again the stump of what must have been once a king of the forest was blazing and crackling like a log fire." Started by lightning, careless hunters, or irresponsible settlers who burned off underbrush for the better growth of edible berries later, Siberia's terrible conflagrations consumed thousands of acres of rich timberlands every year.*

* One of Siberia's most spectacular forest fires was kindled on June 30, 1908, by the "Tunguska Marvel," a cosmic body or nuclear explosion that devastated an area of almost five hundred square miles surrounding the present hunting base of Vanavara, in the taiga about four hundred and fifty miles northeast of Krasnoyarsk. The blast was so tremendous that seismographs of Irkutsk Observatory registered an earthquake; barographic instruments in England recorded an air wave that twice circled the globe;

Little girl selling berries in paper cones; behind her stands a peasant woman with a baked potato for sale

At burgeoning towns and new settlements where the train stopped for anywhere from half an hour to three or four, foreigners took photographs of the dynamic pioneer scene. From these illustrations and the descriptions in their published works, we can see the carpenters hammering together a church, settlers' homes, and warehouses; stethoscoped doctors examining caterwauling babies at station-side clinics; tempo-

and American observatories reported atmospheric turbidity, though there had been no volcanic eruptions to account for this phenomenon. The conclusions of Russian investigating expeditions are in some disaccord, but highly technical evidence indicates that the explosion occurred several kilometers above the earth's surface, and that it may have been produced by atomic energy rather than by a meteor or a comet. The mystery has been so far from being solved that reputable Soviet scientists have even given serious, if somewhat cautious, consideration to a theory advanced by Alexander P. Kazantsev in 1946. This Russian engineer and science-fiction writer maintained that a gigantic nuclear-powered spaceship from somewhere in the universe blew up when it went out of control on an exploratory approach to earth. Most of the Soviet scientific community reject this theory on the grounds that, as one of the investigators has said, "There are no planets with a highly organized life from which such a ship could descend."

rarily stranded immigrants herded together round one of the food stations the government was establishing along the line; convicts stretching out begging hands from the iron-barred windows of an *arestantski* train on a siding, where there might also be a long-haired priest blessing a cluster of peasants and railway employees beside a church car; white-jacketed military bandsmen tooting horns and thumping drums in honor of gold-trimmed officers before their departure with morose conscripts to other garrisons; barefooted, tatterdemalion urchins playing hide-and-seek under boxcars being loaded with hides and tallow beside a newly built processing plant; small girls selling paper cones of blackberries still moist with morning dew; and, at every one of these stations, drunken old muzhiks sprawled over their bundles, sottishly dead to the raw, vigorous life of a Siberia awakened and transfigured by the Trans-Siberian Railway.

A contemporary muzhik lounging on a telega

Sightseers seldom lingered at Omsk. This hub of an extensive agricultural and dairying region was a singularly unattractive, storm-wracked city with wretched hotels and little of touristic interest but a grandiose modern cathedral, a "Yermak Banner" said to have been borne by Siberia's first Russian conqueror, and a small, crescent-crowned mosque for Kirgiz sheepherders and southern Moslem traders who brought wool and hides to market on camels with pads rag-bound, in winter, against the snow and ice.

Tomsk, on the other hand, offered curiosities well worth the two-day journey from Omsk and the nine-hour wait at Taiga station for a decrepit train to take one on the branch line to this "rollicking, wealthy city . . . half full of millionaires and ex-convicts," as Fraser found it in 1901. Tomsk looked down scornfully on rival cities because it possessed Siberia's sole university, though this institution had only medicine and law faculties and an enrollment of not many more than five hundred students in 1900. Fraser describes the university buildings as "handsome," an adjective he would never apply to his hotel, the Europe. ". . . It reeked with paint. The paint on the floor of my room came off like the tar on a freshly asphalted sidewalk," he says in some dudgeon. "Everything was blue, red, and gold. At one end of the dining hall was a huge, up-to-date barrel organ, for all the world like the organs that accompany roundabouts at English fairs, only bigger. There were the harsh brass and rattling drums, clanging cymbals, and in front was a toy figure of a man with right arm jerking up and down, beating time wrong. At present this organ is the sensation of Tomsk. It makes such a row that one's appetite disappears."

Jefferson had been unable to get rooms at the Europe but, more fortunate than Fraser in another respect, he visited the

Imperial gold-smelting laboratory. "I was . . . shown into the safety vaults, where was stored something like two hundred poods [almost 7223 pounds, then worth about $2,389,000] of smelted gold. The deep dungeons of mediaeval history may be compared to the safety vaults at the Tomsk laboratory. Subterranean passages, guarded by heavily armed soldiers; ponderous iron gates and doors; keys a foot long; rusty hinges, bolts; and all that sort of thing. Four soldiers took us into the store-room, where three enormous iron safes let into the walls glared at us. . . . There, reposing on shelves, lay bars of the dull yellow metal, representing some millions of roubles and the work of thousands of men for many months. I had the opportunity of trying to carry as much gold as I could lift . . . it would have been sufficient to have made my Siberian journey distinctly remunerative — if I had been allowed the further opportunity of getting away with it. But there were too many soldiers about; far too many revolvers, guns, swords, big gates, ponderous locks, and such things as that . . . [and so] I went out as poor as I entered . . ."

Wright and Digby were fascinated by the great market on the bank of the Tom, where all the food was frozen: if you wanted less butter or half a fish, you hacked off the piece of your choice with a hatchet. Near the market, the American and the Briton prowled into an eating place of the poor, and were astonished to find that, contrary to American custom of the time, the drinks and not the lunch were free. "At the end of a long table stands a great brass hot water urn, the *samovar,*" they recalled. "Ranged eight a side are the peasants who have come in to market with their rude sledges loaded with produce or logs. They are very dirty and very happy; their garments are an extraordinary sight. A patchwork pure and simple, a patched medley of sheepskin, rabbit pelt, sackcloth, scraps of grimy linen and flannel and shoddy cloth rags, sewn together with string and frayed twine. . . . At the other end of the room, seated at small tables, are the better class customers, hackmen and market porters for the most part, as dirty as the peasants but dressed in good, if shabby, coats, with gaudy girdles around the waist. Entertaining them are the musicians — a derelict with bandaged stumps where his hands should be,* accompanied by a well-dressed little girl of fourteen who plays a discordant harp; a disreputable peasant youth, who also has a harp and plays it even worse; a lad with a one-legged hurdy-gurdy strapped round his neck; and three Jews with an accordion. . . . The beggars are an interesting feature of the market eating-house of Tomsk. The swing doors fling open, and in they stride. After warming their hands at the stove, they walk to the counter and cross themselves. Instantly the bartender hands over a large lump of bread — not stale bread nor crusts; perfectly good new bread. No remark passes on either side. The beggar drops the gift into a tattered rent in his garments, crosses himself and departs to the next eating-house. . . . There are other beggars one likes less, blue-cheeked, shivering little mites of girls, bare-legged, their skirts in rags, who have only just enough strength to push back the heavy door. Often they have no coats nor cloaks, and the snow is their only shawl. They go direct to the counter, too chilled to heed the inviting glow of the stove. The numb little fingers make the Sign of the Cross, and then, hugging the precious slices of bread to their bosoms, the children turn and shuffle away, out into the snows."

* In explanation of the uncommonly large number of men with amputated limbs one saw throughout the empire, it has been said that the victims had collapsed from drink after leaving taverns on winter nights, and, falling asleep in the snow, suffered such severe frostbite that they were lucky to escape at no greater cost than the loss of a hand or a foot.

But for all its mendicants, Tomsk was alive with enterprising citizens. The editor of the daily newspaper was a noteworthy example cited by Wright and Digby. When he received a report that the Russian ambassador at Peking had been murdered, he hurriedly printed the story on handbills, but before these could be hawked about, official denials poured in. The editor was not one to resign himself to the loss of costly paper and ink, and so he rushed through the press a fresh batch of handbills with "Startling Sequel!" as banner head. Handing out both the original and the new bills, he explained his strategy to the newsboys. They ran the streets crying "Horrible Assassination!" until the "Horrible Assassination!"s sold out, then waited ten minutes before running the streets again with the "Startling Sequel!"s which they also sold out, to the immense satisfaction of their employer. The resourcefulness of this editor contrasts strikingly with the folly of the proprietor of the Tomskian weekly journal *Siberian Truth:* when an entire issue was censored out of existence because of the revolutionary effusions of a young reporter he had hired, the proprietor could think of no solution for his difficulties but to get rid of the man, an unpleasant business he disposed of by shooting him dead.

Krasnoyarsk, the next major city beyond Tomsk, was a flourishing Yenisei River port, but offered so few attractions (save for the 80,000-volume library of the distiller Yudin) that most foreigners continued on to Irkutsk. Annette Meakin and her mother were exceptions, and "found Krasnoiarsk a flourishing Russian colony . . . proud of its public gardens, they are the best in Siberia, for in most towns it has been difficult to make the trees grow." While mailing letters to England, Miss Meakin took care to register them, for otherwise the stamps might be removed and sold by postal employees. "If you do not register in Siberia," she remarks, "there is every chance that the stamps will be taken off and the letter destroyed long before it reaches the border. You cannot register after 2 P.M., in which case it is advisable to use a black-edged envelope. Superstition will then prevent its being tampered with."

At Irkutsk, travelers usually stayed at the Hotel Métropole, a large, two-storied, gabled structure of logs with moss stuffed into cracks against the cold. For the extravagant sum of three dollars a day (bed linen, towels and candles being extra, as Baedeker had warned*), one could get a sitting room draped with heavy velvet curtains, and a bedroom in which a straw mattress lay "in the little wooden-bottomed box called a bed," observes an American engineer named Lindon Bates, Jr. Though the month might be June, the double windows would still be hermetically sealed with putty and paper tape except for a single pane that could be swung open in both windows. To call the waiter (not infrequently a time-expired murderer, since this type of criminal was considered more trustworthy as a servant than other ex-felons, Jackson avers), you shouted down the corridor. In the experience of the Meakins, the manager understood German, "but he was invariably out, or asleep in bed when we wanted him to interpret. When surrounded by six gaping waiters I asked for a spoon [but] they brought me a glass of vodka!"

Like most hotels throughout the empire, the Métropole had no lounges, parlors, or smoking room, the lack of which a

* In extenuation, it should be pointed out that hotelkeepers assumed that travelers had their own bedding and towels, and, if not, expected them to pay for any supplied. According to Sir Donald Mackenzie Wallace — a distinguished correspondent of the London *Times* in the nineteenth century — Russians possessed "a kind of fastidiousness to which we are strangers. They strongly dislike using sheets, blankets, and towels which are in a certain sense public property, just as we should strongly object to putting on clothes which had been already worn by other people."

Irkutsk: the Hotel Métropole in 1901

combined restaurant and café chantant supposedly made up for. This rough wooden hall was jammed from 10 P.M. to four in the morning with the usual garrison officers, Jacks-in-office, miners, and merchants, some with wives and others with trollops. All the men swilled liquor and wine as if in passionate defiance of fly-specked wall signs that requested patrons not to get drunk.

"It is very gay — very, very gay," says Bates. "Corks pop, and sweet champagne flows. The call goes up for '*Papirose!*' and more cigarettes and more bottles come thick and fast. Soon there is an air of subdued expectancy, and eager looks are directed to the curtain [of the stage at one end of the room]. Somebody near by leans close and whispers for your enlightenment, 'All-black man!' Out comes an old Southern Negro, who sings to the wondering Russians a Slavonic version of the

'Suwanee River,' between verses delivering himself, with many a flourish, of a clog-dance. Johnson is the man's name. How he drifted so far from Charleston he hardly knows himself. He followed the music-halls to 'Frisco, and somebody, for whom he 'has a razor ready,' told him he would make his fortune in Vladivostok. He kept getting further and further into the interior, picking up the language as he went, and turning his songs into the vernacular. Poor chap, the pathos he puts into the 'Suwanee River'! He is thinking, in frozen Irkutsk, of the old Carolina homestead, and is singing and dancing his way back."

Foreigners who made use of letters of introduction from Prince Khilkov or other important officials found all doors open to them. In Irkutsk, for example, they were usually entertained by the governor-general or, in his absence, the mayor who, in Jackson's experience, "took us happily through his house to show us the electric lights and telephone, all of which were gleamingly new." The photographer was also invited to the monastery of the archbishop of Eastern Siberia. "Far from being a venerable patriarch," Jackson relates in his autobiography, *Time Exposure,* "Archbishop Nikodim was blond, handsome, and not much more than thirty years of age. He was interested in everything, and his charm was irresistible. . . . He received us in a splendid apartment — the Czarevitch had occupied it during his tour of the Empire in 1891 — and served us champagne and chocolates."

Official letters also opened the gates of Aleksandrovski, the only institution of its kind in Siberia. About forty-six miles northwest of Irkutsk, this model penal complex was a disappointment to anyone seeking the horrible conditions George Kennan exposed in the late eighteen-eighties. The great square building looked forbidding enough in contrast to the pretty domes and spires of the convict-built, red-brick church nearby, but inside, the dormitories were clean and the meals moderately well prepared. The twelve hundred-odd inmates, all men without chains, were kept busy as shoemakers, tailors, carpenters, and, ironically enough, locksmiths. Besides a canteen where white bread, cheese, sausages, sardines, and cigarettes could be bought with the small prison wage, there was a joint library and adult school — adorned with lugubrious pictures of the evils of drink — together with a makeshift theater for the performance of concerts and skits by the felons themselves. After a certain period, good-conduct criminals whose wives and children had followed them were permitted to live with them in outside cabins, provided that they reported daily at the prison. For the youngsters, a matron ran a neat, cheerful school.

But Slavophobic journalists could still assert that the Russians had little else to show for their "reforms" since Kennan's revelations. In fact, one of the unsavory, palisaded *étapes* was still in use on the Aleksandrovski grounds. "Every twenty yards there marched hither and thither through the snow a soldier with musket across his shoulder," Fraser reported in his book, *The Real Siberia*. "This was a distributing station, to which batches of convicts are sent from all parts of the Russian Empire to await decision where they shall spend the years of their punishment. Just as we entered a batch of forty men, muffled in heavy grey coats, were starting out in the custody of exactly the same number of soldiers, to walk seventy miles to a small prison up country. . . . The rooms were overcrowded and the stench almost choked me. The men looked dirty and ill-cared for. They had no work; they were just huddled together, waiting often six or eight months before they were sent off. In the yard I caught sight of six . . . boys, the youngest seventeen, the eldest twenty-two, bright and intelligent. . . . They had taken part in some boyish socialistic demonstration against the government. For this they had already been in prison for a year, and were on their way to the dreary frozen province of Yakutsk, under banishment for ten years."

Of all Siberian cities, Irkutsk offered perhaps the most in entertainment. In summer, traveling circuses came to town with jugglers, tumblers, acrobatic bears, and, inevitably, some awesome scientific marvel like "the Hinglishman from Hupper Clapton, who professionally added to the gayety of nations by dying, *coram publico,* thirty-six times a week," Wright and Digby observed. "At least, he held a certificate from a professor at the University of St. Petersburg, stating that he could stop his heart beating for twenty-eight minutes at a stretch, though in Irkutsk he did not make a practice of repeating the full rigor of that feat, for even the satisfying spectacle of a dead Cockney began to bore a Siberian audience after the first ten minutes."

There were band concerts in the park, trotting races, holiday processions of the finest carriages in town, fishing on the Angara, excursion boats to Lake Baikal, and a teeming market to which settlers and Buryats brought crates of woodcock, grouse, and quail, cages of live pigeons and tame white rabbits, and herds of newborn calves. At night, one still had to be on guard against criminals, for murders and robberies were almost as common as they had ever been. But these perils seldom bothered Westerners, who seemed to believe that a passport from Whitehall, Washington, the Quai d'Orsay, or the Wilhelmstrasse bestowed immunity to molestation by the inhabitants of every country save their own. And so they proceeded fearlessly to the banks of the Angara whenever there were evening pyrotechnics of the kind that delighted Fraser at the conclusion of a fête in Omsk. "Then, to wind up, there was a grand explosion of fireworks, whizzing rockets releasing blue and red stars, gorgeous designs, and the mob crying 'O-o-oh!' for all the world like Londoners at the Crystal Palace. The final piece showed the name of the Czar in coloured lights, with a crown above. Everybody cheered and hallooed, and the men waved their hats. And this was in far Siberia, 2,805 versts east of Moscow!"

Until express service was extended from Irkutsk to Baikal, travelers boarded a grubby mail train that took four to five hours to negotiate the innumerable curves and bridges on the forty-two-mile branch. They either sledged or ferried across the lake to another mail train that crawled for three days to Sretensk. Foreigners who knew Russian history or their Baedeker took advantage of a long station-wait at Chita to visit the famous Damskaya Ulitsa, or "Ladies' Street," where the Princesses Volkonskaya and Trubetskaya and other aristocrats had lived in two rows of huts to be near their exiled husbands. But most travelers confined their sightseeing to the station platform which, when Wright and Digby alighted, was thronged with "the hordes of Tartary. Quite 200 Booriats, men, women and children," the writers continue, ". . . surged out to the hack stand and eagerly sifted transportation bids. The tribe in its curious hats and richly colored garments, the women wearing in their hair and dangling on cords handfuls of strange metal trinkets that would have been the envy of a museum curator, bargained fiercely for many minutes with the *istvostchiks* before resigning itself to a minimum rate of forty *kopecks* for as many as could crowd into each little chaise." *

* On Greener's authority, it appears that Buryat girls with several children, preferably by different fathers, were more sought after in marriage than were virgins, for they had produced living evidence "to prove how

The transcontinental track that seemed to go on forever finally came to an end at Sretensk. Passengers with the temerity to continue to the Pacific in winter were now on their own. Before them lay a journey of fourteen hundred miles down the frozen Shilka and Amur rivers to Khabarovsk. Like Jackson, who had traveled in the opposite direction in the winter of 1895-1896, they had to buy sledges, hire horses and drivers, and provision themselves with frozen bread, frozen steaks and cutlets, and blocks of frozen soup and milk, besides tea, sugar, and other essentials. Ordinarily, they stopped only long enough to change horses and driver at post stations and to thaw out and devour a meal. *Yamshchiki* held to a furious pace, bumping and slewing over rough river ice with occupational unconcern for the apprehension and discomfort of their passengers. When the latter reached Khabarovsk more than ten days later and boarded a Ussuri train for Vladivostok, they might look back, again like Jackson, on scenes which had hardly changed since his time: fetid posthouses, broad-antlered reindeer with riders perched high on the shoulders of the beasts, Goldi hunters clad in dogskins from head to feet, and, perhaps most unforgettable of all, one of the Russian military caravans totaling a thousand sledges pulled by as many Bactrian camels winding silently in Indian file like a serpent on the snow.

It is possible but unlikely that someone in a moment of aberration has said a good word for Sretensk as it appeared in summer. This military post and former penal center was inhabited by Russian immigrants, Chinese market gardeners, and

highly esteemed they are by men." The Buryats, it may be mentioned again and not in elaboration of the previous sentence, have long been regarded as the most intelligent of Siberian natives.

Goldi hunter on the snow and ice ripples of the frozen Amur

The American photographer William Henry Jackson took this and the picture on page 74 in the winter of 1895-1896

Cossacks described by a fellow traveler of Miss Meakin's as "great riders, great drinkers and great sleepers." Cows and pigs wandered through the unpaved streets six inches deep in dust, which rain turned to muck. The settlement's shantytown aspect was enhanced by Chinese opium and tea-drinking dens and drab shops with outside signs picturing a fur coat, a kettle, or a chunk of meat for the benefit of the population, more than ninety per cent of which could neither read nor write. The tracks of the Transbaikal line came to an end on the opposite riverbank, where travelers endured long waits for the ferry that carried only a few passengers and baggage carts at a time. Latecomers at the two hotels were turned away and forced to put up at rooming houses little better than the "cowshed" Annette Meakin describes in her book, *A Ribbon of Iron*. "The room contained a wretched bed and a worse sofa; the springs of the latter were broken and rose in lumps with pointed corners . . . A few planks with great spaces between them, and a sheet hung over the whole, was all that separated us from our next neighbour, who snored loudly. Two sides of the room had windows without shutters, and the fourth side a door with cracks." One of the hotels was only a little better, Harold S. Clark discovered. Now a retired teacher living at Sagamore Beach, Massachusetts, Mr. Clark was twelve years old when he kept a diary of his Siberian journey in 1900 with his parents, the Reverend Dr. and Mrs. Clark. "On one side of the river was Stretinsk [*sic*] and on the other the Railway," he recorded in *My Journal*. "We had a very bad room with one bed and a lounge. Papa slept on the bed and Mama and I slept on chairs and the sofa but papa got all the flees [*sic*]."

From this dismal backwater, flat-bottomed steamers and barges conveyed passengers and cargo on the shallow Shilka to Pokrovka, a hamlet near the head of the Amur proper,

Siberian river boat

about two hundred and forty miles northeast of Sretensk. Among the mainstays of the fleet were the *Rurik*, which Burton Holmes called "a sad old corpse of a steamer," and the barge *Diana* that was coaxed along by a tugboat when exceptionally low water held deeper-draft vessels in port. On this virtual scow, there were two first-class cabins, one for men and the other for women, and open deck space for third-class passengers — a horde of Orientals and immigrant peasants who stormed aboard with bedding, bundles, jangling kettles, bawling children, Mongolian sheep, and pet dogs, cats, and hares, the chaos rising to crescendo as cursing deck hands yanked ticketless Chinese coolies ashore by their pigtails. The food was so atrocious, said the elder Clark, that an irascible fellow voyager sprang from the table, flung his plate overboard, and hurled a full bottle of beer at the waiter.

Hardly an hour passed without the jar and scrape of the barge's bottom against the gravelly riverbed. Whenever the *Diana* stuck fast, her tug grunted and churned, in most instances pulling her off in a few minutes. In the summer of

1901, however, the tug itself grounded, narrowly escaped a ramming by the barge, and remained hard-fast on a bar for eighteen hours until the crew, unable to shove off with poles, finally managed to anchor a cable ashore and haul her into deeper water with a windlass. On each approach to lengthy shallows, the *Diana* discharged passengers on a riverbank, then picked up the pedestrian voyagers a mile or so down, or wherever the going was clear.

Since navigation on the shoaly Shilka was even more precarious at night, the barge and towboat anchored alongshore just before dusk. Third-class passengers streamed down a gangplank, put their sheep out to graze, and built bonfires against the chill air and the pests of eastern Siberia — inch-long, green-eyed horseflies whose needle-like sting made victims jump with pain. After the evening meal which they would have otherwise cooked on a stove under one of the ship's hatches, "pipes are smoked," says Holmes, "and stories are told."

Three days and nights out of Sretensk, the *Diana* reached deeper water at Pokrovka, where her voyagers were transferred to the *Admiral Chikhachev,* or a similarly roomy paddle-wheeler with first- and second-class cabins, a dining room, and a lounge; the afterdeck, relegated to third-class rabble, was partly covered to give some protection from the hot noonday sun and billows of funnel smoke and sparks. Among the first-class passengers Clark, Fraser, and other foreign travelers observed on their respective trips were European salesmen, a school inspector who drank Crimean wine all day and snored all night, a Russian officer's frowsy, chain-smoking wife who strewed the floor with cigarette ends and ashes, and a fur merchant's wife who, if asked to pass the butter, did so by handing over a piece with her fingers. Fraser's cabin in the

Chikhachev crawled with cockroaches.* Meals costing all of a dollar and a quarter a day per person were brought in by a waiter who doubled as cook, steward, and general drudge. Midday and evening fare seldom varied from meat-and-onion hash, oily potatoes, and underdone peas and macaroni dumped on a communal platter from which diners fished out their portions with knife and fork.

The *Chikhachev* drew two and a half feet. But some of her skippers seemed to believe that they could navigate on a heavy dew, or even on ice-pitcher sweat, as Clark remarked of Mississippi River captains. They frequently grounded despite the warning cries of two crewmen at the bow who probed the water depth with poles and sang out soundings once a minute. When passengers heard "Four," "Three and a half," "Three," and the electrifying "Two and a half!" they waited for that sudden surge of engine power that would either shoot the ship safely over the shallows or drive her hard on the bar, where, with a subsequent fall in water level, she might lie heeled over like the *Admiral Putyatin,* which had been stranded for seventeen days with two hundred people aboard.

Holmes was an eyewitness to this event in 1901. "The neighboring village has been eaten out of house and home, the last

* Our foreign voyagers in Siberia avoid any mention of fellow passengers in the form of rats, those "agile, bloodthirsty parasites" Sir Donald Mackenzie Wallace encountered on Don River steamers in Russia. When the Briton asked for a cabin, the captain said that he would be only too glad to comply. " 'I have always on board a large body of light cavalry,' he remarked, 'and when I have all this part of the ship to myself they make a combined attack on me; whereas, when someone is sleeping close by, they divide their forces!' " Subsequently, Wallace found a rat in his bunk and gave it a savage kick, greatly to the outrage of a cabin-mate, who protested "on the ground that, though he was willing to take his own share of the intruders, he strongly objected to having other people's rats kicked into his berth." The next day, Wallace told the captain that the rat had escaped. "After listening to me patiently, he coolly replied . . . , 'Ah! I did better than that this morning; I allowed my rat to get under the blanket, and then smothered him!' "

loaf of bread and the last string of Siberian pretzels have been purchased. No one has thought of telegraphing a complaint to the administration for sending out a boat with a three and one-half foot draft to ascend a river two feet deep. It is not the Russian way. It is not considered good form to criticize anything. The proper attitude is one of absolute indifference, the proper thing to say is '*Nitchevo.*' The word means literally 'nothing,' and yet it means everything. It sounds the keynote of the Russian character — 'nitchevo.' There's nothing to be done. Nothing is wrong. Nobody is to blame. What's the use of bothering? It will be all the same in a thousand years. 'Nitchevo.' "

When the *Chikhachev* grounded, all hands followed standard practice by turning to with long, heavy spars to lever the hull free. If the spars broke, the crew then tried the anchor-and-windlass technique to warp her off. This failing, passengers were transferred by boat to the riverbank while the captain made further efforts to float the lightened vessel. Everyone usually enjoyed these obligatory shore excursions in spite of the horseflies, hornets, mosquitoes, and gnats for which the Amur is notorious. In the muggy heat, third-class passengers bathed in the sweet, cool river — women upstream, men downstream, and children all along the bank, as Holmes relates. If a settlement were nearby, the inhabitants promptly showed up, "each woman hugging two or three bottles of milk," says Clark, "or carrying a pail of butter or a basket of eggs or a bowl of sour cream or a great loaf of black bread, with a hole in the middle like a huge doughnut. Sometimes a woman would appear holding a large goose in her arms as tenderly as though it were a baby, the body of the goose being concealed in the blouse that covered her ample bosom, while its long neck craned out, exhibiting as much interest in the passing show as any one on the shore."

From their own mysterious stores, the pigtailed, straw-hatted Chinese concocted mysterious messes and chattered like monkeys with astonishing news to tell. What with mothers in pursuit of straying small fry, men fishing from the river edge or sleeping with cap over eyes, the scene resembled an encampment of holidayers on a carefree outing. "The youngsters . . . would come back from the meadows laden with great armfuls of beautiful wild flowers," Clark continues. "Lilies of the valley seemed to abound everywhere, violets, blue and white forget-me-nots, lady slippers, and another beautiful orchid somewhat similar, which I have never seen elsewhere. In other places, blue honeysuckles were found, and yellow lilies, and Solomon's seal, and the yellowest of buttercups."

Again underway, one began to be bored by the white-birch groves and rolling hills that repeated themselves endlessly. But occasionally the eye was refreshed by a gaudily painted, high-sterned junk anchored off the Manchurian side, or rafts of trussed timbers swarming with immigrant families, horses, cattle, dogs, and household goods towed by one of the new tugs the government subsidized for the development of the Russian "Great East." Every so often, there was a humble Cossack hamlet consisting of a few earth-banked huts, a store, a little church, and, in honor of the Tsarevich Nicholas's visit on his journey westward from Vladivostok in 1891, a weathered triumphal arch of only two rough-hewn uprights topped by a crossbar.

Visibility and water depth permitting, the *Chikhachev* steamed at night as well as by day, for the channel was marked every few hundred yards with oil lanterns on high posts. Before twilight, the setting sun transformed the Amur into what seemed to be a river of claret, over which a purple haze enveloped natives in slim dugouts on their rounds to light the lamps, white on the Russian side and red on the Chinese. As evening darkened, "the moon, seeming larger than we sight it in old England," Fraser was moved to write later, "hung like a great silver lantern in the high south, and the steamer followed its quivering reflection down river as though it were the appointed trail."

Approximately three days after sailing from Pokrovka, the *Chikhachev* reached Blagoveshchensk, " 'The town with the swear name,' as I have since heard it called . . ." Annette Meakin remarks. The inhabitants styled it "the New York of Siberia" because it was a hustling, expensive city with streets laid out at right angles in the American pattern. This capital of the central Amur also had a high rate of violence. ". . . It is a poor week that does not see five or six cold-blooded slaughters," Wright and Digby declared, ". . . [and] fifteen suicides each Easter Week for the past three years." The 1897 census showed a population in excess of thirty-two thousand, the largest urban concentration in the Siberian Far East, Vladivostok not excepted. Although one-storied wooden houses predominated, there were a few three-storied buildings, brick churches and a Public Club of stone, and several big department stores where you could buy almost anything from pipes and pickles to indigo and icons, Clark noted. These emporiums were run mainly by Germans or Russians from the Baltic provinces. One of the best was that of Kunst and Albers, an aggressive German chain that operated in far eastern Siberia. The Blagoveshchensk manager was particularly enterprising: on a Sunday or other sacred holiday, he respectfully locked the front door and drew down all the window curtains, but, "like

The Grand Hotel at Blagoveshchensk

the saloons in Maine," says Clark, the back door was left open so that business could be conducted as usual. One of the prides of the city was the blue and white Grand Hotel, a many-porched and balconied affair with electric lights and a reputation as the finest hostelry in Siberia. In 1900, the management charged as much as five dollars a day for a room, plus a daily supplement of forty-five cents for bed linen and towels. The proportionately expensive meals tasted of bad butter, the eggs were uneatable, and the bread sour, though the coffee — at twenty-five cents a cup — was excellent, in the experience at least of the Meakins, who had left the city only a few days before "the black Crime of Blagoveshchensk." In July 1900, the entire Chinese colony of several thousand innocent men, women, and children were driven at bayonet point into the Amur and forced to drown by panicky Cossack troops who had been fired at from the Manchurian shore during the Boxer Rebellion. The massacre aroused worldwide indignation, but the military governor was merely relieved of command and assigned to another post.

The finest steamers plying between Blagoveshchensk and Khabarovsk were government-owned vessels of the type Dr. Clark has described. ". . . The *Baron Korff* was a stately side-wheeler, such as might have done duty on the Mississippi before the railroads robbed her of her commercial glory. The first-class accommodations were well forward, and consisted of roomy and comfortably furnished staterooms for about twenty people on the upper deck, each room having berths for two people, a long dining-saloon, into which the staterooms opened, and a pleasant saloon in front, handsomely furnished and provided with a good German piano. This saloon made a delightful sitting-room for the passengers, for its abundant glass furnished a splendid view of the river and the banks on either side, between which the *Baron* made her devious way. Behind the first-class cabins was a large open space, sheltered from the wind, and suitable for a promenade. Here was a restaurant and bar, frequently patronized by some of our thirsty fellow-passengers, while behind it were the second-class cabins, which looked to me nearly as comfortable as those at the other end of the ship. Down below were huddled a miscellaneous crowd of peasants — men, women, and children — with their scant piles of bedding and all their worldly possessions; sturdy men in top boots and figured gowns belted at the waist, often with a sleeveless vest worn outside; women in gay calicoes and hobnailed shoes; children clad in little more than nature's original raiment — all were here. On the hard iron floor they spread out their quilts, piled their household goods about them, and prepared to make the best of their six days in the bowels of the *Baron Korff*. Their accommodations were not luxurious, certainly, but when we re-

Shilka-Amur steamers laid up for the winter at Blagoveshchensk

member that they paid but three roubles and six kopeks for the entire 918 versts, more than six hundred miles, to Blagavestchensk [*sic*], or only about one dollar and a half, we cannot think that the accommodations were disproportionate to the price." The first- and second-class fares, Clark records, amounted to the equivalent of approximately $11.50 and $7 respectively.

The downstream voyage came to an end at the magnificently located but drab transportation, trading, and military center of Khabarovsk. There, travelers entrained for Vladivostok, a thirty-hour journey that "was jolt and jerk and bump all day and all night long," Fraser comments. "I felt at times that if only the engine managed to get off the metals the running might have been easier. Long sweeps of the line were under repair, fresh metals being put down and better ballasting provided. All the work was done by soldiers, well-built young fellows, with their shirts open at the throat, their braces hanging loose, and a little yellow-banded cap stuck on the back of their heads."

Had their paths crossed, Fraser might have added to his collection of Siberian characters a river pilot encountered by Jackson on an Ussuri stern-wheeler a few years before. "Everything seemed to me to be going all right," the photographer narrates, "but suddenly a wild bellow of rage issued from the wheel house, and we were treated to as fine a recital of old-fashioned Yankee blankety-blank-blanks as I had heard since I left the Army. The virtuoso completed his damnation of all oriental deck hands and then came out to greet us. His name was Harwood (or Hardman), he came from Maine, he had learned his art on the Mississippi and the Missouri, and he was 'god-damned proud to have some folks from home to visit with.' "

Picture-posing before an Ussuri River stern-wheeler

CHAPTER XV

Ordeal in the Orient

IN the summer of 1897, work began on the Chinese Eastern Railway, a bold, dual-purpose undertaking by Russia to attain economic and political supremacy in China and to shortcut the long and difficult route to Vladivostok via the northern bank of the Amur.

Besides the invaluable roadsteads of Talienwan and Port Arthur coveted by St. Petersburg, Manchuria possessed an abundance of precious-fur animals, gold, iron, coal, and soda; her fertile soil was given over to the raising of cattle, silkworms, grain, rice, beans, tobacco, garden produce, ginseng, and poppies for opium; her import and export trade amounted to something in the neighborhood of $73,000,000 a year — altogether excellent reason why the Russians burned with impatience to complete the Chinese Eastern at the earliest possible moment and to entrench themselves — to the exclusion of Japan and the Western Powers — for exploitation of this rich economic and strategic prize.

Construction commenced first on two single-track branches that were to connect the projected railway with the Ussuri line in the east and the Transbaikal line in the west. The eastern branch extended for seventy-odd miles from the present city of Ussurisk, north of Vladivostok, to the Manchurian border at

Pogranichny, and was opened to provisional traffic early in 1899. In the west, Chief Engineer Pushechnikov started the second link not far from Kaidalovo, between Chita and Sretensk and two hundred and fifteen miles from his destination at the Sino-Siberian frontier, where the western leg of the trans-Manchurian railway was to end. He had been on the job for only ten months when the Communication Ministry directed him to finish it in 1901, a year earlier than planned, to conform with an accelerated timetable for completion of the Chinese Eastern. Pushechnikov was handicapped by a labor shortage, outbreaks of Siberian anthrax, typically bitter Transbaikalian winters, and the necessity to bridge half a dozen rivers. But by working crews round the clock, he managed to reach his goal at Manchuria station (now Man-chou-li) in February 1901, well on time though at a cost of $1,620,600

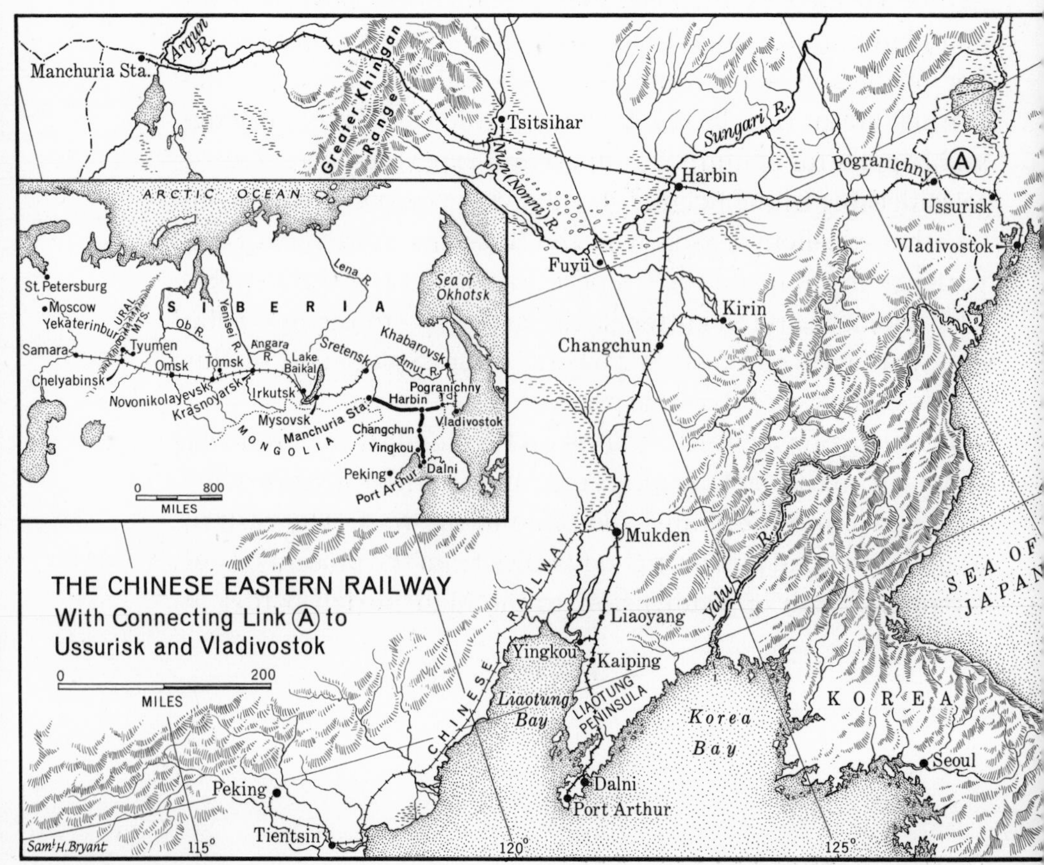

THE CHINESE EASTERN RAILWAY
With Connecting Link Ⓐ to Ussurisk and Vladivostok

0 200 MILES

Alexander I. Yugovich, constructor of the Chinese Eastern Railway

more than the preliminary estimate. Late in October, the branch was opened to regular traffic.

Meanwhile, Alexander I. Yugovich, an exacting and long-experienced chief engineer who had built, among other things, one of the finest railways in central Russia, had begun the Chinese Eastern itself, later described by Witte as having been constructed "under quite peculiar conditions." Other engineers throughout the world have contended with deserts and mountain ranges, arctic cold, rampaging floods, pestilence, bandits, saboteurs, and obstructive officials without number, but Yugovich and his associates were perhaps unique in that they coped with all of these formidable impediments almost simultaneously.

When Yugovich arrived at Vladivostok in April 1897, he lacked detailed knowledge of topographical and climatic peculiarities between the eastern and western terminuses. Surveying parties sent out to explore the proposed route returned with discouraging reports. The few roads were fantastically rough and, during the rainy season, remained impassible quagmires until tediously filled in with brush and innumerable logs. Supply carts could cross the uniformly unbridged rivers and streams only at random fords or on pairs of boats lashed together. In parts of the eastern section, there was wood but no stone; in the western, stone but no wood for upwards of six hundred miles. Fourteen major waterways — icebound for at least four months annually — would require spans of anywhere from eight hundred feet to a half-mile in length. Eight tunnels would have to be bored, one for a distance of nearly two miles through the Greater Khingan Range in the west. Along the entire northern route of nine hundred and twenty-seven miles, there were no utilizable laborers and fewer than six towns, each the periodic prey of Manchurian outlaws, called hunghutzes (literally "red beards"), who terrorized the inhabitants and waylaid traders unless the latter had already taken out insurance.* If not openly hostile to the Russians, local officials were uncooperative. The overwhelming majority of Chinese and Manchus understood not a word of Russian, and interpreters were virtually nonexistent.

For these reasons, Engineer Stanislav I. Kerbedz, the active vice president of the Chinese Eastern Railway Company,

* No one dared to inform against the "red beards," since they were bound together in a loose but fanatically loyal confederation in which each band avenged the betrayal of another. Hence, they operated with such freedom from capture and execution that every sensible shipper of goods to and from the interior submitted to their power. For the convenience of merchants, private insurers (and, it is said, business agents of the hunghutzes themselves) maintained offices in Manchuria's principal cities, where one could pay in advance for immunity and receive a document and little flags which, nailed to carts or river vessels, guaranteed safe passage.

adopted a special construction plan that was approved by Finance Minister Witte, the deciding voice, after the Tsar's, in all matters pertaining to the Russian-held concern. The cardinal requisite of the scheme was to lay a rough work-track at top speed, dispensing with elaborate embankments and even a semblance of ballast, throwing together temporary wooden bridges, and surmounting eminences with gradients limited in steepness solely by the traction power of locomotives to climb them. The makeshift line would then serve for transportation of materials, Russian artisans, and legions of Chinese coolies from Chefoo, Tientsin, and other cities south of Manchuria, who would build the permanent way, erect stone or steel bridges, pierce tunnels, lay heavier, sixty-five-pounds-to-the-yard rails, and, in short, construct a durable single-track railway of the broad Russian gauge. To this end, the first wave of laborers began to work westward from the Ussuri region in August 1897, while others went by rail and water from Vladivostok to Khabarovsk and thence up the Amur and its southern tributary, the Sungari, to the site of Harbin in east-central Manchuria. There, they improved roads and tracked easterly to meet construction parties from the Ussuri, and westerly toward Manchuria station.

As soon as the Russians had wrung Talienwan and Port Arthur from Peking in 1898, the Kerbedz plan of construction was applied also to the South Manchurian line that was to run from Harbin to these two harbors, with a spur to the thriving commercial city of Yingkou (also known as Newchwang), the projected departure point for Chinese trains to Tientsin and Peking. Slightly more than six hundred miles long, the South Manchurian extension-to-be passed through the most densely populated section of the country, a tremendous market for Russian exporters of textiles, hardware, kerosene, and the like, and, in the confident view of the expansionists in St. Petersburg, an open door through which Russia could dominate all of North China to the Central Asian border in the west.

The two hundred thousand and more coolies who ultimately worked on the Chinese Eastern had to be taught, in Witte's words, "processes and kinds of work till then wholly unknown to them," a time-consuming task owing to the scarcity of Chinese interpreters, most of whom were either incompetent or so self-seeking that, in wage-bargaining sessions, they distorted the statements of both sides in order that they themselves might benefit to the greatest degree financially.

Without steam shovels and mechanical earth-movers to help them, coolies dug up soil and dumped it into baskets which they slung on poles and carried to the right of way. As in Transbaikalia, extensive stretches of permanently frozen ground had to be blasted to bits or thawed with fires fueled by wood brought hundreds of miles to the treeless western region, where winter frosts touched almost sixty below. Spring floods and summer cloudbursts of unanticipated violence swept away wooden bridge piers and washed out track for tens of miles, forcing the engineers to rebuild on higher embankments, increase the diameter of drainage culverts, and extend the length of many bridges and trestles half again as much as the previous norms.

Yugovich had fully intended to use a few hundred railway guards for protection of the line, as he was entitled to do under the pact with Peking, but he had not foreseen the need to raise a small army of Cossacks against the roving hunghutzes who raided construction camps for horses and firearms, lay in wait for workers on pay days, and launched piratical attacks on river junks and other supply vessels. Since Chinese officials were antipathetic and shrugged off his demands for troops to deal with the brigands, Yugovich was obliged to increase his initial force of seven hundred police to five thousand, build barracks and watch towers, and maintain mounted patrols along the route. These measures were far from effective, for the hunghutzes infiltrated into camps apparently as workers, and, at the first opportunity, seized rifles, shot the guards, and pillaged the barracks. More often, however, they struck at night from sheltered positions nearby. While one group fired volleys to distract the defenders, another swooped into the workers' compound and snatched off foremen and others as hostages for arms, ammunition, or money. These assaults were executed with such speed and coordination that the hunghutzes usually suffered few casualties and vanished without trace into the hills. Punitive expeditions ran them down only with the utmost difficulty. A typical offensive was that mounted in June 1899 by the chief of railway police after night raiders had slaughtered the sentry and all but one of the sleeping guards at a military post some sixty miles west of Harbin. Fanning out in separate groups, forty-two Cossacks scoured the unfamiliar countryside for ten days until they finally caught up with their quarry. In the subsequent brief engagement, the bandits scattered so swiftly on fresh horses that no more than three were killed and two taken prisoner — a meager reward for the Cossacks, who straggled into Harbin after having ridden eight hundred miles in sixteen days, often without food and water for themselves and their horses.

The "red beards" sometimes joined forces to loot large communities of silver, horses, and weapons. Southwest of Harbin, the city now called Fuyü was sacked and occupied by seven hundred desperadoes, including renegade Russians, until relieved by a Cossack cavalry squadron. The summary decapitation of prisoners (whom the Russians turned over to the

Chinese authorities for punishment) and the display of their severed heads on poles or the limbs of trees failed to deter other hunghutzes from continued forays against construction camps, where kidnapings for ransom occurred almost daily at one point or another along the line. Terrified of capture, Chinese gang-bosses and laborers alike put only halfhearted effort into their jobs and stopped work altogether at the slightest hint of marauders in the vicinity. Consequently, construction lagged while expenses soared; the police alone cost $1,250,000 a year. Yugovich must have found small comfort in the fact that the interpreter problem was resolving itself as Russians and Chinese picked up each other's language.

In the summer of 1899, this stout and deceptively dull-eyed chief engineer was beset by a calamity without parallel in any sector of the Trans-Siberian. At Yingkou, where his subordinates had been receiving supplies and pressing on with construction of the South Manchurian branch, a particularly virulent epidemic of bubonic plague broke out. Yugovich rushed railway doctors to the port while St. Petersburg dispatched additional physicians, bacteriologists, and surgeon's assistants, together with vaccines and disinfectants. With the aid of an international sanitary board under the chairmanship of the British consul at Yingkou, the medical task forces acted swiftly to prevent the contagion from spreading beyond the city. Near Talien, troops cordoned off land approaches to the isthmus; inspection teams boarded steamers and junks at Yingkou and rigidly enforced sanitation rules; vessels making runs between Yingkou and other ports were quarantined for ten days at each harbor; hospital and medical examination stations were established in or near towns and cities as far distant as Mukden, Manchuria's capital, more than a hundred miles to the north. At the Russian-administered railway construction settlement about two miles from Yingkou, sanitation squads removed sewage, filled in refuse pits, dug drainage canals, built an isolated barracks for plague patients, and improvised a disinfecting chamber and quarantine quarters for everyone known to have come in contact with the stricken.

As the panicky employees were on the verge of flight, the Chinese Eastern's board of directors imported a highly revered monk to inspire fortitude, and appointed a priest to live in the camp and relieve anxiety further by his spiritual ministrations. To this incorporeal balm the board added a financial inducement to discourage desertion: if an employee died of plague, his relatives would receive a grant of two thirds of his annual wage multiplied ten times (for example, $4000 in the case of a man making $600 a year). These shrewd measures calmed the workers who, a Russian historian records, "remained at their posts . . . and carried out their duties with selfless devotion." Thanks to the medical corps' vigorous control program, no more than three deaths occurred among the twenty-six hundred persons in the railway construction settlement.

A dramatically different and frustrating situation existed in Yingkou itself. The governing Chinese could not be convinced that plague was infectious and, on the grounds that ancient traditions would be violated, refused to assist in the immediate burial of the dead in a separate plague cemetery, or to remove offal that blanketed the narrow streets of the city, or to disinfect polluted houses and shops. On their part, the foreigners could not adopt a hard line without enraging the people, who might rise against them in bloody defense of the old, familiar pattern of "organized filthiness," as the American author and senator Albert J. Beveridge stigmatized Chinese towns of the period. In the opinion of Yingkou's municipal authorities, the white busybodies were making needless fuss over a matter that could be easily set to rights merely by taking a liberty with the calendar. Since epidemics were released by evil demons, the officials announced, we will advance the date of the New Year; the demons will hear the noisy celebration and, in the belief that they had inexplicably lost track of time, will depart in confusion, taking the epidemic with them.

The inefficacy of this ruse failed to weaken Chinese resistance to the medical staffs even after the distribution of thousands of warning notices in Chinese. Living plague-sufferers were hidden from inspectors for fear that a quarantine would be clamped down on the quarter and thereby hurt trade. Among the poorest classes, corpses were spirited to the city walls, dumped on fields to rot, or simply thrown into the street. Not only the bodies but also the clothing and bedding of the deceased added to contagion, as their relatives used these contaminated belongings without a thought for sterilization.

Better-off Chinese spread the pestilence by their strict adherence to time-honored funeral customs. It was unthinkable to them that anyone should be interred in other than the region from which he had sprung, and so bodies were left outside some shrine or placed in the mortuary of Chinese traders' guildhouses until relatives arrived to escort them to the homeland. There, according to Chinese practice, the coffins were not buried but only covered with earth to form a mound, which wind and rain swept away, exposing the boxes and, eventually, their grisly contents. Relatives went to bizarre lengths to satisfy investigators that their kin had not died from plague: one family, reported a railway doctor, hanged a victim by the neck *after* death in the hope that he would be mistaken for a "healthy" suicide and spared the profane plague cemetery.

The Russians and other foreigners combated Chinese recalcitrance as best they could without inflaming the populace, carted away exposed corpses and coffins, disinfected shops and dwellings, and isolated suspected cases in quarantined observation stations. By November, when the epidemic ended, the death count had mounted to nearly fourteen hundred, not including concealed mortality. But the Russian medical department had achieved its primary objective: the plague had been bottled up in the Yingkou area and prevented from infecting the vitally important railway construction camps. On the other hand, building progress had suffered from the exodus of coolies and by matériel shortages during the height of the shipping season, a number of vessels having been quarantined for a total of fifty and more days at various ports of call. These delays, to say nothing of those imposed by Nature's ravages and hunghutze depredations, put Yugovich behind schedule. Nevertheless, by the spring of 1900, he had obtained labor reinforcements from Russia and had built railway stations and employee housing, replaced some of the wooden bridges with those of metal or stone, and work-tracked more than half of the Chinese Eastern's ultimate fifteen hundred and seventy-six miles. At Harbin, operating headquarters of the railway were under construction; military and naval installations were springing up at Port Arthur; and the development of a garden city and great commercial port had been begun at Talien, which had been renamed Dalni. Their Excellencies in St. Petersburg were determined that nothing should halt the Russian advance into Manchuria.

In May 1900, the antiforeigner Chinese Boxers derailed a train or two and burned a few bridges, but no extensive damage was done until the latter part of June, when Chinese regulars — now aligned with the Boxers — destroyed a hundred and thirty miles of telegraph and railway installations in the Mukden region. Railway police retreated to the south, skirmishing with ambushers on the way. Employees and their families fled north from Mukden in forced marches to Harbin, from which women and children were evacuated in July by Sungari riverboats and barges to Khabarovsk. Sanctioned by Peking, a provincial Chinese governor-general with six thousand men then besieged Harbin, but was temporarily driven off by the numerically inferior though well organized railway police and civilian workers. Meanwhile, two hundred thousand Russian troops had been mobilized by War Minister Alexis N. Kuropatkin, who had welcomed the Boxer Rebellion. "I am very glad," he told Witte. "This will give us an excuse for seizing Manchuria."

Just as Harbin's defenders were running perilously short of ammunition, Russian vessels steamed into sight and disgorged a corps of frontier guards who, like United States Marines in Hollywood productions of a later period, could not have arrived at a more providential moment or made shorter work of the besiegers. In September, Russian detachments left Peking to launch an offensive against Mukden and other Manchurian cities held by rebels and enemy Chinese army units. No match for the Tsar's better-equipped battalions, the insurgents cleared out after an orgy of plundering and burning. In the interim, Kuropatkin's military divisions had been pouring into the country from Transbaikalia and the Amur and Ussuri territories, purportedly to keep the peace but actually to impose a supervisory protectorate over Manchuria to the exclusion of other nations. As a surprisingly outspoken engineer under Yugovich later wrote, ". . . It is an open secret that from the very beginning of the campaign it was the desire of the military party not only to punish the Boxers but also permanently to annex Manchuria."

Well before the last pockets of resistance had been wiped out in December, more than two thirds of the Chinese Eastern built so far had been destroyed. In the ruined sections — totaling five hundred and sixty miles of the eight hundred-odd that had been tracked under an unparalleled combination of adversities — ties, rails, and spikes had been torn up and carried off; telegraph poles had been cut down and the wires stolen; stations and employees' quarters had been burned to the ground; looters had swept administrative buildings clean of every coin, ruble note, and bar of silver bullion; surviving warehouses and workshops were as bare as orchards stripped by locusts; rolling stock had been reduced to irreparable wreckage. In all, the losses came to nearly $35,873,000, for which Russia demanded compensation from China and later received it in part.

Although shorthanded by the flight of Chinese laborers during the insurrection, Yugovich began reconstruction immediately after liberation of each sector from the rebels. Additional workers from Russia were augmented by returning coolies, who were reassured by the presence of the army of occupation; rolling stock was taken from China; locomotives were unshipped from the Baldwin plant in the United States; and the erection of houses and barracks for railwaymen began once again. The chief engineer drove his men so relentlessly that, in November, trains were running from Harbin westward to the vicinity of Tsitsihar, where new track was being laid to meet that under construction easterly from Manchuria station. Three months later, in February 1901, the line from Harbin to Ussurisk, the junction for Vladivostok, was opened to provisional traffic. That July, the particularly hard-hit

South Manchurian branch was restored despite another outbreak of bubonic plague at Yingkou; a special antiplague commission managed to keep fatalities down to a hundred and fourteen persons, of whom only two were Russians.

Finally, on November 3, 1901, the entire Chinese Eastern from Manchuria station to Harbin and Vladivostok and from Harbin to Port Arthur was opened to provisional traffic. About a third of a century before, in 1869, President Ulysses S. Grant and parading throngs had jubilantly saluted the driving of the last spikes on America's first transcontinental railway. But in the Russian empire no such national celebration took place when Yugovich's crews joined the east- and westbound tracks at a point two hundred miles east of Manchuria station. To mark the memorable occasion, however, Witte sent the following message to his sovereign:

"On May 19, 1891 [Old Style], your Majesty, at Vladivostok, turned with your own hand the first sod of the Great Siberian Railway. Today, on the anniversary of your accession to the throne, the East Asiatic Railway is completed. I venture to express to Your Majesty from the bottom of my heart my loyal congratulations on this historic event. With the laying of the rails for a distance of 2,400 versts, from the Transbaikal territory to Vladivostok and Port Arthur, our enterprise in Manchuria is practically, though not entirely, concluded. Notwithstanding exceptionally difficult conditions and the destruction of a large portion of the line last year, temporary traffic can, from today, be carried on along the whole system. I hope that within two years hence all the remaining work to be done will be completed and that the railway can be opened for permanent regular traffic."

To his faithful if often irritatingly opinionated subject, to this indefatigable champion of Russian aggrandizement by means of the Trans-Siberian and Chinese Eastern railways, the Emperor Nicholas telegraphed: "I thank you sincerely for your joyful communication. I congratulate you on the completion within so short a time and amid incredible difficulties of one of the greatest railway undertakings in the world."

Now that trains ran throughout the full length of the Chinese Eastern, Yugovich set about to make improvements, construct additional railway buildings, and finish the erection of permanent bridges, of which there were to be more than six hundred. One of the most arduous tasks that confronted his engineers was the boring of a tunnel more than ten thousand feet long in the desolate, wind-swept Greater Khingan Range, three hundred and fifty miles west of Harbin. Except for the fabrication of workers' barracks, little was accomplished until the westbound track reached the mountains in the autumn of 1901 and was continued to the opposite flank with a circuitous deviation that was to be used by trains pending completion of the tunnel. In September, steam boilers, electrical generators, pumps, compressors, and pneumatic drilling gear arrived by rail and were distributed so that excavation could proceed from both sides.

As in Siberia, Nature seemed determined to thwart the Russians. From September until May, cold waves dropped the thermometer to fifty-eight below and halted outside activities. Less frigid temperatures inside the tunnel allowed drilling to continue, but masonry work was impossible. During spring thaws, water gushed from the unlined walls and inundated the diggings in spite of continual pumping. Foreigners who caught a glimpse of the project were convinced that it would take years to complete, but they were wrong. Ever since the delivery of mechanized equipment, an army of laborers had toiled day and night in three shifts and sometimes bored forty-five feet in twenty-four hours. As the almost incredible result, they holed through in less time than it had taken to pierce the Suram tunnel, longer by about two thousand feet but located in southernmost Russia, where a more temperate climate permitted full-scale operations the year round.

Elsewhere, Yugovich built at a gratifying rate, for he had tens of thousands of coolies whose sheer weight in numbers more than made up for their lack of technical skills save in stonecutting, which they did well. At the beginning of summer in 1902, however, construction suffered another severe setback. An epidemic of Asiatic cholera, which had enveloped a huge area from Shanghai to Tientsin and Chefoo, entered Manchuria through Yingkou. Everyone remembered the terrible summer of 1892, when the last great wave had swept from India and wiped out more than a hundred thousand lives in Persia, Russia, and western Europe. Faced with the possibility of a similar catastrophe, Yugovich and his colleagues moved swiftly to suppress the pestilence in their areas. Special cholera commissions were set up at Yingkou and Harbin. Incoming coolies were segregated and examined, the sick quarantined in the plague barracks of 1899, and the healthy restricted to new quarters prior to their departure northward in disinfected trains, each with a carful of surgeon's assistants and pharmaceutical supplies. Construction camps were cleaned and policed by sanitation squads. Nevertheless, the disease reached Harbin, by that time a mushrooming railway and commercial complex created by the Russians on nine thousand acres bought from China by the railway company. Rigorous measures stopped the epidemic in the city itself but failed to brake its advance along the railway. By the middle of July, only two large centers on the main line and another two on the southern branch remained free from cholera; at other points, fresh cases among Russians varied from one to five a day and, among Chinese, from five to thirty. Almost fourteen hundred Europeans and more than three thousand Chinese were stricken in the railway zone alone; less than half of the former and only a third of the latter survived.

Thousands of still healthy coolies fled from the railway works. Immediate replacements were out of the question, for cholera was also raging in Shantung province, the main source of labor. To make matters worse, bubonic plague erupted again in cities near Yingkou; in a single month, three hundred Chinese died in Kaiping. Yugovich lost practically all of the best working season in the afflicted districts, as well as his hope to complete the permanent way that summer. But at last, in February 1903 — two years behindhand — he opened the Chinese Eastern to regular traffic. Experts generally agreed that it was a solidly built railway, and singled out for special praise the stone bridges of "Roman massiveness."

Witte hailed the enterprise as "a superb work that will do honor to the knowledge of Russian railway engineers." But it had been expensive. Surveys, construction, rolling stock, railway buildings, police, losses in the Boxer Rebellion, and special projects such as the Khingan tunnel had raised costs to almost $173,000,000, not counting financing charges. With the addition of the sums spent on the eastern and western branches to the Trans-Siberian, the total rose to $192,493,100, or nearly $5,550,000 more than the entire Trans-Siberian main line, including the Ussuri section, the abandoned Amur extension, the Tomsk and Irkutsk-Baikal branches, and Khilkov's improvements. However, the government was playing for the highest of stakes — Russian hegemony in China. It was also following a policy that was soon to result in one of the greatest military debacles in the history of the empire.

CHAPTER XVI

The Trans-Siberian Comes of Age

> As far as they can be determined, the results of the construction of the Trans-Siberian indicate that the fundamental intentions which governed the conception of this colossal enterprise have now been realized. On one hand, Russia has ceased to be separated from the extremities of her Far Eastern possessions, and, on the other, Siberia has been brought firmly within the sphere of economic and cultural evolution which the other parts of the Russian empire are experiencing.
>
> — ANATOLI N. KULOMZIN: *Le Transsibérien* (1904)

WITH the opening of the Chinese Eastern to regular traffic, the through railway to the Great Ocean was complete save for a 162-mile segment round the southern rim of Lake Baikal. Construction had been postponed indefinitely, but at a meeting of the Trans-Siberian Committee in the spring of 1898 the Emperor declared that new surveys must be undertaken without delay. These were concluded in the following year and confirmed previous findings that the worst construction difficulties would be encountered between Irkutsk and Kultuk, a village on Baikal's extreme southwestern bank. From Kultuk easterly to Mysovsk, there were fewer obstacles, and so Their Excellencies authorized an immediate building start on this stretch of slightly more than a hundred miles. The surveyors had mapped out four possible routes through the formidable Irkutsk-to-Kultuk terrain; Communication Minister Khilkov narrowed these down to two — one up the Irkut valley from Irkutsk, and the other alongshore from the end of the Mid-Siberian track at Port Baikal. Unable to make up their minds which to adopt, the Committeemen decided to dump the problem into the lap of a team of geologists headed by the eminent Professor Ivan V. Mushketov of the University of St. Petersburg. After more than a year of field work, Mushketov produced a stack of technical evidence that convinced Their Excellencies the line should follow the lake shore from Port Baikal to Kultuk.

In 1901, construction was begun by private Russian contractors, who readily agreed to take the job now that men and equipment could be transported by rail from the mother country. Among them was Alexander N. Pertsov, a dynamic architect and civil engineer who preferred hard jobs to easy ones. He dug in at Maritui, about halfway between Port Baikal and Kultuk, for a protracted assault in both directions against the worst sector, comprising fifty-odd miles of precipitous cliffs broken by capes, ravines, bays, and narrow shelvings. With him in a spacious new log house were his wife and children, and, quartered in nearby barracks, a labor force of somewhat less than ten thousand Russian, Turkish, Persian, and Italian workers, together with a garrison of tough Circassian guards to break up brawls, patrol warehouses, and intercept bootleggers, predominantly women who wrapped up jugs of vodka to resemble swaddled babies.

Committeeman Kulomzin scarcely exaggerated when he wrote in 1904 that the Circumbaikal line "surpassed in difficulty and amount of work all those constructed in the Russian empire up to the present." Much of the route was inaccessible by road and could be reached by water solely in those brief periods when Baikal was comparatively calm and free of fog. Hurricane winds and lashing waves not only delayed operations but also necessitated miles of masonry walls to anchor the artificial embankments that had to be built up from the sinuous, rocky shoreline with an average of 101,720 cubic yards of earth and stone per mile. Pertsov and the other contractors were forced to dynamite cuttings through mountain folds that fell sheer into the water, and to bore thirty-three tunnels. Inlets, gorges, and Baikal's tributaries required more than two hundred bridges and trestles.

In winter, paralyzing cold halted major activities except tunneling and such preliminary bridgework as could be done within heated shelters. By the end of 1903, however, the contractors had cleared nearly eighteen hundred acres of forest, completed ninety-three per cent of the embankments,

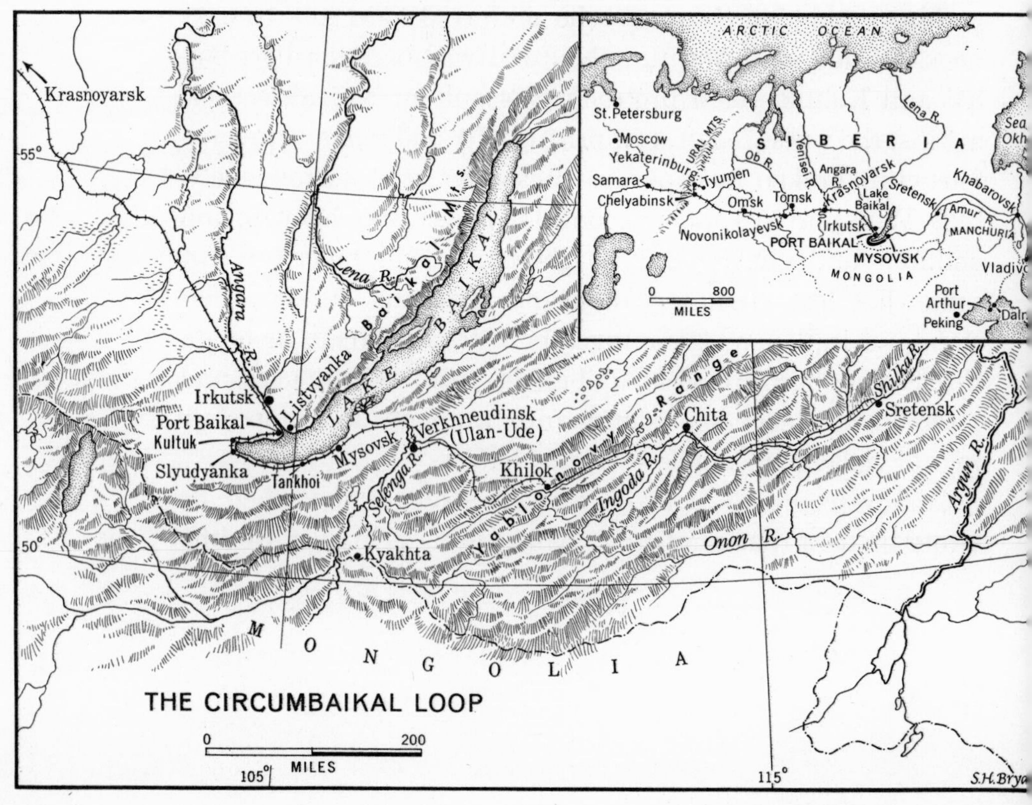

erected most of the bridges, and dug four miles of tunnels; the majority of stations and freight sheds were up, and rails had been laid for seven miles in the Port Baikal-to-Kultuk area, and, on the opposite shore, from Mysovsk to Tankhoi, a distance of thirty-five miles.

After Japan's devastating torpedo-boat attack against the Russian naval squadron at Port Arthur on the night of February 8, 1904, the contractors worked at a furious pace to complete the line. In mid-September, they turned it over to the Communication Ministry with so many defects that the first test train derailed ten times, failed to pass through one of the tunnels until the tops of car-roof ventilators were removed, and limped along for three days before it reached Port Baikal from Kultuk. For all that, Prince Khilkov and his inspection party officially opened the long-deferred and desperately needed loop on September 25. Luck and the fruits of feverish repairs were with them, for their seven-coach "special" left the track only once between Port Baikal and Mysovsk.

The cost of this vital ligament had risen out of all proportion to its length, as Khilkov was fully aware when he returned to Maritui.* Including $225,000 spent for a steamer wharf at

* Constantin A. Pertzoff, one of Alexander Pertsov's sons and now an American citizen practicing architecture in Cambridge, Massachusetts, recalls that Prince Khilkov and Finance Minister Witte were among the notables his parents put up as house guests, twenty at a time often descending on the Maritui ménage. If on their first visit, these travelers to and from the distant parts of the empire were asked to autograph a fine linen tablecloth laid out at dinner for the occasion. Mr. Pertzoff's mother then embroidered the penciled autographs to preserve them. However, the tablecloth vanished during the October Revolution in 1917, when the family left St. Petersburg for Siberia. They survived two years of civil war and eventually reached the United States via Japan.

More vivid in Mr. Pertzoff's memories than the illustrious visitors at Maritui were the pet bear cubs he and his brother kept in a pen underneath the dwelling. "We had at least two sets of them," he recalls in a letter to the writer, "but they had to be released each fall because of the habit of their species, when entering their dormant period, to suck their paws in a most noisy way all through the night. They had come to us through the guards,

Tankhoi Bay, which was deep, sheltered from winds, and closer to Port Baikal than was Mysovsk, expenditures had soared to nearly $26,630,000. With subsequent improvements, the total advanced to $35,000,000, or a record-breaking $216,000 per mile.

But for the first time, the Atlantic shores of Europe were joined to the eastern coast of Asia by uninterrupted rails. Thirteen years and four months had elapsed since those windswept inaugural ceremonies at Vladivostok on the last day of May 1891, and within that time 5500 miles had been tracked from the Urals at an average annual rate of 414 miles. This was considerably below the world record of 466 miles set by Canadian Pacific engineers when they tracked 2097 miles in four and a half years and completed the Dominion's transcontinental railway in 1885. However, if one excludes the Circumbaikal link, 5338 miles had been covered in about ten and a half years, or at an annual mean of 508 miles. As Kulomzin proudly noted, this remarkable speed in construction "confers all the more honor on the engineers who had to overcome such great and unusual difficulties."

From official statistics published by Kulomzin in 1904, one finds that the Trans-Siberian — including surveys, construction, rolling stock, working capital, river steamers and navigational improvements on waterways, the two Baikal ferries, the abandoned Amur line, the branches to the Chinese Eastern, and miscellaneous projects associated with the railway — had cost $250,702,202, twice as much as Communication Minister Posyet's estimate in 1875 for a track from the Volga

who had picked them up after having shot the mothers in the street. The wild beasts kept on going to their accustomed watering place in spite of the huge camp which arose overnight. In fact, if I remember correctly, even a Manchurian tiger was killed in the middle of Maritui. It was a wild country, all right."

to the Amur, and some $69,000,000 more than Von Hubbenet's appropriation submitted in 1890.

Ironically, the greatest rewards from the enterprise accrued not to its creators but to the followers of Lenin, who dedicated himself to the overthrow of emperors and capitalists, without whom the Trans-Siberian, the Chinese Eastern, and the economic aggrandizement of Siberia might not have materialized for years.

In broad terms, the Russo-Japanese War resulted from the competition of two nations for mastery over alien territories to which neither had the slightest shred of legal or moral right. Avowedly to protect the Chinese Eastern under construction during the Boxer upheaval, Russia had occupied Manchuria and showed no intention of leaving. Japan, backed by Britain and the United States, demanded that Russia withdraw her forces and restore China's sovereignty. Apparently yielding, St. Petersburg removed some troops in 1902, as the Soviets did in Cuba sixty years later, but reneged on a promise to evacuate the rest, on the ground that Peking refused to fulfill certain guarantees, some highly prejudicial to Japan and the Western Powers. Russia's militaristic expansionists, now influenced by an erratic adventurer in the Imperial court named Bezobrazov, began to drive a wedge into Korea under the cover of Cossack-guarded timber concessions in the Yalu River valley. Nicholas favored the incursion, for possession of Korea — a peninsula washed on the east by the Sea of Japan and on the west by the Yellow Sea — would give his navy control of the approaches to Vladivostok and northern China. On her part, Japan looked on the aggressive Russian move not only as a menace to her security but also to her own designs on the independent kingdom, which she planned to take over with all the brazenness of her rival in Manchuria. However, Tokyo was prepared to make a deal for the sake of peace: Stay out of Korea and recognize our paramount interests there, said the Mikado's envoy at St. Petersburg, and we will recognize yours in Manchuria. This proposal was tepidly received despite the warnings of Witte, whose opposition to the provocative policy of the Tsar was partly responsible for his dismissal as Finance Minister in August, 1903.* In the meantime, Japan had been building up an efficient modern army while her diplomats continued to seek an accord with the dilatory and evasive Russians. Finally, Witte's eclipse and the further ascendancy of Bezobrazov convinced Tokyo that all hope for an amicable settlement had vanished. On February 5, 1904, Japan broke off diplomatic relations and, three days later, opened hostilities without formal declaration of war, precisely as she was to do at Pearl Harbor on December 7, 1941.

The Japanese astutely struck before the Trans-Siberian had reached a state of readiness for the transportation of overwhelming legions from Russia. The crippling rail-gap at Lake Baikal had still to be closed; rolling stock and experienced engine crews were inadequate for the movement of a twentieth-century war machine; and many portions of the track were in no condition to bear trainloads of heavy artillery. It was at this early stage of the conflict that St. Petersburg paid dearly for forty-odd years of hesitancy, tergiversation, and frugality, since the single-track railway and its insufficient equipment, sidings, marshalling yards, and water-supply depots meant

* Professor Von Laue, author of *Sergei Witte and the Industrialization of Russia,* has pointed out that Witte always put the financial well-being of the empire before an expansionist foreign policy. He stood for economic penetration of China "with a rather cautious political orientation — one that would not threaten war or any other costly expedition. But the Foreign Ministry, the Court, and the Army pressed for territorial as well as economic gains, to Witte's immense distress."

that Russian effectives, so urgently needed to stem the Japanese, reached Manchuria only after five to six weeks of broken and fatiguing travel. The chaos of congestion reached its peak in the spring and summer of 1904 at Irkutsk, where whole regiments piled up while awaiting passage on the *Baikal* and the *Angara,* which together could manage no more than four daily roundtrips when not delayed by fog and mechanical breakdowns.

But traffic accelerated in succeeding months, thanks to the single-minded efforts of the Communication Ministry, the military, the Circumbaikal contractors, and an army of workers who laid heavier rails and ballast in critical sectors, modified sharp curves and inclines, added two hundred sidings, and rerouted the track from various steep, train-slowing grades northwest of Irkutsk. Supplementary rolling stock had been rounded up from other parts of the empire, and new locomotives were being produced at unprecedented speed by Russian works. In consequence, Khilkov could assert without straining the truth in a March 1905 issue of *Collier's Magazine* that 300,000 men had already been carried by rail to the front, and that 400,000 more were on the way. A British expert had gone even further and estimated that 510,000 men and 93,000 horses had been delivered between February and December 1904. At any rate, the sweeping railway improvements swung the preponderance of land forces in Russia's favor during the latter part of the struggle.

And yet, to the stupefaction of the world, the "little apes" (as the Russians had dismissed the Japanese) gave the Great Bear a mauling such as he had never known. Confusion in the high command, incompetent leadership in the field, and futile maneuvers by the Imperial navy led to one disastrous defeat after another. Officers and men by the tens of thousands had been killed, wounded, or taken prisoner; the Tsar's turreted battleships and cruisers were all but annihilated; and, partly because of the unpopularity of the war, the nation was engulfed in a wave of workers' and students' strikes, agrarian riots, and ominous revolutionary rumblings. In the peace treaty signed at Portsmouth, New Hampshire, on September 5, 1905, Russia surrendered to Japan her lease of the precious ice-free anchorages at Port Arthur and Dalni, together with the South Manchurian branch of the Chinese Eastern from Port Arthur to Changchun (an important soybean entrepôt not quite four hundred and seventy miles to the north), and the southern half of Sakhalin. Witte, St. Petersburg's chief plenipotentiary at the peace conference, saved for Russia the rest of the Chinese Eastern and its holdings in the railway zone, but had to acknowledge Japan's claim to Korea as her exclusive sphere of influence. "I acquitted myself with complete success," the former Finance Minister remarks with customary self-esteem, "and I was extolled and praised to the skies, so that in the end the Emperor Nicholas was morally compelled to reward me in an altogether exceptional manner by bestowing upon me the rank of Count. This he did in spite of his and, especially, Her Majesty's personal dislike for me, and also in spite of all the base intrigues conducted against me by a host of bureaucrats and courtiers, whose vileness was only equaled by their stupidity."

Russia had been far from humbled by Japan's stunning victories, as David J. Dallin pointed out in his *The Rise of Russia in Asia* (1949). "The Russian army was still a formidable force; Russian resources were not diminished; France continued to provide assistance to her eastern ally; Russian economy had not sustained any lasting losses from the war to any significant degree; in the realm of politics, the revolutionary movement of 1905-6 was soon crushed and suppressed. The Russian Government was again master of the situation."

During and after the war, the American railway builder Edward H. Harriman (father of the prominent State Department official W. Averell Harriman) and a group of Wall Street financiers developed a grandiose plan for a round-the-world transportation system that involved the acquisition of track rights on the Trans-Siberian and control of both the Chinese Eastern and Japan's newly won line from Port Arthur to Changchun. At first, Russia seemed ready to cooperate, for she desired better relations with the United States in hope of stalemating Japan. But owing to complicating factors — chiefly Tokyo's adamant opposition — St. Petersburg turned down the project and ultimately killed it by concluding a series of secret agreements with Japan for joint hegemony in Manchuria.

Harriman's ambitious and politically significant scheme was one of several that had captured the imagination of newspaper readers in the nineties and early nineteen-hundreds. Under the aegis of the *Pall Mall Gazette*, Harry de Windt investigated the feasibility of a continuous railway — variously referred to as the "All-World Railway," the "Leviathan Railway," and the "Franco-American Railway" — from Paris to New York via Bering Strait, and nearly lost his life when he reached northeastern Siberia in 1896. Five years later, he set out again for the *Daily Express* and discovered that Bering Strait presented quite a problem: a tunnel would be fabulously expensive, bridge piers would probably not withstand the spring ice breakup, and a balloon crossing suggested by a helpful Parisian gentleman was beyond sober consideration. Nothing came of this expedition, but the versatile De Windt may have made enough money from his book, *From Paris to New York by Land* — the account of his 11,000-mile journey by train, horses, reindeer, and sledge dogs across Europe and Asia — to take time off for the pursuit of his scientific hobby "Moleosophy," and the lighthearted writing of *Moles and their Meaning . . . With regard to the Mind, Morals, and Astral Indications in both Sexes, being a modernised and easy Guide to the Ancient Science of Divination by the Moles of the Human Body* . . . a book published in 1907 by a usually level-headed London firm.

Somewhat similar to the "All-World" line was the "Trans-Alaska-Siberian Railway," incorporated in New Jersey in 1906 by sponsors who mapped out a course more or less along the route of Collins's overland telegraph to Bering Strait and the Amur country, where connection would be made with Russian and European communications to the Atlantic. This undertaking aroused no more capitalistic enthusiasm than had the "London, Bombay, and Hong Kong Railway," whose backers proposed to tunnel under the Strait of Dover, follow French and Spanish lines to Gibraltar, tunnel from there to North Africa, and continue by way of Egypt, Persia, Baluchistan, India, Burma, the eastern Himalayas, and China to Hong Kong. Hardly less vaulting in conception was the "Cosmopolitan Railway" favored by a former governor of Colorado who envisioned a permanent way down the west coast of Africa to Cape Town, up the east coast to Turkey, then across the Russian empire to Bering Strait, Canada, and the United States, from which passengers could, if they still felt up to it, travel on a Pan-American railway-to-be as far south as Patagonia. "Bold as this scheme is," observed a commentator of the day, "there is really nothing impracticable about it . . ." Quite possibly, he expressed this optimistic view because he had no desire to be caught out like the derogators of the Trans-Siberian.

Not long after the war with Japan, the Trans-Siberian and Chinese Eastern resumed normal civilian service. By the summer of 1907, three "fast" trains operated every week in each direction between Moscow and Vladivostok, as well as Changchun, northern head of the Japanese-controlled South Manchurian section that assured connections with Dalni, Port Arthur, and Peking. Two were the state-owned *trains de luxe,* which continued to be as good, bad, or indifferent as Annette Meakin, Harry de Windt, Pastor Clark, and others had found them some years before. The third — Wagons-Lits' "International" — showed startling improvement since prewar days. Finally granted fare increases that promised to bring profits instead of the previous losses, the Sleeping Car Company had taken practical steps to attract a rich, if demanding, clientele.* Although the management could not bring itself to use the magnificent equipment displayed at the Paris Exposition in 1900, it diverted some of its second-best cars to the Siberian run; staffed them with solicitous attendants speaking Russian, French, German, and English; provided good foods and wines; and widely publicized the fact that, via the rail route, one could travel from London or Paris to the Extreme Orient in less than half the time and cost of the sea voyage by way of the Suez Canal. Or, in the opposite direction, one could sail westerly from European ports across the Atlantic, take

* One did not have to be so very rich to travel on the International. Mrs. John Clarence Lee — a Philadelphia clergyman's wife who crossed Siberia alone, rejecting the advances of three importunate Frenchmen and "a gorgeously clothed Russian officer in white and blue and gold" — says in her book *Across Siberia Alone* (1914) that the first-class fare from Shanghai to Moscow by way of Harbin amounted to £44 8*s*. [about $215], as against £30 via the Russian State Express. Mrs. Lee paid $1.75 for three meals a day in the Sleeping Car Company's *wagon-restaurant.*

American or Canadian trains to the Pacific, embark there for the Far East, and complete a world tour on the Chinese Eastern, Trans-Siberian, and European railways. Most American globe-trotters visited Japan and China, then entrained for Moscow at Vladivostok or Dalni, which the Japanese had renamed Dairen and completed as a thoroughly modernized city with broad, radiating avenues like those in Washington, D.C.

At Dalni, travelers boarded American-built Pullmans of the South Manchuria Railway and proceeded to Mukden, northern terminus of a weekly Chinese through-express from Peking. At Changchun, they changed to either the Russian government's or the Sleeping Car Company's carriages. The latter consisted of four first- and second-class sleepers, a *wagon-restaurant,* and a couple of *fourgons* for baggage and supplies. First-class cars differed from second in that they had a lavatory between every two compartments, each with only two berths instead of four. North of Changchun, Cossack guards boarded every train to protect it from hunghutze raiders and to assert Russia's authority over the railway zone.

The next important stop was Harbin, "the Aladdin City" that had sprung up from nothing at the turn of the century and become a Russian metropolis within the land concession obtained from Peking. "The police are largely Russian," Wright and Digby reported. "Kharbin is so Russian that they dare to hang printed notices in hotels telling you to lodge your Russian passport [or that issued by any other nation] for inspection at the Russian police station before you have unstrapped your trunks. The colossal impertinence of the thing — Russian police surveillance in the heart of a Chinese province!"

This conglomeration of railway shops and administrative headquarters, military barracks, flour- and sawmills, a distillery that produced three million gallons of vodka a year (or thirty gallons a year for every one of the city's 100,000 inhabitants), stockyards, ornate commercial buildings, and unpainted wooden dwellings, was Russia's base for the exploitation of Manchuria. It was also a crowded, unsanitary, wide-open city, "a magnet for all the adventurers in Russia," as Fraser had noted. Wright and Digby effectively described it after their stay in 1911.

"Saturday night. Everyone is on the Kitaiskaia, China Street. Caucasians, handsome swashbucklers with pointed black beards and a swagger in their walk. In spite of the summer heat each wears an Astrakhan fez tilted rakishly over one ear, and the long plum-colored national coat with a dummy bullet belt slung across the breast. In the belt is a silver-handled dagger in a beautifully chased sheath. Numbers of women, women of the upper classes, well dressed and with pretty faces — a rare sight, indeed, in Asiatic Russia. Their poorer sisters, too, have not the slipshod air of the Siberian women, who have always appeared to have robed themselves with the fire engine at the door. Nor do you see any women in peasant dress. They wear becoming scarfs of filmy black lace over their heads. There are plenty of mounted police, Chinese and Russian soldiers with bayoneted rifles slung across their backs and big wooden revolver holsters at the hip. The little Russian school girls, in smart straw hats and a bunch of lilies-of-the-valley tucked in their blouses, have come out to sit demurely on the benches along the broad plank pavements. A tall, bearded Sikh, with a bright pink turban, enormous button-hole bouquet, cutaway frock coat, lavender gloves, brown shoes, silver-headed cane and other splendors, has drifted up from India. Students and schoolboys of innumerable sorts and sizes stroll about in their long brass-buttoned military coats and military peaked caps. Officers and soldiers of a dozen regiments and ranks you see — a continuous performance of saluting and acknowledging salutes.

"A profusion of color prevails. Red-shirted Russians, girded with gleaming black belts are here, and gorgeous cabbies in brown Holland smocks, with scarlet scarfs around their waists. . . . Now and then a group of Germans, arm-in-arm, and chattering volubly, drifts by. There are men in dark blue military capes fastened with a smart silver clasp, men in Panamas, in the wide-brimmed Stetson, in snowy pith helmets, in flat English motoring caps. You see Japanese, the men invariably in western dress and more often than not with gold-rimmed spectacles. Their women folk do not take so kindly to skirt and blouse. They wear their pretty native dress, and clatter along on their high-heeled wooden shoes, here and there one with a slant-eyed, gayly-clad, animated little doll of a Nippon baby packed up in the fold of the *obi* behind her shoulder. And the Chinese, in their thousands, gliding here and there in the throng, noiseless in their cloth shoes. . . . A very dirty and very picturesque old Chinaman pokes along, smoking his long pipe, hand in hand with a little Chinese boy robed in pale blue canvas and wearing a decrepit derby hat on the back of his head. When the Chinese of Kharbin want to pass a really satisfying evening, they get hold of a dusty, battered derby and parade the streets, wearing it with visible *éclat*. . . . Soldier, sailor, tinker, tailor, of half the races of the Occident and the Orient pass to and fro with gay laughter and chatter. Under the lovely purple evening sky of the East, diamond-powdered with scintillating stars, the concourse flows up and down the cobbled Kitaiskaia."

Daniel A. de Menocal, manager of the Peking office of the International Banking Corporation from 1909 to 1914 and now a resident of Nantucket, Massachusetts, describes an overnight stop at Harbin with his bride in 1909. "We gathered together our mass of luggage, signaled a Chinese coolie and walked close behind him to the hotel," he says in his memoirs. "It was mandatory to keep these coolies and your luggage always in sight, as it is well known that otherwise they might easily disappear in the flash of an eye and never be seen or heard of again. It was really cold, for winter had already arrived. What we found at the hotel was certainly a new experience. It was like one of our Western movies: a milling gang of bearded, husky, half-drunken and fully drunken, noisy Russians in circulation from the bar to the billiard table. . . . There were Buriats who were half-Russian, half-Mongol, some Japanese, and mixing with these frenetic groups some women, big tough creatures. It was all very forbidding for two strangers from the Western world, particularly when one was a beautiful young girl. We were eventually discovered by the owner's daughter, who said that there were no rooms available, but that we might sit in the entrance hall until our train left in the morning. But when she took another look at my lovely Beatrice she realized that something else must be improvised. So she very kindly offered us her own bedroom.

"This squalid room was probably about six feet by twelve. The bedclothes in the bunk had probably not been changed for many months, and the prevailing smell was from sour to fetid; naturally, we did not disrobe, but we were most grateful for this generous hospitality. We were, however, fearful that when we arrived at Peking we might bring along with us in our clothes or in our pile of luggage some unspeakable vermin from this combination railway hotel, Manchurian saloon, night club and brothel.

"The next morning we took our seats in the train. . . . Almost at once we first only sensed and then were almost overpowered by a poisonous stench unlike anything we had ever known, so I left my seat to investigate. It seems that the Russian Minister Plenipotentiary had a compartment at the end of the car, and as he was for the time being on the platform or elsewhere, there was stationed at the door of his room a Russian Cossack in full uniform, his rifle with bayonet fixed. It appears that at the beginning of these northern winters the Russian soldiers all seal themselves in a leather undergarment which is never removed until they dig themselves out in the Spring. The effect I leave to your imagination."

Westward from Harbin, passengers regarded a boundless plain of little interest save for an occasional Chinese village, clusters of railwaymen's huts, and the watchtowers and loopholed blockhouses of the railway guard corps. A knowing few may have looked twice at Tsitsihar station, in western Manchuria, the junction for the old provincial capital that was notorious for its Field of Death, where a Chinese executioner slashed off the heads of criminals while picnicking throngs looked on. The decapitated heads were taken to the Russian consulate for inspection, then handed over to relatives who had to sew them to the appropriate bodies for decent Chinese burial. "But here the Government steps in," says Wright, who visited Tsitsihar alone. "It would obviously lower the moral tone of Heaven, explains Peking, to have the executed criminals strolling about like any gentleman, corrupting the innocent outlook of who knows how many guileless angels; yet we do not want to interfere with the enjoyment of Heaven by men who have expiated their crimes here below. So it is ordered that the heads of the executed criminals shall be sewn on the wrong way, facing backwards. Thus, in the world to come, men who have not been all they might have been may

Execution Day at Tsitsihar

Decapitated heads of hunghutzes

be recognized at sight and treated with a necessary tinge of hauteur by law-abiding citizens of Zion."

From Manchuria station, at the western Sino-Siberian frontier, Wagons-Lits' carriages bounced across Transbaikalia and round Lake Baikal to Irkutsk. One day in the latter part of June 1907, passengers whose eyes happened to fall on an embankment between Mysovsk and Tankhoi must have rubbed them in disbelief, for there, surrounded by three men in muddy motoring costumes, was a European automobile, a rare enough sight in Russia and such an unknown machine in Siberia that railwaymen at Lake Baikal mistook it for a new kind of locomotive undergoing tests. Not many on the train would have known that the car was an Itala three-seater Prince Scipione Borghese was driving in the Peking-to-Paris "road trial" promoted by the Parisian newspaper *Le Matin*. Borghese, the *grand-pilote* of one of the four surviving autos, had taken to the railway bed itself. He was driving on the flush-to-the-surface ties as the easiest way to reach Baikal's western shore, and had barely got off the track when the train approached.

Most passengers had only the vaguest notion of the hour of day or night, since the railway management ignored the Asian sun and ran trains and station clocks on St. Petersburg time. But dining-car meals were served according to local time wherever the train happened to be. At Irkutsk, for example, it was 4:56 P.M. but only noon at the capital. And so one seldom knew what to expect — breakfast, lunch, or dinner. However, the food was generally good, and sometimes excellent, according to Mr. de Menocal, who traveled across Siberia several times on Wagons-Lits' trains. "The food in the dining car was superb," he recalls, "an abundance of game, unlimited caviar which came from Lake Baikal en route, thick Siberian cream, rich sauces, good cigars. Occasionally at a neighboring table there would be a great hulking, bearded, ruddy-faced, big-gutted man drinking copiously of brandy, eating to repletion, smoking the most expensive cigars. . . . The evidence of his success would be, among other things, a large diamond ring and a jeweled stickpin."

At major stations — where car attendants locked momentarily vacated compartments against Baedeker's "*Thieves*" — foreigners could buy innocuous journals and magazines in languages other than Russian; admire the icons of an altar or a chapel conveniently close to the buffet bar; haggle with peddlers hawking miniature wooden or waxen models of convicts in chains; and marvel at the foolhardiness of virtually all Russian travelers. If blocked by temporarily halted coaches between them and a train they meant to catch on another track, they saved themselves walking distance by diving under the cars. These were higher from the track than those in Europe and America but none the less likely to start suddenly and mangle anyone who tripped or fell between the wheels. Impoverished peasants in particular seemed to think that their lives were charmed as far as railway hazards were concerned. They waited until cars got underway, then leapt on the bumpers and scrambled to the roof, often a dependable refuge from train guards. But if the latter were not too lazy to climb up and give chase, free-riders faced the prospect of being shoved off from a twelve- to fourteen-foot height and of hitting the ground at forty miles an hour if the engineer were trying to make up lost time. Today, Soviet citizens continue to dive under cars and ride on roofs despite the risk of heavy fines.

In 1910, the American, Lindon Bates, Jr., wrote that the Trans-Siberian "is deemed, like the Pyramids, a monument to colossal effort and achievement but of little service to mankind." Foreigners who knew the old and the new Siberia would have contested this judgment. To be sure, the railway ran at a heavy loss to the Treasury; ordinary passenger trains were late, crowded, and dirty beyond belief; the bulk of stationmasters, ticket clerks, and train crews were given to slipshod ways and excessive drinking. But in enormous counterweight, the Trans-Siberian opened up the country and brought unparalleled benefits to hundreds of thousands.

With the advance of the steel rails, no longer did parties of convicts, exiles, and voluntary followers march for month after month along the seemingly endless road to oblivion in wild Siberia; no longer did they suffer the cold, rain, winds, and heat on the Trakt and in prison barges. The pestilential *étapes* of the Trakt went the happily forsaken way of the posthouses, where proprietors and *yamshchiki* grieving the loss of bribes and drink money were infinitesimal in relation to the multitudes of travelers whom the Trans-Siberian spared the detestable accommodations of the former, the reckless driving of the latter, and the adversities of river transits on ferries and paddle-wheelers.

Siberia escaped serfdom because it escaped the gentry which, in European Russia, had received lands and peasants to help bulwark the Crown against Tartars, Turks, and other invaders. In Asia, the gentry class was unneeded, as Donald W. Treadgold explains in his *The Great Siberian Migration* (1957). "The Central Asian Turks might harass the Siberians, but they were not particularly warlike, and there was practically no armed friction with China once the border was fixed. The gentry did not wish to leave the amenities of the capitals for the valleys of the Yenisei and the Lena, and fortunately the military needs of Siberia could be cared for without them, by Cossacks and small regular detachments."

However, the inhabitants were gripped in an economic squeeze by trading cartels in Russia, Siberian merchant coalitions, and transportation monopolies, all of which fleeced the public without fear of rivals or government intervention. But the advent of the Trans-Siberian forced the profiteers to loosen their stranglehold, for the railway and Witte's tariff reforms opened the country to competition from Russia and abroad. And so the era passed when families could buy meat only from certain butchers favored by wholesalers, when tremendous markups were the rule for consumer goods, when Siberia's few industries were hamstrung by the prohibitive cost of importing more efficient machinery and equipment. Factories and workshops sprang up where none had existed before; new firms began to work rich deposits of iron ore and other minerals discovered by geologists seeking coal for the Trans-Siberian's locomotives; imports and exports moved across the country in unparalleled volume. In 1902, carloadings on the Chelyabinsk-Irkutsk division alone amounted to 1,033,200 metric tons, a gratifying state of affairs to Their Excellencies who, ten years before, had estimated the prospective annual average at a mere 270,000 tons.*

And now we come to the early railway's supreme role in the transformation of Siberia: the conveyance of myriads of Rus-

* Siberia's principal imports at this time were iron and ironware, machines and agricultural implements, kerosene, textiles, sugar, tobacco, and building materials such as cement, lime, gypsum, and hardwoods. Exports included wheat, oats, and rye, tea from China, coal, meat, lard, tallow, hides and sheepskins, wool, poultry, eggs, and butter. In the nineties, a handful of Danes introduced their own dairy methods into Western Siberia and revolutionized butter production. Exports to the London market alone leapt from slightly less than 10,834,000 pounds in 1899 to more than 162,508,000 pounds in 1913.

sian emigrants and of incalculable tons of materials, supplies, and equipment for their welfare in new settlements east of the Urals.

Freed from serfdom in 1861, peasant families in the crowded central Russian provinces had struck out for Siberia as an asylum from agrarian and other restrictions which, combined with periods of famine or economic slump, had reduced them to almost unmitigated want. They walked beside a horse-drawn cart, overloaded with household goods and useless knickknacks of sentimental value, for weeks and months until they came to a promising site. It could be had for the taking, since the state or the Crown owned practically all the land and countenanced squatters.* But the government did little to ease their hardships on the road. An estimated ten per cent of the adults and thirty per cent of the children died of malnutrition, exposure, or disease. A good many survivors tried homesteading only to straggle back to Russia, nearly destroyed by the rigors of the Utopia that never was.

---

* As distinguished from state property, Crown lands and mines belonged to the sovereign, who pocketed the income. A relatively tiny part of Siberia had been given or sold to Russian nobles, Cossacks, monasteries, two communities, and a few merchants.

Alexander Michie, a Briton who traveled across Siberia in 1863, stated that "there is but one Siberian nobleman and proprietor of serfs in existence, — Mr. Rodinkoff, Councellor of State and Vice-Governor of the Province of Yeniseisk, a kind-hearted, good old man." Rodinkoff's grandfather had received from Catherine the Great a grant of lands and peasants, but neither he nor his children exercised proprietary rights over the latter. A brother of Rodinkoff broke the custom and tried to exact contributions from the peasants, who killed him in consequence. Probably not relishing a similar fate, his fraternal survivor — so Michie related — "seldom interferes with, or visits his peasants, but contents himself with the modest imposts of wood for winter fuel for his town residence, and hay for his horses, with which they cheerfully supply him."

Michie's statement that there was only one Siberian proprietor of serfs is not correct, as Professor Treadgold points out. He cites a Russian authority who "asserts that there were some 3,700 serfs in Siberia, of whom 2,800 were peasants and the rest household serfs. The 2,800 were distributed on 36 estates, of which 28 were in Tobolsk, 6 in Tomsk, and 2 in Yeniseisk province."

In the eighteen-eighties, St. Petersburg decided to encourage emigration as a means to relieve congestion in chronically depressed areas and to help colonize Siberia's virgin territories. In July 1889, the government promulgated a law which, among other provisions, granted allotments of about a hundred and forty acres to the average family of three adults and two children. For three years, settlers would be exempt from military conscription and from taxes, reduced by fifty per cent for another three. Long-term, interest-free loans were made available for the purchase of seed grain, agricultural implements, and wood for housing.

These measures spurred emigration but failed to give it orderly direction. On the way to the chief settlement region — west-central Siberia's fertile Tomsk Province — the peasants moved in disorganized masses and, while waiting for overtaxed barges to carry them on river portions of the journey, camped under such unhygienic conditions that typhus and other epidemics wiped out innumerable families. Government offices, called "points of emigration," had been set up at various key locations to provide financial and medical aid, but staffs and funds were inadequate for an influx that had swept from about 48,000 in 1890 to more than 82,000 in the following year.

Then, in 1893, the Trans-Siberian Committee took over as one of its functions "the settlement of the country within the range of the Siberian line, and the regulation of the emigration movement to the East." In consequence, the fortunes of the itinerant Russian plowmen and their families were to take a remarkable turn for the better after several years of rolling-stock shortages that stranded emigrants for weeks at a time. By the autumn of 1896, the West Siberian sector from Chelyabinsk to the Ob was open to regular traffic, and, in the summer of 1900, one could ride on almost continuous rails to Krasnoyarsk, Irkutsk, and Sretensk. At first, the Committee-men had established a migrant fare of a fifth of a cent per mile per person, children under ten years of age being carried free. In 1898, they reduced this rate to the point where the average family of five could travel from, say, the central Russian city of Kursk, to Tomsk — a distance of approximately 2530 miles — for $7.50 in rubles.

These ultra-economy-class passengers were assigned to special emigrant trains — long strings of boxcars like those Wright and Digby saw near Irkutsk in 1911. ". . . There were cars for families and cars for single men. The former were simply stables on wheels. In them, three human generations — grandparents, the man and his wife in their prime, the children — and the population of their little farmyard back in Russia. Three cows and half-a-dozen sheep lie in straw and knee-deep filth, munching hay and green stuff. Bales of hay and straw are stacked to the roof, the home of the wandering fowls and turkeys and ducks. A couple of big lean dogs crouch in a corner. A Russian log hut has not much furniture. All there is fits comfortably into a box car, even when cows and sheep, backed by a small haystack, swell the family circle. Goods and chattels are disposed here and there, chairs are placed around the rude table, a lamp and even a pair of religious prints hang on the wall. . . . The single men's quarters are populated by an intimidating band of ruffians, bare-headed, bare-footed, shaggy-bearded creatures with flat animal faces and wild, bloodshot eyes, one's conception of a ship-wrecked crew after ten years on the desert island."

These and the hundreds of thousands of rail-borne migrants who had preceded them had been far from "shipwrecked." "Toward the tail of the immigrant train," the journalists noted,

Emigrant train, with stationmaster (in white)

"was a coach of dazzling white — the hospital, a very necessary adjunct to a journey taken under the conditions and lasting from one to three weeks. Through the open door we caught a glimpse of a brass and white enameled bed, a spotless white counterpane across it, and surrounded by all the dainty fittings of a private room in a good metropolitan hospital. The uniformed nurse sat by the window embroidering." In addition to this rolling infirmary, there was a permanent hospital at each of the big emigrant-receiving stations such as Chelyabinsk, Omsk, and Novonikolayevsk, where medicine and treatment were free, as was also true at clinics in smaller stations. By 1898, mortality among migrants of all ages had been reduced to hardly more than a fifth of one per cent, quite a drop from the death rate that had averaged twenty per cent for both adults and children in pre-railway days.

No longer did emigrants whose money had given out have to subsist on occasional handouts from villagers and on roots, berries, and whatever fish and small game they could catch. As the rails progressed eastward, government feeding facilities soon followed, together with heated barracks, laundries, bathhouses, and medical and pharmaceutical corps. Provisions and hot food were sold at rock-bottom prices, or given to young children, the sick, and the needy. Apparently, the commissary managers had soft hearts, for Kulomzin records that, out of nearly 3,947,000 hot meals consumed by adults from 1894 to 1901, no charge had been made for 3,072,600, nor for 2,793,000 pounds of bread.

Except for many "irregulars" who took over any good piece of vacant land, emigrants settled on registered allotments which had been surveyed by government topographers at the instance of the Committee; these holdings were parceled out for indefinite rental by the tenants, and could not at that time be sold or mortgaged. Tracts abutting the main line soon filled up after the western railway divisions had become operational, and so hitherto inhospitable terrain had to be prepared for extensive colonization. For example, hydrographic engineers of the Ministry of Agriculture and State Domains worked over an area of 3,460,000 acres in the Barabinskaya Steppe — in summer, a mosquito-infested jungle of reeds, sedge grass, and stagnant lakes and ponds between Omsk and Novonikolayevsk — and, by clearing out vegetation and digging drainage ditches, opened more than 1,200,000 acres for grain cultivation. In areas devoid of potable water, other engineers drilled hundreds of artesian wells or brought it from a distance in canals.

The occupation of these western lands meant that succeeding migrants were forced to push eastward. Relatively few had gone as far as the Amur and Ussuri territories, since the trek by road took all of two years. But from 1900 onward, the Trans-Siberian enabled them to reach Sretensk in a few weeks. Then it was only a matter of days by barge or raft to new allotments in the Far East, which the government was so anxious to colonize with potential defenders that it granted settlers greater privileges and almost twice the acreage allowed in other parts of Russian Asia. These inducements drew an unprecedented twenty percent of all migrants crossing the Urals in 1907, and, as Professor Treadgold adds, reached the ears of pious Old Believers in distant Rumania and Austria-Hungary, five thousand of whom received permission to settle in the Amur and Ussuri regions.

Russian figures on the emigration movement are the "statistician's nightmare" noted by Professor Treadgold, but it appears that more than 4,900,000 peasants had entered Siberia from 1894, when the Trans-Siberian track reached Omsk, to 1914. Unlike the American pioneers who had settled much of the West before completion of the first transcontinental track, these migrants were heavily dependent on rail transport for their well-being. The Trans-Siberian brought them seed grain, food to tide them over until the harvest, and lumber for cabins on poorly wooded steppes, where dwellings would otherwise have been half-subterranean, unhealthy sod huts. In country with trees, the "old-settlers" — descendents of Russians and others who had fled from serfdom, military service, religious persecution, or arrest for crime — had taken all the newcomers' government-lent money for wood and supplied the worst stock in return. Their Excellencies ended this swindle by directing the railway administration to deliver carloads of fine timber from state forests for distribution at nonprofit prices.

Similarly, the old-settlers had charged exorbitantly for ancient agricultural implements which, broken-down though they were, the emigrants could not do without. Again, the gougers were put out of this business when the Trans-Siberian carried thousands of modern plows, harrows, and American mowers and reapers to be sold cheaply at "Agricultural Implement Depots" — highly successful affairs that multiplied from nineteen in 1902 to three hundred in 1913. In addition, artisans could now obtain inexpensive tools for such village industries as shoe-, saddle-, and harness-making, blacksmithing, coopering, weaving, and tanning.

With a series of $75,000 allocations voted by Their Excellencies, the Trans-Siberian's engineers had begun to erect chapels and shrines at principal stations for railway employees as well as for the agricultural population. Churches, schools, and orphan asylums were built with money from the "Fund of the Late Emperor Alexander III," which had raised $900,000 from public subscribers. Aside from materials for these structures, the railway delivered Nicholas's gift of 60 silver ornaments for altars and 93 church bells cast in brass from government armories. To all appearances, His Imperial Majesty believed learning to be of less importance than divine worship, for he authorized the creation of 218 churches as against only 184 schools. Kulomzin — who must have been a sadly secular man, since he chose to donate a harmonium and a magic lantern to a school near Novonikolayevsk rather than candlesticks or something else to the church — does not specify the number of orphanages, but makes clear that the girls were kept busy with needlework and lacemaking, and the boys with blacksmithing, metalworking, and shoemaking.

Indecisive and procrastinating though the Committeemen had been in railway construction matters, they moved quickly to protect the hordes of new settlers from the centuries-old scourges of the empire — epidemics, famines, and fires. In exemplification, they sent out additional doctors and nurses to eradicate typhus, and augmented medical personnel with teams of oculists who traveled from place to place along the railway and, in the course of a typical nine-month tour, treated or operated on 12,500 persons suffering from eye afflictions.

The crop failures of 1900 and 1901 in western Siberia would have produced much greater hunger if Their Excellencies had not thwarted speculating monopolists by shipping low-priced grain to the inhabitants, who also received advances for storage bins in which to maintain reserves during future famines. With respect to the fires that frequently left villagers destitute of homes, clothing, livestock, and food stored for the long, barren winters, the Committee sponsored measures that extended insurance benefits, lent money for community fire-fighting equipment, and promoted the use of brick — quantities of which could now be transported on freight cars for long distances from kilns — in lieu of wood for new houses and buildings.

By the end of 1905, the Committeemen had guided the trans-Asian railway to completion, organized subsidiary undertakings for Siberia's development, and set aside land and facilities for a tide of emigration that was to reach full flood in 1908, the year when nearly 759,000 peasants and artisans entered the country. In spite of Nature, rebellion, plague, war, and themselves, Their Excellencies had fulfilled the mission entrusted to them by Alexander III thirteen years before. They had already delegated most of their responsibilities to individual ministries and commissions. Accordingly, on December 22, 1905, Nicholas issued a decree that went practically unnoticed amid the general strikes and revolutionary turmoil of the period. "Declaring our royal gratitude to all who have honestly labored for the construction of the Great Siberian Way and for the realization of the auxiliary enterprises," His Majesty — the Committee's president — dissolved the august conclave of ministers, administrators, and Siberian governors-general. From then on, the destinies of the railway and of Siberia were to be determined successively by the leaders of a quasi-parliamentary government, a republic, a Bolshevist state, and, until some time in the unforeseeable future, the Communist oligarchy of the Soviet Union.

CHAPTER XVII

Chaos

> Never had the steppes and forests of Siberia, accustomed to the spectacle of gangs of Czarist prisoners moving into exile, witnessed such confusion and misery.
>
> — George Stewart: *The White Armies of Russia*

AFTER the Revolution of 1905, the fortunes of the empire lay in the hands of both the Tsar and a bicameral legislative body that comprised a State Council and a State Duma, for Nicholas had been compelled to yield a measure of constitutional government to his subjects. The public was indifferent to the loss of Port Arthur and Dalni, half of Sakhalin, and the South Manchurian branch of the Chinese Eastern, but certain nationalistic journals and members of the court circle clamored for revenge. They realized, however, that an attack on Japan might lead to her seizure of the rest of the Chinese Eastern and consequent isolation of the Maritime Province, in which Vladivostok lay. To guard against the latter eventuality, leaders of the militant faction urged construction of a strategically safe railway north of the Amur sector that had been abandoned in 1896. Witte opposed the project. "Above all, I insisted, the new line meant the expenditure of huge sums which could be spent, with better results, on defending our

Far-Eastern possessions and the existing Eastern-Chinese Railroad." The war party, in which Witte included the Emperor and the Grand Duke Nicholas Nikolayevich, head of the Committee on State Defense, ignored his protests and directed the Communication Ministry to resurvey the Siberian side of the Amur.

The formal proposal to build the railway was approved by the Duma in November 1907 after much impassioned debate among the parliamentary representatives. As mapped by the Communication Minister — a military engineer and practical railwayman named Nicholas K. Schauffhausen-Schönberg och Schaufuss but nonetheless a Russian — the new route branched off from the Transbaikal rails at Kuenga, a junction thirty miles west of Sretensk, and followed an irregular arc to Khabarovsk through a forbidding, unpopulated wilderness of mountains, forests, boglands, and marshy plains, all beyond artillery range of the Amur's Manchurian bank. Only one track would be laid, but tunnels and major bridges would be wide enough for double-tracking in the future. Schauffhausen-Schönberg estimated costs at approximately $109,000,000, not counting rolling stock and, at Khabarovsk, a great multi-piered span nearly a mile and a half long. Except for an undetermined number of convicts and a few thousand Koreans who had become Russian nationals, laborers would be imported from the homeland. They were considered potential colonists and, unlike itinerant Chinese coolies, would keep their earnings within the country to the benefit of the economy. In the aggregate, these earnings reached a rather impressive sum: in 1912 alone, wages of the 80,000 Russian workers came to $15,000,000.

Construction of the 1200-mile Amur railway began at Kuenga in the spring of 1908 and was assigned to four chief

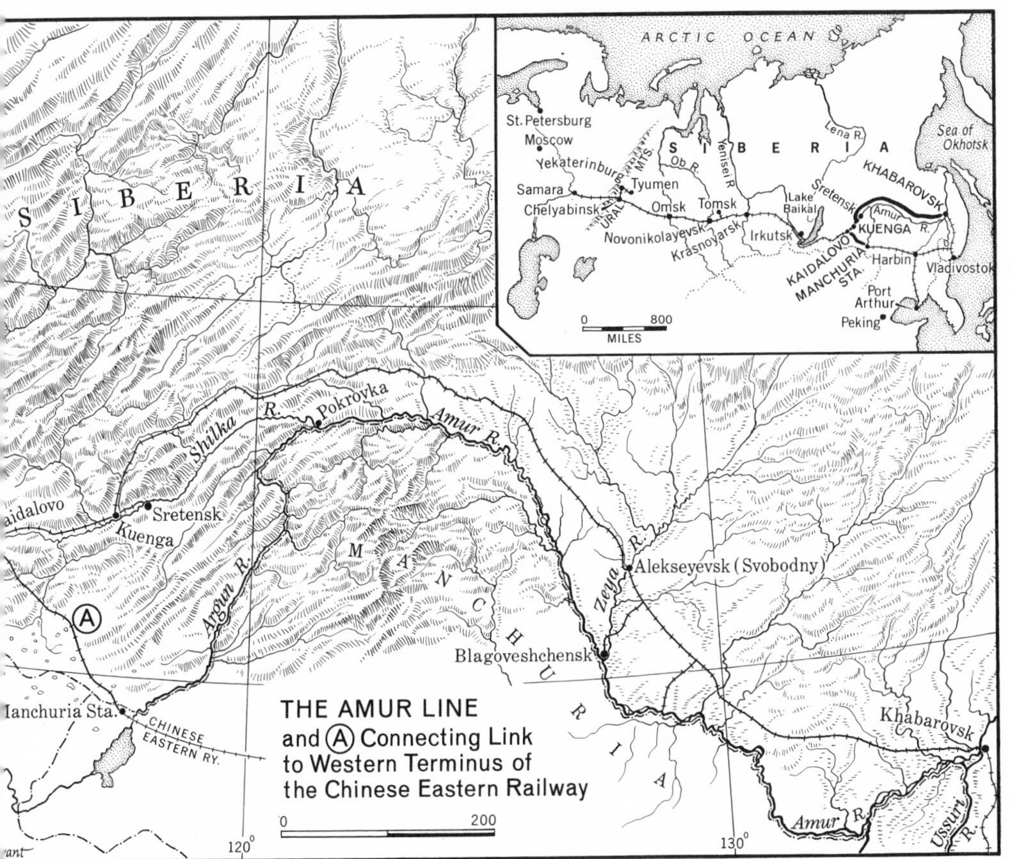

engineers, the most prominent of whom was Alexander V. Liverovski, who later became Communication Minister. Tunneling and bridge-foundation work could be carried on throughout the winter, but other activities were limited to hardly more than four months, starting in June and ending no later than the first week or so in October. To save wages and maintenance costs in the slack period, eighty per cent of the laborers were sent back to Russia and returned in the following year; the rest had brought out their families and remained as settlers.

The summer season was hot, humid, and often rainy, with men and horses under almost constant attack by swarms of gnats, flies, and a breed of small mosquito peculiar for its painful sting. (Maud D. Haviland, a British naturalist who voyaged down the Yenisei in 1914 and was taken for a suffragette exiled by her government to Siberia, observed that "If Siberia is ever in need of a national emblem, she cannot do better than to quarter her arms with a cloud of mosquitoes rampant.") While building miles of access roads, clearing a broad swath through the taiga, filling in seemingly bottomless bogs, and coping with permafrost, seventy-five per cent of the Russians reportedly came down with scurvy and disorders induced by drinking stagnant swamp water where there were no rivers or streams.

The worst was not over until late in 1913. Easterly portions of the track and a few of the longer bridges and tunnels had yet to be finished, but stretch after stretch of hitherto unusable terrain had been cleared for new settlers. In arid areas, wellholes had been sunk through perennially frozen layers of bedrock, gravel, sand, silt, clay, organic material, and ice, not infrequently to a depth of more than three hundred and fifty feet before reaching water beneath the permafrost floor. Long-armed, steam-powered excavators had drained miles of marsh fields and transformed them into arable fields from which colonists had already gathered harvests of grain and vegetables. Villages had sprung up on forest clearings and the sites of former quagmires. Towns such as Alekseyevsk (renamed Svobodny) on the Zeya River, one of the Amur's principal northern tributaries, had been laid out with wide boulevards, rows of log houses, an orphanage, and a school for children. Under the direction of the railway medical superintendent, hospitals had been erected at the larger stations. "We went through several of them," says the celebrated Norwegian polar explorer and pioneer oceanographer Fridtjof Nansen, who toured the length of the line in October 1913, "and saw the wards, operating rooms, baths, etc.; they were all light, clean and well arranged, and it was a pleasure to see them. . . . [Schoolrooms] were large and airy, and on the walls hung all kinds of plates illustrative of botany, geography, geology, zoology, demonstrations of industry, and so on. Some of these schools had mistresses, others masters. Sometimes there were so many children that they had to be divided, some coming in the morning and others in the afternoon. The children all looked happy; it could not be seen that the climate had done them any harm."

With completion in 1916 of the Khabarovsk bridge — the longest in Russia or Siberia to the present day — the Amur line was opened to traffic. It had been an extravagant undertaking, as Witte had predicted and Nansen confirms with a statement, based on official sources, that at least $150,000,000 had already been spent at the time of his 1913 trip. Ironically, the enemy Japan, against which the railway had been built as a military weapon, had become a valuable if acutely distrusted ally and, at the very moment when the last girder was riveted into place on the Amur span, was helping to arm Russian troops some six thousand miles west of Vladivostok.

For St. Petersburg and Tokyo had concluded a series of secret pacts which had as their main object mutual aggrandizement at the expense of China. Japan was therefore willing to sell rifles and munitions to Russia during the World War that began in August 1914. During the later stages of hostilities with the Central Powers — Germany, Austria-Hungary, Turkey, and Bulgaria — these supplies and others purchased in America and elsewhere accumulated at Vladivostok in mountainous lots far beyond the capacity of the Chinese Eastern and the Trans-Siberian to move all of them westward. In 1917, Russia was in turmoil. Her armies had suffered crushing defeats and were rapidly disintegrating; strikes, mutinies, and bread riots had been climaxed by the February-March Revolution and the abdication of Nicholas, who was later interned in Siberia by the new Provisional government. The republic proclaimed by Alexander F. Kerensky in September was overthrown by the Bolsheviks on October 25 (November 7 according to the Western calendar). On March 3, 1918 (New Style), these Communists, as they renamed themselves, abrogated an agreement to stand firm with France, Britain, the United States, Japan, and the other Allies, and signed a separate peace treaty with the Central Powers at Brest-Litovsk. In the interim, civil war had broken out between the Reds (Bolsheviks) and the Whites, or counterrevolutionists consisting chiefly of former tsarist military officers and civil administrators, landlords bereft of estates, moderate Socialists, and, in the rank and file, peasants and factory workers outraged by Bolshevik requisitions.

The Trans-Siberian is inseparable from the history of this bloodshed, and so we must follow the flow of events in some detail.

When the Bolshevik government withdrew from the World War in the winter of 1917-1918, the only effective Allied force left in the former empire was the Czechoslovak Corps, composed of forty to fifty thousand well-armed Czechs and Slovaks who had made their home in Russia or had been unwillingly conscripted into the Austro-Hungarian armies, and later defected to the Russians. These troops had been fighting the Central Powers in hope that an Allied victory would free their native Slovakia, Moravia, and Bohemia from the tyranny of the Hapsburgs. The Brest-Litovsk peace precipitated an arrangement between the French government and the Czechoslovak nationalist leader Thomas G. Masaryk to evacuate the Corps, then in the Ukraine, and utilize it on the battlefront in France. Since access routes to western Europe from the Ukraine were blockaded by the Germans, Masaryk sought and received Soviet permission for free passage of the Czechs to Vladivostok, on condition that they surrender most of their arms. At the end of March 1918, the first trainloads departed eastward. Twelve thousand men reached Vladivostok by mid-May, but the greater part of the Czech Legion, as it was also known, was strung out in groups at broad intervals along the railway, with some near the Volga, some at Chelyabinsk and Novonikolayevsk, and others farther east of the latter. Tensions mounted as the Bolsheviks delayed the exodus for fear that, among other things, the Czechs might be used in a surmised Allied plot to invade Siberia. The legionaries on their part became increasingly suspicious of Soviet good faith, and secreted rifles and ammunition in violation of Soviet terms.

"Under these circumstances a small incident led to big consequences," William Henry Chamberlin writes in his monumental *The Russian Revolution 1917-1921*. "On May 14 a group of Hungarian war prisoners came into contact with a number of Czech soldiers in one of their trains [at Chelyabinsk]. Nationalist antipathy soon flared up; one of the Hungarians threw a piece of iron at the Czechs and hit one of the soldiers; a scuffle followed and the Hungarian who threw the missile was killed. . . . The Cheliabinsk Soviet, investigating the incident on May 17, arrested several Czech soldiers. Their comrades demanded their release; and when this was not forthcoming they marched with arms into the

Camouflaged and armored car of the Czech Legion

town, forcibly released the prisoners, occupied the station and disarmed the Red Guards — apparently no very difficult task."

Bolshevik leaders reacted explosively to this fracas and, more particularly, to the news that all the Czechs en route had resolved to shoot their way across Siberia if necessary. Local Soviet war commissars were ordered to halt, disarm, and dissolve the entire Corps at once, and to shoot every Czech found thereafter with a weapon. In the belief that Germany was behind the action, the scattered legionaries seized munitions, supplies, and trains, which they serviced themselves and converted into rolling barracks and fortresses. By mid-August, they and underground anti-Communist organizations had taken over practically the whole railway and telegraph system from Penza, a city west of the Volga, to the eastern bank of Lake Baikal.* At Port Baikal, a Czech column blew up a trainload of high explosives with which the Reds had planned to demolish the shoreline tunnels and block the Legion's escape route to Vladivostok. The same column set the ferry *Baikal* afire and ended her rather sporadic career as she lay off Mysovsk. On July 25, it may be noted, another detachment had captured Yekaterinburg (Sverdlovsk), in the Urals, where Nicholas II, last of the Tsars, and his wife and children had been massacred by Bolshevik agents in the early hours of the seventeenth.

Meanwhile, the Czechs already in Vladivostok had decided in June to join their western comrades and fight with them and the Whites against the Bolsheviks. On the twenty-ninth, they ousted the Soviet municipal authorities and appealed for Allied help against armed Austro-Hungarian and German prisoners-at-large who, they believed, stood between them and their nearest compatriots, then in the vicinity of Irkutsk. This plea brought America into one of the most

* At the height of their power, the Czechs controlled, roughly, two hundred trains, including *broneviki*, or armored railway cars of the sort described by the American Major R. Ernest Dupuy. "This offensive vehicle, in its original state, consisted of any kind of car, preferably of the gondola type, which was reenforced [*sic*] by wooden baulks and iron plating. Buttressed by sand-bags banked along its sides and bristling with machine guns peering through embrasures, it presented a formidable, moving fortress. Sometimes a field-piece, anchored on a concrete base, peered from above the sides. Ahead rolled a flat-car loaded with rails. Behind the *bronevik* came the locomotive, and in rear of it rolled the box-cars of the crew. . . . In any movement the spear-head of the attack was the *bronevik*. It was pushed as far forward as possible, consistent with reconnaissance, which was carried out on foot or on commandeered horses. A reasonable distance behind came the troops of the main body. Once contact was established, the troops detrained and pushed ahead under the cover of the *bronevik's* fire. . . . In retirements the *broneviki* constituted the support and at times the refuge of the rear guard." Circular steel gun turrets sprouted from later versions of these roving citadels, the most famous of which was the ever-victorious *Orlík*, or "Little Eagle."

The Legion was remarkable for its large proportion of men from the educated classes. Among them were civil engineers who directed the repair of damaged bridges and, in one instance, devised a quick method by which a

The Orlík (*"Little Eagle"*), *a renowned armored train of the legionaries*

curious sideshows of the World War and postbellum years — the Allied intervention in the Russian civil strife. We shall confine the description of this fiasco as far as possible to our Siberian sphere of interest.

1260-foot river causeway was constructed in only sixteen days; doctors and chemists who compounded medicines for the troops; former financial experts and postal officials who set up a bank and a letter and parcel service; artists who painted the exteriors of the Czechs' boxcar quarters with patriotic motifs and hometown landmarks that served to identify the occupants to fellow countrymen along the line. On one train, a poet-schoolteacher and a lawyer in civilian life edited and published a peripatetic military newspaper, so many copies of which had to be printed to meet demand that the original type from Kiev wore out and had to be twice replaced, the last time by a font that reached the journalists by some miraculous means from the United States.

Ever since the Treaty of Brest-Litovsk, the United States had been under increasing pressure from France and Britain to mount a joint Allied expedition at Vladivostok for restoration of the war front the Bolsheviks had abandoned in western Russia late in 1917. A military threat to the contiguous Austro-German back door, the Allied Supreme War Council reasoned, might divert the Central Powers' full attention from their offensives in France and Italy. Neither the French nor the British were in a position to commit sizable forces to the undertaking, and hence they proposed that America and Japan contribute the lion's share. President Wilson regarded the scheme as politically and militarily impractical, and resisted the unceasing importunities of its supporters. After the Czech appeal, however, he was wrongly led to believe that the Vladivostok echelons intended to rescue those in the west and return with them for transportation on Allied shipping to France. In addition, he had received erroneous reports that the Austrian and German prisoners — estimated at eight hundred thousand in Siberia and supposedly being freed and armed by the Bolsheviks — might halt the rail movement of the Czechs and seize Vladivostok's billion-dollar store of accumulated war matériel as well. Under these fateful misapprehensions, the President adopted a line that fell far short of French and British desires. On July 17, he informed the Allies that "Military action is admissible in Russia, as the Government of the United States sees the circumstances, only to help the Czecho-Slovaks consolidate their forces and get into successful co-operation with their Slavic kinsmen and to steady any efforts at self-government or self-defense in which the Russians themselves may be willing to accept assistance. . . . [The United States] proposes to ask all associated in this course of action to unite in assuring the people of Russia . . . that none of the governments . . . contemplates any interference of any kind with the political sovereignty of Russia, any intervention in her internal affairs, or any impairment of her territorial integrity either now or hereafter . . ." America, the President also declared in his aide-mémoire, was prepared to send a small force, to be supplemented by a Japanese one of comparable modesty, for the protection of the supplies at Vladivostok and the rear of the Czechs operating from Vladivostok.

No sooner had the President spoken than Tokyo set its own plans in motion for a self-seeking military intervention that breached every principle of his hands-off policy with respect to Russia's internal affairs. Wilson had suggested that Japan send troops not in excess of the seven thousand America was prepared to commit to Siberia. To his dismay, the Japanese replied that they would dispatch twelve thousand and, if necessary, even more. The President was tempted to call off the venture, but he had already pledged himself in the aide-mémoire and could scarcely rescind it without appearing faithless to the Czechs. After several diplomatic exchanges, he reluctantly countenanced the twelve thousand figure and left the matter of additional troops in a haze of equivocation.

Early August saw the landing at Vladivostok of Japanese regiments and of much smaller British and French units whose activities in Siberia can henceforth be ignored as relatively insignificant. On September 2, Major General William S. Graves also debarked and assumed command of the American Expeditionary Forces (Siberia), whose maximum strength amounted to less than nine thousand officers and enlisted men. Graves, warned by Secretary of War Newton D. Baker that "you will be walking on eggs loaded with dyna-

Major General William S. Graves at his headquarters in Vladivostok

mite," had been adjured only to aid the Czechs and "to guard military stores which may subsequently be needed by Russian forces . . ." The General's orders — no more than an unsigned copy of Wilson's aide-mémoire — failed even to hint which "Russian forces" were meant, the Bolsheviks or the counterrevolutionists.

Graves, a capable, conscientious, and politically inexperienced West Pointer, had served in the Philippines, on the Mexican border, and in Washington as Secretary of the General Staff. After his arrival, he learned that power in Manchuria and eastern Siberia was divided among the Japanese, Chinese, Whites, and two Japanese-supported freebooters, one a half-Russian, half-Buryat anti-Communist cutthroat, the Ataman (or chieftain) Gregory M. Semenov,

General Gregory M. Semenov, "a murderer, robber and a most dissolute scoundrel," said Graves

also known as General Semenov. The Czechs in Vladivostok had long since taken matters into their own hands, battled Bolshevik forces north of the city (the Reds rather than the Austrian-German prisoners-at-large had been the threat all along), and entrained on the Chinese Eastern to meet their western brethren. These legionaries had been aiding the counterrevolutionists from central Siberia to the Volga, for most were convinced that the Bolshevik government was in Germany's pocket and had tried to disarm the Corps as a preliminary step toward German seizure of Siberia's granaries and other resources. The Legion was warmly encouraged in this mistaken conviction by the Whites and by primarily French and British military or diplomatic representatives hostile to the Communists for their "traitorous"

Vice Admiral Alexander V. Kolchak

desertion of the Allies, repudiation of Russia's foreign debts, and confiscation of private property. These representatives gave the Czechs to infer that Allied armies would soon be rolling from Vladivostok to help in the overthrow of the Soviets and the constitution of a White setup friendly to the Great Powers. Two counterrevolutionary governments, one at Samara and the other at Omsk, had formed a democratic, anti-Bolshevik coalition called the Directory. To the anger of the Czechs, this regime was liquidated in a coup d'état at Omsk. On November 18, 1918, Vice Admiral Alexander V. Kolchak, a small, highstrung, and humorless former commander-in-chief of the Black Sea Fleet, proclaimed himself Supreme Ruler of Russia and assumed dictatorial powers.

Japan immediately capitalized on President Wilson's unhappy acquiescence in her military program. Instead of

12,000 men, she poured 72,000 into the Amur-Ussuri region and 12,000 more into Manchuria. She had grabbed German holdings in China and the Pacific archipelagoes at the beginning of the World War, gained predominant influence over China, and viewed Russia's troubles as a priceless opportunity to move in on eastern Siberia and the rest of the Chinese Eastern. If the Russian Far East could be won, Japan would gain an expanse of land and sea from Formosa to Kamchatka. She would then be in a position to dominate both Asia and the Pacific Ocean.

Protection of the Trans-Siberian from Vladivostok to Lake Baikal — the only portion not in Czech or White hands by the end of summer in 1918 — was assigned by Allied accord to America and Japan. A tacit agreement between Reds and counterrevolutionists allowed the regular railway employees to go about their jobs presumably without fear of molestation by either side. Graves's forces, as finally disposed, were concentrated in the Vladivostok and South Ussuri regions, and spaced out at intervals along a hundred-mile stretch between Verkhneudinsk (the present Ulan-Ude) and Mysovsk. The Japanese took charge of the other sectors, including the Amur line, either with their own soldiers or the Cossack, Buryat, and Mongol brigands led by Semenov or by his nominal subordinate, General Ivan P. Kalmykov, who operated out of Khabarovsk and was described by Graves as "the worst scoundrel I ever saw or ever heard of."

Tokyo obviously had no desire to speed the evacuation of the Czechs, whose departure would remove all reason for the continued presence of eighty-four thousand Japanese troops on Russian and Chinese territories. The policy of the island empire was threefold: to shun aid to the Supreme Ruler Kolchak, who might conceivably build a strong White government capable of thwarting Japan's ambitions; to foster the nefarious activities of Semenov and Kalmykov in the hope that America, in Graves's words, "would become disgusted with conditions, withdraw her troops and request Japan to go in and clean up the situation"; and, lastly, to hamper the efforts of Colonel George H. Emerson to bring some degree of efficiency to the Chinese Eastern and the oriental divisions of the Trans-Siberian. Emerson, in ordinary life general manager of the Great Northern Railway Company and "the best mechanical railroad man in the United States" in the judgment of a knowing contemporary, was technical chief of the Russian Railway Service Corps, organized in 1917 to help the Provisional government improve rail communications in northern Manchuria and far eastern Siberia for the transport of munitions and supplies to the front. Shortly after the October Revolution of that year, Emerson and some three hundred American engineers sailed from San Francisco to Vladivostok, where they remained for only a few days because no one seemed to be in full charge of the railways. In March 1918, they returned from Japan and set up headquarters at Harbin. About a year and a half later, Graves reported to Washington that "our railway men are accomplishing very little." He adds in his *America's Siberian Adventure 1918-1920*, "No sincere person could come to any conclusion other than that the Japanese and Semeonoff were trying to block the Technical Board in the operation of the railway, and thereby delay the evacuation of the Czechs, which would give an excuse for Japanese troops to remain in Siberia."

Throughout his entire tour of Siberian duty, Graves was left without a single directive from Washington to clarify his inadequate orders. He could not determine which Russians he was to steady in "efforts at self-government or self-defense," and so he followed a neutral course that satisfied few besides the President and the War Department. Pro-Kolchak officials in the Department of State, the General asserts, tried to have him relieved from command when he thwarted their hopes that he "would use American troops as they wished them used, rather than as ordered by the Secretary of War." His British and French colleagues, whose enmity for the Communists was heightened by fear that bolshevism would spread to other European countries, also sought his removal because he repeatedly refused to take sides. For instance, Graves resisted the suggestion of the British Military Mission's chief — Major General Alfred W. F. Knox, who once referred to the Russians as "only swine" — to bar Bolsheviks from all points within six miles of the railway. The Japanese tried vainly to usurp Graves's command and undermine his authority in other ways, then instigated savage press attacks against him and his men, who were vilified as degenerates and Communist sympathizers. Exasperated by the General's obduracy, the White leader Kolchak impugned the United States forces as "the offscourings of the American Army, Jewish emigrants, with a corresponding commanding staff . . ." Graves relates that "During the period of these violent outbursts I was notified through a Kolchak liason [*sic*] officer, that two Czarist Russian General officers, both supporters of Kolchak, would stop this propaganda against me and other Americans, if I would pay them twenty thousand dollars a month." Both the White and the Red factions accused him of guarding the railway for the exclusive benefit of the other. "I could not give a Russian a shirt," the General comments, "without being subjected to the charge of trying to help the side to which the recipient of the shirt belonged." In the light of these harassments, it is understandable why their victim described as "very significant and agreeable" the letter he received from Chief of Staff General Peyton C. March, who enjoined him to "Keep a stiff upper lip, I am going to stand by you until - - - - freezes over."

The capitulation of the Central Powers in November 1918 automatically invalidated the Allies' justification for their activities on Russian and Chinese soil. Now there was no necessity for the contra-German front in western Russia or for the protection of Vladivostok's military stores and the encouragement of counterrevolutionists on the grounds that their enemies, the Bolsheviks, were German pawns. Nevertheless, the Allies stayed on. Early in 1919, President Wilson tried to bring the Reds and their antagonists together for peace talks, but failed because the Whites refused to treat on equal terms with what they called "traitors, murderers, and robbers." This gloomy contretemps left the French, British, and Americans with several choices which they narrowed down to two: one was to retire from the scene, the other was to give Kolchak further aid. The Japanese did neither, and remained for their own imperialistic purposes. Britain and France adopted the second course. Not only did they fear that the Communists would infect Europe with the doctrine of socialist revolution, but they also foresaw, among other certainties, the nonrecovery of Western investments in Russian mines, oil fields, railways, and other enterprises if the Soviets triumphed. At the time, there seemed a healthy chance that Kolchak might win with continued Allied support, and so the British and French decided to stand by him.

Neither ever sent more than token forces to Siberia, but Britain shipped tons of equipment while France contributed high-ranking staff officers in hope that they might "somehow or other contrive to take command of the whole situation," as George F. Kennan says in *Russia and the West under Lenin and Stalin.* America, however, dragged her feet. President Wilson placed little confidence in Kolchak and, in May 1919, was only dissuaded by Prime Minister Lloyd George and Premier Clemenceau from withdrawing the American troops. With both of these statesmen under the mistaken impression that the Omsk government had the upper hand, the President — overspent by the strains of the Versailles Peace Conference — finally consented on June 12 to go along with the British and French if Kolchak guaranteed to establish a democratic regime and fulfill various other inter-Allied desires in the event of victory. Accordingly, Clemenceau dispatched an interrogatory note to the Supreme Ruler. The latter's reply could have scarcely dissatisfied Wilson, for it is said to have been drafted at Omsk mainly by the Anglo-French representatives, who had a good idea of Wilsonian views. Although the President stood firm against direct intervention by United States forces in opposition to the Soviets, he promised "to assist the Government of Admiral Kolchak and his associates with munitions, supplies, and food." It was then made known that Graves's troops would stay in Siberia solely in compliance with an Allied agreement to hold the eastern railways open to traffic. Their other, unannounced purpose was to keep a watchful eye on the Japanese.

What of the Czechs? They, too, stayed on, but solely as railway guards. Exhausted by months of combat and resentful of the Allied failure to give them substantial manpower in the struggle against the Bolsheviks,* the legionaries saw no point in further sacrifices. The World War was over and the independent Czechoslovakian democracy for which they had been fighting on the Allied side had been created. Most of the troops had no stomach for battle on behalf of Dictator Kolchak. He was surrounded by decadent reactionaries and had alienated the Corps by disparaging its aid to the White cause. In short, the Czechs were sick of the Russians and the Allies, and wanted to go home. But the Allies withheld evacuation transports from Vladivostok and convinced Masaryk, now President of the new republic, that the Czechs should remain where they were. It was finally decided that they should patrol the Trans-Siberian from Omsk to Lake Baikal.

Throughout his nineteen months with the American Expeditionary Forces in Siberia, General Graves proceeded cautiously and exploded none of the "eggs loaded with dynamite." His men settled down to comparatively quiet guard duty interrupted now and then by clashes with Red partisan bands which tried to interfere in railway or coal-mining operations and were almost invariably driven off with heavy losses. The Japanese also gave trouble on several

* In his history of the Revolution, Chamberlin offers an interesting explanation for this failure. "The inability of the Allies either to make war effectively on Soviet Russia or to come to an amicable settlement with it can only be understood if one takes into account the political and social conditions which prevailed in Europe immediately after the end of the [World] War. The statesmen in Paris were sitting on a thin crust of solid ground, beneath which volcanic forces of social upheaval were seething. Two of the most pronounced psychological characteristics of the time were immense war-weariness, in the victorious as well as in the defeated countries, and acute labor unrest. So there was one absolutely convincing reason why the Allied powers could not fulfill the hopes of the White Russians and intervene with large numbers of troops: no reliable troops were available. It was the general opinion of leading statesmen and soldiers alike that the attempt to send large numbers of soldiers to Russia would most probably end in mutiny."

occasions. In July 1919, for example, they arrested nine Russians in an American sector as suspected Bolsheviks and executed five against the protests of the sector's commander. "The five Russians were marched to some graves that had been dug in the vicinity of the railroad station; they were blindfolded and forced to kneel at the edge of the graves, bending forward with their hands behind them," the official American report read. "Two Japanese officers, removing their coats and drawing their sabers, then proceeded to slash the victims on the back of the neck, while as each one fell forward into the grave, three to five Japanese soldiers bayonetted him several times with cries of pleasure. Two were beheaded at once by the saber strokes; the others were apparently alive as the earth was thrown in upon them."

Graves warned the Japanese Chief of Staff that another such massacre would lead to a conflict between American and Japanese troops. The Chief of Staff replied that he would make an investigation. "After about five weeks," Graves observes, "he came to my office and said they would have to admit the truth of the report I had received, but he wanted me to know that [the deed] was not in accordance with the practice of the Japanese Army."

Tokyo's hireling General Semenov, Graves asserts, "had openly boasted that he could not sleep at night when he had not killed some one during the day." He and his followers — said to have reached a peak strength of sixty thousand — cruised up and down Transbaikalia in a fleet of armored railway cars bearing such appropriate names as *The Merciless* and *The Destroyer,* the latter armed with ten machine guns, two one-pounders, and two three-inch guns behind steel plating and reinforced concrete eighteen inches thick. From these roving bases, Semenov — reportedly paid almost

$152,000 a month by the Japanese — murdered, ravaged, and looted on the pretense that he was suppressing bolshevism. Requisitioning parties would corral the leading citizens of a village and accuse them of collaboration with Red guerrillas. "If money and supplies were not instantly forthcoming," Major Dupuy narrates, "these people were executed out of hand, being shot, burned, tortured. In winter-time a favorite method was to cut a hole in the ice of a nearby stream or pond, dip the victims in several times until they were ice-coated and then leave them as frozen monuments. Men and women were strung up by the ears to the fronts of their houses, loot was collected by the wagon-load and car-load . . ."

Colonel Charles H. Morrow, commanding officer in the Transbaikal sector, confirmed "a most cruel, heartless, and almost unbelievable murder of an entire village by Semeonoff," Graves writes. "When his [Semenov's] troops reached the village, the inhabitants apparently tried to escape by flight from their homes, but the Semeonoff soldiers shot them down, men, women, and children, as if they were hunting rabbits, and left their bodies where they were killed. They shot, not one, but everyone in the village."

At a town near Kyakhta on the Mongolian border, Semenov put to death eight hundred prisoners between the sixteenth and twenty-first of January 1920. "In order to prevent the executioners from being bored, a different process was used on each day," Henry Baerlein records in his *The March of the Seventy Thousand*. "During the first day the victims were slaughtered by the firing of volleys, on the second day by the sword, on the third by poison and asphyxiation, on the fourth — as a grand finale — by being burned alive."

Ludovic H. Grondijs, a Dutch war correspondent who was in the thick of things as a captain attached to the French Military Mission, describes another mass execution by Semenov officers. Halting a train with nearly three hundred and fifty men, women, and children aboard, Cossacks led by two colonels herded these travelers into a field in the Chita area and mowed them down with machine guns simply because one of the colonels was not disposed to feed them as prisoners. (Why the Russian travelers were on the train and for what reason they were held are questions left unanswered by both Grondijs and General Graves, who received an account of the slaughter from two Americans in the Russian Railway Service Corps.) "The same evening," says Grondijs, "the Cossacks publicly sold the bloody clothes of the victims."

Semenov and his underlings were the sharpest thorns in Graves's side. They shot at trains, stole rolling stock, arrested railway employees, and insulted the American guards when they appeared. "We regarded them as a bunch of swashbuckling bandits and they termed us foreign interlopers and even accused us of being sympathetic with the Bolsheviki, simply because we didn't go around dealing blows to the general public and paid for what we got instead of requisitioning it and handing out worthless promissory notes as they did," Corporal Leslie H. Head recalled. ". . . Our trigger fingers often itched as we saw the obscene gestures to us and heard their epithets as their frowsy and lousy but heavily armed train guards contemptuously looked us over while their armored train passed our lonely posts. I think it a credit to our discipline and common sense that we didn't 'let them have it.' "

In January 1920, one of Semenov's henchmen, General

Nicholas Bogomolets, arrested the stationmaster at Verkhneudinsk with the announced intention of executing him for Bolshevist activities. The prisoner was released only when Colonel Morrow threatened to call out twenty-five hundred soldiers under his command. Bogomolets continued down the line in his armored train for some seventy miles to Posolskaya, where he opened fire at 1 A.M. on the boxcar barracks of an American garrison comprising one officer and thirty-eight enlisted men. These soldiers swarmed out of their quarters, dropped into skirmish line, and blazed away while Sergeant Carl Robbins, a "lanky boy from Concord, Tennessee" (in Dupuy's words), ignored enemy bullets and disabled the *bronevik*'s locomotive with a hand grenade before he was killed. At a cost of two dead and one wounded on their side, the Americans captured the train, General Bogomolets, six of his officers, and forty-eight other men, who later told interrogators that, between January 1 and 10, they had robbed and murdered at least forty-three persons, including three women whom they had previously raped. "I was sorry," Graves remarks, "that Lieutenant Kendall, who first got hold of Bogomoletz [*sic*], did not hang him to a telegraph pole . . ."

Second Lieutenant Paul W. Kendall later received the Distinguished Service Cross, an award given posthumously also to Sergeant Robbins. Since Morrow was about to pull out of Transbaikalia, Bogomolets and the other prisoners were turned over to a Kolchak agent at Verkhneudinsk. The General fled the country in 1923 and became, of all things, a cobbler in Hollywood. Investigation of his marital status when he applied for first citizenship papers led to a federal court order for his deportation to the Soviet Union, where he might well have been shot for his crimes in Siberia. Sensibly enough, Bogomolets fought the order and managed to get himself shipped to Latvia instead. The American charge against him was not for complicity in the deaths of two United States infantrymen and the wounding of one other. It was for moral turpitude.

One must return to the summer of 1919, when initial White advances along the Volga and elsewhere were rolled back by a Red army greatly strengthened through Commissar for War Leon Trotsky's fiery efforts. Kolchak was a brave, well-meaning but uninspired patriot completely out of touch with the masses, and had never won popular support. He had infuriated the peasantry by the barbarous excesses of his impressment gangs; at the slightest resistance, villages were put to the torch and the inhabitants shot, hanged, or driven into holes cut through river ice. White headquarters overflowed with superfluous personnel. "Nine hundred officers constituted the admiral's military staff; fifty-eight officers of all grades were employed in the work of censoring," Baerlein reports. "And the Grand Headquarters Staff at Chantilly which directed the world war consisted of scarcely 200 men! At Omsk the afore-mentioned 900 were surrounded by a further 5,000, who were ready for anything except to fight." Generals created useless departments and bureaus as havens for themselves and their retainers. Less exalted self-servers wangled soft administrative jobs or command posts with gunless artillery batteries unlikely to be sent into action. Still others sought safety in counterespionage that involved no more peril than the drowning of government critics in the river which Captain Grondijs sardonically calls "the Republic of the Irtysh." Kolchak, lacking the ruthlessness of a true dictator, could not bring himself to punish the skulkers who encircled him. Instead of shooting a few as examples, he merely remarked that "the Bolsheviks have done enough killing in Russia without our extending it to Siberia."

Grondijs makes vividly clear that graft and venality plagued the Supreme Ruler's supply lines. At Harbin, Manchuria, his officers turned over empty military-freight cars to enterprising merchants for twenty to fifty thousand rubles each.* Once a merchant had loaded his car with fancy foodstuffs, cigarettes, and luxury goods, he had many palms to grease. A waybill clerk collected two hundred rubles for certifying the shipment as "suitable for travel"; the Harbin stationmaster received a thousand rubles for allowing the car to be attached to a westbound train; the workers who did the actual coupling had to be paid off at the rate of fifty rubles per man; locomotive crews demanded "reasonable" compensation for proceeding at something better than a crawl and cutting short otherwise prolonged station waits; passenger seats were unavailable to the merchants (and to other civilians as well) unless they entered ticket offices by the back door and paid four times the regular fare, plus ten rubles to the conductor. The merchants must have regarded these extortions as chicken feed, for they themselves exacted

* Gold rubles — paper rubles? Grondijs does not say. According to the United States Department of Commerce, currency in circulation included " 'Czarist money' [with the gold ruble at a par value of $0.51455], 'Kerenskies,' and 'Duma money' (the paper money of the Provisional Government)." There were also "Penza" notes printed at Penza by the Soviets, and, for a brief period, "Omsk money" printed for the Kolchak government on the Czechs' railway press. Commerce Department figures indicate that the average exchange rate of the "former Russian ruble" in 1918 and the first quarter of 1919 was a trifle less than fourteen cents. In 1922, it dropped to $0.00000046, or forty-six cents per million rubles.

In an explanatory letter to the present writer, the Bank of England summed up its view with the statement that "It is not really practicable to assess the sterling equivalent of the 20–50,000 Roubles in Harbin, Manchuria between 1918 and 1920." And so we must regretfully leave it to someone who was in Harbin at the time to determine how well knavery and black-marketing paid off in terms of dollars or pounds sterling.

slightly more than a million rubles for the contents of every one of their cars delivered to black marketeers in Omsk.

In one instance mentioned by Grondijs, transportation officers accompanying a shipment of tobacco for the troops sold eighty-five per cent en route from Harbin, with the balance going to staff officers at headquarters. Between Omsk and the White forces to the west, 30,000 uniforms and the greater part of 300,000 pairs of boots were also sold along the way. During the first half of 1919, an entire army corps received no sugar, no tobacco, and no habiliments other than a thousand trouser braces for officers; everything else had been pilfered by the White commissariat. Most soldiers were in rags and carried their ammunition in potato sacks. Military withdrawals were so indifferently executed that, for example, nearly 172,000 metric tons of wheat and 65,525 tons of oats were left in July 1919 to the advancing Reds at Ufa and Chelyabinsk alone. Also falling to the Soviets were numerous consignments of armaments and clothing provided by Britain as part of her over-all anti-Communist aid program, the cost of which War Minister Winston Churchill estimated at £100,000,000, or almost $403,000,000 at the average exchange rate throughout the period. "One hundred thousand men clothed, armed, and equipped by the British had joined the anti-Kolchak forces by December, 1919," Graves declares, "and the Bolsheviks wired General Knox thanking him for supplying clothing and equipment for the Soviet forces." An important official in the Kolchak war ministry epitomized conditions when he wrote in his diary: "In the army, decay; in the Staff, ignorance and incompetence; in the Government, moral rot, disagreement and intrigues of ambitious egoists . . . in public life, panic, selfishness, bribes and all sorts of scoundrelism."

Although Czech guards were spread out along the fifteen hundred and sixty-odd miles between Omsk and Lake Baikal, Kolchak's rail communications were frequently disrupted by Red partisans, an assortment of escaped or freed convicts, White defectors, and vagrant Red soldiers who raided from forest hideaways in groups ranging from a dozen or so to several thousand. Among other activities, the larger companies pounced on White troop trains and finished off the occupants with rifles, shotguns, and scythes after trapping the cars between two bridges set on fire. Smaller bands operated mainly at night and tore up the permanent way with teams of horses hitched to the rails; others stole into station yards and sabotaged switches, brakes, and journal boxes of car axles. Railway employees, seething with discontent because their wages from the Kolchak government were three months in arrears, connived at collisions that not only wrecked rolling stock but also blocked other trains often for a half day or more.*

When shorthanded, the Czechs forced local peasants to stand sentry at bridges between every two Legion posts. If the peasants failed to raise the alarm against saboteurs, their villages were burned to the ground. In this event, they usually joined the partisans and mutilated every Czech they could lay hands on. In retaliation, Legion cavalrymen hunted them down and paid them back in kind. The savagery of Reds, Whites, Czechs, and partisans knew no bounds. It is irrelevant to go into details of tortures, flayings, and

* Except for any graft they could pick up, an engineer, a conductor, or trainman had to live on the equivalent of $3.75 a month after the fall of the ruble in 1918. "This was the average," General Graves says, "some a little less and some a little more. This was better than nothing, and if they left the railroad they could get no other work. In one case, the men struck for higher wages, the Kolchak management called it bolshevistic, and executed some of the leaders of the strike."

mutilations, but we may mention one of the "milder" atrocities Chamberlin reports. On entering a certain village, a Red leader found partisans whose ears and noses had been cropped by White troops. "As a reprisal he had the leg of a prisoner hacked off and tied to his body and sent him back in that condition to the Kolchak forces."

And so "the Russian Washington," as some had hailed the Supreme Ruler, drifted down to ruin. "Well authenticated reports justify the statement," General Graves cabled the War Department during an on-the-spot assessment of the situation at Omsk in July and August 1919, "that officers are leaving the troops and fleeing to the rear, staff officers preceding line officers in this flight, soldiers are throwing away their arms and ammunition and in some cases their heavy clothing so as to enable them to move more rapidly to the rear. I have been unable to discover any enthusiasm for the Kolchak Government."

On the city outskirts, Graves found a trainload of the dictator's sick and wounded perishing in boxcars not twenty-minutes' travel from "a gay crowd" of a thousand people dancing to a band in the municipal park. "Many of these men were too ill to help themselves," he recounts, "and there was only one nurse to five or six hundred men. There were no arrangements for food and only a very limited quantity of water carried in canteens. No help was provided for the seriously sick in attending to the calls of nature. We looked into the first box car and saw two dead men in the car and a third was dying, while a sick comrade held his head and tried to give him a drink of water. Many of the sick had mustered sufficient strength to crawl out of the cars, but this effort exhausted them and they were sprawled on the ground by the train, a helpless mass of humanity." *

Graves had traveled to Omsk on the Chinese Eastern and the Trans-Siberian railways with armed American guards and the United States ambassador to Japan, Roland S. Morris, whom President Wilson had asked to determine the true state of affairs in the Kolchak camp. After conferring with the dictator's foreign minister, Morris reported that the Omsk government was in urgent need of twenty-five thousand American soldiers and a loan of $200,000,000. The report, coupled with Graves's wholly pessimistic evaluation of military prospects and the realization that Congress would never approve either the loan or the allotment of troops, decided Washington to leave the Whites to their fate.

The curtain began to fall on the final act of the Kolchak drama that November. The Soviets had swept over the Urals and continued to advance eastward almost without opposition. Before them fled hundreds of thousands of refugees — the families of White officers and government functionaries, together with shopkeepers, priests, and journalists and other professional men with a Red price on their heads. Many

* In the ambulance cars Grondijs visited in the vicinity of Ufa, he found ninety-five per cent of the soldiers with no other injury than a wounded right or left index finger. "I doubt that any such blatant acts of cowardice," he observes, "are committed with the same impunity under the Bolsheviks, whose severe and bloody discipline there is reason to admire."

Further demonstrations of funk are given by Baerlein. "If it happened that a train set out for the front a good many of the officers used to jump out of the cars on the way. This courageous example was followed by the men, so that, for instance at the end of July, 1919, when a force was dispatched to the region of Ischin [Ishim, about a hundred and eighty miles northwest of Omsk] only 150 soldiers arrived at their destination. Later on in the evening the number had dwindled to forty-three, and the local commandant locked them up in order to prevent them from escaping."

streamed into Omsk with the shattered remnants of Kolchak divisions. One can imagine the scene from a 1923 American magazine article based on the observations of a Czech officer. "The normal population of a hundred and twenty thousand had grown almost overnight to six hundred thousand. Kolchak's housing commission had compelled every door to open and admit refugees. Many a one-story log house held fourteen to twenty people. Sanitary conditions had become frightful with the advent of the dread spotted typhus. The dead contaminated the living, and Omsk had become a city of living dead. . . . Day after day the retreating soldiers of Kolchak's army continued to straggle through the city. It required no prophet to predict that they would soon drift into the Bolshevik ranks. Emissaries of the latter were everywhere, and the promised pay of twenty to thirty roubles a day together with the best of food and clothing seemed like paradise to the poor fellows. Realizing that the troops could no longer be depended upon, Kolchak's generals decided not to hold the city, and at the close of the month ordered evacuation. Frightful were the scenes as all those hundreds of thousands of refugees who had put their homes behind them and fled to Omsk for shelter now found that they must flee again, out into the frozen wastes . . . with no destination, no place to lay their heads. They crowded the railroad station and yards. . . . Packing *teplushkas* [*teplushki:* heated freight cars] to the last limit of capacity, the refugees rolled away day after day to the east without seeming to make any sensible diminution in the remaining hordes. . . . And along the railroad for hundreds of miles after leaving Omsk ran the never ending line of refugees, a long, thin, black line of sorrow and suffering and death traced upon the white background of the snow."

In the autumn of 1919, the Allies accepted the inescapable reality that the White cause was doomed as surely as their efforts to support it. Shortly before the Red Army entered Omsk on November 14, the foreign military missions left the city and were followed by Kolchak's ministers on their way to reinstate the government at Irkutsk. The dictator and his entourage departed in six or seven trains. One contained the major part of the Russian State Bank's reserve confiscated in eastern Russia and valued at 633,600,000 gold rubles (approximately $326,019,000 at par) by an assistant finance minister in the old Provisional government. In the course of his prolonged journey eastward, Kolchak abdicated his supreme powers and entrusted himself, with the state treasure, to Allied protection under convoy of the legionaries. The latter, ever loath to risk their skins for the detested Admiral, surrendered him on January 15, 1920, to the Political Center at Irkutsk. This newly formed antidictatorial government had lasted less than a week before it was taken over by Communists. In return for Kolchak and the gold bullion, the Czechs were allowed to proceed toward Vladivostok. Early in the morning of February 7, Kolchak was executed by a Red firing squad outside the Irkutsk prison.

Previously, numerous White generals at Omsk, Novonikolayevsk, and other centers had foreseen defeat and had each appropriated a separate train for themselves, their suites, and an abundance of baggage. En route, they depleted coal supplies and forced stationmasters to halt and sidetrack traffic for considerable distances so that they could pass. This highhanded blockage of their escape route inflamed the Czechs, who saw themselves as a deserted Lost Legion about to be overwhelmed by the superior might of the approaching Bolsheviks. With the formidable armored car *Orlík* to help enforce their orders, the legionaries commandeered the railway they had hitherto merely guarded. Parts of the Trans-Siberian had been double-tracked to Verkhneudinsk some years before, but since both lines were choked, the Czechs cleared the northern one for themselves and confined refugees to the southern. From then on, it was devil take the hindmost on a deep-winter cortege of death, disease, degradation, and suffering without parallel since the days when armies of convicts and exiles had been driven on foot for thousands of miles into the depths of Siberia.

The Trans-Siberian was in chaos. The south track had been heavily clogged even before the Czechs had diverted the mainstream of traffic to it. Now, in the frost and snow of a country notorious for the cruelty of its winters, the congestion reached fantastic proportions. Jammed almost to the point of suffocation with men, women, children, the sick, and the wounded, trains in mile-long queues moved at a creep, if at all, while others stood stranded on sidetracks for lack of locomotives. Of those the Czechs had left, many broke down and were deserted by their unpaid and hungry crews. The Kolchak government had neglected to lay in sufficient coal stocks save in the Omsk region, with the result that engine pipes froze and burst when fireboxes cooled; frost put thirty locomotives out of action at the small station of Bogotol alone. Carshops became cemeteries of inoperable rolling stock the payless mechanics refused to repair. Untended pumps for water towers congealed in the cold. The refugees turned out in glacial temperatures to gather snow for engine boilers, or to pass buckets from a hole chopped through river ice.

Medicines, opiates, and antiseptics were nonexistent, and food was desperately hard to come by. At some stations,

Russian civil war refugees

Red partisans forbade peasants to sell it; at others, vendors put no faith in paper rubles, and were deaf to the entreaties of everyone without coins or articles of intrinsic value. Starvation took its greatest toll among the very old and the very young. Typhus, which had already erupted before the flight, also claimed them and countless fellow sufferers in the lice-infested, unspeakably filthy conveyances. "The dead were thrown along the tracks to rot and contaminate the district!" George Stewart exclaims in his *The White Armies of Russia.* ". . . Every station was a graveyard, with hundreds and in many places thousands of unburied dead. At Taiga, where the branch line runs north to Tomsk, over fifty thousand were slain by hunger and disease."

In the meantime, the Czechs had been rolling eastward in their cozy, typhus-free boxcars, which they insulated with wood ashes tamped down between double walls. In areas without coal, they organized its extraction and transport from deposits eighty miles northwest of Irkutsk, and left any surplus to the refugees. Altogether, the condition of the legionaries must have been nearly as enviable as that of the resourceful Scotsman who took possession of an empty boxcar, equipped it with a stove and other amenities, printed the Russian words for "English Mission" on its exterior, and, by inveigling stationmasters and trainmen with promises or threats, was conveyed in solitary, if primitive, grandeur for three thousand miles to Vladivostok.*

Not far from the railway, there was one other path that led to possible havens from the Red Army. This was the Trakt. Eastward from Omsk, the old highroad was a last resort for those who had been stranded at wayside stations or had abandoned immobilized trains, a hundred and eighty of which had fallen to the Reds by December 18. On foot or on horseback, in sledges, sleighs, telegas, and military transport carts drawn by horses which were beaten forward until they dropped in their tracks, civilians and the flotsam and jetsam of a wrecked army struggled ahead in hope that they might yet escape the Bolsheviks. Those who walked were in a state of destitution so destructive to the sense of compassion that many snatched away the blankets of women,

* We cannot vouch for this anecdote by George Stewart, nor for Baerlein's, about another "fortunate person who, in lieu of a British passport, traversed Siberia with no other document than a six-monthly ticket to the reading-room of the British Museum."

children, and the sick or aged in vehicles, and left them to freeze to death. No one stopped to cover cadavers with even a shroud of snow as a makeshift mark of Orthodox respect. Villagers barricaded their doors and hid food and fodder from the same soldiers whom they had joyfully welcomed a year before with the traditional bread, salt, and holy icons. As Peter Fleming was to write forty-three years later in *The Fate of Admiral Kolchak*, "Misery and squalor and cowardice, pain and fear and cold, carrion and excrement — these were the ingredients of the White migration."

When Red troops crossed the Ob in mid-December 1919, they found more than thirty thousand dead in the streets and buildings of Novonikolayevsk. By April of the next year, sixty thousand of the city's inhabitants and refugees had died from typhus alone. Stewart estimated in 1933 that a million persons lost their lives during the macabre flight by rail and Trakt. Some survivors joined the Bolsheviks or were captured by them; others reached Manchurian towns, Peking, or Shanghai, and settled there permanently.

There is little to add to the story of the civil war as it affected Siberia and the Trans-Siberian.

Intervention had been an ignominious failure from the Allied standpoint and had, in fact, strengthened the Communists' determination to preserve their regime against domestic and foreign enemies. With the exception of Japan, the Allies withdrew from Siberia. On April 1, 1920, while echelons of the Czech Corps were still en route through Transbaikalia to Vladivostok, Graves and the balance of his troops sailed from that port to "the good old American tune, 'Hard Times Come Again no More,'" played by a Japanese band at dockside, as the General recollects with no discernible pleasure.* By winter, all the Czechs had been evacuated on Allied transports and the *Legie,* a vessel which the legionaries had bought through their own bank; the *Legie* later became the first merchantman of the Czechoslovak Republic.

The Japanese remained for two more years on the pretext that their "special interests" needed protection until conditions stabilized. They had disengaged themselves from Transbaikalia in the summer of 1920 only to plunge into tortuous maneuvers in Manchuria and the Maritime Province to maintain dominance over North China and the Russian Far East. Nothing came of their stratagems chiefly because a post-Kolchak succession of Japanese-backed White leaders was unable to halt the oncoming Communists. The unproductive Siberian adventure had already cost Tokyo at least 900,000,000 yen (roughly $450,000,000) and was under increasing diplomatic fire from the United States. But it was

---

* Graves, a Texan by birth, received the Distinguished Service Medal and, together with his men, was highly commended by General March in a report dated June 30, 1920. "The expedition," the Chief of Staff wrote, "affords one of the finest examples in history of honorable, unselfish dealings with an unfortunate people and of a dignified and sincere attempt under very difficult circumstances to be helpful to a people struggling to achieve a new liberty and a self-government. The situation which confronted the commanding general, his subordinate commanders and troops was a peculiarly difficult and hazardous one. The manner in which this difficult and arduous task was performed is worthy of the best traditions of the Army."

Graves's later commands included the 1st Division; the 6th Corps Area, Chicago; and the Panama Canal Department. He retired in 1928 at his own request and wrote *America's Siberian Adventure 1918–1920.* Published in 1931, these reminiscences provoked a former White Russian general, living in European exile, to write a letter in which he challenged the author to a duel for having "represented the bolsheviki as the whole people of Russia and their opponents as 'Kolchak's few adherents.' " When American newspapermen questioned Graves about the letter, he remarked that "It's amusing, but I won't do anything about it. I'll just ignore it."

The Major General died from a coronary thrombosis in his home at Shrewsbury, New Jersey, on February 27, 1940, about one month short of his seventy-fifth birthday.

not until the Washington Naval Disarmament Conference of 1921-1922 that largely American pressure forced Japan to retire from both the Siberian mainland and northern China. Her troops sailed from Vladivostok on October 25, 1922, only a few hours before the Communists occupied the city and completed their take-over of continental Siberia. The northern half of Sakhalin island, seized by Japan in reprisal for the Red-partisan massacre of hundreds of Japanese soldiers and civilians near the mouth of the Amur in March 1920, was not restored to the Soviets until 1925.

"At the close of the bloodiest civil war in history," Stewart writes in one of his purple patches, "men whose names had been known only upon the files of the Secret Police now controlled the destiny of half a hundred tribes and tongues scattered over a vast domain conquered and annexed by a score of Czars in the long years of Russian history."

Grave's "worst scoundrel" General Kalmykov had fled early in 1920 to China, where he was shot after several attempted escapes from his Chinese captors. When the Japanese retired from Transbaikalia in the same year, Semenov found himself endangered by Red partisans and hastily departed southward from Chita. Later, he turned up at Port Arthur and, in 1922, visited America. His past quickly caught up with him and he was deported after a governmental hearing at which General Graves and Colonel Morrow testified to his atrocities. Thenceforth, Manchuria became his base for anti-Communist intrigues masterminded by Japan. Just before the end of the Second World War, Soviet security agents at Dairen arrested Semenov, then in his mid-fifties. He was brought to trial in Moscow about a year later, and was executed by hanging, a merciful death for a merciless killer of thousands of innocents.

CHAPTER XVIII

The New Siberia

"ONE feature of the history of old Russia was the continual beatings she suffered because of her backwardness," Joseph V. Stalin said in a speech to a conference of Soviet industrial managers on February 4, 1931. "She was beaten by the Mongol khans. She was beaten by the Turkish beys. She was beaten by the Swedish feudal lords. She was beaten by the Polish and Lithuanian gentry. She was beaten by the British and French capitalists. She was beaten by the Japanese barons. All beat her — because of her backwardness, because of her military backwardness, cultural backwardness, political backwardness, industrial backwardness, agricultural backwardness. . . . Do you want our socialist fatherland to be beaten and to lose its independence? If you do not want this, you must put an end to its backwardness in the shortest possible time and develop a genuine Bolshevik tempo in building up its socialist economy. There is no other way. That is why Lenin said on the eve of the October Revolution: 'Either perish, or overtake and outstrip the advanced capitalist countries.' We are fifty or a hundred years behind the advanced countries. We must make good this distance in ten years. Either we do it, or we shall go under."

As all the world knows, the achievements of the Soviet

Union have been nothing short of spectacular. In fewer than ten years after Stalin's speech, she revolutionized her antiquated economy and created a war machine that was to crush the greatest armies ever to invade her territory. Despite frightful devastation and manpower losses in the millions, she entered the early nineteen-fifties as an industrial and nuclear Power unrivaled by any other nation but the United States. One can visualize a totally different outcome if the Russians had lacked the Trans-Siberian to transport the infinite treasures of iron ore, coal, and countless other natural resources in Soviet Asia.

Within a few years after the civil war of 1918-1920, damaged rolling stock had been replaced or patched up by the People's Commissariat of Ways of Communication. Roadbed improvements were evident here and there, but one looked vainly for "genuine Bolshevik tempo" in the restoration of operating efficiency. When Junius B. Wood, European correspondent of the *Chicago Daily News,* crossed Siberia in the summer of 1926, he found even the Express in poor mechanical condition, seldom on time, and without enough cars to accommodate way-station throngs clamoring to get aboard.

"Half an hour before the train arrives," Wood writes in his *Incredible Siberia,* "the ticket office opens, usually a round hole in the wall no larger than a saucer, and the riot starts. The waiting crowd, some of whom may have been living, eating and sleeping on the station floor for days rushes the window. . . . There may be 200 who want to go, 40 places on the train and 35 of these preempted by individuals who have a pass or 'pull.' The first five who have stood patiently in line for hours get the surplus places and the cashier slams his window and turns down the others as coldly as a pay-car passes a wayside tramp. They can take a local train which is not so crowded and more leisurely, very leisurely, with many stops and changes of fares."

After the 1917 revolution, the Bolshevik government had confiscated the International Sleeping Car Company's *wagons-lits* and *wagons-restaurants* without compensation to their Franco-Belgian owners.* The once impeccably maintained cars were now quite dilapidated. Wood remarks on cracked windows, torn carpets, and "a few hot boxes, a cracked wheel to be replaced, airbrakes that occasionally locked, a sagging truck which made each night a gamble . . ." The dining-car cuisine was grim. "At 3:30 a plate of soup appeared — greasy hot water poured over cold pieces of fish which had been cooked earlier in bulk. The next course was pre-cooked cauliflower warmed with a sauce of unknown texture. Roast veal, cooked weeks earlier and now dry and hard, smothered in warm brown gravy, without vegetables, was the main course. A compote of fruit completed the hurried meal. The price was 1.75 roubles. Drinking water, butter or a napkin cost extra." One of Wood's fellow diners, "a haughty Norseman," was treated to what was literally a Tomato Surprise. "In the dim light," the journalist relates, "a beautiful confection of tomatoes and lettuce appeared. He [the Norseman] deftly speared a tomato with a fork but it did not connect. On top was a hard thick slice of pink soap. The diner[s] roared. The waiter shouted that an enemy was trying to ruin him. The fat

* The Sleeping Car Company's losses were slight compared to those of foreign investors in Russian railway bonds, repudiated with other tsarist financial obligations by the Bolshevik government early in 1918. In November 1955, the *New York Times* reported the face value of the various rail issues as $2,350,000,000. According to Great Britain's Council of the Corporation of Foreign Bondholders, all defaulted Russian debts amounted to $4,591,794,883, not counting interest due.

Georgian concessionaire dashed down the aisle from his counter, visioning a protocol and the loss of his concession, offering 100 roubles reward for the perpetrator. The soap was returned to the kitchen, the salad eaten. A Soviet dining car furnishes much which is not on the menu."

The American noted that the railway commissariat, in keeping with the Party vow to abolish bourgeois class distinctions, had done away with the first, second, and third categories of accommodation. Coaches were simply designated "hard" or "soft." The change was only in semantics and the removal of class-identification numerals from cars. As in the unreconstructed days of the Tsars, the common herd rode in cramped space on the hard wooden benches of the old third class while ranking government personnel and other privileged persons enjoyed cushioned seats in the roomy compartments of the former first and second classes. Abhorrence of "capitalist exploiters" apparently gave the Communists no immunity to the lure of profits, for the use of two sheets and a pillowcase cost Wood the equivalent of a dollar a night, twice the charge under the old Imperial Communication Ministry.

It was obvious that the Soviet government cared nothing then about the betterment of passenger service. From the inauguration in 1928 of the First Five-Year Plan, all its energies were devoted to the massive expansion of industry, agricultural production, and mineral extraction from known deposits or from fabulous discoveries by far-roving teams of geological prospectors. Stated in simplest terms, Stalin had determined to transform a mainly agrarian country into a self-sufficient industrial behemoth "capable of producing on a mass scale," as he said, "all modern means of defense and of equipping its army with them in the event of an attack from abroad."

To attain this goal, Stalin required a vast pool of additional laborers who could be rigidly controlled, moved about at will, and sustained at minimal cost to the state. He therefore developed a system of mass slave labor that played a major — and horrifying — role in the Soviet economy until after his death in 1953. Beginning in the late nineteen-twenties, hundreds of concentration camps, or "corrective labor camps" in Communist terminology, were established in European Russia, Central Asia, and in Siberia under the super-police rule of the OGPU (Federal State Political Administration) and of its successors, the NKVD (People's Commissariat of Internal Affairs) and the MVD (Ministry of Internal Affairs). Peasants who had resisted Stalin's farm-collectivization program, priests, real or merely suspected malcontents and political dissidents, accused saboteurs, embezzlers and bribe-takers in the bureaucracy, malingering workers, victims of wholesale Stalinist purges after the assassination of the high-ranking Party leader Sergius Kirov in 1934 — these and many others were sentenced, often without judicial trial, to forced labor terms of up to ten years. Together with common criminals, they were transported under subhuman conditions in cattle-car trains, open trucks, or ships to the sites of the stockaded and barbwired encampments they themselves had to build. From there, they were marched every day to work from ten to eighteen hours on whatever projects the camp administration had been assigned: chiefly lumbering, mining, or oil-drilling; construction of canals, hydroelectric dams, roads, railways, airfields, and industrial installations; and manual labor in diversified mills and factories. Undernourished, denied all but the most primitive and grudging medical care, overworked to meet staggering daily quotas in labor performance, hundreds of thousands perished from starvation, disease, and exhaustion. A former prisoner in northern Russia, Gennadius Khomyakov, estimated a mortality rate of twenty to thirty per cent a year and, at times, more than fifty per cent. Another ex-prisoner in the Kolyma gold-mining camps of northeastern Siberia stated that "mortality was high and ran up to one-fourth of the inmates." From the accounts of survivors, death was often a longed-for release from the Soviet camps' almost unbelievable oppressions and barbarities, all too numerous and diverse to be within the scope of this final chapter.*

During the Second World War, the slave labor camps were swelled by deported armies of "socially hostile" Poles, "unreliable" residents of the Baltic States, and "traitorous" Soviet ethnic minorities which had allegedly collaborated with the Germans. To their numbers were added thousands of Axis and Japanese prisoners-of-war. Responsible estimates of the Soviet forced labor population have ranged from three to

* Among the many graphic and harrowing personal narratives by former slave laborers is Elinor Lipper's *Eleven Years in Soviet Prison Camps* (Chicago: Henry Regnery Co., 1951). Mrs. Lipper's calmly factual memoirs describe the infamous Kolyma camps, reached from the Okhotsk seaport of Magadan, which itself was built from scratch by slave labor transported on the Trans-Siberian to Vladivostok and thence north by ship. Soviet penal labor has been comprehensively covered in the book, *Forced Labor in Soviet Russia,* by David J. Dallin and Boris I. Nicolaevsky (Yale University Press, 1947). The most recent authoritative account is available in the *Report of the Ad Hoc Committee on Forced Labor,* pp. 426-528, published by the International Labor Office (Geneva, 1953).

After Stalin's death, the almost unbearable lot of slave laborers was somewhat ameliorated. Former prisoners have testified that the population of the camps declined owing to shortened terms and a considerably larger number of releases. It has also been reported that wages have been "reintroduced," well-stocked canteens opened, and working hours limited to eight hours a day. However, forced (if not "slave") labor remains very much a part of the Soviet Union's penal system. Those sentenced to corrective labor camps include "parasitic elements," or idlers, beggars, and job-slackers, persons engaged in illegal private enterprise, and speculators, often youths who buy articles from visiting foreigners and sell the former at a profit.

twelve million, and there is a great deal of evidence that the network of corrective labor camps was very large. The Soviet government has consistently repudiated these estimates, but has not offered any alternative figures.

Under the initial Five-Year Plan, the Communication Commissariat adopted a turn-of-the-century proposal of Witte and others to connect the Trans-Siberian with the tsarist-built Trans-Caspian Railway so that cheap West Siberian grain could be exchanged for the cotton of Central Asia. Construction of this Turkestan-Siberian Railway through barren, waterless terrain commenced in 1928 at Semipalatinsk, to which a single track had been laid in 1915 from Novonikolayevsk (now called Novosibirsk). At Semipalatinsk — the garrison town where Dostoyevski had served in the army after his release from the Omsk prison in the eighteen-fifties — Soviet engineers and slave laborers continued the rails southwestward by way of Alma Ata, the capital of Kazakhstan, to the present Lugovoi for a total distance of roughly nine hundred miles. From Lugovoi, an existing section ran westerly to a junction for the Trans-Caspian from Tashkent and Samarkand to a Turkestan port across the Caspian Sea from the famous Baku oil district. Fully completed in 1931 at a cost somewhat in excess of $104,700,000, the Turksib brought cereal food to Central Asian cotton growers and thus freed their artificially irrigated grain land for greater cotton output to northern textile mills.

While this railway was under construction, work had begun on two Siberian industrial complexes of tremendous import to the Soviet Union, for the sites of both contained mineral reserves that could make Russia independent of the militarily vulnerable Ukraine, her chief source of coal and iron ore since the eighteen-seventies. The complexes were known collectively as the Ural-Kuznetsk Combine. The first lay along the Urals, described by the State Planning Commission as "the natural defense base of the U.S.S.R." The second centered round the present city of Novokuznetsk, in the Kuznetsk coal basin (or Kuzbass), about twelve hundred and fifty rail miles to the east.

The Urals possess an incalculable wealth of iron and manganese ore, copper, nickel, bauxite (used in aluminum production), chromite, zinc, asbestos, silver, gold, platinum, semiprecious stones, oil, and chemical raw materials such as potassium and common salts, phosphorites, and pyrites. But with that same perversity mentioned earlier in this book, Nature had largely deprived the region of good coking coal, an essential for iron and steel production. The charcoal fuel used for the relatively small, prerevolutionary smelters was unsuited to the mammoth blast furnaces blueprinted by Soviet planners, and so the latter had looked eastward to the Kuzbass, which further exploration had revealed as a coal area then surpassed in richness only by the American Appalachians. A Soviet estimate of 400 to 450 *billion* metric tons of proven, probable, and possible reserves has since been revised upward to 905.3 billion tons, sufficient to meet all consumer requirements of the U.S.S.R. for centuries.

As the Combine took shape, Trans-Siberian hopper cars hauled Uralian iron ore eastward to Novokuznetsk (until recently, Stalinsk), where the first of several big blast furnaces had been "blown in" early in 1932. The cars returned to the Urals with coking coal primarily for the monolithic iron foundries and steel mills just erected at Magnitogorsk, a totally new city named for its nearby mountain that contained, by Soviet claim, 485,000,000 metric tons of high-grade iron ore. For the information of those interested in statistical fancies, this tonnage from a single deposit would provide enough steel for the frames of 7938 Empire State Buildings, or for 3,969,140 Diesel locomotives, or 26,807,700 standard six-passenger automobiles.*

Simultaneously with the development of Magnitogorsk and Novokuznetsk, an immense tractor plant rose at the old town of Chelyabinsk, which had been linked to Magnitogorsk by a 258-mile branch via Kartaly in 1930. At Sverdlovsk, machine-building works began to turn out heavy industrial equipment "giving birth to new plants," as a Soviet writer puts it. Farther north at Nizhni Tagil, what was to be the Soviet Union's largest railway-car factory went into operation. Not even in America had there ever been such a sudden, turbulent burgeoning of new metallurgical colossi, machine-tool and metalworking combines, electric-power stations, and innumerable other enterprises. Several of the biggest installations built during this period of Soviet-admitted "gigantomania" were designed by American consultants and technologists paid by the Russians. The influx of free workers, peasants forcibly uprooted from the mother country, and masses of slave laborers created a population explosion in the newly industrialized centers. In the twelve years between 1926 and 1939, population more than tripled in Novosibirsk and Sverdlovsk, and quadrupled in Chelyabinsk, which later manufactured high-quality rolled steels as well as tractors. Novokuznetsk developed from a community with about 3900 inhabitants to a city of almost 170,000, while the combined

* These figures were made available to the author through the generosity of Mr. Charles M. Parker, Vice President, Research and Technology, American Iron and Steel Institute.

population of Irkutsk, Ulan-Ude, Chita, and Khabarovsk increased by 269 per cent.

The boom imposed a staggering burden on the Trans-Siberian. Not only did the railway shuttle coal, coke, and ore for the Ural-Kuznetsk Combine. It also hauled coal deriving from a freshly exploited field at Karaganda, a subsequently notorious forced labor center in mineral-rich Kazakhstan, to which a branch southward from the main-line city of Petropavlovsk had been extended in 1931. Capacity was further overtaxed by shipments of petroleum, industrial machinery, agricultural equipment, and military material for eastern Siberia and the Soviet Far East; grain and timber for farther transport on the Turksib to Central Asia; animal and fish products, foodstuffs, and tea for European Russia. Between Omsk and Novosibirsk, for example, east- and westbound freight increased from not much more than 5,400,000 tons in 1931 to nearly 8,105,000 tons two years later. Responsibility for the resulting congestion, the mounting backlogs of unshipped consignments, and the sharp rise in accidents and wrecks lay squarely with the Party leaders. In the belief that better organization and higher labor productivity would prevent bottlenecks, they had denied the rail system sufficient personnel as well as capital funds for much-needed improvements and rolling stock.

The failure of the incumbent Communication Commissar to resolve the crisis led to his replacement in February 1935 by Stalin's chief trouble man and alleged brother-in-law Lazar M. Kaganovich, then Commissar of Heavy Industry. Described by John Gunther as a former tanner and shoemaker remarkable for "impressive force, animation, and volubility," this self-educated administrator was given a free hand

and the necessary resources, with the consequence that the railways recovered substantially by the summer of 1937.

During Kaganovich's eight-year administration, corrupt or obstructive officials were executed or shipped off to forced labor camps along with workers repeatedly guilty of "criminal" carelessness, absenteeism, or slipshod workmanship. On the other hand, successful innovators and top producers were rewarded with cash prizes, wide publicity as national heroes or heroines, and rapid promotion. "Relatively few women reached the glamorous post of locomotive engineer," Professor Holland Hunter says in his *Soviet Transportation Policy,* "but many became assistant engineers; in September 1939 there were forty-four of the former and forty-five hundred of the latter." Among the full engineers was Zinaida P. Troitskaya, a young woman who received the Order of Lenin for her exceptional proficiency as a driver of passenger trains. She was later appointed assistant head of the Moscow subways which, incidentally, had been constructed under Kaganovich's direction. As one honored by the Lenin order — the U.S.S.R.'s highest award — Madame Troitskaya was elevated to the peak later attained by Stalin, Kaganovich, the novelist Michael Sholokhov (author of *And Quiet Flows the Don*), and the composer Dmitri Shostakovich. (In 1945, holders of the Order were entitled to a monthly stipend of twenty-five rubles for life; a one third reduction in the required number of years of work or service to qualify for a pension; income-tax exemption; housing accommodations at ten to fifty per cent less than the normal rent, a prerogative extended to the decorated person's family and disabled dependents after his or her death; an annual free roundtrip within the Soviet Union by train or ship; and free rides on streetcars anywhere in the U.S.S.R. Equal privileges did not accrue to "Heroes of Socialist Labor," such as the embalmer who preserved Lenin's remains for permanent exhibition in the mausoleum on Red Square.)

The training of railway employees received more attention than ever before. Middle-grade workers such as station- and yardmasters, dispatchers, and foremen were assigned to full- or part-time studies at railway engineering institutes and technical schools. Additional apprentice schools were opened for prospective mechanics, engine-drivers, shunters, and permanent-way men. As preliminary training, boys and girls were taught how to operate scaled-down engines and cars that ran on narrow-gauge track a mile or so long in various cities. Like its big brothers, the miniature locomotive seen in a Krasnoyarsk park by the American traveler and Far East expert Owen Lattimore was embellished with the features of Lenin on the front; it was not the familiar adult profile shown on main-line engines but a portrait of the Father of Bolshevism as a baby.

Kaganovich augmented the rolling-stock fleet with more powerful locomotives, large, four-axle freight cars, and all-metal passenger coaches. In 1936, workshops for the overhaul of nearly eleven hundred engines annually began to rise at Novokuznetsk. A year later, the largest plant east of the Urals for building and repairing locomotives and cars went into operation at Ulan-Ude, a producer of glass, chemicals, and processed foods. Heavily worked sectors of the Trans-Siberian had been double-tracked and strengthened with more ballast, additional ties, and heavier rails. Other improvements included automatic brakes and couplings, automatic or semiautomatic block-signaling systems over part of the line, centralized switches, and semaphores and colored lights in lieu of flags and hand-swung oil lanterns. The number of sidings and marshaling yards was notably increased. Bottlenecks at single-track bridges were eliminated by the erection of a second span.

It is difficult to evaluate the benefits from Kaganovich's personnel-training plan, but there is clear evidence that his modernization program added significantly to train capacity and speed. For instance, in 1940 the railways of the U.S.S.R. hauled twice the freight tonnage of 1934 with nothing like the difficulty encountered earlier, while average freight-train speed showed a gain from barely nine miles an hour to twelve miles an hour. Including stops, the terminal-to-terminal pace of the Siberian Express remained constant at about twenty-seven miles an hour, but since tsarist days Soviet railwaymen had reduced the scheduled Moscow-Irkutsk running time by practically a whole day.*

* A strictly unpublicized "fast" train of the Stalin period was the Lux Blue Express, reserved exclusively for Communist Party leaders, supreme military commanders, and their wives. The Express made its first trip on May 1, 1933, and ran every spring, summer, and autumn between two groups of pleasure resorts in southern Russia, and occasionally to and from Moscow. In his *The New Soviet Empire* (1951), David J. Dallin draws on a description of the train by its former chief, Vladimir Tregubov. "Tregubov to begin with had to see to the building of the train. He selected ten of the best cars from various lines and began to rebuild them. The first requisite was that no noise of the wheels be heard inside the cars, and that they move smoothly. To achieve this a thick coat of lead was poured over the floor of each car; this was covered with a layer of felt, a layer of cork, another layer of felt, a wooden flooring, and yet another layer of felt. Over this was laid a covering of linoleum, and on top of everything a soft rug. The resulting floor was like a feather bed. The rugs laid in the lounge cars cost 5,000 rubles apiece in a special restricted store in Moscow. They could not have been bought in the open market for 50,000. In testing a car a glass brim-full of water was put on a table in one of the compartments; not a drop must spill on the table during the entire trial run. On the outside the cars were painted a deep azure and the roofs sky blue. The paint was covered with a coat of lacquer and polished until not a rough spot or a scratch could be found. . . . Each car of the Blue Express . . . consisted of eight compartments (for two persons each), with toilets between every two compartments, and one bathroom. Equipped with every convenience, the compartments outshone the most comfortable trains in Europe. . . . The dining car provided a wide selection of exquisite delicacies, a great variety of fruits, and the choicest drinks. Before every trip the conductor passed

For a reason that shall be seen, double-tracking of the seventeen hundred and eighty-seven miles from Ulan-Ude to Khabarovsk had been hastily begun in 1933 with work crews that included ten thousand forced laborers. Three years later, when Khabarovsk was reached, the construction gangs turned south and, in 1939, joined rails with the existing two tracks from Ussurisk to Vladivostok, which was the focus of maritime trade, shipbuilding, and fishing as well as a great naval base. From there, short branches were built to regional coal mines and smaller commercial ports such as Nakhodka. In 1940, a 213-mile section from a town slightly west of Khabarovsk was officially opened to Komsomolsk-na-Amure, a northern shipbuilding center called "the City of Youth" to honor pioneering members of the Young Communist League who had built it. In the same year, a 158-mile track was laid

from compartment to compartment, spraying eau de cologne and putting flowers on the tables. During the journey he brought around fruit, candy, and the best cigarettes. The most extravagant whims of the generals, marshals, people's commissars, secretaries of regional party committees were to be satisfied. . . . Stalin's car has two bedrooms, a sitting room, an office, another office for his secretary, a compartment for the persons accompanying him, a bathroom, and a kitchen. The walls and all the furniture are of mahogany. The cars of other leaders are built along the same lines, but the paneling and the furniture in each are of different styles and materials. Kaganovich's car, for instance, is done in Karelian birch, while Molotov's is exactly like Stalin's. . . . Behind the 'leader's' car there was always another car, exactly like it in appearance, as a 'blind,' carrying a detail of NKVD men, and others were distributed through all the cars, entrances, and platforms; two or three of them sat in the dining car. . . . Before the train passed a station all incoming and outgoing switches were locked and each was guarded by the switchman and a NKVD agent assigned to the station. Troops and agents from the railroad's NKVD section were stationed as guards in all the tunnels and along the entire length of the tracks. . . . Ordinary Soviet citizens were not even permitted near the station when the train was due. . . . The NKVD kept two girls [*sic*] agents permanently in the train. It was their duty to strike up an acquaintance with the passengers, engage them in conversations in the dining cars, and generally keep their ears open. They were good looking, always well dressed, knew how to behave in society and were always accessible to the important passengers. . . . The job of chief of the Blue Express is a very profitable one: Tregubov was paid as much as the top engineers of the largest factories; twice a year he received new uniforms, and there were from Ulan-Ude to Naushki, near the old caravan-tea entrepôt of Kyakhta and only two hundred and fifty miles north of Ulan Bator, capital of the Mongolian People's Republic with which the Soviet Union maintained close ties.

Meanwhile, two western extensions had been under construction in Kazakhstan, a prairie and semidesert land nearly four times the size of Texas and the source of half of the U.S.S.R.'s zinc, a third of its copper, and a quarter of its lead. By means of the first extension — a 296-mile single track running southeast from Karaganda via Mointy to Lake Balkhash — Karaganda coal was exchanged for copper from deposits near the lake. This line was opened to traffic in 1939. The second, completed in the next year, comprised a 273-mile section from the Karaganda-Balkhash track southwest to the copper mines of Dzhezkazgan and Karsakpai.

Twenty-one years later in the vicinity of Baikonur, perhaps thirty miles west of Karsakpai, the Soviet Air Force pilot Major Yuri A. Gagarin was launched into the ionosphere. He completed one orbit round the earth and became the first human space traveler to return safely. On June 16, 1963, Junior Lieutenant Valentina V. Tereshkova was also launched from the Baikonur area and became the first spacewoman. Undoubtedly much heavy equipment for their flights was transported to the cosmodrome by the Trans-Siberian and the Karsakpai extension, but Commissar Kaganovich, under

numerous perquisites. There was such an abundance of goods around the train that no one kept any account of them. One could bring home from these trips whole cases of caviar, canned goods, wines, and cigarettes. Tregubov lived like a Soviet dignitary — yet in ever-present fear of arrest. He was always being called for questioning by the NKVD and various party commissions. And his fears were well founded. He was finally arrested and sentenced to be shot on the charge that he had allegedly plotted to assassinate Kaganovich but for some reason had not gone through with it. The sentence was commuted, and later during the [Second World] war Tregubov had the chance to leave Russia."

whose aegis the first railway had been modernized and the second built, was unremembered in the celebrations. For this old-line Stalinist had been driven into obscurity by the miner's son, Nikita S. Khrushchev, in 1957, roughly fifty-four years since the Emperor Nicholas had dismissed from the Finance Ministry that other brilliant administrator Sergius Yulyevich Witte.

The role of the Trans-Siberian during the "Great Patriotic War" is singularly lacking in drama. Unlike the railways in western Russia, it was never blitzed, seized, and ultimately destroyed by the Germans. The Kremlin had concluded a nonaggression pact with China and maintained peaceful relations with Japan, and so there were few alarms and excursions in the Soviet Far East. The part played by the Trans-Siberian, then, was the rather colorless one of an overstrained yet faithful workhorse offstage from the lurid theatricals of combat. But without this workhorse the Soviets might well have gone down to overwhelming defeat. For the railway and its subsidiary lines filled the breach in food supplies, minerals, and oil when the Wehrmacht isolated western Russia, the Ukraine, and the Caucasus. Round-the-clock for almost four years the Trans-Siberian helped to keep Russia alive with grain, fed coking coal and iron ore to the feverishly worked Ural-Kuznetsk Combine, and hauled inestimable tons of war matériel. In addition, the railway aided in the transport of labor and equipment from more than eight hundred West Russian airplane, munitions, and other factories for safe relocation in the Urals and such centers farther east as Novosibirsk and Krasnoyarsk, a mushrooming city to which the machinery of a huge Ukrainian locomotives works was transplanted.

Under the exigencies of war, the Soviets rushed through several railway construction jobs, in most of which Axis prisoners-of-war formed part of the labor force. The first, completed in 1942, consisted of a 334-mile single track from the Caspian Sea port of Guryev northeast to Kandagach, not far from the Kazakh-Emba fields that yielded high-quality oil for the refinement of aviation gasoline, desperately needed at the front.* In the following year, another single-track railway was opened from Akmolinsk (the present Tselinograd, in northern Kazakhstan) westward for five hundred miles to the Kartaly junction for Magnitogorsk. This line was doubly important to the war effort: it shortened the haul of Karaganda coal to Magnitogorsk via Petropavlovsk by three hundred miles and freed the Trans-Siberian for the transport of other vital freight between Petropavlovsk and the Urals.

In the Soviet Far East, new construction was confined to a branch from Pivan, across the Amur from Komsomolsk, southeastward to the newly developed naval and fishing base of Sovetskaya Gavan, on the Strait of Tartary. The 277-mile link was hurried to makeshift completion in the latter part of July 1945, just in time to be useful for the seizure of southern Sakhalin and the Kuril Islands from the Japanese, who lost, at the war's end, all their gains in China, including Port Arthur, Dairen, and every mile of the Chinese Eastern Railway.

Before we explain how Tokyo had gained control of this North Manchurian offshoot, we can dispose of a grandiose and as yet unrealized railway project called the Baikal-Amur

* In July 1964, a 440-mile extension from the Guryev-Kandagach line was opened between Makat, seventy-seven miles northeast of Guryev, and the new town of Shevchenko, south of Fort Shevchenko, on the Caspian Sea. The branch provides rail-access to a rich oil-bearing region on the Mangyshlak Peninsula.

Silver-painted statue of Stalin, now removed from the platform of Taishet station

Magistral. Writers in the West have described it as a "Second Trans-Siberian," begun in the thirties largely by slave labor to exploit virgin mineral and forest resources in eastern Siberia and to provide a second line of communications if the Japanese knocked out the Amur track with long-range bombers. The route is not to be found in the latest definitive Soviet atlas, but many British and American publications show it, in its entirety, as lying between Komsomolsk and Taishet, a distance of roughly sixteen hundred miles as the crow flies over savage, partly mountainous, and largely uninhabited terrain north of the Amur and Lake Baikal. Yet, as far as is known, no more than a 434-mile section has been completed. Beginning at Taishet, a town on the Trans-Siberian between Krasnoyarsk and Irkutsk, the track follows a winding course easterly to the Bratsk hydroelectric power station — the world's largest — and terminates at Ust-Kut, on the Lena

River about a hundred and seventy miles northwest of the upper extremity of Lake Baikal. This railway has undoubtedly been invaluable in the development of the renowned diamond fields discovered in the Yakutsk Autonomous Republic in 1954 and thereafter.

Although some Western experts on the Soviet Union believe that the whole B.-A.M. would be hardly worth the cost — estimated in 1941 at more than one and a third billion rubles, or approximately $250,000,000 at the foreign exchange rate for a decade after 1937 — one should not assume that it will never be built. For the Russians, as Paul E. Garbutt, a British authority on Soviet railways, points out, "regard their railways, just as we do our merchant fleets, as the main physical factor in binding together their vast empire. They consider, too, that in this connection their railways have a political and social, as well as a purely economic, function to perform." *

The events leading to Japan's acquisition of the entire Chinese Eastern began at the height of the Russian civil war,

* Mr. Garbutt's description of steam locomotives used on the Trans-Siberian will be found in Appendix D.

Ernest W. Williams, Jr., offers additional reasons why railways still outbalance all other carriers in the Soviet Union. "The United States since the middle 1920's and Western Europe since the second war have developed mainly by expanding the nonrail forms of transport," he says in his *Freight Transportation in the Soviet Union* (1962). "No counterpart is observable in Soviet history. It is likely, indeed, that no major nation has ever been so completely dependent on the railroad as the Soviet Union is today. . . . The natural waterways of the Soviet Union which are capable of improvement do not mesh well with the traffic flows required by the economy. Pipeline transportation has been of limited usefulness because of the want of concentrated flows which could fill large-diameter pipe. . . . Motor transport could not be developed, except for local purposes, because of the lack of an improved highway system. No importance has been attached to highway development, doubtless because it is recognized that, by comparison with the railroad, truck or bus transportation is highly inefficient except on the shortest hauls and requires unacceptable inputs of fuel, labor, and repair parts, and a rate of vehicle replacement which cannot be sustained without very massive expansion of the automotive industry."

when the Bolsheviks made a dramatic bid for friendship with China. In 1919 and again in 1920, they declared their willingness to renounce tsarist privileges, concessions, and railway rights in Manchuria without compensation. The offer made a profound impression on the Chinese people, but the Peking government, exacerbated by Russian penetration into Chinese-claimed Outer Mongolia, reacted coldly and refused to open diplomatic relations with Moscow. By May 1924, however, the Soviet position had been strengthened by agreements with Britain, Germany, and several smaller Powers for mutual trade and de jure recognition. China, on the other hand, was weakened by incessant strife among her powerful war lords. Soviet negotiators stood by their promises to abolish the old privileges in Manchuria, but now they refused to consider return of the railway unless Peking accepted a special treaty "on the way of working the Chinese Eastern Railway with due regard for the interests of the U.S.S.R." Peking reluctantly capitulated, assented to a face-saving adjustment of the Mongolian issue, and opened diplomatic relations with Moscow. On May 31, 1924, the high contracting parties signed a treaty which, among other articles, called for provisional operation of the railway as a commercial enterprise on a half-and-half basis. It was agreed that a conference would convene in the near future to arrange financial and other terms for China's future redemption of the line. In the interim, five Chinese and five Russians would comprise the board of directors; disputes unresolved by the board would be referred to the two governments; the general manager was to be a Soviet citizen, aided by one Soviet and one Chinese assistant manager; Chinese and Soviet nationals were to be equally represented among railway personnel. One paragraph in the agreement stated explicitly that the future of the line was to be determined by the U.S.S.R. *and* the Republic of China, to the exclusion of any third party.*

Since actual control of Manchuria rested with the celebrated war lord Marshal Chang Tso-lin, Moscow concluded a nearly identical pact with him at Mukden in September. The Soviets then proceeded to violate both treaties in a drive to squeeze out the Chinese and reestablish the Chinese Eastern as an all-Russian sphere of influence. On one pretext or another, they postponed the conference that was to arrange for reversion of the railway to China. They ignored her rights and stalled the settlement of disputes at both directorial and governmental levels. The Chinese assistant manager was overruled by the Soviet general manager and his assistant, who appointed fellow countrymen to top railway posts and hired so many others that only twenty-five per cent of the total personnel in 1929 were Chinese.

Under Soviet rule, the Chinese Eastern again became a Russian state on China's soil. ". . . It ran its own schools, had its own museums, engaged in construction activities, maintained its own river flotilla and owned land in excess of its actual needs," Dallin declares. ". . . The telephone and telegraph systems of northern Manchuria likewise were in the hands of the Russian-dominated Chinese Eastern. Finally, Communist cells and clubs were operated in the area of the

---

* According to an official publication issued by the Chinese Eastern Railway Company in 1924, the railway had on January 1 of that year 16,584 employees, 533 locomotives, 739 passenger coaches, and 10,823 freight cars. Of the passenger equipment, 221 were four-axle, 15 three-axle, and 503 two-axle; the freight stock included 324 American four-axle cars and 1054 four-axle gondolas, also American. Thirteen and a half per cent of the locomotives, 25 per cent of the passenger coaches, and 5.3 per cent of the freight cars were "in bad order."

The railway's one deluxe train at that time consisted of a baggage car with an electric-power generator; a dining car; two first-class and one second-class car, a drawing-room car, and one observation car with "verandah-platform, large plate glass windows, a drawing room, bar, reading room, barber shop and bath room."

railroad, and a variety of ties connected them with the Chinese Communists who were being persecuted by the Manchurian Government. . . . The manager used a Soviet bank to keep the assets of his company, and in this way considerable profits of the enterprise were used by the Soviet side without any control by China.

Marshal Chang Tso-lin, anti-Communist in his views and backed financially for some years by Japan, tried to halt the Russian inroads. From time to time he arrested the Chinese Eastern's manager and other employees, seized its river vessels, and took over its schools and museums on the grounds that they disseminated subversive propaganda. Despite these inflammatory tactics, the Soviets avoided an all-out conflict until 1929. By that time, Chang had proved troublesome also to the Japanese, who had occupied southernmost Manchuria since the 1904-1905 war with Russia. In June 1928, they allegedly exploded a bomb beneath a train in which he was riding. The Marshal died of injuries and was succeeded by his son Chang Hsueh-liang. By agreement with Chiang Kai-shek — head of the Nationalist government — the "Young Marshal" confiscated the Chinese Eastern in July 1929, replaced the manager and other executives with Chinese, and incarcerated hundreds of Soviet citizens. Moscow retaliated by arresting a similar number of Chinese and severing diplomatic relations. Stalin undertook no large-scale military operations, however, until assured of Japan's nonintervention. She made this role clear by declining to join the United States and leading European Powers in a plan to place the Chinese Eastern under neutral control while negotiators tried to settle the quarrel. Such action, the Japanese feared, would make it easier for the Western mediators to hand over the entire railway direction to China. They might then turn to Tokyo's holdings in southern Manchuria and press for their restoration to the Chinese.

With the tacit consent of Japan and in successful defiance of Western attempts to intervene, Stalin mobilized more than a hundred thousand troops in Siberia, launched extensive raids into Manchuria, and forced the Young Marshal and Chiang Kai-shek to sue for peace. On December 22, 1929, a protocol signed at Khabarovsk reinstated the status quo ante. The farcical "joint" management continued until September 1931, when the Japanese launched an invasion that culminated in their incorporation of Manchuria and other Chinese territory into the puppet state of Manchukuo. The Russians still ran the railway, but only under increasingly chaotic conditions created or encouraged by the Japanese military.

"Brigandage along the whole length of the Chinese Eastern has become more serious than ever before," Dr. Wang Ching Ch'un, a former director-general of the railway, wrote in 1933. "Sabotage, train-wrecking and burning of stations have become an everyday affair. Numerous demands of the most irritating and costly sort, such as for the free transportation of Japanese troops and Manchukuo guards, the restriction of train movements, etc., have been made in dictatorial language and carried out by force. Valuable properties belonging to the railway have been seized; many Russians have been summarily arrested; numerous railway employees have been killed, disabled or kidnapped by bandits for ransom. Even the railway itself has been cut several times by Japanese officers in the employ of Manchukuo . . . for the purpose of stopping all traffic between Manchuria and Siberia. Life and property, the Soviets declare, 'have never been so insecure along the Chinese Eastern as they are today.' . . .

The Soviets' forbearance has only led to ever-increasing encroachments." But in one instance at least, Soviet forbearance did not preclude the execution of a quiet order by which 83 locomotives, 194 passenger coaches, and 3200 freight cars on the Chinese Eastern were rolled out of Manchukuo to Siberia. Manchukuo demanded their return, but the Russians maintained that they owned the equipment, and never sent it back.

By the spring of 1933, the situation had worsened to such degree that the Soviets realized they would either have to give up the railway or resist Japanese aggressions by force of arms. Stalin followed the first course, for war was the last thing he wanted during his monumental industrialization program. Warily on guard, however, he strengthened Soviet defenses in the Far East and, in anticipation of the Chinese Eastern's loss, ordered the double-tracking of the Trans-Siberian from Ulan-Ude through Khabarovsk to the Ussurisk approach to Vladivostok. In June 1933, a Soviet delegate opened negotiations at Tokyo for the sale of the Chinese Eastern to Manchukuo — that is, Japan — at the asking price of 250,000,000 gold rubles (nominally $128,637,500). Manchukuo countered with an offer of 50,000,000 yen ($13,-500,000). The Russians responded to this disdainful bid by cutting their figure to 200,000,000 gold rubles. After many acrimonious exchanges and protracted stalemates, the deal was finally closed at 140,000,000 yen, one third to be paid in cash and the remainder in Manchukuan and Japanese goods and commodities. The purchaser also had to pay 30,000,000 yen as a retirement pension fund for Soviet employees. Tokyo thus bought the enterprise for a total of 170,000,000 yen, or $48,280,000 (in reporting the agreement, a *New York Times* dispatch from Tokyo quoted the value of the yen at the time as $0.284 and added that compensation was provided in case the exchange rate fluctuated more than eight per cent). On its part, the Soviet government received a windfall in cash and goods for an inherited line that was rapidly deteriorating and, moreover, in peril of outright take-over by the Japanese.

The sale agreement was signed at Tokyo on March 23, 1935. Japan's Foreign Minister hailed it as marking an epoch in Russo-Manchukuan relations and assuring "the steady growth of their mutual cordiality." The Soviet envoy replied that it "should bring genuine satisfaction to every peace-lover in every part of the world." Two years before, China had protested the proposed sale as the crowning infringement of the 1924 treaties, in which a special paragraph had established her joint right to determine the future of the railway. Foreign Affairs Commissar Maxim M. Litvinov answered that the Chinese "have ceased to be the active partners of the U.S.S.R. on the Chinese Eastern Railroad for more than a year and a half." The failure of China "to fulfill the obligations incumbent upon it under the Peking and Mukden agreements for a period of eighteen months," he added, "deprives it both formally and morally of the right to refer to these agreements. . . . Our proposal is still another manifestation of the desire of the Soviet Government to maintain peace." Shortly before the consummation of the sale, China filed another protest. It received no Russian notice save in the government organ *Izvestia*. "Every thinking Chinese patriot knows that the U.S.S.R. would have been deeply happy if it had been possible to turn over the railroad to the representatives of the great Chinese people," an editorial said in part. "But the Chinese people are not masters of the situation in Manchuria and they would gain nothing if the C.E.R. became the object of a war which might have destroyed this Far Eastern railroad." And with that convenient line of argument the Soviets virtually ended the controversy. The Japanese promptly changed the broad Russian track to the standard Western gauge of the South Manchuria Railway and merged operations with the latter.

Only a few days before the end of the Second World War, the U.S.S.R. joined forces with the Allies against Japan. The Russians poured thousands of troops into Manchukuo, where they captured the Japanese army and seized millions of dollars' worth of raw materials and Japanese industrial equipment for shipment to the Soviet Union. On August 14, 1945 — the day of Japan's formal surrender — the Kremlin concluded a thirty-year treaty of friendship and alliance with the Nationalist government of Generalissimo Chiang Kai-shek. Under this covenant, the Manchurian lines were renamed the Chinese Changchun Railway and placed yet again under Russo-Chinese "joint" administration dominated by the Soviets. Ostensibly, the two governments shared equally in control of Port Arthur and Dairen, which was declared a free port open to international shipping and trade, but actually Russia ruled both. On September 21, 1949, the Chinese Communists proclaimed the People's Republic of China, then drove Chiang and his government from the mainland to Formosa, or Taiwan. In the following February, the Soviets repudiated their 1945 pact with the Generalissimo, signed a thirty-year treaty of friendship, alliance, and mutual assistance with Communist Premier Chou En-lai, and agreed to surrender participation rights in Port Arthur, Dairen, and the Changchun Railway without compensation. Late in 1952, China at long last became sole owner of the former Chinese Eastern after more than fifty stormy years, perhaps the stormiest in the history of any modern transportation system. Conceived by tsarist expansionists and beset by plague, cholera, banditry, rebellion, and declared or undeclared warfare, the railway — as Dr. Tao-hsing Chang wrote in 1936 — had been "born in sin . . . [and] reared in tragic adversity."

While the railways in European Russia were being rehabilitated after their devastation in the Second World War, the Ministry of Ways of Communication commissioned a number of new construction projects.* In 1949, an extension of the Transbaikalian branch between Ulan-Ude and the frontier town of Naushki became fully operational to Ulan Bator. Four years later, Russia, Mongolia, and China began a southeasterly extension across the Gobi Desert to connect Ulan Bator with Peking. This Trans-Mongolian Railway was opened to traffic on January 1, 1956. Aside from its value as an inland link to the most populous areas of China, it shortens the rail distance between the Soviet and Chinese capitals by more than seven hundred miles and assures transport communications if the more vulnerable Manchurian tracks were ever to be demolished by enemy action. The Trans-Mongolian connects at Chining with a Chinese railway that has been built, at the date of this writing, in a westerly

* According to figures presented by Professor Hunter and converted by the present writer from kilometers to miles, destruction of the railway network in European Russia included almost 62,100 miles of first, second, and yard track, of which roughly eighty-seven per cent was restored during hostilities; more than 2300 large and medium-sized bridges; and nearly 2460 stations. Soviet postwar reparations claims charged the loss or damage of 15,800 locomotives and 428,000 freight cars. Professor Hunter and others offer evidence that these last two statistics were exaggerated.

In 1946, the "People's Commissariats" of Finance, Trade, and so forth were renamed "Ministries," possibly in recognition of the brief thaw in Soviet relations with the West, to which "Commissariats" and "Commissars" were rather opprobrious terms.

direction as far as Wulumuchi (or Urumchi), capital of the Chinese province of Sinkiang. A continuation of the line would bring it to Dzungarian Gate, at the Soviet border, to which a 186-mile branch was completed in 1960 from Aktogai, a town about midway between Alma Ata and Semipalatinsk. The Soviets constructed this "Road of Friendship" to aid in the promotion of trade and exploitation of Sinkiang's mineral resources.

Meanwhile, two important lines in Kazakhstan and western Siberia had been quickly completed by forced laborers in 1953 with the help of time-saving equipment that laid and ballasted prefabricated track. The first line consisted of an extension of the Magnitogorsk-Karaganda railway — double-tracked and electrified today — northeastward for nearly seven hundred miles to the Kuznetsk coal basin. The extension begins at Tselinograd and passes through the textile and food-processing center of Barnaul, on the upper reaches of the Ob River. It continues to the Kuzbass, now a nucleus of machine-building, metal-working, chemical, and nonferrous metallurgical plants in addition to steel mills. Often referred to as the South Siberian, the whole railway between the two extremities of the Ural-Kuznetsk Combine relieves congestion on the Trans-Siberian. Recently, a 200-mile branch was opened from Novokuznetsk eastward to Abakan, a city in a mining and agricultural region which had been joined to the Trans-Siberian in 1926 by a somewhat longer branch from the flour-milling community of Achinsk, where a large aluminum plant was under construction in 1964. The new line not only hauls ore to the Kuznetsk complex, but also serves as another transportation outlet for timber from Trans-Siberian collection points to Kazakhstan and Soviet Central Asia. Another new line from Abakan northeastward to Taishet will

Station at Taiga, the junction for Tomsk

provide a through route from the southern republics to the Lena River.

The second construction project completed in 1953 comprises a single-track extension from Mointy, not far from Lake Balkhash, southward to Chu. This junction is on the Turksib between Tashkent and Alma Ata which, as guidebooks chorus with unfaltering unanimity, means "Father of Apples" in the Kazakh tongue, one of the eighty main languages indigenous to the present area of the U.S.S.R. By delivering coal from Karaganda, the 281-mile extension ended Tashkent's dependence on the Kuzbass, more than seven hundred miles farther away. It should be pointed out here that the reduction in length of haul is considered important by Soviet authorities. In most Western countries, freight rates per mile decrease as the distance increases, but

Irkutsk station, now reached by a steel and concrete bridge across the Angara

in the U.S.S.R. they rise progressively with mileage increments. This system is set up to discourage excessively long hauls and to spur the use of local or neighboring resources by industry. Conversely, passenger rates per mile diminish in proportion to the distance traveled: the longer the run, the less the rate per mile.

Today, the largest Trans-Siberian stations are at Sverdlovsk, Omsk, Novosibirsk, Taiga (the junction for Tomsk), Irkutsk, Khabarovsk, and Vladivostok. They are monolithic, many-windowed, and sometimes ornamentally pillared buildings of brick, stone, or concrete stuccoed or painted in pastel colors. They show remarkably little soot from locomotives, and so far have been spared outdoor billboards save for a few poorly lithographed panels of official exhortations and architectural landmarks of Moscow. There is a restaurant-buffet

The old station at Mariinsk

The new, adjoining Mariinsk station, since completed

Pajamas, a favorite traveling costume on the Trans-Siberian

Passengers buying bread and sandwiches at a pushcart buffet

Soft-drink stand ·n station platform

The line-up at food stalls

inside the stations, but most passengers on express trains, which stop for only twenty minutes, head for the more accessible snack bars on the platform or for canvas-canopied pushcarts where women sell sandwiches, doughnut-shaped meat pastries, portions of fried chicken or fish, ice cream on sticks, and bottles of beer. Kiosks display Soviet magazines and paperbound books, *Izvestia,* the Communist Party organ *Pravda,* and occasionally the London *Daily Worker* and the Parisian *l'Humanité,* both communist in their views.

No Soviet railway station seems complete in summer without at least one bed of pansies and other flowers enclosed by a neat border of pebbles. Frequently, close-set plants are trimmed to portray the name of the station, a slogan such as the ubiquitous "Glory to the Communist Party," or, at Irkutsk during the writer's visit, the life-sized

Boiled-water taps at practically every station

figure of a bear standing with paws extended in greeting; only a close view revealed the tiny, growing foliage that entirely blanketed it.

On the platform of practically all stations but whistle-stops, you see a silver-painted statue of Lenin. At some, he is shown with an arm oratorically outstretched or merely raised as if — to be utterly truthful — he were hailing a taxicab. At others, he stands with hand in pocket or sits while holding a book.

Many of the smaller stations would be easily recognized by Trans-Siberian passengers of the early nineteen-hundreds. Now, as then, the ticket office and waiting room are housed in a single-storied wooden structure surmounted at the center by a high, steep roof with one or more gables overhanging the façade. Almost invariably, the station is painted light brown and ornamented at the rooftop and along the eaves with jigsaw gingerbread. By the entrance hangs a brass bell of the type Robert Jefferson observed in 1897, but no longer is it rung with "a terrific tintinnabulation," since an outdoor loudspeaker now announces train arrivals and departures. A picket fence surrounds most platforms, still wood-planked as a rule and perilously slippery on wet days. On the station wall facing the tracks, several brass faucets deliver boiled water just as they did years ago when ordinary water might be contaminated by the stationmaster's livestock. An old-fashioned outdoor clock gives Moscow time, which the Trans-Siberian still follows to the continued confusion of long-distance passengers, for there are eight different local time zones between Moscow and Vladivostok, including the zones of these two cities.

Probably like their mothers, grandmothers, and great-grandmothers before them, kerchiefed peasant women stand behind board counters laden with bread, bottles of milk, roasted chickens, and such. Others walk past car windows with buckets of meat pies and plates of baked potatoes while small girls trail behind with pails of red currants or baskets of raspberries and wild strawberries in paper cones. Essentially, the scene at most wayside stops has changed very little from the descriptions by early rail travelers.

In 1950, work began on the Angara Dam, about six miles from Irkutsk center, and the first of several installations designed to harness the Angara and Yenisei rivers for hydroelectric power. As the reservoir would eventually flood part of the Trans-Siberian between Irkutsk and Port Baikal, a double-tracked and electrified roadway was built up the Irkut valley and across the Primorski Range directly to Slyudyanka, on the lake's extreme southwestern shore. The 84-mile bypass of Port Baikal is equipped throughout with automatic block signals, runs through two tunnels, and has the steepest grades — two per cent — on the entire Trans-Siberian. It was opened to traffic in 1956, three years before completion of the Angara 660,000-kilowatt station. Irkutsk now has a population greater than 370,000, heavy machinery works, an airframe factory, ship-repair yards, an oil refinery, and many other enterprises. It is also the transportation hub, military-supply depot, and cultural center of eastern Siberia. In addition to the oldest university in this region, the city possesses eight technological institutes and a new scientific research and student-training academy near the Angara Dam.*

From the observations of the writer during a visit limited by Soviet authorities to five days, Irkutsk has become as prosaic and respectable as any contemporary city in the once-gaudy American West. One can walk the streets at night without fear of strangulation by lurking *varnaki*, and one sees no modern counterparts of gold-mine laborers gallivanting around town on flamboyant sprees. So circumspect is this former "Paris of Siberia" that uncultured pedestrians who discard as much as a cigarette stub on sidewalks are likely to be accosted by a Citizen Volunteer and required to pick up the stub and put it into one of the aluminum-painted

* The Trans-Siberian has proved indispensable in the construction of the eastern hydroelectric power grid that centers on Irkutsk, Bratsk, and Krasnoyarsk, where the Yenisei is being harnessed for a ten-turbine plant of 5,000,000-kilowatt capacity. At the Angara installation, for instance, the Trans-Siberian delivered turbines from the Ukraine, generators from Novosibirsk, and other electrical equipment from Leningrad. Some idea of the Soviet investment in Siberian "white power" may be gained from knowledge that the Angara dam and station — smallest of the three — cost $133,000,000. The writer was taken on a tour of the station from Lenin's silver-painted effigy in the reception room to the water-splashed depths of the eight-turbine area about a hundred and sixty feet underground. The plant is so fully automated, we were told, that it is usually operated by shifts of only four engineers each, some of them women.

Irkutsk: the Central Hotel

ashtrays or urns at curbstones. Roisterous cafés chantants have disappeared as completely as the old Métropole and its restaurant where John Foster Fraser observed "a troupe of girls from Warsaw [who] sang lewd songs, and then came and drank champagne with the audience." The nearest thing to these honky-tonks today is the main restaurant of the Central Hotel. Noisy and smoke-filled from 10 P.M. until the small hours, this cavernous hall is stripped of tablecloths for the evening and given over to thirsty Irkutskian young fellows in sport shirts and baggy trousers. From the running fire of talk and explosions of laughter, they seemed to be enjoying themselves thoroughly despite the absence of cards and girl entertainers.

Intourist, the state travel organization, obliges foreign

visitors to stay at the Central. It is a five-story steel and concrete building more than thirty years old, and, though renovated in 1960, just barely escapes the spartan, cheerless look of low-rental housing projects in the United States and Britain. Bedrooms for even those who travel in Intourist's most expensive class are small, carelessly painted, cheaply furnished, and remarkable for color-blind décors if our quarters were typical. Room 340 had pale green walls, purple window drapes that inexplicably turned red at night, highly varnished brown bedsteads and chairs with red plush seats, a quilted green stool before a dressing table, a student lamp with emerald-green plastic shade, and brown linoleum to supplement a thin red and blue runner between the beds. As in almost every Intourist hotel, a woman employee on each floor sits at a table by stairs or elevator and allows no one to descend without turning in the room key. She also never fails to note on a ledger the time of one's departure and return.

For all its blocks of austere new apartment houses, grandiose governmental buildings of the Stalin architectural period, and paved, well-lit main streets, much of Irkutsk could be quickly identified by the pioneer travelers. The handsome rose and buff Drama Theater at one end of Karl Marx Street (the former Bolshaya) remains unchanged save for a background of trees not evident in the old photographs. Part of the nearby Museum of Regional History, established in 1782 and housed in a brick and stone Russian-baroque building, may still be seen through the eyes of Marcus Lorenzo Taft, an American Methodist minister and missionary who crossed Siberia with his wife and baby daughter in the summer of 1910. There on the second floor are the "utensils and implements pertaining to the primitive ages of man, systematically arranged and labeled," as he writes in

Early travelers on the Chinese Eastern and Trans-Siberian railways: the Reverend and Mrs. Marcus Lorenzo Taft and daughter Marian

his *Strange Siberia Along the Trans-Siberian Railway.* More interesting to the present writer were the exhibits added since Taft's time: convicts' iron fetters and chains, lethal-looking whips of leather and metal, and yellowed photographs of prisoners branded on cheek and forehead, and of one felon stretched out on a sleeping platform with his wrist manacled to a wheelbarrow. Even George Kennan could not speak with greater eloquence than these melancholy relics of the Siberian exile system.

It is odd that comparatively few foreign visitors since Harry de Windt and the Meakins have commented on what struck the writer as the most beautiful building in Irkutsk, far superior to any of the gold-mine proprietors' show places which have long since been taken over for civic use or multiple housing. This is the present scientific library of the university and was once the residence of the governors-general of Eastern Siberia. Overlooking a bluff above the Angara, it is a white-stuccoed, three-story edifice (and edifice *is* the word for a structure of such dignity) embellished by a Corinthian colonnaded portico that delights the eye from every angle. The mansion dates from the beginning of the last century and was occupied some forty years later by General Muravyev, who entertained Collins at the sumptuous banquets the latter described. An exterior plaque commemorates certain revolutionists of 1917, but Muravyev — the empire-builder who won the vast Amur territory from China for the Bolsheviks eventually to inherit — is ignored.

At the city's other extremity, the green-spired eighteenth-century Church of the Holy Cross exists as "a superb example of Russian craftsmanship," a recent Soviet guidebook says in agreement with admirers of this exquisite national monument, "and is preserved as such by the state." Orthodox services are held at the older, less impressive Church of the Saviour, where we saw a handful of old women kneeling on

Irkutsk: scientific library of the university; formerly the governor-general's residence

Irkutsk: the Church of the Holy Cross

the steps. We were informed by an Intourist interpreter — a twenty-year-old girl who had to be asked repeatedly to show us this "working" church — that the practice of kneeling was very unsanitary. In a somewhat neglected plot on the grounds are the tombstones of several exiled Decembrists and that of Princess Trubetskaya.

Steel and concrete spans supersede the old pontoon bridge across the Angara, but a number of the city's side streets have yet to be paved, and, on the outskirts, one still sees the plank sidewalks and trestles over ditches almost every British and American visitor used to remark on. The walks are now kept in tolerable repair and have ceased to be the "man-traps for the unwary" Dr. Clark termed them in 1900. Although our interpreter said, quite rightly, that they were "untypical," she made no objection to our photographing them. It may be

Irkutsk: Kirov Square, formerly Speranski Place

added in passing that Irkutskians seem to take a more relaxed view of foreigners with cameras than do Muscovites who, in our experience, frown disapprovingly if one snaps unfavorable aspects of their city. In Irkutsk, we could wander alone on photographic expeditions and take pictures of any number of mud-holes and run-down houses without passersby paying us the slightest attention.

One of the most charming smaller thoroughfares is First Red Army Street, tree-shaded and partly lined with prerevolutionary wooden houses Mrs. John Clarence Lee described as "a cross between a sea-shore cottage and an Alpine chalet." Solid and squat, the log houses among them are cozy-looking little affairs, with fanciful fretwork decorating the eaves and with window frames and shutters sometimes painted blue, or

The old and the new in Irkutsk: wooden house and modern apartment building on Krasni By-Street

green, and white. The contrast between the old and the new Irkutsk is particularly striking on Krasni By-Street, in the heart of the city, where a square log house of tsarist vintage stands in low silhouette against a new apartment house rearing behind it. In its other aspects, Irkutsk failed to impress us as anything else than a spacious commercial and industrial metropolis with pretensions as a cultural rival to Tomsk, whose university was rather summarily referred to as "also good" by our female interpreter, a native Irkutskian.

In summer, one reaches Lake Baikal on slim, Diesel-powered ferries or the much faster hydrofoil vessel we shall later describe. There is also the old, forty-mile post road, now asphalted, that follows the Angara's northern bank and undulates over pine- and larch-covered hills to historic Listvyanka, near the Angara outlet. Today, it is a somnolent

One of the conventional summer ferries plying between Irkutsk and Lake Baikal

A side road at Listvyanka

little port of interest chiefly for its Limnological Institute, where scientists devote themselves exclusively to study of the lake and its flora, fauna, and marine life. Set into the wall of an exhibit room is a large plastic reproduction in color, done to scale, of Baikal's crevasse in cross section and in perspective from south to north. On the right of this ingenious pictorial creation, you see the eastern lake bed descending until it plunges to a depth of more than a mile almost beneath the pictured Listvyanka dwellings, which seem about to plummet down the almost sheer wall of the western abyss. From observations taken in the lake itself for the benefit of science and the local fishing industry, the courses of schools of *omul* and other fish are regularly plotted with simulated schools in the model crevasse. Also on view are preserved specimens of most of the creatures that inhabit the lake.

Listvyanka can scarcely be regarded as a commercial summer resort, for it has no hotels and only one small restaurant. But it is frequented by Irkutskians on day-long excursions and is a sightseeing attraction for visiting domestic and foreign delegations. By the lakeside, we ran into a group of Mongolian tourists — the men in Western clothes but the women in red or yellow native dress — all escorted by a young man who introduced himself to us as a Buryat and a professor of Mongolian at the university in Irkutsk. He was short and genial, and spoke in intelligible French.

A mile or so across the water, Port Baikal lies as a forlorn reminder of the great summer days of the *Baikal*, the once-famous train-ferry which the Meakins observed "puffing dark smoke from its three [*sic;* four] funnels, and standing so high above the water level that we shuddered to think how it would roll if caught in a storm." Breakwaters remain, but the

On the shore of Lake Baikal: the Buryat professor of Mongolian, with Mongolian delegation in background

fork-shaped slipway is no more. The still active *Angara* (somewhere else on the lake during our visits) now ties up with barge-tugs and small, black-hulled cargo ships at the port's conventional wharf. A yellow and white wooden station rises near sidings from the double tracks now used only for freight to and from Kultuk, fifty-odd miles down the shore. A few metal-roofed sheds are scattered about, but they seemed disused, and not a freight car was visible. Port Baikal, in short, is a ghost of itself in the early nineteen-hundreds, when the bustle was such that Fraser imagined himself at Folkstone. "Porters seized the baggage," he recalled, "and, losing pieces of it, scampered along the pier, where lay a steamer belching black smoke . . . and another steamer laden with horses was snorting its way seawards."

On the return voyage downriver, one can see the old Irkutsk–Port Baikal track where it has not yet been submerged by the dammed Angara. Here and there little wooden

A lake freighter at Port Baikal; at lower right, the skipper of the Raketa

Steam tug at Port Baikal

railway bridges span tributary streams, and beneath the no-longer-traveled roadbed Engineer Pushechnikov's wall of flat stones still protects it from erosion by the swift Angara. Occasionally, a black-and-white-striped signal standard can be glimpsed along the track. On one, the arm was raised to the stop position. It was a fitting epitaph. We disembarked from the hydrofoil of the new Siberia and were glad to return to the lively traffic of Irkutsk. After sleepy Listvyanka and all-but-deserted Port Baikal, Irkutsk appeared to be indeed the Paris of Siberia.

Nineteen fifty-six marked the end of the production of steam locomotives. With the proliferation of electric-power plants and high-voltage transmission lines, the railway ministry had been shifting over to electric, Diesel, and Diesel-electric engines in the interest of greater efficiency, economy, and adaptability to the climate.* Electrification of the Trans-Siberian and of main lines in European Russia was proceeding rapidly with the aid of army labor on some sections and

* "By the end of the seven-year period (1959-1965) only lines with moderately dense traffic will continue to use steam traction, and steam locomotives will handle only 13 per cent of the rail freight turnover instead of the 74 per cent of 1958," say the authors of a Soviet publication entitled *Soviet Seven-Year Plan, Transport and Communication 1959-1965*. ". . . If the railways continued to use steam locomotives in 1965, it would require nearly 140,000,000 tons of coal transported each year in 30,000 wagons only to fire the locomotives. The use of diesel and electric traction will increase the carrying capacity of double-track lines 50-100 per cent and of single-track lines 100-150 per cent. With these types of traction labour productivity on the railway transport will increase about 15 per cent and transportation costs will drop 20-25 per cent. . . . The replacement of steam engines with diesel and electric locomotives will reduce the personnel of the engine crews about 36 per cent and that of the water, coal, etc., supply departments 85 per cent. An additional 15 per cent reduction in engine crews will result from the greater train speeds and weights. . . . All railwaymen released as a result of the technical reorganization will be taught new trades in special classes and will then be re-employed on new jobs."

The author has not verified these statements, but includes them for whatever interest they may hold for railwaymen in the Western community.

A P–36 steam locomotive, the postwar 4-8-4 modification of the former JS Class

Eight-axle N–8 electric locomotive, since renumbered VL–8

An E–723 2-8-0, a successor of the old Shch Class

An antique E Class now used for freight switching; at left, brick water towers

of specially designed machinery which, Soviet sources reported in the *Railway Gazette*, installed as many as a hundred reinforced concrete pillars for overhead-current wires in two or three hours. On October 9, 1961, the Soviets announced that the trunk line from Moscow to Lake Baikal via Ryazan, Kuibyshev, Chelyabinsk, and Novosibirsk had been electrified.

Today's equivalent of the Russian State Express completes the run from Moscow to Irkutsk in four days and to Vladivostok in seven days, sixteen and a half hours. Hauled alternately by electric, steam, Diesel, and Diesel-electric locomotives, it includes a baggage car, a diner, a deluxe "International Class" sleeper, several soft coaches with eight four-berth compartments, and a string of hard cars, each with "lying places" (in Soviet timetable terminology) for up to fifty-eight persons. The massive, high-riding, all-steel equipment is painted pea-green with two narrow horizontal stripes of what Gogol called "the everlasting shade of yellow," so common it was and still is in Russia. Each car bears the U.S.S.R. coat of arms and detachable black and white signs that give its terminal destination.

All carriages have electric fans but no air-conditioning. Except at stations, windows are kept tightly shut against showers of cinders and soot. Every compartment and hard car is rigged with a radio loudspeaker that delivers a barrage of Soviet news, songs, and now and then excerpts from Western operas. There is a volume-control button in each compartment, but its location — in our car, under a table by the window — is seldom easy to find the first time.

The deluxe sleeper is a ponderous Soviet version of a European prewar *wagon-lits* and comprises nine two-berth compartments, each separated by a toiletless, lavishly mir-

Car attendant and the author at Sverdlovsk

rored washroom. There is a distinct Victorian elegance about the compartments that would have surely been familiar to Annette Meakin and her mother, who traveled on the State *train de luxe* in 1900: the glistening mahogany-finished paneling; the massive, highly polished brass door lock and other fittings; the white, semitransparent window curtains and side drapes of thick blue plush; the weighted table lamp with its fringed silk shade; the upholstered easy chair by the window; the multicolored Oriental carpet; the solid mahogany stepladder on which one climbs precariously to a narrow upper berth; the ashtrays and water decanter as heavy as lead crystal; the pungent aroma of burning charcoal when an attendant fires up the corridor samovar for tea. Both water taps in the adjacent washroom usually run cold. In the often sooty but otherwise inoffensive toilet-washroom — one at each end of the car — there is a communal roller towel and a

Dining car on the Moscow-Vladivostok express

shower, with no curtain or stall-door to prevent all the water and suds from drenching the basin, toilet, walls, and floor. The soft coaches are much simpler but quite comfortable affairs with washing and toilet facilities limited to a cubicle at each end of the corridor. The hard cars are generally uncompartmented, with three tiers of berths, some extending across the car, others lengthwise between the side wall and the aisle.

As in tsarist times, the diner is partitioned, but the old lounge section with its piano and library has vanished as irrevocably as the menus in French and the male waiters. Now as you sit at one of the cloth-covered tables for four you are served by a white-bloused and aproned woman, two to a car and each crowned with a white, paper-lace tiara. Near the cash register and the time-honored abacus with which the waitresses calculate diners' bills, a glass cabinet displays Russian cigarettes, candies in paper wrappers, preserves and relishes in jars, and, dominating them all, bottles of Georgian champagne and brandy, but none of vodka, the most popular hard drink in the nation. Rather reluctantly, the dining-car supervisor told the writer (through his interpreter) that the sale of vodka, much less expensive than champagne and brandy and within the means of most passengers, might lead to "uncultured" behavior on their part. Presumably all those who can afford the higher priced stuff know how to drink like ladies and gentlemen. Except for the usually excellent fish or meat soups, the food reminded us of Junius Wood's description when he crossed Siberia years ago.

The coaches seldom jerk or sway, but how they bounce at times. "The truck-riding qualities are definitely inferior and are aggravated to a certain extent by the fact that the rail is laid with square or opposite joints, rather than staggered joints," an exchange delegation of American railwaymen reported in 1960. "This imparts a characteristic bouncing quality to the ride, particularly when the speed is increased." * At big stations after a long run, crews of women wash down

* This was the first official American group to inspect Russian railways since 1930, when other Americans led by Ralph Budd, then president of the Great Northern Railway, were invited by the Soviet government to examine operations on the Trans-Siberian and to suggest improvements. The head of the 1960 delegation, Curtis D. Buford, has said that "the state of Russian railroad technology is at least 30 years behind American railroad development. . . . There is little or nothing like our widespread use of centralized traffic control, two-way train radio and microwave relay systems, push-button freightyards with radar-activated retarders and remote-controlled switches. . . . People work in 8 or 12-hour shifts and after 42 hours have been completed, the worker is relieved until his next work week period. There is virtually no overtime for extra hours. . . . Rail operations are

the car exteriors with water and long-handled brushes, while workmen inspect axle boxes and give car wheels a hammer-tap to test their soundness.

The observations of the writer and of the American railway experts indicate that the danger of accidental electrocution has yet to stop the old custom of the poor or thrifty to ride on train roofs. "The Russian name for such riders is 'flyers,' because there is some frequency of such passengers flying from the top of cars into a ditch when [a] train gives a sudden lurch," the delegation explained. "This roof riding practice is frowned upon and has diminished a great deal in recent years. However, passengers were observed on the roof, even in electrified territory under the high voltage wire."

There are no more cabooses on Soviet freight trains today than there were when Civil Engineer Lodian deplored their absence sixty-five years ago. In their *Railroads of the U.S.S.R.*, the railwaymen of 1960 stated that ". . . the only facility provided for the trainmen consists of a shelter with open sides and open end, which is installed on approximately 10 per cent of the freight car fleet. This shelter is 3 ft. or less in length, and in some cases does not extend for the full width of the car. A narrow board seat is available, but it is

generally overstaffed, due to lack of mechanization. They use 3,500,000 workers or about 10 times as many employees per route mile and three times as many employees per traffic unit as in the U.S."

However, the Soviet authorities are steadily improving their equipment, installing time-saving machinery, and adding electronic control systems. Even with their present plant, the railways seem to make money. On May 9, 1962, the *New York Times* reported a speech in which the railway minister declared that "the railroad revenues since 1955 not only had covered all operating costs and capital expenditures but had supplied 'significant funds' to the budget. These, he said, amounted to 1,800,000,000 rubles ($1,988,000,000 at the official rate) last year, or 2.2 per cent of Government revenues." But an editorial in the *Times* a few days later pointed out that "Soviet railroads pay no interest on the huge capital investment they represent, much of which came from luckless foreign investors before the Bolshevik Revolution."

without cushioning or upholstering of any kind. The Soviets stated that the railroad issues heavy winter clothing free to the trainman in order to protect him from the severe winter weather, which may reach 40° F. below zero or lower. No heat is provided in the trainman's shelter nor is there any protection against the elements from the open sides and rear of the shelter."

However, the Soviet Union's 3,500,000 railway employees — about a third of whom are women engaged mostly in permanent-way maintenance, car-cleaning, and car attendance — are better off than many other industrial workers in the U.S.S.R. "Every railway line has its own medical-sanitary service, its own hospitals, clinics and outpatient departments where all services are free," the English-language *Moscow News* reported in July 1961. "The home health service has a staff of doctors and nurses who take care of calls from small stations and watchmen's cabins. . . . Last year alone 22 new hospitals and maternity homes with 1,650 beds were opened for this industry. In the course of the Seven-Year Plan some 150 hospitals and 30 clinics will be built. . . . In case of the wage earner's death the family receives a pension for those of its members who cannot work. . . . Railway workers are eligible for old-age pensions upon reaching 60 years for men and 55 for women. Pensions are issued on privileged terms for those employed in difficult conditions such as locomotive engineers of all types and their assistants, stokers, locomotive washers, furnace cleaners, freight train conductors, etc. Men working in these trades are eligible for pensions at the age of 55 and women at 50."

According to railway authorities in Leningrad, electrification of the rest of the Trans-Siberian to Vladivostok is scheduled for completion by 1971. Electric engines will prevail between Khabarovsk and Komsomolsk, which had a population of 177,000 according to the 1959 census, steel mills, and a pipeline from the Sakhalin oil fields across the Strait of Tartary. Unconfirmed reports say that this pipeline is being extended southward to Khabarovsk, the largest Soviet city east of Irkutsk. It has a population in excess of 320,000, an oil refinery, machine-building works, armament factories, an aircraft-assembly plant, sawmills, and extensive facilities for handling a large volume of rail, river, and air traffic. Like every other major center in Siberia, Khabarovsk is served by transport planes of the state-run Aeroflot, one of the world's largest airlines. Mainstays of the long-distance fleet are the TU-104 jet and the TU-114, a turboprop so big that Americans have called it "the aluminum overcast." It can carry 220 passengers and flies the Moscow-Khabarovsk route of roughly 3800 miles nonstop in about six hours. Feeder lines connect with mining, reindeer-breeding, and other isolated communities even farther north than Norilsk, originally developed by forced labor and now a thoroughly modern nickel-producing city almost two hundred miles above the Arctic Circle and with more than 100,000 inhabitants.

In 1960, the head of the American railway delegation stated in an interview that "Development of nuclear locomotives is not now contemplated in the U.S.S.R. We were told positively that instead of motive power, nuclear technology would be applied to the development of central power stations to produce electricity for railroad electric locomotives and for the electrification of areas where other power sources are not economic." Nuclear power has been applied, however, in a region that had successfully defied Man for centuries. This is the arctic territory where the Northern Sea Route follows the waters north of European Russia, passes the Soviet nuclear testing ground of Novaya Zemlya, skirts the Ob, Yenisei, and Lena estuaries, and terminates round Siberia's northeasternmost tip.

In 1879, the Swedish explorer Nils A. E. Nordenskjöld completed the first through voyage in the 357-ton bark *Vega.* The British Captain Wiggins, one may recall, also negotiated the Northeast Passage as far as the Yenisei in his attempt to deliver a cargo of English rails to Trans-Siberian construction engineers in 1893. The Imperial regime had recognized the seaway's potentialities for trade to and from the Siberian interior, but no significant commercial breakthrough between western Russia and the Far East occurred until the early nineteen-thirties, when three Soviet ships circumnavigated the polar route from northern Russia to Vladivostok. Subsequent lighthouses, meteorological observation posts, and radio stations led to routine freighter operations that lasted anywhere from ten weeks to four months, depending on the severity of the "open" season. These operations are of great economic and military importance to the Soviet Union. Siberian raw materials shipped down the Ob, Yenisei, and Lena are exchanged for commodities and manufactures from both European Russia and the Far East. In addition, the Arctic fleet transports equipment and supplies to the network of early warning and ground control intercept sites, forward air strips, and missile-launching installations that rings the Soviets far eastern seaboard. Navigation continues for longer periods than ever before, largely owing to reconnaissance aircraft and formidable icebreakers such as the Diesel-electric *Moskva,* her sister ship the *Leningrad,* and the nuclear-powered *Lenin.* Commissioned in 1959, this first atomic icebreaker displaces almost four times the tonnage of that earlier Siberian wonder, the *Baikal,* and develops nearly twelve times her horsepower. The *Lenin* can navigate for two or three years without calling at port, the Soviets aver, "while conventional icebreakers [presumably the 5000-tonners also employed to clear the Northern Sea Route] must discontinue their voyages every month or two." *

Among the new river craft east of the Urals are *rakety,* or "rockets," which were almost as amazing to young Siberians as the *Baikal* had been to their great-grandparents. These sleek *rakety* are hydrofoil passenger vessels fitted with underwater wings that enable them to skim over water and attain high nautical speeds. According to the captain of *Raketa N.4* that races between the Angara Dam and Lake Baikal in the ice-free season, there were seven of these hydrofoils on Siberian watercourses in 1961. Since then, faster models of 140- to 300-passenger capacity have been tested and perhaps put into serial production. The ship he himself skippered with the aid of a first mate and a young woman boatswain was a low-slung, rakish yacht 85 feet long and 15 feet in beam; it develops 1250 horsepower, cruises at 38½ mph, attains a top speed of 52 mph, and puts out for the 40-mile run to Lake Baikal even when waves are four feet high. The passenger cabin resembles the interior of an airliner: a middle aisle divides two rows of three-abreast but spacious foam-rubber

* The *Lenin* is 440 feet long, 109 feet in beam, displaces 16,000 metric tons, develops 44,000 shaft-horsepower, and reaches a maximum speed of 18 knots in clear water. The *Moskva* and the *Leningrad* are slightly smaller, with an approximate length and beam of 400 feet and 80 feet respectively, and 22,000 shaft-horsepower. By comparison, the largest American icebreaker, the United States Navy's *Glacier* (the conventionally powered AGB-4, commissioned in 1955) is 310 feet long, 74 feet in beam, and displaces 8775 tons full; her engines develop 16,900 shaft-power and drive her at speeds up to 16 knots. In the spring of 1964, the Navy Department informed the author that it "currently has no plans" for building a nuclear-powered icebreaker.

The Raketa *("Rocket") that speeds between Irkutsk and Lake Baikal in summer*

Interior of the Raketa *hydrofoil*

Siberian youngsters on the "Rocket"

seats for possibly sixty persons. The large plate-glass windows are bordered by semitransparent pull-back curtains with the familiar Victorian fringes which still seem as pleasing to Russian eyes as the buffet in the stern. As if to announce that she is no conventional vessel, the *Raketa* signals her advent and departure with a siren instead of a marine horn.

Siberian river-port installations have been enlarged and mechanized for the transshipment of water-borne grain, timber, mineral building materials, and related bulk freight to the railway, from which petroleum, chemicals, machinery, consumer goods, and tons of other products are unloaded for farther transport by barges and freighters to northern and southern Siberia. (A pipeline from the rich Ural-Volga oil region — the "Second Baku" developed during the thirties — has been laid to Omsk, Novosibirsk, and Krasnoyarsk, and is being continued to the Irkutsk area.) On the Irtysh River, windy, inclement Omsk has far outstripped its old rival

Auto tail fin and Buryat boy at hydrofoil landing place near Irkutsk

Tomsk in population and industrial growth. Omskians outnumber Tomskians by more than two to one and outproduce Tomsk with their oil refinery, machine-building and chemical works, sawmills, and processing plants for agricultural and animal products. Tomsk, however, is still the educational center of western Siberia and, besides its decades-old university, has a technological institute said to have been the model for dozens of others elsewhere. As both Omsk and Tomsk have been closed to practically all non-Communist nationals, the author cannot compare the hotels of either city with those Robert Jefferson and other foreigners endured years ago.

In spite of fog for an average of ninety-five days a year, Novosibirsk is without doubt the busiest river port in Siberia, for products converge on it from the northern and southern reaches of the Ob as well as from the tracks of the Trans-Siberian, the Turksib, and a 180-mile connection with the Kuzbass. This youngest and greatest of Siberian metropolises — the unofficial capital of western Siberia — has a population that has risen from 887,000 in 1959 to more than 980,000 today, not counting the transients who throng the railway station, the largest in Siberia. Since the Second World War, acres of outlying land have been covered with new factories, now powered by a 420,000-kilowatt hydroelectric station. Novosibirsk's products include aircraft, machinery, steel, rubber, and textiles. Along an artificial lake formed by the Ob Dam, a great scientific center has been established since Harrison E. Salisbury visited the site with the party of the then Vice President Richard M. Nixon in the summer of 1959. "When . . . [it] is complete," Mr. Salisbury wrote in *To Moscow — and Beyond*, "there will be a self-contained community of 35,000 scientists and their assistants and between 1,500 and 3,000 students with 4,000 teachers in a new graduate university. . . . The role of the center will be to coordinate all scientific work in Siberia. It will direct the program to transform Siberia into the most productive region of the Soviet Union. Here will be devised the strategy for unlocking the untold mineral resources of the great continent. And here will be devised plans for exploiting these riches most economically and efficiently."

One hopes that this journey through infinite plains, taiga, and mountains has shown how the Trans-Siberian was built by a relatively poor and backward nation under the severest adversities ever encountered in railway construction. For all its early frailty, it bound Siberia inseparably to the motherland and kept the eastern regions within a European rather than an Oriental civilization. It revolutionized Siberia's archaic transportation and mercantile systems and helped millions of peasants to make new lives for themselves on extensive acreage far from the oppressions of the gentry class west of the Urals. Under the influence of the railway, the "rich but forsaken country" of Alexander the Third's time burgeoned economically and became the industrial bulwark of Russia against the seemingly invincible war machine of Nazi Germany. When one adds the Trans-Siberian's contributions in the development of the Soviet Union as a whole, one can only conclude that no other single transcontinental railway has ever done so much for so many.

APPENDIX A

Partial List of Place Names Adopted by the Board on Geographic Names

PLACE-NAME spellings different from those recommended by the United States Department of the Interior's Board on Geographic Names and by the Permanent Committee on Geographical Names for British Official Use are followed by (BGN) and the approved BGN spelling, complete with diacritical marks and addenda. In the text of this book, the writer has used a simplified form recommended by the editors of *Soviet Geography,* for he believes that "Muravyev-Amurski," "Gorki," "Changchun," and "Pogranichny," for instance, are somewhat easier to read than BGN's "Murav'yëv-Amurskiy," "Gor'kiy," "Ch'ang-ch'un," and "Pogranichnyy." However, many modern maps and atlases follow the BGN/PCGN spellings of Russian and Chinese names, and so the list relates the author's variants to these. It also gives the old and new names, together with conventional spellings, of certain cities and towns in the Soviet Union and in China.

Aigun — (BGN) Ai-hui [Communist], Ai-hun [Nationalist]
Akmolinsk — now (BGN) Tselinograd
Aktogai — (BGN) Aktogay
Alekseyevsk — now Svobodny (BGN, Svobodnyy)
Altan Bulag — formerly Mai-mai-ch'eng
Archangel (conventional) — (BGN) Arkhangel'sk
Babushkin — formerly Mysovsk
Baikal (conventional) — (BGN) Baykal

Baikonur — (BGN) Baykonur
Brest-Litovsk — now (BGN) Brest
Changchun — (BGN) Ch'ang-ch'un
Chefoo (conventional) — (BGN) Yen-t'ai
Chiao-chou Wan — formerly Kiaochow Bay
Ch'i-ch'i-ha-erh — formerly Tsitsihar
Dalni [Russian] or Dairen [Japanese] (conventional) — now (BGN) Lü-ta [Communist], Ta-lien [Nationalist]
Ekaterinburg or Yekaterinburg — now (BGN) Sverdlovsk
Formosa — now (BGN) Taiwan
Gorki — (BGN) Gor'kiy (formerly Nizhni Novgorod)
Guryev — (BGN) Gur'yev
Harbin (conventional) — (BGN) Ha-erh-pin
Kaidalovo — (BGN) Kaydalovo
Kaiping — (BGN) Kai-p'ing
Karsakpai — (BGN) Karsakpay
Kazan — (BGN) Kazan'
Kiaochow Bay — now (BGN) Chiao-chou Wan
Kiev (conventional) — (BGN) Kiyev
Komsomolsk-na-Amure — (BGN) Komsomol'sk-na-Amure
Kuibyshev — (BGN) Kuybyshev (formerly Samara)
Lugovoi — (BGN) Lugovoy
Lupin — formerly Manchuria station
Lü-shun — Port Arthur (conventional)
Lü-ta — formerly Talien [Chinese], Dalni [Russian], Dairen [Japanese]
Mai-mai-ch'eng — now (BGN) Altan Bulag
Manchuria station — now (BGN) Man-chou-li [Communist], Lupin [Nationalist]
Molotov — now Perm; (BGN) Perm'
Mukden (conventional) — now (BGN) Shen-yang
Muravyev-Amurski — (BGN) Murav'yëv-Amurskiy
Mysovsk and its station Mysovaya [Stantsiya Mysovaya] — now (BGN) Babushkin and Mysovaya
Newchwang or Yingkou — (BGN) Ying-k'ou
Nikolayevsk — now (BGN) Nikolayevsk-na-Amure
Nizhni Novgorod (BGN, Nizhniy Novgorod) — now Gorki (BGN, Gor'kiy)
Nizhni Tagil — (BGN) Nizhniy Tagil
Norilsk — (BGN) Noril'sk
Novokuznetsk — formerly Stalinsk
Novonikolayevsk — now (BGN) Novosibirsk
Ob — (BGN) Ob'
Oktyabrski — (BGN) Oktyabr'skiy
Perm — formerly Molotov
Petropavlovsk (in Kamchatka, not western Siberia) — now (BGN) Petropavlovsk-Kamchatskiy
Pivan — (BGN) Pivan'
Pogranichny — (BGN) Pogranichnyy
Port Arthur (conventional) — (BGN) Lü-shun
Primorski — (BGN) Primorskiy
Ryazan — (BGN) Ryazan'
Samara — now Kuibyshev; (BGN) Kuybyshev
Shen-yang — Mukden (conventional)
Sofisk — (BGN) Sofiysk
Sovetskaya Gavan — (BGN) Sovetskaya Gavan'
Stalinsk — now (BGN) Novokuznetsk

Stanovoi Range — (BGN) Stanovoy Khrebet
Sverdlovsk — formerly Yekaterinburg or Ekaterinburg
Svobodny — (BGN) Svobodnyy (formerly Alekseyevsk)
Taiga (conventional) — (BGN) Tayga
Taishet — (BGN) Tayshet
Taiwan — formerly Formosa
Talien [city] — (BGN) Ta-lien; now Lü-ta [Communist], Talien [Nationalist]; formerly Dalni [Russian], Dairen [Japanese]
Talienwan [Chinese] — Talien Bay
Tankhoi — (BGN) Tankhoy
Tbilisi — Tiflis (conventional)
Tientsin (conventional) — (BGN) T'ien-ching
Tobolsk — (BGN) Tobol'sk
Tselinograd — formerly Akmolinsk
Tsitsihar (conventional) — (BGN) Ch'i-ch'i-ha-erh
Tyumen — (BGN) Tyumen'
Ulan Bator — (BGN) Ulaan Baatar
Ulan-Ude — formerly Verkhneudinsk
Ussurisk — (BGN) Ussuriysk
Ust-Kut — (BGN) Ust'-Kut
Verkhneudinsk — now (BGN) Ulan-Ude
Yablonovy Range — (BGN) Yablonovyy Khrebet
Yekaterinburg or Ekaterinburg — now (BGN) Sverdlovsk
Yenisei — (BGN) Yenisey
Yeniseisk — (BGN) Yeniseysk
Yen-t'ai — Chefoo (conventional)
Yingkou or Newchwang — (BGN) Ying-k'ou

APPENDIX B

Chronology of the Conquest of Siberia

1581 — Yermak invades the kingdom of Khan Kuchum beyond the Urals and presents the conquered territory to Tsar Ivan IV (the Terrible).

1633 — Blockhouses are established as far east as Yakutsk, on the Lena River.

1639 — Cossacks attain the Sea of Okhotsk, thereby spanning Siberia.

1643 — The Cossack Vasili Poyarkov reaches the Amur and sails downriver to the Sea of Okhotsk.

1648 — Siberia's northeastern cape is rounded for the first time by the Cossack Semen Dezhnev, who also sails through the strait later named for the Danish navigator Vitus Bering.

1649 — The Russian trader Yerofei Khabarov leads a force to the Amur territory and subsequently oppresses the inhabitants.

1689 — Russian and Chinese ambassadors sign the Treaty of Nerchinsk, defining the Sino-Siberian frontier and barring Russians from the Amur region.

1728 — In Russian employ, Bering rediscovers the strait first navigated by Dezhnev.

1784 — The first Russian colony in North America is founded on Kodiak Island, east of Alaska Peninsula.

1799 — The Tsar Paul I charters the Russian-American Company to trade in Alaska, the Aleutians, and the Kuril Islands.

1847 — Nicholas I appoints Lieutenant-General Nicholas Muravyev governor-general of Eastern Siberia.

1849-1850 — Captain Gennadius Nevelskoi discovers Sakhalin to be an island and, in 1850, raises the Imperial standard at the present Nikolayevsk-na-Amure, twenty-eight miles upriver from the Amur's mouth.

1854 — Outbreak of the Crimean War. Muravyev leads a large flotilla down the Amur to strengthen Russian settlements and military installations against attack by British and French forces.

1856 — End of Crimean War. Muravyev consolidates his gains.

1858 — Muravyev organizes the Amur Company to operate steamers and trading stations along the Amur. Founds Khabarovsk, at confluence of the Amur and the Ussuri River.

1858 — The Chinese sign the Treaty of Aigun and surrender to Russia all of the territory north of the Amur as far as Khabarovsk, and north from Khabarovsk to the Sea of Okhotsk.

1860 — The Russian diplomat Nicholas Ignatyev secures the Treaty of Peking from China. The pact reaffirms the Treaty of Aigun frontiers and cedes Chinese territory eastward from the Ussuri and as far south as the Korean border, including Vladivostok, which had been seized by Muravyev's forces.

1861 — Muravyev resigns as governor-general and receives the title of Count Muravyev-Amurski.

APPENDIX C

Chronology of the Trans-Siberian Railway*

1857 — The American Perry McDonough Collins makes the first proposal for a steam railway in Siberia, to run from Chita to Irkutsk via Kyakhta. Proposal rejected.

1857 — Collins followed by the English engineer Dull, who offers to build a horse-tramway between Nizhni Novgorod and the Pacific. Offer refused.

1858 — Governor-General Muravyev mistaken in his belief that St. Petersburg will approve his projected railway from De Kastri Bay to Sofisk, on the lower Amur.

1858 — The Britons Morison, Sleigh, and Horn offer to construct a steam railway from Nizhni Novgorod to the Strait of Tartary. Offer turned down.

1875 — Communication Minister Constantine Posyet advocates a trunk line from Russia to the Far East. Not approved.

1885-1887 — Siberian Governors-General Count Alexis Ignatyev and Baron Korff press for a railway from Tomsk to Sretensk, and from Vladivostok to the Ussuri River.

1887-1889 — Topographical surveys undertaken Tomsk-Sretensk and in the Vladivostok area.

1889-1890 — Communication Minister Adolf von Hubbenet urges construction of the through railway.

1891 — The enterprise is approved. The Tsarevich Nicholas inaugurates construction of the Great Siberian Railway at Vladivostok.

1891-1897 — Construction of the South Ussuri section by Engineer Alexander Ursati, succeeded late in 1892 by Engineer Orest Vyazemski, who also completes the North Ussuri track.

1892 — Sergius Witte becomes Finance Minister after serving briefly

* The second date stated for construction projects refers to the year when the section was opened to regular traffic.

as Communication Minister. Creation of the Trans-Siberian Committee.

1892-1896 — Construction of the West Siberian sector (Chelyabinsk to the Ob River) by Engineer Constantine Mikhailovski.

1893-1899 — Construction of the Mid-Siberian sector (Ob to Irkutsk) and a branch from Taiga to Tomsk by Engineer Nicholas Mezheninov.

1894-1896 — Construction of the Chelyabinsk-Yekaterinburg section by Engineer Mikhailovski.

1895-1900 — Construction of the Transbaikal sector (Mysovsk, on Lake Baikal, to Sretensk, on the Shilka River) by Engineer Alexander Pushechnikov.

1896-1900 — Construction of the Irkutsk-Baikal extension by Engineer Pushechnikov.

1897-1901 — Construction of connecting lines in Transbaikalia and the Ussuri area to the Chinese Eastern Railway under construction; Pushechnikov in charge in Transbaikalia, and Engineer Alexander Yugovich in the Ussuri.

1897-1903 — Construction of the Chinese Eastern (Manchuria Station to Pogranichny and from Harbin to Dalni and Port Arthur) by Engineer Yugovich.

1899-1904 — Construction of the Circumbaikal loop (Port Baikal to Mysovsk) by Engineer-Contractor Alexander Pertsov and others.

1900 — The new icebreaking ferries *Baikal* and *Angara* begin service on Lake Baikal.

1908-1916 — Construction of the Amur sector (Kuenga to Khabarovsk) by Engineer Alexander Liverovski and others. Completion of uninterrupted rails on Russian soil from the Urals to Vladivostok.

APPENDIX D

Description of Steam Locomotives on the Trans-Siberian Railway

PAUL E. GARBUTT, a British authority on Soviet railways, describes the various types of steam locomotives used on the Trans-Siberian. "When the line was first built," he writes in the *Journal of Transport History,* "the motive power was largely provided by Class O 0-8-0 [that is, no front or "pony" wheels, eight driving wheels, and no trailing wheels] freight and Class B and G 4-6-0 passenger engines; with axle-loads of only 13–13.5 metric tons, these were well suited to the flimsy nature of the original track. Class 'Shch' 2-8-0 locomotives were first built in 1906; originally used on the Chinese Eastern Railway, this class was later employed generally throughout Russia. From 1908, Class F Mallet 0-6-0+0-6-0 locomotives came into production and engines of this design also were introduced on the Trans-Siberian line. Class S 2-6-2 heavy passenger engines (axle-load 15.5 metric tons) first appeared in 1911, and locomotives of this type were in 1938 hauling Trans-Siberian expresses through from the Polish frontier. . . . [There were also] Class E 2-10-0 engines supplied by American builders to increase the capacity of the Trans-Siberian route during the First World War. The Class I 2-10-2 tank engines built by the [Czechoslovakian] Skoda Works in

1929 were another interesting type, having been designed for use on the Khingan mountain section of the Chinese Eastern Railway. Evidence of improved track standards on the Trans-Siberian in the 1930s was provided by the use of heavier Soviet-designed locomotives over the line. In 1936, an FD Class 2-10-2 engine (axle-load 20 metric tons) successfully hauled a trial train of 568 axles, weighing 11,310 tons, between Chelyabinsk and Kurgan [a distance of 160 miles], and in February 1937 an SO Class condenser-equipped 2-10-0 locomotive (axle-load 17.5 metric tons) performed an endurance test by, it was claimed, hauling a 1,200 ton train from Moscow to Vladivostok and back, an aggregate distance of over 11,600 miles, in a total running time of only 240 hours."

The weights and maximum speeds of several of the above locomotives Mr. Garbutt gives as follows (his kilometric miles have been converted to English statute miles): "S," 75 tons, 71.5 mph; "E," 99.3 tons, 46.6 mph; "FD," 133 tons, 59 mph; "SO," 96.6 tons, 46.6 mph. Other types are the "JS," a 2-8-4 type now known as "FDp," 128.6 tons, 87 mph; and the "AA," 4-14-4, the largest ever built in Europe. It weighed 206 tons and attained a speed of 44 mph.

APPENDIX E

Table of Equivalents

LENGTH

1 sagene (*sazhen*) — 7 ft.
1 verst — 0.663 mi.; 3500 ft.
1 meter — 39.37 in.
1 kilometer — 0.62137 mi.; 3280.8 ft.

AREA

1 hectare — 2.471 acres
1 dessiatine — 2.70 acres
1 sq. verst — 0.4394 sq. mi.; 1.14 sq. km.; 281 acres
1 sq. meter — 1.1960 sq. yards
1 sq. kilometer — 0.3861 sq. mi.; 247.1 acres; 100 hectares

WEIGHT

1 pood — 36.113 lbs. avoirdupois
1 Russian pound (*funt*) — 14.44 oz. av.
1 centner — 100 kg.; 220.46 lbs. av.
1 kilogram — 2.2046 lbs. av.
1 metric ton — 1,000 kg.; 2,204.6 lbs. av.

VOLUME

1 cubic meter — 1.308 cu. yards

VALUE

1 ruble — $0.515 (gold ruble before the First World War). Except where indicated, ruble values have been converted in this book at the rate of $0.50 per ruble to avoid awkward odd numbers.
1 kopeck — 1/100th of a ruble, or about half a cent
1 English pound sterling — $4.87 (mint par value of $4.866564 to the pound, which ruled from 1837-1931) has been uniformly followed in this book save where otherwise noted. Rates varied as follows: $5.58 to the pound in 1862; $7.12

in 1863; $9.92 in 1864; $7.46 in 1865; $6.75 in 1866, before returning to normal. The sterling/dollar exchange rate was stabilized at $4.76½ to the pound from January 6, 1916, until March 20, 1919; thereafter, it fell to $3.378 in February 1920, recovering to $3.933 in April 1920. Over the period 1850-1900, the cost of living fluctuated considerably, but on the average the pound then had a purchasing power between four and five times as great as in 1960. (Source: Bank of England)

TEMPERATURE

To convert Centigrade to Fahrenheit, multiply Centigrade degrees by 1.8 and add 32. To convert Fahrenheit to Centigrade subtract 32 from Fahrenheit degrees, multiply by 5, and divide by 9.

To convert Reaumur to Fahrenheit, multiply Reaumur degrees by 9/4 and add 32. To convert to Centigrade, multiply Reaumur degrees by 5/4.

TIME

The Julian (or Old Style) Calendar was dated earlier than the Gregorian (or New Style) Calendar as follows: 10 days, from 1582-1699; 11 days, 1700-1799; 12 days, 1800-1899; 13 days, 1900-1918. For example, May 19, 1891 (Old Style), becomes May 31, 1891 (New Style). In February 1918, the Bolshevik government adopted the New Style Calendar used by other nations. Foreigners in Russia sometimes used Old Style to date a Russian event, such as a Tsar's coronation, and New Style when referring to personal matters, such as the date of arrival in Russia from, say, England or America, where the New Style Calendar prevailed. When stated jointly, as $\frac{24}{13}$th June 1757, the upper date designates New Style.

St. Petersburg time was 2 hours, 1 minute ahead of Greenwich time; that is, 12 noon at St. Petersburg was 9:59 A.M. at Greenwich. Today, the difference is three hours. In comparison with Eastern Standard Time in the United States, the spread amounts to eight hours; when it is noon in New York, it is 8 P.M. in Leningrad and Moscow.

Acknowledgments

THE writing of this book has led me into so many areas of inquiry that I must thank quite a number of individuals, organizations, and specialized institutions and agencies for their generous assistance. My wife excepted, I am most deeply indebted to Mr. Marshall S. Shatz, a young American scholar in Russian history who has been invaluable to me as a highly literate translator from the Russian and as an indefatigable detective in the pursuit and discovery of elusive facts. I thank Mr. Shatz also for his speed and thoroughness in resolving innumerable questions, his counsel on technical points, and his good-humored willingness to tackle pressing problems even when busiest with his own professional projects. It has been a fruitful and pleasant experience to have been associated with him for more than two years. I should say at this point, however, that neither Mr. Shatz nor my other benefactors are to be held responsible for my use of their contributions to the book. If any errors should be theirs through inadvertence, it is I who should be blamed for letting them slip by. I also accept responsibility for the illustrations but not for the maps, which were completed when I was abroad and unable to check them properly.

I am greatly indebted to Dr. Meredith F. Burrill, Executive Secretary of the Department of the Interior's Board on Geographic Names, and to his assistants, who went out of their way to supply information from sources not readily available to me during much of my writing. I am almost equally obliged to Mr. P. J. M. Geelan, Secretary of the Permanent Committee on Geographical Names for British Official Use, in London, who did much to clarify various systems of geographical nomenclature. In England, too, Dr. M. E. M. Herford, D.S.O., of Farnham Royal, Buckinghamshire, has been most generous with information about his aunt, Annette M. B. Meakin, and in giving me a copy of her out-of-print and very scarce *A Ribbon of Iron*.

Mr. D. S. M. Barrie, Assistant General Manager of the North Eastern Region of British Railways, York, has been very helpful, as have Mr. L. R. Jones, of the Photographic Section, Department of Printed Books, British Museum, and members of the staff of the Royal Geographical Society, The Institution of Civil Engineers, The Institution of Mechanical Engineers, the Science Museum, and the *Daily Express*. My debt is perhaps greater to Mr. R. L. Thomas, Principal of the Balance of Payments Office of the Bank of England, who went to considerable trouble to compile statistics on the American dollar values of the ruble and the pound sterling during parts of the nineteenth and twentieth centuries; to Mr. W. G. Hall, of Vickers-Armstrongs (Engineers), Ltd., who sent the picture of the train ferry *Baikal,* together with her specifications, and to Mr. A. Young, of Vickers-Armstrongs (Shipbuilders), Ltd., who supplied the various names of the Armstrong shipbuilding firm before it became Vickers-Armstrongs.

My Trans-Siberian journey would have been far less rewarding without the utmost cooperation I received from Mr. Vladimir I. Babkin, manager of the Anglo-American Department of Intourist, in Moscow; Madame Nadya Kulikova, the Intourist interpreter who accompanied my wife and me on our Siberian travels and who must never be confused with the twenty-year-old guide assigned us in Irkutsk; Mr. Vladimir V. Vladimirov, then manager of the Intourist office in New York and an experienced hunter who filled me in on the habits of Russian wolves; and Mr. Fred B. Petera, at the time manager of the Forty-second Street office of The American Express Company, in New York, who relieved me of several travel worries en route to the U.S.S.R. My very special thanks are due Mr. Leslie S. Brady, now Counselor for Public Affairs at the American Embassy in Paris. When Cultural Affairs Officer at the American Embassy in Moscow, he was an exceptionally gracious host and made various arrangements I would have been hard put to work out myself. Subsequently, he enabled me to obtain certain geographical data which, though unclassified by the government, I probably would not have found elsewhere in such clear and concise form.

For many facts relating to Perry McDonough Collins, it is a pleasure to thank Miss Ethel M. Harker, Assistant Secretary of The Western Union Telegraph Company, in New York, who could have hardly been more assiduous in detailing Collins's transactions with the organization and in locating material on his later career; Mr. Ashley T. Day, Librarian of the Gould Memorial Library of New York University, for his contribution of an unpublished monograph on Collins; Mr. H. P. Gundy, Librarian of Queen's University, Kingston, Ontario, who helped to round out the story of the overland telegraph to Siberia; Mr. John Buchanan, Assistant Archivist of the Albert R. Mann Library, Cornell University, who kindly did the same; and Mr. W. N. Davis, Jr., Historian of the State Archives of California, in Sacramento, for a search bearing on Collins's title of Major; Mrs. Mary M. Moses, of the San Francisco Public Library, for bibliographical material; Mr. James B. Rhoads, Archivist in Charge, Foreign

Affairs Branch of the National Archives and Records Service, and Mr. Fred W. Shipman, Librarian, Department of State, for data on Baron Edward de Stoeckl; Mr. William Bloor, Treasurer of Columbia University, and Mr. Tredwell H. Hopkins, Controller of New York University, for the specific amounts of Collins's bequests, through his niece, to these institutions.

Mrs. Eugene Hotchkiss, of Highland Park, Illinois, has been the epitome of generosity and a delightful correspondent as well. She lent original photographs of George Kennan, of whom she is a first cousin twice removed, and corrected some widely circulated misconceptions of Kennan's father. In addition, she provided several biographical details I had not encountered before. To my profound thanks to her I must add a word of gratitude to her brother, Mr. George F. Kennan, the writer and former American ambassador to the Soviet Union and to Yugoslavia, who gave me Mrs. Hotchkiss's address.

Mr. Harold S. Clark, of Sagamore Beach, Massachusetts, entrusted to me the original copy of his boyhood account of his Siberian journey in 1900 and also lent photographs taken then by his mother, Mrs. Francis E. Clark. My warm thanks to him.

Without the aid of Mrs. Laura Allyn Ekstrom, Assistant Librarian of The State Historical Society of Colorado, in Denver, I might not have located the negatives of William Henry Jackson's superb photographs taken during his trip through Siberia in 1895-1896. Mrs. Ekstrom told me about the rather odd circumstances under which a part of Jackson's 52,900 negatives had gone to The Library of Congress. In Washington, the library's photographic department finally found the negatives — still in their original wrappers and without identification of scenes and persons — in one of its outlying repositories.

It would have been practically impossible for me to tell the story of the International Sleeping Car Company's operations in the Russian empire had it not been for the courtesy of Mr. Sheridan H. Garth, Manager of the Public Relations Department of Thos. Cook & Son, Inc., in New York, and the wholesale generosity of M. Olivier Chermiset, Secrétaire de la Direction Générale of the Compagnie Internationale des Wagons-Lits et des Grands Express Européens, in Paris. M. Chermiset not only arranged for photographs of Wagons-Lits' deluxe equipment to be sent me, but answered a long list of questions and supplied historical papers as well.

For railway and other technical information of many sorts I am much obliged to Mr. Charles E. Fisher, President of the Railway and Locomotive Historical Society, Inc., in Boston; Mr. John H. White, Jr., Curator of Land Transportation, Smithsonian Institution; Dr. Robert F. Legget, Director of the Division of Building Research, National Research Council, Ottawa, Ontario, who read my pages dealing with permafrost and contributed a number of the Council's publications; Dr. Vladimir Walters, Associate Professor of Zoology in the University of California at Los Angeles; Messrs. George D. Drechsler, Chief of the Section of Foreign Solid Fuels, and W. C. Elliott, Jr., Chief of the Division of Petroleum, both of the Department of the Interior's Bureau of Mines; Mr. Paul Swain, International Editor of the *Oil and Gas Journal;* Mr. Harrison E. Salisbury, Moscow correspondent for the *New York Times* from 1949 to 1955 and now an assistant managing editor of the same newspaper; Mr. John F. Doran, of New York; and Mr. Charles M. Parker, Vice President, Research and Technology, American Iron and Steel Institute, whose help I have also acknowledged in a footnote. For information about Siberian anthrax, I thank Edward B. Miller, M.D., of New York, and for that about plague and cholera, Charles Sziklas, M.D., of Nantucket, Massachusetts. Dr. Hiroshi Shinjo, Professor of Money and Banking at Kobe University, in Japan, was so good as to send me an exhaustive compilation of Japanese yen and Russian ruble values in the nineteen-thirties; I greatly appreciate his whole-hearted aid.

I owe a particularly heavy debt to Mr. Constantin A. Pertzoff, of Cambridge and Lincoln, Massachusetts, to his late mother, and to his late uncle, Mr. Kornely Pokrovski, the last a resident of Harbin for many years after the Russian civil war. Born in Chelyabinsk, Mr. Pertzoff enlightened me about daily life in Siberia and described the family ménage at Maritui. His mother contributed recollections of Engineer Mikhailovski, while Mr. Pokrovski explained unusual aspects of tsarist railway construction.

For the tracking down of the Reverend Mr. Marcus Lorenzo Taft — a Methodist minister who seemed at first to be almost as unidentifiable as the English engineer Dull — I am grateful to Miss M. Dorothy Woodruff, Research Librarian of the Board of Missions of The Methodist Church, in New York; Mrs. Mabel R. Schell, Genealogist of the History and Literature Department, The Public Library of Cincinnati and Hamilton County; one of his daughters, Mrs. Frederick M. Pyke, of Timonium, Maryland; and Mrs. Wilbur F. Cannon, of Bettendorf, Iowa, another daughter who lent me photographs. It is one of the peculiarities of writing that, after this involved research, I had occasion to mention the Reverend Mr. Taft and his Siberian journey only once.

Mr. J. Edward Nève, of the Public Relations Department

of Canadian Pacific, devoted time and care to a summary of the dates and mileages concerned in the trans-Canadian railway's construction, and sent a privately printed history of the company. For biographical information on Colonel George H. Emerson and Ralph Budd, I am almost equally indebted to Mr. Charles W. Moore, Executive Assistant, Public Relations-Advertising, the Great Northern Railway Company.

Mr. Charles F. Montgomery, Jr., Assistant Curator of the Virginia Museum of Fine Arts, in Richmond, was so kind as to contribute a copy of Alexander the Second's photograph in the Fabergé-Aarne frame. Mr. Marvin C. Ross, of Washington, generously supplied a description of Fabergé's craftsmanship. I wish to thank Mr. Kenneth Snowman especially for permission to reproduce the photograph of the Great Siberian Railway Easter egg and the tiny scale-model of the train. This picture is from Mr. Snowman's *The Art of Carl Fabergé* and was supplied through the courtesy of his London publishers, Faber and Faber, Ltd. Since the Boston Book and Art Shop published the American edition, I thank that firm as well as Faber and Faber for permission to reproduce the illustration.

In the library field, I have received valuable help from Mr. Sergius Yakobson, Chief of the Slavic and Central European Division, and Mr. K. T. Wu, Chief Bibliographical and Reference Librarian, Chinese Section, both of The Library of Congress; Mr. Bernard L. Koten, Librarian of The Library for Intercultural Studies, in New York; Mr. Harry L. Eddy, Librarian of the Bureau of Railway Economics, Association of American Railroads, in Washington; Mr. Robert C. Goodrich, Head Reference Librarian of the Engineering Societies Library, in New York; and Mr. Harold L. Roth, Librarian of the Public Library of East Orange, New Jersey. I am most grateful to all of these as well as to the reference staffs of The New York Public Library, *Railway Age,* and the British Museum.

Among librarians, however, there is one whom I must single out for my highest thanks. She is Mrs. Raymond P. Smith, Librarian of The Nantucket Atheneum, in the New England island community where I have a summer home. When I needed a book not on her shelves, she obtained it from The Library of Congress or other sources. Countless times she interrupted her own work and cheerfully looked up an essential fact to spare me a twelve-mile round trip to and from town. She allowed me to borrow many of the Atheneum's rarest books and hard-to-replace bound copies of old magazines such as the *Century,* and she unearthed long-out-of-print volumes with the thought that they might be useful, as they almost invariably proved to be. It is impossible for me to express adequate thanks to Mrs. Smith.

I am also deeply indebted to Mr. Daniel A. de Menocal, of Nantucket, for his oral recollections of his several trips on the Trans-Siberian and for permission to quote from his memoirs. In the same community, Colonel Charles P. Porter gave me a copy of the "Order Book" which accompanied the Soviet Union's award to him of the Order of the Patriotic War, First Degree; among other things, the Order Book states the privileges accruing to holders of the Order of Lenin. My thanks are also due Mrs. John W. McCalley, who lent me her copy of the Siberian railway picture album, *The Great Way;* her husband, a commercial photographer, made photo-copies of a number of old pictures for inclusion in the present volume. I am indebted to Mrs. Allen E. Norcross, Librarian of the Maria Mitchell Library, for materials obtained from the Boston Public Library and for early editions of the *National*

Geographic Magazine and *Scientific American.* Mrs. Alexander M. Craig kindly lent me two rather scarce volumes of *Burton Holmes Travelogues,* and Mrs. Charles Clark Coffin and Mrs. Robert D. Congdon gave me two out-of-print books by foreign travelers whose narratives I have quoted in part. I wish that I could properly thank the late Messrs. Donald Craig and Burnham N. Dell for help, respectively, on several engineering and philological questions.

Dr. Cyril E. Black, Professor of History at Princeton University, has been so good as to read the manuscript in its entirety, and I have profited from his scholarship. For reading portions pertaining to their specialized interests and for permission to quote from their own books, I am indebted to Professors Theodore H. Von Laue, of the University of California at Riverside, Donald W. Treadgold, of the University of Washington, in Seattle, and Holland Hunter, of Haverford College. Mr. Harrison E. Salisbury, Mr. Paul E. Garbutt, of London, and the Association of American Railroads, in Washington, have graciously allowed me to quote from their respective publications.

Next to last but far from least, Mr. Alan D. Williams, editor in New York for Little, Brown and Company, has shown the utmost patience while waiting four years for delivery of the manuscript. More important to the book, he has given me the benefit of his perceptive critical judgments.

I cannot begin to catalog the contributions of my wife Elsie, who has collaborated in the writing of this book as well as numerous earlier publications, some of which were issued under our joint names. I shall only say that, without her, *To the Great Ocean* would have never materialized.

Bibliography

Administration de la Construction des Chemins de Fer de l'Empire. Exposition Universelle de 1900 — Russie — Ministère des Voies de Communication. Paris: Librairies-Imprimeries Réunies, 1900.

ALEXANDER, GRAND DUKE OF RUSSIA. *Once a Grand Duke.* New York: Farrar & Rinehart, 1932.

ANSPACH, ALFRED. *La Russie Économique et l'Oeuvre de M. de Witte.* Paris: Librairie H. LeSoudier, 1904.

ATHOLL, DUCHESS OF. *Conscription of a People.* London: Philip Allan & Co., Ltd., 1931.

ATKINSON, THOMAS WITLAM. *Oriental and Western Siberia . . .* London: Hurst & Blackett, 1858.

——— *Travels in the Regions of the Upper and Lower Amoor and the Russian Acquisitions on the Confines of India and China . . .* New York: Harper & Bros., 1860.

Atlas skhem zheleznykh dorog SSSR [Atlas of Railroad Networks of the USSR]. Moscow: Chief Administration of Geodesy and Cartography of the MVD SSR, 1960.

AVERITT, PAUL. *Coal Reserves of the United States — A Progress Report January 1, 1960*, pp. 7-11; 91-93. Geological Survey Bulletin 1136, Department of the Interior. Washington: Government Printing Office, 1961.

Aziatskaya Rossiya [Asiatic Russia]. 3 vols. St. Petersburg: Resettlement Administration, 1914.

BABEY, ANNA M. *Americans in Russia 1776-1917.* New York: Comet Press, 1938.

BAEDEKER, K. *La Russie* (3e édition). Leipzig: Karl Baedeker, 1902.

———, KARL. *Russia, with Teheran, Port Arthur, and Peking.* Leipzig: Karl Baedeker, 1914.

BAERLEIN, HENRY. *The March of the Seventy Thousand.* London: Leonard Parsons, 1926.

BAIEVSKY, BORIS. *Siberia: Its Resources and Possibilities.* Department of Commerce Trade Promotion Series No. 36. Washington: Government Printing Office, 1926.

BARANSKY, N. N. *Economic Geography of the U.S.S.R.* Translated by S. BELSKY. Moscow: Foreign Languages Publishing House, 1956.

BARBER, NOEL. *Trans-Siberian.* London: George G. Harrap & Co., Ltd., 1942.

BATES, LINDON, JR. *The Russian Road to China.* Boston & New York: Houghton Mifflin Co., 1910.

BEAZLEY, C. RAYMOND. "The Siberian Railway," *The Scottish Geographical Magazine,* Vol. XVI, No. 11 (November, 1900), pp. 617-630.

BEEBE, LUCIUS. *Mr. Pullman's Elegant Palace Car.* Garden City: Doubleday & Co., Inc., 1961.

BEHREND, GEORGE. *The History of Wagons-Lits 1875-1955.* London: Modern Transport Publishing Co., Ltd., 1959.

BERG, L. S. *Natural Regions of the U.S.S.R.* Translated by OLGA ADLER TITELBAUM; edited by JOHN A. MORRISON and C. C. NIKIFOROFF. New York: Macmillan Co., 1950.

BEVERIDGE, ALBERT J. *The Russian Advance.* New York: Harper & Bros., 1903.

BONSAL, STEPHEN. "Eastern Siberia," *Harper's New Monthly Magazine,* Vol. XCVII, No. 578 (July, 1898), pp. 240-259; "The Convict System in Siberia," *ibid.,* No. 579 (August, 1898), pp. 327-342.

BOOKWALTER, JOHN W. *Siberia and Central Asia.* Springfield, Ohio: Privately printed, 1899.

BORZUNOV, V. F. "Rabochiye sibirskoi zhelezhodorozhnoi magistrali v 1891-1904 gg." [The Workers of the Siberian Railroad in the Years 1891-1904], *Istoriya SSSR,* 1959, No. 4, pp. 116-126.

BOULANGIER, EDGAR. *Notes de Voyage en Sibérie.* Paris: Société d'Éditeurs Scientifiques, 1891.

Bradshaw's Continental Railway, Steam, Transit, and General Guide for Travellers Through Europe (August, 1902; July, 1903; April, 1904). London.

Bradshaw's Through Routes to the Capitals of the World and Overland Guide to India, Persia, and the Far East. London: Henry Blacklock & Co., Ltd., 1903.

Bradshaw's Through Routes to the Chief Cities of the World. Edited by A. H. KEANE and STANLEY REED. London: H. Blacklock & Co., Ltd., 1913.

BREITIGAM, GERALD B. "The Retreat of the Hundred Thousand," *Adventure,* Vol. XLIII, No. 6 (November 30, 1923), pp. 174-175.

BRESHKOVSKAIA, KATERINA. *Hidden Springs of the Russian Revolution.* Stanford: Stanford University Press, 1931.

[BROCKHAUS-YEFRON] *Entsiklopedicheski slovar* [Encyclopedic Dictionary]. Edited by F. A. BROKGAUS and I. A. YEFRON. 41 vols. St. Petersburg: 1890-1904. 2 supplementary vols. St. Petersburg: 1905-1907.

——— *Novy entsiklopedicheski slovar* [New Encyclopedic Dictionary]. 29 vols. St. Petersburg: 1911-1916.

BROWN, ARTHUR JUDSON. *The Mastery of the Far East.* New York: Charles Scribner's Sons, 1919.

BROWNE, C. C. L. "The Mammoth and Its Ivory," *The Field,* Vol. 219, No. 5712 (July 5, 1962), p. 15.

BRYCE, VISCOUNT JAMES. "Western Siberia and the Altai Mountains," *National Geographic Magazine,* Vol. XXXIX, No. 5 (May, 1921), pp. 469-507.

BURR, MALCOLM. *In Bolshevik Siberia.* London: H. F. & G. Witherby, 1931.

BUSH, RICHARD J. *Reindeer, Dogs, and Snow-Shoes . . .* New York: Harper & Bros., 1871.

CARY, CLARENCE. "The Trans-Siberian Railway: Its New Terminal in China," *The Forum,* Vol. XXV (May, 1898), pp. 285-299.

——— *The Trans-Siberian Route . . .* New York: Evening Post Job Printing House, 1902.

CHAMBERLIN, WILLIAM HENRY. *The Russian Revolution 1917-1921* (Revised edition). 2 vols. New York: Macmillan Co., 1957.

CHANG, TAO-HSING. *International Controversies Over the Chinese Eastern Railway.* Shanghai: Commercial Press, Ltd., 1936.

CHANNING, C. G. FAIRFAX. *Siberia's Untouched Treasure.* New York: G. P. Putnam's Sons, 1923.

CHAPIN, WILLIAM WISNER. "Glimpses of the Russian Empire," *National Geographic Magazine,* Vol. XXIII, No. 11 (November, 1912), pp. 1043-1078.

CHARLES, J. L. "Permafrost Aspects of Hudson Bay Railroad," Proceedings of the American Society of Civil Engineers, *Journal of the Soil Mechanics and Foundations Division,* Vol. 85, No. SM6 (December, 1959), pp. 125-135. Reprinted as NRC 5574, National Research Council, Division of Building Research, Ottawa.

CHARQUES, RICHARD. *The Twilight of Imperial Russia.* London: Phoenix House, 1958.

CHENG, TIEN-FONG. *A History of Sino-Russian Relations.* Washington: Public Affairs Press, 1957.

CHEVIGNY, HECTOR. *Lost Empire: The Life and Adventures of Nicolai Petrovich Rezanov.* New York: Macmillan Co., 1937.

——— *Lord of Alaska: Baranov and the Russian Adventure.* New York: Viking Press, 1942.

Chudodeĭ Baikal [Baikal the Miracle-Worker]. Irkutsk: Irkutskoye knizhnoye izdatelstvo [Irkutsk Publishing House], 1960.

Cinquantenaire de la Compagnie Internationale des Wagons-Lits et des Grands Express Européens 1876-1926. Paris: Privately printed, 1926.

Citizen's Atlas of the World, The (Tenth edition). John Bartholomew. Edinburgh: John Bartholomew & Son Ltd., 1952.

CLARK, EUGENE FRANCIS. *A Son's Portrait of Dr. Francis E. Clark.* Boston & Chicago: Williston Press, 1930.

CLARK, REV. FRANCIS E., D.D. *A New Way Around an Old World.* New York & London: Harper & Bros., 1901.

——— *Memories of Many Men in Many Lands.* Boston & Chicago: United Society of Christian Endeavor, 1922.

CLARK, GROVER. *The Great Wall Crumbles.* New York: Macmillan Co., 1935.

CLARK, HAROLD S. *My Journal: Around the World Jan. 24, 1900.* Unpublished diary, 68 pp.

CLARK, M. GARDNER. *The Economics of Soviet Steel.* Cambridge: Harvard University Press, 1956.

COCHRANE, CAPT. JOHN DUNDAS, R.N. *Narrative of a Pedestrian Journey Through Russia and Siberian Tartary, from the Frontiers of China to the Frozen Sea and Kamtchatka; Performed During the Years 1820, 1821, 1822, and 1823.* Philadelphia: H. C. Carey, & I. Lea, and A. Small, and Collins & Hannay, New York, 1824.

COLLINS, HENRY B., JR., CLARK, AUSTIN H., WALKER, EGBERT H. *The Aleutian Islands: Their People and Natural History.* Smithsonian Institution War Background Studies No. 21. Washington: Smithsonian Institution: February 5, 1945.

COLLINS, PERRY MCDONOUGH, United States Commercial Agent at the Amoor River. *A Voyage Down the Amoor: With a Land Journey Through Siberia, and Incidental Notices of Manchooria, Kamschatka, and Japan.* New York: D. Appleton & Co., 1860.

———, MAJOR PERRY MCD. *Overland Explorations in Siberia, Northern Asia and the Great Amoor River Country; Incidental Notices of Manchooria, Mongolia, Kamschatka, and Japan, with Map and Plan of an Overland Telegraph Around the World, Via Behring's Strait and Asiatic Russia to Europe.* New York: D. Appleton & Co., 1864.

——— *Abridged from a Lecture by P. McD. Collins, Before the Traveler's Club and Other Societies, on Overland Telegraphic Communication Via Behring Strait, and Across Asiatic Russia to Europe.* New York, December 1865, pp. 143-163. Privately printed, n.d.

——— *Siberian Journey: Down the Amur to the Pacific 1856-1857.* A New Edition of *A Voyage Down the Amoor by Perry McDonough Collins.* Edited with an introduction by CHARLES VEVIER. Madison: University of Wisconsin Press, 1962.

[COLLINS, PERRY MCDONOUGH] *Statement of the Origin, Organization and Progress of the Russian-American Telegraph Western Union Extension, Collins' Overland Line, Via Behring Strait and Asiatic Russia to Europe.* Rochester: Privately printed, May, 1866.

——— "Material Relating to Collins Overland Telegraph to Russia, 1865." McNichol Collection, Douglas Library, Queen's University, Kingston, Ont.

COLQUHOUN, ARCHIBALD R. "The Great Trans-Siberian-Manchurian Railway," *The Journal of the Royal United Service Institution,* Vol. XLIV, No. 274 (December, 1900), pp. 1408-1430.

——— *Overland to China.* New York & London: Harper & Bros., 1900.

[COMPAGNIE INTERNATIONALE DES WAGONS-LITS ET DES GRANDS EX-

PRESS EUROPÉENS (Sleeping Cars)] *Bilan et Compte de Profits et Pertes* (1898-1908). Privately printed.

Complete Pronouncing Gazetteer or Geographical Dictionary of the World, A (Revised edition). 2 vols. Philadelphia: J. B. Lippincott Co., 1872.

Cook's Handbook for Tourists to Peking, Tientsin . . . Dalny, Port Arthur . . . London: T. Cook & Son, 1910.

[COOKE, HENRY] "Report on Russian Railways by Mr. Henry Cooke, British Commercial Agent in Russia," *Diplomatic and Consular Reports*, No. 522, Miscellaneous Series (March, 1900). Foreign Office, London: Printed for Her Majesty's Stationery Office, by Harrison and Sons.

——— "Report on the Trans-Siberian Railway by Mr. Cooke, British Commercial Agent in Russia," *ibid.*, No. 533, Miscellaneous Series (July, 1900).

COVILLE, LILIAN GROSVENOR. "Here in Manchuria," *National Geographic Magazine*, Vol. LXIII, No. 2 (February, 1933), pp. 233-256.

CRESSON, W. P. *The Cossacks, Their History and Country.* New York: Brentano's, 1919.

CROLY, HERBERT. *Willard Straight.* New York: Macmillan Co., 1924.

CURTIN, JEREMIAH. *A Journey in Southern Siberia.* Boston: Little Brown & Co., 1909.

CUSTINE, THE MARQUIS DE. *Journey for Our Time.* Edited and translated by PHYLLIS PENN KOHLER. New York: Pellegrini & Cudahy, 1951.

[DALLAS, GEORGE MIFFLIN] *Diary of George Mifflin Dallas While United States Minister to Russia 1837 to 1839, and to England 1856 to 1861.* Edited by SUSAN DALLAS. Philadelphia: J. B. Lippincott Co., 1892.

DALLIN, DAVID J. *The Real Soviet Russia.* Translated by JOSEPH SHAPLEN. Revised and enlarged edition. New Haven: Yale University Press, 1947.

——— *The Rise of Russia in Asia.* New Haven: Yale University Press, 1949.

——— *The New Soviet Empire.* New Haven: Yale University Press, 1951.

DALLIN, DAVID J. and NICOLAEVSKY, BORIS I. *Forced Labor in Soviet Russia.* New Haven: Yale University Press, 1947.

Dark Side of the Moon, The. Anonymous. London: Faber & Faber, Ltd., 1946.

Data on the Principles of the Study of Frozen Zones in the Earth's Crust, Issue II, 74 pp. Academy of Sciences of the U.S.S.R. Moscow: V. A. Obruchev Institute of Permafrost Studies, 1955. Technical Translation 1006, National Research Council, Division of Building Research, Ottawa.

DAVIDSON, JAMES W. "The Great Siberian Railway from Recent Personal Investigation," *The Century Illustrated Monthly Magazine,* Vol. LXVII [New Series, Vol. XLV] (April, 1904), pp. 940-950.

DAVIES, RAYMOND ARTHUR and STEIGER, ANDREW J. *Soviet Asia.* New York: Dial Press, 1942.

DAVIS, JAMES W. "Russian Exile Special . . ." *Railroad Man's Magazine,* Vol. II, No. 1 (April, 1930), pp. 88-97.

DAWES, ANNA LAURENS. "George Kennan," *The Century Magazine,* Vol. XXXVI, No. 4 (August, 1888), pp. 625-631.

[DE LONG, GEORGE W.] *The Voyage of the Jeannette: The Ship and Ice Journals of George W. DeLong . . .* Edited by EMMA DE LONG. Boston: Houghton, Mifflin & Co., 1893.

DE MENOCAL, DANIEL A. *My Memoirs.* Unpublished manuscript in progress, 77 pp. 1964.

DENNETT, TYLER. *Americans in Eastern Asia.* New York: Macmillan Co., 1922.

DEPPERMANN, W. H. "Two Cents an Acre," *The North American Review,* Vol. CCXLV, No. 1 (Spring, 1938), pp. 126-133.

DEUTSCH, LEO. *Sixteen Years in Siberia: 1884-1900.* Translated by HELEN CHISHOLM. London: John Murray, 1903.

DE WINDT, HARRY. *The New Siberia.* London: Chapman & Hall, Ld., 1892.

——— *Siberia As It Is.* London: Chapman & Hall, Ltd., 1892.

——— *Through the Gold-Fields of Alaska to Bering Straits.* London: Chatto & Windus, 1898.

——— *From Paris to New York by Land.* London: George Newnes, Ltd., 1904.

——— *From Pekin to Calais by Land* (Second edition). London: George Newnes, Ltd., 1904.

——— *Through Savage Europe.* Philadelphia: J. B. Lippincott Co., 1907.

——— *Russia As I Know It.* Philadelphia: J. B. Lippincott Co., 1917.

——— *My Note-Book at Home and Abroad.* London: Chapman & Hall, 1923.

DICKENS, H. B. "Construction in Permafrost: Obstacles of Soil and Climate," *Canadian Consulting Engineer,* Vol. 2, No. 1 (January, 1960), pp. 33-37. Reprinted as NRC 5539, National Research Council, Division of Building Research, Ottawa.

——— "Water Supply and Sewage Disposal in Permafrost Areas of Northern Canada," *Polar Record,* Vol. 9, No. 62 (May, 1959), pp. 421-432. Reprinted as NRC 5169, National Research Council, Division of Building Research, Ottawa.

DIGBY, BASSETT. *The Mammoth and Mammoth-Hunting in North-East Siberia.* New York: D. Appleton & Co., 1926.

——— *Tigers, Gold, and Witch-Doctors.* New York: Harcourt, Brace & Co., 1928.

——— [and WRIGHT, R. L.] *Through Siberia, an Empire in the Making.* London: Hurst & Blackett, Ltd., 1913.

DOBBIE, I. "The Trans-Siberian Railway," *The Living Age,* Vol. CCXLII,

No. 3130 (July 2, 1904), pp. 96-103 [Reprinted from *Macmillan's Magazine*, London].

DOBELL, PETER. *Travels in Kamtchatka and Siberia; with a Narrative of a Residence in China.* 2 vols. London: Henry Colburn & Richard Bentley, 1830.

DOMINIQUE, PIERRE (pseudonym of Pierre Lucchini). *Secrets of Siberia.* Translated by WARRE B. WELLS. London: Hutchinson & Co., Ltd., 1934.

DOUGLAS, WILLIAM O. *Russian Journey.* Garden City: Doubleday & Co., Inc., 1956.

DULLES, FOSTER RHEA. *Eastward Ho! The First English Adventurers to the Orient.* Boston: Houghton Mifflin Co., 1931.

DUMAS, ALEXANDRE. *Adventures in Czarist Russia.* Translated and edited by ALMA ELIZABETH MURCH. Philadelphia & New York: Chilton Co., 1961.

DUPUY, R. ERNEST. *Perish by the Sword: The Czechoslovakian Anabasis and Our Supporting Campaigns in North Russia and Siberia 1918-1920.* Harrisburg, Pa.: Military Service Publishing Co., 1939.

DURBAN, WILLIAM. "The Trans-Siberian Railway," *The Contemporary Review* (London), Vol. LXXVI, No. 404 (August, 1899), pp. 261-271.

——— "From Moscow to Vladivostok," *The Outlook,* Vol. LXIII, No. 10 (November 4, 1899), pp. 587-595.

Eastern Siberia. "Handbooks Prepared Under the Direction of the Historical Section of the Foreign Office," No. 55. London: H.M. Stationery Office, 1920.

Economic Geography of the USSR. Edited by S. S. BALZAK, V. F. VASYUTIN, and YA. G. FEIGIN. American edition edited by CHAUNCY D. HARRIS; translated by ROBERT M. HANKIN and OLGA ADLER TITELBAUM. New York: Macmillan Co., 1956.

EDEN, CHARLES H. *Frozen Asia: A Sketch of Modern Siberia.* London: Society for Promoting Christian Knowledge, 1879.

Englishwoman in Russia; Impressions of the Society and Manners of the Russians at Home, The. By a Lady, Ten Years Resident in That Country. London: John Murray, 1855.

[ENNIS, WILLIAM H.] "Journal of William H. Ennis." Transcribed, with introduction and notes by HAROLD F. TAGGART. *California Historical Society Quarterly,* Vol. XXXIII, No. 1 (March, 1954), pp. 1-12.

ERMAN, ADOLPH. *Travels in Siberia . . .* Translated by W. D. COOLEY. 2 vols. Philadelphia: Lea & Blanchard, 1850.

FALK, EDWIN A. *From Perry to Pearl Harbor: The Struggle for Supremacy in the Pacific.* Garden City: Doubleday, Doran & Co., 1943.

Far Eastern Review, The (Shanghai). "History of the Railways in Manchuria," Vol. XXXVI, No. 1 (January, 1940), pp. 19-25.

FISCHER, EMIL S. "My 1932 Journey Around the World," *Peking and Tientsin Times,* May 31, 1932.

FISCHER, LOUIS. *The Soviets in World Affairs* (Second edition). 2 vols. Princeton: Princeton University Press, 1951.

FISHER, RAYMOND H. *The Russian Fur Trade 1550-1700*. "University of California Publications in History," Vol. 31. Berkeley & Los Angeles: University of California Press, 1943.

FLEMING, PETER. *One's Company: A Journey to China*. New York: Charles Scribner's Sons, 1934.

——— *The Fate of Admiral Kolchak*. New York: Harcourt, Brace & World, 1963.

FLORINSKY, MICHAEL T. *Russia: A History and an Interpretation*. 2 vols. New York: Macmillan Co., 1953.

FOORD, JOHN. "Siberia and Its Railway," *Asia*, Vol. XVII (June, 1917), pp. 265-270.

FRANCK, HARRY A. *Wandering in Northern China*. New York: Century Co., 1923.

FRANKLAND, NOBLE. *Imperial Tragedy*. New York: Coward-McCann, 1961.

FRASER, JOHN FOSTER. *Round the World on a Wheel*. London: Methuen & Co., 1899.

——— *The Real Siberia*. New York: D. Appleton & Co., 1902.

——— *Red Russia*. London: Cassell & Co., Ltd., 1907.

GALLOWAY, JOHN DEBO. *The First Continental Railroad*. New York: Simmons-Boardman, 1950.

GARBUTT, P. E. *The Russian Railways*. London: Sampson Low, Marston & Co., Ltd., 1949.

——— "The Trans-Siberian Railway," *The Journal of Transport History* (University College of Leicester), Vol. I, No. 4 (November, 1954), pp. 238-249.

Geografiya SSSR [Geography of the USSR], by N. I. LYALIKOV, R. M. KABO, E. M. DAVYDOV, S. S. VOSKRESENSKI. Moscow State Educational and Pedagogical House of the Ministry of Education of the RSFSR, 1955.

Geographical Journal, The (London). "The Hydrographic Exploration of Lake Baikal," Vol. XI, No. 2 (February, 1898), pp. 143-145.

GEORGE, PIERRE. "Le Transsibérien," *Géographia*, No. 30 (March, 1954), pp. 33-37.

GERHARDI, WILLIAM. *The Romanovs*. New York: G. P. Putnam's Sons, 1939.

GERRARE, WIRT (pseudonym of William Oliver Greener). *Greater Russia*. New York: Macmillan Co., 1904.

GILDER, WILLIAM H. *Ice-Pack and Tundra*. New York: Charles Scribner's Sons, 1883.

GLEASON, GEORGE. "How the Yanks Are Speeding Up the Longest Railway in the World," *The Independent*, Vol. XCIX (August 16, 1919), pp. 220-221; 235-236.

GLIKSMAN, JERZY G. *Tell the West*. New York: Gresham Press, Inc., 1948.

GOLDER, F. A. *Russian Expansion on the Pacific 1641-1850*. Cleveland: Arthur H. Clark Co., 1914.

GOWING, LIONEL F. 5000 *Miles on a Sledge*. London: Chatto & Windus, 1889.

GRAJDANZEV, A. J. "The Trans-Siberian Railway and the Problem of Soviet Supply," *Pacific Affairs*, Vol. XIV, No. 4 (December, 1941), pp. 389-415.

GRAVES, WILLIAM S. *America's Siberian Adventure 1918-1920*. New York: Jonathan Cape & Harrison Smith, 1931.

[*Great Way, The*] *See Veliki put — Vidy sibiri i yeya zheleznykh dorog*.

GREELY, A. W. "The Siberian Transcontinental Railroad," *National Geographic Magazine*, Vol. 8, No. 4 (April, 1897), pp. 121-124.

———, MAJOR GENERAL A. W. "The Land of Promise," *ibid.*, Vol. XXIII, No. 11 (November, 1912), pp. 1078-1090.

[GREENER, WILLIAM OLIVER] *See* GERRARE, WIRT.

GREY, IAN. *Peter the Great*. Philadelphia: J. B. Lippincott Co., 1960.

GRIBAYEDOFF, VALERIAN. "The Great Trans-Siberian Railway," *Cosmopolitan Magazine*, Vol. XIV (March, 1893), pp. 559-565.

GRONDIJS, LUDOVIC H. *La Guerre en Russie et en Sibérie*. Avant-propos de MAURICE PALÉOLOGUE; Préface de ÉMILE HAUMANT. Paris: Éditions Bossard, 1922.

Guide to the Great Siberian Railway. Edited by A. I. DMÍTRIEV-MÁMONOV and A. F. ZDZIÁRSKI, Railway Engineer. English translation by MISS L. KÚKOL-YASNOPÔLSKY, revised by JOHN MARSHALL. St. Petersburg: Ministry of Ways of Communication, 1900.

GUNTHER, JOHN. *Inside Asia* (Thirteenth edition). New York: Harper & Bros., 1939.

——— *Inside Russia Today*. New York: Harper & Bros., 1958.

HALPERN, ADA. *Conducted Tour — Soviet Style*. London: Sheed & Ward, Ltd., 1945.

HAMM, WALTER C. "Great Engineering Projects," *Cosmopolitan Magazine*, Vol. XXVIII (December, 1899), pp. 163-170.

Handbook for Travellers in Russia, Poland, and Finland; Including the Crimea, Caucasus, Siberia, and Central Asia. London: John Murray, 1893.

Handbook of Siberia and Arctic Russia, A. Vol. I. Compiled by the Geographical Section of the Naval Intelligence Section, Naval Staff, Admiralty. London: His Majesty's Stationery Office, 1920 [?].

HANDY, ISAAC O. "Some Notes on the Erection of the Baikal Railway Steamers," *Transactions of the North-East Coast Institution of Engineers and Ship-Builders*, Vol. 26, 26th Session, 1909-1910. Newcastle-upon-Tyne & London: Andrew Reid & Co., Ltd., 1910.

HAVILAND, MAUD D. *A Summer on the Yenesei (1914)*. London: Edward Arnold, 1915.

HERLING, ALBERT KONRAD. *The Soviet Slave Empire*. New York: Wilfred Funk, Inc., 1951.

HERLING, GUSTAV. *A World Apart.* Translated by JOSEPH MAREK. New York: Roy Publishers, 1951.

HERZEN, ALEXANDER. *My Exile in Siberia.* 2 vols. London: Hurst & Blackett, 1855.

HILL, EBENEZER J. "A Trip Through Siberia," *National Geographic Magazine,* Vol. XIII (February, 1902), pp. 37-54.

HILL, S. S. *Travels in Siberia.* 2 vols. London: Longman, Brown, Green, and Longmans, 1854.

HINDUS, MAURICE. *House Without a Roof.* Garden City: Doubleday & Co., Inc., 1961.

HODGKINS, JORDAN A. *Soviet Power: Energy Resources, Production and Potentials.* Englewood Cliffs, N. J.: Prentice-Hall, Inc., 1961.

HOLMES, E. BURTON. *Burton Holmes Travelogues.* 10 vols. "The Trans-Siberian Railway," Vol. VIII, pp. 227-236. "Down the Amur," Vol. IX, pp. 5-112; *ibid.,* "Peking," pp. 115-224; *ibid.,* "The Forbidden City," pp. 227-336. New York: McClure Co., 1908.

HOSIE, ALEXANDER. *Manchuria.* London: Methuen & Co., 1901.

HOUGH, RICHARD. *The Fleet That Had to Die.* New York: Viking Press, 1958.

HUNTER, HOLLAND. *Soviet Transportation Policy.* Cambridge: Harvard University Press, 1957.

——— "Soviet railroads Since 1940," *Bulletin on Soviet Economic Development,* Series 1, No. 4 (September, 1950), pp. 8-20, 33. Birmingham, England: Department of Economics and Institutions of the U.S.S.R., Faculty of Commerce, The University, Edgbaston.

——— "Soviet Railroads in World War II," *National Defense Transportation Journal,* Vol. 11, No. 5 (September-October, 1955) pp. 52-58.

HUPPERT, HUGO. *Men of Siberia.* Translated by H. G. SCOTT. Moscow-Leningrad: Cooperative Publishing Society of Foreign Workers in the U.S.S.R., n.d.

Illustrated Guide for the Use of Passengers to the Far East by the Trans-Siberian Railway. London: International Sleeping Car Co., 1911.

Industries of Russia, The. "Siberia and the Great Siberian Railway," Vol. V. Editor of English translation JOHN MARTIN CRAWFORD. St. Petersburg: Department of Trade and Manufactures, Ministry of Finance [Russia] for the World's Columbian Exposition at Chicago, 1893.

INNIS, HAROLD A. *A History of the Canadian Pacific Railway.* London: P. S. King & Son, Ltd., 1923.

Irkutsk, A Short Guide. Moscow: Foreign Languages Publishing House, 1958.

Istoricheski ocherk razvitiya zheleznykh dorog v Rossii s ikh osnovaniya po 1897 g. vklyuchitelno [Historical Outline of the Development of the Railroads in Russia from Their Beginning through 1897 Inclusive]. Second edition. St. Petersburg: Ministry of Ways of Communication, 1899.

IVANOV, VSEVOLOD. *The Trans-Siberian Express.* Moscow: Intourist, [193-?].

JACKSON, WILLIAM HENRY. *Time Exposure.* New York: G. P. Putnam's Sons, 1940.

JEFFERSON, ROBERT L. *Awheel to Moscow and Back.* London: Sampson Low, Marston & Co., Ltd., 1895.

——— *Roughing It in Siberia.* London: Sampson Low, Marston & Co., 1897.

JOHNSON, ALFRED S. "The Trans-Siberian Railway," *The Technical World* (Chicago), Vol. I, No. 2 (April, 1904), pp. 125-134.

JOHNSON, HENRY. *The Life and Voyages of Joseph Wiggins . . .* New York: E. P. Dutton & Co., 1907.

JOHNSON, ROBERT UNDERWOOD. *Remembered Yesterdays.* Boston: Little, Brown and Co., 1923.

Johnson's Universal Cyclopedia (New edition). 8 vols. New York: D. Appleton & Co.–A. J. Johnson Co., 1895.

KAREISHA, SERGE. *Methods of Dealing With Snow on Russian Railways.* St. Petersburg: Ministry of Ways of Communication, 1904.

KAUS, GINA. *Catherine: The Portrait of an Empress.* New York: Viking Press, 1935.

KENNAN, GEORGE. *Tent Life in Siberia* (Revised edition). New York: G. P. Putnam's Sons, 1910.

——— *Siberia and the Exile System.* 2 vols. New York: Century Co., 1891.

——— *E. H. Harriman's Far Eastern Plans.* Garden City: Country Life Press, 1917.

——— "The Last Appeal of the Russian Liberals," *The Century Magazine,* Vol. XXXV, No. 1 (November, 1887), pp. 50-63; "Prison Life of the Russian Revolutionists," *ibid.,* No. 2 (December, 1887), pp. 285-297; "Russian Provincial Prisons," *ibid.,* No. 3 (January, 1888), pp. 397-406; "A Russian Political Prison," *ibid.,* No. 4 (February, 1888), pp. 521-530; "Russian State Prisoners," *ibid.,* No. 5 (March, 1888), pp. 755-766; "The Russian Penal Code," *ibid.,* No. 6 (April, 1888), pp. 880-886.

KENNAN, GEORGE F. *Soviet-American Relations, 1917-1920,* Vol. I, *Russia Leaves the War.* Princeton: Princeton University Press, 1956. Vol. II, *The Decision to Intervene.* Princeton: Princeton University Press, 1958.

——— *Russia and the West under Lenin and Stalin.* Boston: Little, Brown and Co., 1961.

KENT, PERCY HORACE. *Railway Enterprise in China.* London: Edward Arnold, 1907.

KERNER, ROBERT J. *The Urge to the Sea.* Berkeley & Los Angeles: University of California Press, 1942.

KINLOCH, ALEXANDER. "Trade and the Siberian Railway," *The Monthly Review* (London), Vol. II, No. 6 (March, 1901), pp. 60-71.

Kitaiskaya vostochnaya zheleznaya doroga. Istoricheski ocherk [The Chinese Eastern Railroad. An Historical Outline]. Vol. I (1896-

1905). Compiled by the Chancellery of the Board of the Chinese Eastern Railroad Company. St. Petersburg, 1914.

KITCHIN, GEORGE. *Prisoner of the OGPU*. New York: Longmans, Green & Co., 1935.

KNOX, THOMAS W. *Overland Through Asia*. Hartford: American Publishing Co., 1870.

——— *The Boy Travellers in the Russian Empire*. New York: Harper & Bros., 1887.

——— "To and Upon the Amoor River," *Harper's New Monthly Magazine*, Vol. XXXVII, No. 219 (August, 1868), pp. 289-306; "Traveling in Siberia," *ibid.*, No. 220 (September, 1868), pp. 449-466.

KOULOMZINE, A. N. DE. *Le Transsibérien*. Translated by JULES LEGRAS. Paris: Hachette et Cie., 1904.

KRAVCHENKO, VICTOR. *I Chose Freedom: The Personal and Political Life of a Soviet Official*. New York: Charles Scribner's Sons, 1946.

KROPOTKIN, P. *Memoirs of a Revolutionist*. Boston & New York: Houghton, Mifflin & Co., 1899.

——— "The Great Siberian Railway," *The Geographical Journal* (London), Vol. V, No. 2 (February, 1895), pp. 146-154.

KRYPTON, CONSTANTINE (pseudonym). *The Northern Sea Route*. New York: Research Program on the U.S.S.R., 1953.

[KULOMZIN, A. N.] *See* KOULOMZINE, A. N. DE.

LABBÉ, PAUL. "Les Progrès du Transsibérien," *Bulletin de la Société de Géographie Commerciale de Paris*, Tome XXXII, No. 10 (October, 1910), pp. 648-655.

LABOULAYE, EDOUARD DE. *Les Chemins de Fer de Chine*. Paris: Émile Larose, 1911.

LANE, FERDINAND C. *The World's Great Lakes*. Garden City: Doubleday & Co., Inc., 1948.

LANSDELL, HENRY. *Through Siberia*. 2 vols. Boston: Houghton, Mifflin & Co., 1882.

LANTZEFF, GEORGE V. *Siberia in the Seventeenth Century: A Study of the Colonial Administration*. "University of California Publications in History," Vol. 30. Berkeley & Los Angeles: University of California Press, 1943.

LATTIMORE, OWEN. "New Road to Asia," *National Geographic Magazine*, Vol. LXXXVI, No. 6 (December, 1944), pp. 641-676.

LAUT, AGNES C. *The Romance of the Rails*. New York: Tudor Publishing Co., 1936.

LAUTERBACH, RICHARD E. *Through Russia's Back Door*. New York: Harper & Bros., 1944.

LEE, MRS. JOHN CLARENCE. *Across Siberia Alone: An American Woman's Adventures*. New York & London: John Lane & Co., 1914.

LEGGET, R. F. "Permafrost Research," *Arctic Research*, Vol. 7, Nos. 3 and 4 (December, 1955), pp. 153-158. Reprinted as NRC 3787, National Research Council, Division of Building Research, Ottawa.

LEGRAS, JULES. *En Sibérie*. Paris: Armand Colin et Cie., 1899.

LENGYEL, EMIL. *Siberia*. New York: Random House, 1943.

LENIN, V. I. *Collected Works.* "Concerning the State Budget," Vol. V, pp. 331-336. Moscow: Foreign Languages Publishing House, 1961.

LENSEN, GEORGE ALEXANDER. *The Russian Push Toward Japan.* Princeton: Princeton University Press, 1959.

LE RICHE, H. "Quinze Jours dans le Transsibérien," *l'Illustration,* No. 3562 (June 3, 1911), pp. 459-461.

LEROY-BEAULIEU, PIERRE. *The Awakening of the East.* New York: McClure, Phillips & Co., 1900.

——— "La Sibérie et le Transsibérien, Le Pays et ses Habitans," *Revue des Deux Mondes,* Vol. CXLVI (March 15, 1898), pp. 324-358; *ibid.,* Vol. CXLVIII (August 15, 1898), pp. 808-844.

LESSNER, ERWIN. *Cradle of Conquerors: Siberia.* Garden City: Doubleday & Co., Inc., 1955.

Life Pictorial Atlas of the World. Prepared by the Editors of *Life* and Rand McNally. New York: Time, Inc., 1961.

[LI HUNG CHANG] *Memoirs of Li Hung Chang.* Edited by WILLIAM FRANCIS MANNIS. Boston: Houghton Mifflin Co., 1913.

LIN, CHENG. *The Chinese Railways Past and Present.* Shanghai: China United Press, 1937.

LIPPER, ELINOR. *Eleven Years in Soviet Prison Camps.* Translated by RICHARD and CLARA WINSTON. Chicago: Henry Regnery Co., 1951.

LITTLE, MRS. ARCHIBALD. *Li Hung Chang.* London: Cassell & Co., Ltd., 1902.

LITTLEPAGE, JOHN D. and BESS, DEMAREE. *In Search of Soviet Gold.* New York: Harcourt, Brace & Co., 1938.

LOBANOV-ROSTOVSKY, PRINCE A. *Russia and Asia.* New York: Macmillan Co., 1933.

LOCKHART, R. H. BRUCE. *British Agent.* Introduction by HUGH WALPOLE. New York: G. P. Putnam's Sons, 1933.

LODIAN, L. "Review of Progress on the Trans-Siberian," *Railway and Locomotive Engineering,* Vol. XIV (April, 1901), pp. 147-150; *ibid.* (May, 1901), pp. 224-226; *ibid.,* "Trans-Siberian Construction" (November, 1901), pp. 471-473.

LYASHCHENKO, PETER I. *History of the National Economy of Russia to the 1917 Revolution.* New York: Macmillan Co., 1949.

MCCARROLL, W. J. "Russian Railways," *Locomotive Engineering,* Vol. X, No. 2 (February, 1897), pp. 146-150.

MCDONALD, PHILIP BAYAUD. "Perry McDonough Collins, A Generous Benefactor of New York University," Unpublished manuscript, Gould Memorial Library, New York University, n.d.

MACKAY, CORDAY. "The Collins Overland Telegraph," *The British Columbia Historical Quarterly,* Vol. X, No. 3 (July, 1946), pp. 187-215.

MACLEAN, SIR FITZROY. "Trans-Siberian Journey," *The Sunday Times* Colour Section (London), May 6, 1962, pp. 5-13.

MACLEAN, J. M. "The Great Russian Railway Across China," *The Magazine of Commerce* (London), Vol. II, No. 7 (May, 1903), pp. 281-283.

MANNING, CLARENCE A. *The Siberian Fiasco.* New York: Library Publishers, 1952.

MARIE, GRAND DUCHESS OF RUSSIA. *Education of a Princess.* Translation from the French and Russian under the editorial supervision of RUSSELL LORD. New York: Viking Press, 1930.

MARSDEN, KATE. *On Sledge and Horseback to Outcast Siberian Lepers* (Twelfth edition). London: Simpkin, Marshall & Co., 1895.

MARSH, CODY. "Glimpses of Siberia, the Russian 'Wild East,'" *National Geographic Magazine,* Vol. XXXVIII, No. 6 (December, 1920), pp. 513-536.

MEAKIN, ANNETTE M. B. *A Ribbon of Iron.* London: Constable & Co., 1901.

——— *Russia.* Philadelphia: J. B. Lippincott Co., 1906.

MÉTIN, ALBERT. "Le Transsibérien et la Guerre," *Revue Économique Internationale,* Vol. III, No. 2 (October, 1904), pp. 290-313.

MICHIE, ALEXANDER. *The Siberian Overland Route from Peking to Petersburg . . .* London: John Murray, 1864.

MIKHAILOFF, M. "The Great Siberian Railway," *The North American Review,* Vol. CLXX, No. 522 (May, 1900), pp. 593-608.

MIKHAILOFF, NIKOLAI. *Glimpses of the U.S.S.R., Its Economy and Geography.* Translated by RALPH PARKER and VALENTINA SCOTT. Moscow: Foreign Languages Publishing House, 1960.

Minutes of Proceedings of the Institution of Civil Engineers. "Railway round Lake Baikal" (Abstract from *Annalen für Gewerbe und Bauwesen,* Berlin, 15 November, 1904, p. 194), Vol. CLX. London: Published by the Institution, 1905.

MIROV, N. T. *Geography of Russia.* New York & London: John Wiley & Sons, Inc., 1951.

MITCHISON, LOIS. "Trans-Siberian, 1956," *The Geographical Magazine* (London), Vol. XXIX, No. 9 (January, 1957), pp. 451-459.

Modern Transport. "Electrification of Trans-Siberian Railway," Vol. LXXX, No. 2062 (October 4, 1958), p. 1.

MOORE, FREDERICK F. *Siberia To-Day.* New York: D. Appleton & Co., 1919.

MOORE, HARRIET L. *Soviet Far Eastern Policy 1931-1945.* Princeton: Princeton University Press, 1945.

MOWRER, LILIAN T. *Arrest and Exile: The True Story of an American Woman in Poland and Siberia, 1940-41.* New York: Wm. Morrow & Co., Inc., 1941.

MORPHY, COUNTESS. *Recipes of All Nations.* New York: Wise & Co., 1935.

MULLER, G. F. and PALLAS, PETER SIMON. *Conquest of Siberia . . .* Translated from the Russian of G. F. MULLER and of PETER SIMON PALLAS, M.D., F.R.S. London: Smith, Elder & Co. Cornhill, 1842.

NAGRODSKI, V. A. "General Presentation of the Present Condition of the Railway System in Russia," *Transactions of the International Engineering Congress, 1915,* Vol. IV, pp. 170-184. San Francisco, 1916.

NANSEN, FRIDTJOF. *Through Siberia, the Land of the Future.* Translated by ARTHUR G. CHATER. London: William Heinemann, 1914.

National Geographic Atlas of the World. Editor-in-Chief MELVILLE BELL GROSVENOR; Chief Cartographer JAMES M. DARLEY. Washington: National Geographic Society, 1963.

New York Herald, The (European Edition). "Across Siberia in a Modern 'Train de Luxe,'" 66th Year, No. 160 (Paris, June 9, 1901), Third Section, p. 1.

NICHOLSON, T. R. *Adventurer's Road.* New York: Rinehart & Co., Inc., 1958.

NOLDE, BORIS. *La Formation de l'Empire Russe.* 2 vols. Vol. I. Paris; Institut d'Études Slaves, 1952.

NOMAD, MAX. *Apostles of Revolution* (Revised edition). New York: Collier Books, 1961.

NORDENSKIÖLD, A. E. *The Voyage of the Vega Round Asia and Europe, With a Historical Review of Previous Journeys Along the North Coast of the Old World.* Translated by ALEXANDER LESLIE. New York: Macmillan & Co., 1882.

NORMAN, HENRY, M.P. *All the Russias.* New York: Charles Scribner's Sons, 1902.

North Manchuria and the Chinese Eastern Railway. Harbin: C. E. R. Printing Office, 1924.

Oil and Gas Journal, The, Vol. 61, No. 52 (December 30, 1963), pp. 102-103; *ibid.,* Vol. 62, No. 4 (January 27, 1964), p. 157.

OLENĪN, ALEKSEI NIKOLAYEVICH. *Piśmo o portrete Yermaka, zavoyevatelya Sibiri* [Letter on a Portrait of Yermak, Conqueror of Siberia]. St. Petersburg, 1821.

ORR, CHARLES A. *Stalin's Slave Camps: An Indictment of Modern Slavery.* Boston: Beacon Press, 1952.

OSSENDOWSKI, FERDINAND (in collaboration with LEWIS STANTON PALEN). *Man and Mystery in Asia.* New York: E. P. Dutton & Co., 1924.

OUKHTOMSKY, PRINCE E. E. *Voyage en Orient de son Altesse Impériale le Césarevitch.* Traduction de LOUIS LEGER. Paris: Librairie Charles Delagrave, 1893.

[PALLAS, PETER SIMON] *See* MULLER, G. F. and PALLAS, PETER SIMON.

PARES, BERNARD. *The Fall of the Russian Monarchy.* London: Jonathan Cape, 1939.

——— *A History of Russia* (Fifth edition). New York: Alfred A. Knopf, 1947.

[PARIS UNIVERSAL EXPOSITION, 1900] *Catalogue Général de la Section Russe,* "Commission Impériale de Russie à l'Exposition Universelle de 1900." Paris: Imprimerie Paul Dupont, 1900.

——— *Exposition Illustrée.* Paris: Librairie Montgredien & Cie., 1900.

——— *The Great Siberian Railway* (*Universal Exhibition of 1900 in Paris*). Edited by the Chancery of the Committee of Ministers. St. Petersburg: Government Printing Office, 1900.

——— *Paris Exposition Reproduced from the Original Photographs.* Akron: R. S. Peale Co., 1900.

PARRY, ALBERT. *Whistler's Father.* Indianapolis & New York: Bobbs-Merrill Co., 1939.

——— "Cassius Clay's Glimpse into the Future," *The Russian Review,* Vol. II, No. 2 (Spring, 1943), pp. 52-67.

PASTERNAK, BORIS. *Doctor Zhivago.* New York: Pantheon Books, Inc., 1958.

PASVOLSKY, LEO. *Russia in the Far East.* New York: Macmillan Co., 1922.

PATALEYEV, A. V. *Istoriya stroitelstva velikogo sibirskogo zheleznodorozhnogo puti* [History of the Construction of the Great Siberian Railway]. Khabarovsk: Local Department of the All-Union Society Dealing With Distribution of Political and Scientific Knowledge, 1951.

PAVLOV, YURY and KHRAKOVSKY, YEFIM. "The Trans-Siberian Railway of the U.S.S.R.," *Railway Gazette,* Vol. 116, No. 14 (April 6, 1962), p. 398.

PENROSE, R. A. F., JR. *The Last Stand of the Old Siberia.* Philadelphia: William F. Fell Co., 1922.

PHILLIPS, G. D. R. *Dawn in Siberia: The Mongols of Lake Baikal.* London: Frederick Muller, Ltd., 1942.

PIHLAINEN, J. A. "Permafrost and Buildings," Better Building Bulletin No. 5 (September, 1955), 27 pp. National Research Council, Division of Building Research, Ottawa.

——— "Pile Construction in Permafrost," Proceedings of the American Society of Civil Engineers, *Journal of the Soil Mechanics and Foundations Division,* Vol. 85, No. SM6, Part 1 (December, 1959), pp. 75-95. Reprinted as NRC 5515, National Research Council, Division of Building Research, Ottawa.

Police State Methods in the Soviet Union. Prepared by the International Commission Against Concentrationist Regimes, under the direction of David Rousset. Translated by CHARLES R. JOY. Boston: Beacon Press, 1953.

PRICE, JULIUS M. *From the Arctic Ocean to the Yellow Sea.* New York: Charles Scribner's Sons, 1892.

PRICE, M. P. *Siberia.* London: Methuen & Co., Ltd., 1912.

PRICE, WILLARD. "Japan Faces Russia in Manchuria," *National Geographic Magazine,* Vol. LXXXII, No. 5 (November, 1942), pp. 603-634.

PUMPELLY, RAPHAEL. *Across America and Asia.* New York: Leypoldt & Holt, 1870.

Questions Diplomatiques et Coloniales. Revue de Politique Extérieure. "L'État Actuel du Chemin de Fer Transsibérien," Tome I (May 1, 1897), pp. 285-288.

R——, BARON (Andreas Rosen). *Russian Conspirators in Siberia.* Translated by EVELYN ST. JOHN MILDMAY. London: Smith, Elder & Co., 1872.

RADO, A. (Compiler). *Guide Book to the Soviet Union.* New York: International Publishing Co., 1928.

Railroads of the U.S.S.R. Report on the Visit of the United States Railroad Exchange Delegation to the Soviet Union During June, 1960. Washington: Association of American Railroads, 1960.

Railway Age & Northwestern Railroader, The, Vols. XXV through XXVIII (1898-1899).

RALPH, JULIAN. "The Czar's People," *Harper's New Monthly Magazine,* Vol. XCVII, No. 577 (June, 1898), pp. 3-24.

RASKIN, GEORGE S. "Railroads in the U.S.S.R.," *National Defense Transportation Journal,* Vol. 15, No. 2 (March-April, 1959), pp. 41-43.

RAVENSTEIN, E. G. *The Russians on the Amur.* London: Trubner & Co., 1861.

READY, OLIVER G. *Through Siberia and Manchuria by Rail.* London: Chapman & Hall, 1904.

Red Gaols. Anonymous. London: Burns Oates & Washbourne, Ltd., 1935.

Red Paper on Forced Labor, A. U.S. Information Service. Washington: Government Printing Office, 1952.

REID, ARNOT. *From Peking to Petersburg.* London: Edward Arnold, 1899.

——— "The Siberian Railway," *The Living Age,* Vol. CCXIX, No. 2843 (December 31, 1898), pp. 867-873.

REID, JAMES D. *The Telegraph in America.* New York: Derby Bros., 1879.

REID, WILLIAM JAMESON. "The Great Trans-Siberian Railway," *The National Magazine,* Vol. IX, No. 2 (November, 1898), pp. 154-160.

Report on Railways of U.S.S.R. 1930. Vol. 1, Record Group 219, Office of Defense Transportation Advisory Committee, Council of National Defense. Washington: National Archives and Records Service microfilm, 1964.

Report of the Ad Hoc Committee on Forced Labor. Geneva: International Labor Office, 1953.

RONALDSHAY, THE EARL OF. *On the Outskirts of Empire in Asia.* Edinburgh & London: William Blackwood & Sons, 1904.

ROSTOW, W. W., in collaboration with ALFRED LEVIN, and with the assistance of others at the Center for International Studies, Massachusetts Intitute of Technology. *The Dynamics of Soviet Society.* New York: W. W. Norton & Co., Inc., 1953.

Royal Engineers Journal, The. "The Siberian Railway at the Opening of the Russo-Japanese War" (Reprint of article in *Kriegstechnische Zeitung*), Vol. I (January-June, 1905), pp. 209-213.

RUDOI, Y. and LAZARENKO, T. *Soviet Seven-Year Plan: Transport and Communication 1959-1965.* Translated by XENIA DANKO; edited by DAVID MYSHNE. Moscow: Foreign Languages Publishing House, n.d.

Russki biograficheski slovar [Russian Biographical Dictionary]. 25 vols. St. Petersburg (–Petrograd) & Moscow: Imperatorskoye Russkoye

Istoricheskoye Obshchestvo [Imperial Russian Historical Society], 1896-1918.

SALISBURY, HARRISON E. *To Moscow — and Beyond.* New York: Harper & Bros., 1960.

SCHUMAN, FREDERICK L. *Soviet Politics at Home and Abroad.* New York: Alfred A. Knopf, Inc., 1946.

SCHWARTZ, HARRY. *Russia's Soviet Economy* (Second edition with appendix). New York: Prentice-Hall, Inc., 1960.

——— *The Red Phoenix: Russia Since World War II.* New York: Frederick A. Praeger, 1961.

——— *Tsars, Mandarins, and Commissars: A History of Chinese-Russian Relations.* Philadelphia: J. B. Lippincott Co., 1964.

SCOTT, JOHN. " 'Magnetic City,' Core of Valiant Russia's Industrial Might," *National Geographic Magazine*, Vol. LXXXIII, No. 5 (May, 1943), pp. 525-556.

——— *Behind the Urals.* London: Secker & Warburg, Ltd., 1943.

Secret Letters of the Last Tsar, The. Edited by EDWARD J. BING. New York & Toronto: Longmans, Green & Co., 1938.

SEEBOHM, HENRY. *Siberia in Asia: A Visit to the Valley of the Yenesay in East Siberia.* London: John Murray, 1882.

SEMYONOV, YURI. *The Conquest of Siberia.* Translated by E. W. DICKES. London: George Routledge & Sons, Ltd., 1944.

——— *Siberia: Its Conquest and Development.* Translated by J. R. FOSTER. London: Hollis & Carter, 1963.

SENN, NICHOLAS. *Around the World Via Siberia.* Chicago: Conkey & Co., 1902.

72 Years of C.P.R. Progress (October 21, 1880 to December 31, 1952). Privately printed by Canadian Pacific, n.d.

SHABAD, THEODORE. *Geography of the USSR.* New York: Columbia University Press, 1951.

SHIMKIN, DEMETRI B. *Minerals: A Key to Soviet Power.* Cambridge: Harvard University Press, 1953.

SHINJO, HIROSHI. *History of the Yen — 100 Years of Japanese Money-Economy.* Kobe, Japan: The Research Institute for Economics & Business Administration, Kobe University, 1962.

SHOEMAKER, MICHAEL MYERS. *The Great Siberian Railway from St. Petersburg to Pekin.* New York & London: G. P. Putnam's Sons, 1903.

Sibir pod vliyaniyem relsovago puti [Siberia Under the Influence of the Railway]. St. Petersburg: Ministry of Finance, 1902.

SIMPICH, FREDERICK. "Manchuria, Promised Land of Asia," *National Geographic Magazine*, Vol. LVI, No. 4 (October, 1929), pp. 379-428.

SIMPSON, JAMES YOUNG. *Side-Lights on Siberia.* Edinburgh & London: William Blackwood & Sons, 1898.

——— "The Great Siberian Iron Road," *Blackwood's Edinburgh Magazine*, Vol. CLXI, No. 975 (January, 1897), pp. 2-19.

SISOYEV, V. *The Taiga.* Translated by V. SHNEERSON. Moscow: Foreign Languages Publishing House, 1958.

SOKOLSKY, GEORGE E. *The Story of the Chinese Eastern Railway.* Introduction by DR. HU SHIH. Shanghai: North-China Daily News & Herald, Ltd., 1929.

SOWERBY, ARTHUR DE CARLE. *The Naturalist in Manchuria.* Tientsin: Tientsin Press, Ltd., 1923.

SPARKS, JARED. *The Life of John Ledyard, the American Traveller.* Boston: Charles C. Little & James Brown, 1847.

STADLING, J. *Through Siberia.* Edited and with a preface by F. H. H. GUILLEMARD. London: Archibald Constable & Co., Ltd., 1901.

[STAEHLIN VON STORCKSBURG, JAKOB] *Original Anecdotes of Peter the Great Collected from the Conversation of Several Persons of Distinction at Petersburgh and Moscow by Mr. Staehlin, Member of the Imperial Academy at Petersburgh.* London: Printed for J. Murray, 1788.

STAF, KARL. *Yakutia As I Saw It.* Translated by W. PERELMAN. Moscow: Foreign Languages Publishing House, 1958.

STALIN, J. V. *Works.* Vol. 13, July, 1930–January, 1934. "The Tasks of Business Executives," pp. 40-41. Moscow: Foreign Languages Publishing House, 1955.

STANFORD, DOREEN. *Siberian Odyssey.* New York: E. P. Dutton & Co., Inc., 1964.

STARR, JOHN W., JR. *One Hundred Years of American Railroading.* New York: Dodd, Mead & Co., 1928.

STEAD, ARTHUR L. "Russians Travel 'Hard' or 'Soft' on Vast Rail Network," *Illinois Central Magazine,* January, 1953, pp. 6-8.

STEAD, W. T. *Truth About Russia.* London: Cassell & Co., Ltd., 1888.

STEFANSSON, VILHJALMUR. *Northwest to Fortune.* New York: Duell, Sloan & Pearce, 1958.

STEKLOV, V. Y. *Electrification in the U.S.S.R.* Translated by DAVID SKVIRSKY. Moscow: Foreign Languages Publishing House, n.d.

STEWART, GEORGE. *The White Armies of Russia.* New York: Macmillan Co., 1933.

Stolitsa i usadba [Capital and Country-Seat]. No. 55 (April 1, 1916). St. Petersburg.

SUMNER, B. H. *Tsardom and Imperialism in the Far East and Middle East, 1880-1914.* Raleigh Lecture on History, May 7, 1940. London: British Academy, 1940.

———, BENEDICT H. *A Short History of Russia.* New York: Harcourt, Brace & Co., 1947.

TAFT, MARCUS LORENZO. *Strange Siberia Along the Trans-Siberian Railway.* New York: Eaton & Mains; Cincinnati: Jennings & Graham, 1911.

TAYLOR, BAYARD. *Travels in Greece and Russia, with an Excursion to Crete.* New York: G. P. Putnam, 1859.

TCHERNAVIN, VLADIMIR. *I Speak for the Silent Prisoners of the Soviets.* Boston: Hale, Cushman & Flint, Inc., 1935.

Technical Considerations in Designing Foundations in Permafrost (SN 91-60), 64 pp. State Committee of the Council of Ministers

(U.S.S.R.) for Building Problems. Moscow: State Publishing House of Literature on Building, Architecture and Building Materials, 1960. Technical Translation 1033, National Research Council, Division of Building Research, Ottawa.

THIEL, ERICH. *The Soviet Far East.* Translated by ANNELIE and RALPH M. ROOKWOOD. New York: Frederick A. Praeger, 1957.

Time the Weekly Newsmagazine. "Atom Blasts & TV Sets," Vol. LXXVIII, No. 12 (September 22, 1961), pp. 32-41.

TOLMACHOFF, INNOKENTY P. *Siberian Passage.* New Brunswick: Rutgers University Press, 1949.

TOMPKINS, PAULINE. *American-Russian Relations in the Far East.* New York: Macmillan Co., 1949.

TOMPKINS, STUART R. "Witte as Finance Minister," *Slavonic Review* (London), Vol. XI, No. 33 (April, 1933), pp. 590-606.

Trans-Siberian Express, the Fastest and Most Comfortable Route Between Europe and the Far East. New York: American Express Co., 1936.

TREADGOLD, DONALD W. *The Great Siberian Migration.* Princeton: Princeton University Press, 1957.

TROTZKY, LEON. *My Flight from Siberia.* New York: American Library Service, 1925.

TURNER, SAMUEL. *Siberia: A Record of Travel, Climbing, and Exploration.* London: T. Fisher Unwin, 1905.

TVERSKOI, K. N. *The Unified Transport System of the USSR.* "New Soviet Library," No. 10. London: Victor Gollancz, Ltd., 1933.

[UKHTOMSKI, E.] *See* OUKHTOMSKY, PRINCE E. E. ESPER.

U.S. BUREAU OF FOREIGN COMMERCE. "Siberian Railroad Extension in China," by JOHN KAREL [Report dated December 28, 1896], *Consular Reports*, Vol. LIII, No. 197 (February, 1897), pp. 270-274; "Estimates of Siberian Railroad Traffic," by J. C. MONAGHAN [Report dated December 4, 1896], *ibid.*, pp. 274-276; "The Trans-Siberian Railroad," by W. R. HOLLOWAY [Report dated August 24, 1900], *ibid.*, Vol. LXIV, No. 242 (November, 1900), pp. 328-329. Washington: Government Printing Office.

U.S. DEPARTMENT OF COMMERCE. *Handbook of Foreign Currency and Exchange, 1930*, Trade Promotion Series No. 102, pp. 106-107; 152-156. *Ibid., 1936*, Trade Promotion Series No. 164, pp. 117, 203. Washington: Government Printing Office, 1930; 1936.

U.S. MINT. *Annual Report of the Director of the Mint for the Fiscal Year Ended June 30, 1944.* Washington: U.S. Government Printing Office, 1945.

U.S. TREASURY DEPARTMENT, BUREAU OF STATISTICS. "The Russian Empire and the Trans-Siberian Railway," *Monthly Summary of Commerce and Finance of the United States, April, 1899*, No. 10, Series 1898-1899. Washington: Government Printing Office, 1899.

UVACHAN V. *Peoples of the Soviet North.* Translated by FAINNA SOLASKO. Moscow: Foreign Languages Publishing House, 1960.

VALLÉE, LÉON. "La Sibérie et le grand Transsibérien," *Revue de Géographie,* Vol. XLVIII (January, 1901), pp. 181-200.

VANDERLIP, WASHINGTON B. *In Search of a Siberian Klondike* (As Narrated by Washington B. Vanderlip the Chief Actor and Herein Set Forth by Homer B. Hulbert). New York: Century Co., 1903.

VAN DER POST, LAURENS. "A View of All the Russias," *Holiday,* Vol. 34, No. 4 (October, 1963), pp. 58-141; 150-157; 160-169; 172.

Veliki put — Vidy sibiri i yeya zheleznykh dorog [The Great Way — Views of Siberia and Its Railroads]. *Vypusk I, ot r. Obi do r. Yeniseya i Tomskaya vetv* [Part I, From the Ob R. to the Yenisei R. and the Tomsk Branch]. Photos by I. P. TOMASHKEVICH. Krasnoyarsk: M. B. Akselrod i K.°, 1899.

VERNE, JULES. *Michel Strogoff.* 2 vols. Paris: Librairie Hachette, 1928.

VICKERS, C. E. "The Siberian Railway in War," *The Royal Engineers Journal,* Vol. II (July-December, 1905), pp. 130-138.

VLADIMIR (pseudonym of Zenone Volpicelli). *Russia on the Pacific and the Siberian Railway.* London: Sampson Low, Marston & Co., Ltd., 1899.

VON LAUE, THEODORE H. *Sergei Witte and the Industrialization of Russia.* New York: Columbia University Press, 1963.

WAHL, O. W. *The Land of the Czar.* London: Chapman & Hall, 1875.

WALLACE, SIR DONALD MACKENZIE. *Russia* (Revised edition). New York: Henry Holt & Co., 1905.

WANG, C. C. (Wang Ching Ch'un). "The Sale of the Chinese Eastern Railway," *Foreign Affairs,* Vol. 12, No. 1 (October, 1933), pp. 57-70.

WEALE, B. L. PUTNAM (pseudonym of Bertram Lenox Simpson). *Manchu and Muscovite.* London: Macmillan & Co., Ltd., 1904.

WELZL, JAN. *Thirty Years in the Golden North.* Translated by PAUL SELVER. New York: Macmillan Co., 1932.

WENYON, CHARLES. *Across Siberia on the Great Post Road.* London: Charles H. Kelly, 1896.

WESTWOOD, J. N. *Soviet Railways Today.* Hampton Court: Ian Allan, Ltd., 1963.

WETTERHOF-ASP, S. DE. *La crise russe — Nicholas II Tel qu'il est.* Paris: Librairie Universelle, 1905 [?].

WHISTLER, GEORGE WASHINGTON. "The Gauge of Russian Railways." Letter to His Excellency, the Count Kleinmichel, n.d.

WHITE, WILLIAM L. *Report on the Russians.* New York: Harcourt, Brace & Co., Inc., 1945.

WILLIAMS, ERNEST W., JR. (with the assistance of George Novak and Holland Hunter). *Freight Transportation in the Soviet Union Including Comparisons with the United States.* National Bureau of Economic Research No. 76, General Series. Princeton: Princeton University Press, 1962.

WILLIAMS, W. A. *American-Russian Relations 1781-1947.* New York: Rinehart & Co., 1952.

WILSON, B. G. and DAY, JOHN R. *Famous Railways of the World.* London: Frederick Muller, Ltd., 1957.

WILSON, HELEN CALISTA and MITCHELL, ELSIE REID. *Vagabonding at Fifty.* New York: Coward-McCann, Inc., 1929.

WILSON, J. TUZO. *One Chinese Moon.* New York: Hill & Wang, 1959.

[WITTE, SERGIUS YU.] *The Memoirs of Count Witte.* Translated and edited by ABRAHAM YARMOLINSKY. London: William Heinemann, 1921.

WOHL, PAUL. "Transport in the Development of Soviet Policy," *Foreign Affairs,* Vol. XXIV, No. 3 (April, 1946), pp. 466-483.

WOLDMAN, ALBERT A. *Lincoln and the Russians.* New York: Collier Books, 1961.

WOLFE, BERTRAM D. *Communist Totalitarianism: Keys to the Soviet System* (Revised edition). Boston: Beacon Press, 1961.

WOLKONSKY, PRINCE SERGE. "The Decembrists," *Thought, A Quarterly of the Sciences and Letters,* Vol. III, No. 2 (September, 1928), pp. 216-239.

WOOD, JUNIUS B. *Incredible Siberia.* New York: Dial Press, 1928.

——— "The Far Eastern Republic," *National Geographic Magazine,* Vol. XLI, No. 6 (June, 1922), pp. 565-592.

WOODS, K. B. and LEGGET, R. F. "Transportation and Economic Potential in the Arctic," *Traffic Quarterly,* October, 1960, pp. 435-458. Reprinted as NRC 5952, National Research Council, Division of Building Research, Ottawa.

WRANGEL, FERDINAND VON. *Narrative of an Expedition to the Polar Sea, in the Years 1820, 1821, 1822 and 1823 . . .* Edited by MAJOR EDWARD SABINE. Translated from G. ENGELHARDT's German translation of the then unpublished Russian manuscript. London: J. Madden & Co., 1840.

WREN, MELVIN C. *The Course of Russian History.* New York: Macmillan Co., 1958.

WRIGHT, GEORGE FREDERICK. *Asiatic Russia.* 2 vols. New York: McClure, Phillips & Co., 1902.

WRIGHT, R. L. and DIGBY, BASSETT. *Through Siberia, an Empire in the Making.* London: Hurst & Blackett, Ltd., 1913.

YACOBSON, SERGIUS. "An Autobiography of Gennadiĭ Vasil'evich Yudin," *The Library of Congress Quarterly Journal of Recent Acquisitions,* Vol. 3, No. 2 (February, 1946), pp. 13-15. Washington: Government Printing Office.

[YUDIN, GENNADIUS I.] U.S. Library of Congress. *Report of the Librarian of Congress and Report of the Superintendent of the Library Building and Grounds for the Fiscal Year Ending June 30, 1907,* pp. 20-24. Washington: Government Printing Office, 1907.

ZABRISKIE, EDWARD H. *American-Russian Rivalry in the Far East.* Philadelphia: University of Pennsylvania Press, 1946.

ZDZIARSKI, A. "The First Section of the Great Siberian Railroad," *The Railroad and Engineering Journal* (New York), Vol. LXIV, No. 6 (June, 1890), pp. 258-261; "The Second Section of the Great Siberian Railroad," *ibid.,* No. 9 (September, 1890), pp. 397-400; "The Beginning of the Great Siberian Railroad," *ibid.,* No. 11 (November,

1890), pp. 503-504; "The Government Surveys for the Great Siberian Railroad," *ibid.*, No. 12 (December, 1890), pp. 555-557; *ibid.*, Vol. LXV, No. 1 (January, 1891), pp. 24-27; *ibid.*, No. 2 (February, 1891), pp. 57-59; *ibid.*, No. 3 (March, 1891), pp. 113-115.

ZENZINOV, VLADIMIR (with the collaboration of ISAAC DON LEVINE). *The Road to Oblivion.* London: Jonathan Cape, 1932.

ZIGEL', F. YU. *Nuclear Explosion Over the Taiga (Study of the Tunguska Meteorite).* Washington: Office of Technical Services, U.S. Department of Commerce, 1962.

ZLOBIN, A. *The Baikal Meridian.* Translated by IVANOV-MUJIEV. Moscow: Foreign Languages Publishing House, n.d.

Included in newspaper and magazine sources consulted by the author are *Izvestia, Moscow News, Pravda, Soviet News, Soviet Union, Soviet World, U.S.S.R., The Times* (London), *The New York Times, The New York Herald Tribune, Scientific American, Railway Review, Railroad Gazette, Railroad Age Gazette, Railway Age, The Railway and Engineering Review.*

Sources of Illustrations

Page

11. Collections of the Library of Congress; photo by W. H. Jackson
12. *Ibid.*
16. Henry Lansdell, *Through Siberia;* Boston: Houghton, Mifflin, 1882
18. *Veliki put* [The Great Way]; Krasnoyarsk, 1899
25. Collections of the Library of Congress
32. E. G. Ravenstein, *The Russians on the Amur;* London: Trubner & Co., 1864
35. The Collection of the Virginia Museum of Fine Arts, Bequest of Lillian Thomas Pratt, 1947
43. Picture Collection of The New York Public Library
48. Collections of the Library of Congress; photo by W. H. Jackson
56. *Ibid.*
57. *Ibid.*
58. *Ibid.*
70. *Guide to the Great Siberian Railway;* St. Petersburg: Ministry of Ways of Communication, 1900
74. Collections of the Library of Congress; photo by W. H. Jackson
75. *Veliki put, op. cit.*
84. Picture Collection of The New York Public Library
89. Henry Norman, *All the Russias;* New York: Charles Scribner's Sons, 1902
96. *Guide to the Great Siberian Railway, op. cit.*
102. *Ibid.*
103. *Veliki put, op. cit.*
104. *(Upper and lower) ibid.*
105. *Ibid.*
108. R. L. Jefferson, *Roughing It in Siberia;* London: Sampson Low, Marston & Co., Ltd., 1897
117. *Veliki put, op. cit.*
125. *Guide to the Great Siberian Railway, op. cit.*
126. Collections of the Library of Congress; photo by W. H. Jackson
127. *Ibid.*
133. *Veliki put, op. cit.*
138. Henry Lansdell, *op. cit.*
139. *Ibid.*
140. J. Y. Simpson, *Side-Lights on Siberia;* London & Edinburgh: Wm. Blackwood & Sons, 1898
141. *Ibid.*
143. Harry de Windt, *From Pekin to Calais by Land* (2nd ed.); London: George Newnes, Ltd., 1904
144. J. Y. Simpson, *op. cit.*
145. The American Museum of Natural History
146. J. F. Fraser, *The Real Siberia;* New York: D. Appleton & Co., 1902
148. *(Left and right) The Century Magazine,* 1888
149. F. E. Clark, *A New Way Around an Old World;* New York & London: Harper & Bros., 1901
151. *The Century Magazine,* 1888
163. Mrs. Eugene Hotchkiss, Highland Park, Ill.
171. *Guide to the Great Siberian Railway, op. cit.*
172. Collections of the Library of Congress; photo by W. H. Jackson
173. *Ibid.*
174. Henry Lansdell, *op. cit.*
176. Collections of the Library of Congress; photo by W. H. Jackson
180. *Guide to the Great Siberian Railway, op. cit.*
181. *Ibid.*
183. Collections of the Library of Congress; photo by W. H. Jackson
186. Henry Landsell, *op. cit.*
195. J. F. Fraser, *op. cit.*
196. Harmon Tupper
198. *Ibid.*
199. *Ibid.*

204. Collections of the Library of Congress; photo by W. H. Jackson
205. Harmon Tupper
208. Collections of the Library of Congress
210. Harry de Windt, *From Paris to New York by Land;* London: George Newnes, Ltd., 1904
213. *Veliki put, op. cit.*
217. Collections of the Library of Congress
226. Vickers-Armstrongs (Shipbuilders), Ltd., Newcastle upon Tyne
229. Wirt Gerrare, *Greater Russia;* New York: Macmillan Co., 1904
241. *Guide to the Great Siberian Railway, op. cit.*
243. The American Museum of Natural History
247. Collections of the Library of Congress
250. *Veliki put, op. cit.*
252. Wirt Gerrare, *op. cit.*
253. F. E. Clark, *op. cit.*
254. *Ibid.;* also Mr. Harold S. Clark, Sagamore Beach, Mass.
255. *Ibid.*
256. *Veliki put, op. cit.*
257. *Ibid.*
258. Wirt Gerrare, *op. cit.*
260. (*Upper and lower*) *Veliki put, op. cit.*
267. *Guide to the Great Siberian Railway, op. cit.*
268. (*Upper and lower*) *ibid.*
270. Mr. Kenneth Snowman, author of *The Art of Carl Fabergé;* London: Faber & Faber, Ltd., 1962, Boston: The Boston Book and Art Shop, 1964
271. *Guide to the Great Siberian Railway, op. cit.*
272. (*Upper and lower*) Compagnie Internationale des Wagons-Lits et des Grands Express Européens, Paris; Thos. Cook & Son, Inc., New York
273. *Ibid.*
277. A. M. B. Meakin, *A Ribbon of Iron;* London: Constable & Co., 1901
291. Harmon Tupper
292. *Ibid.*
293. *Ibid.*
294. *Ibid.*
295. *Ibid.*
301. *Burton Holmes Travelogues;* New York: McClure Co., 1901-1908
307. (*Upper and lower*) Collections of the Library of Congress; photo by W. H. Jackson
309. The American Museum of Natural History
315. F. E. Clark, *op. cit.*
317. Wirt Gerrare, *op. cit.*
318. Collections of the Library of Congress; photo by W. H. Jackson
321. *Kitaiskaya,* etc. [The Chinese Eastern Railroad]; St. Petersburg: Chancellery of the Board of the Chinese Eastern Railroad Co., 1914
353. (*Upper and lower*) R. L. Wright and Bassett Digby, *Through Siberia, an Empire in the Making;* London: Hurst & Blackett, Ltd., 1913
361. Mr. Harold S. Clark, Sagamore Beach, Mass.
374. U.S. Signal Corps, 111-SC-75872, National Archives
376. Henry Baerlein, *The March of the Seventy Thousand;* London: Leonard Parsons, 1926
379. U.S. Signal Corps, 111-SC-75758, National Archives
380. Henry Baerlein, *op. cit.*
381. Ludovic H. Grondijs, *La Guerre en Russie et en Sibérie;* Paris: Éditions Bossard, 1922
401. U.S. Signal Corps, 111-SC-75491, National Archives
423. Harmon Tupper
434. *Ibid.*
435. *Ibid.*
436. (*Upper and lower*) *ibid.*
437. (*Upper, middle, and lower*) *ibid.*
438. *Ibid.*
439. *Ibid.*
442. *Ibid.*
444. Mrs. Wilbur F. Cannon, Bettendorf, Iowa
445. Harmon Tupper
446. *Ibid.*
447. Russian postcard
448. Harmon Tupper
449. (*Upper and lower*) *ibid.*
451. *Ibid.*
452. (*Upper and lower*) *ibid.*
454. (*Upper and lower*) *ibid.*
455. (*Upper and lower*) *ibid.*
457. *Ibid.*
458. *Ibid.*
465. (*Upper and lower*) *ibid.*
466. *Ibid.*
467. *Ibid.*

Index

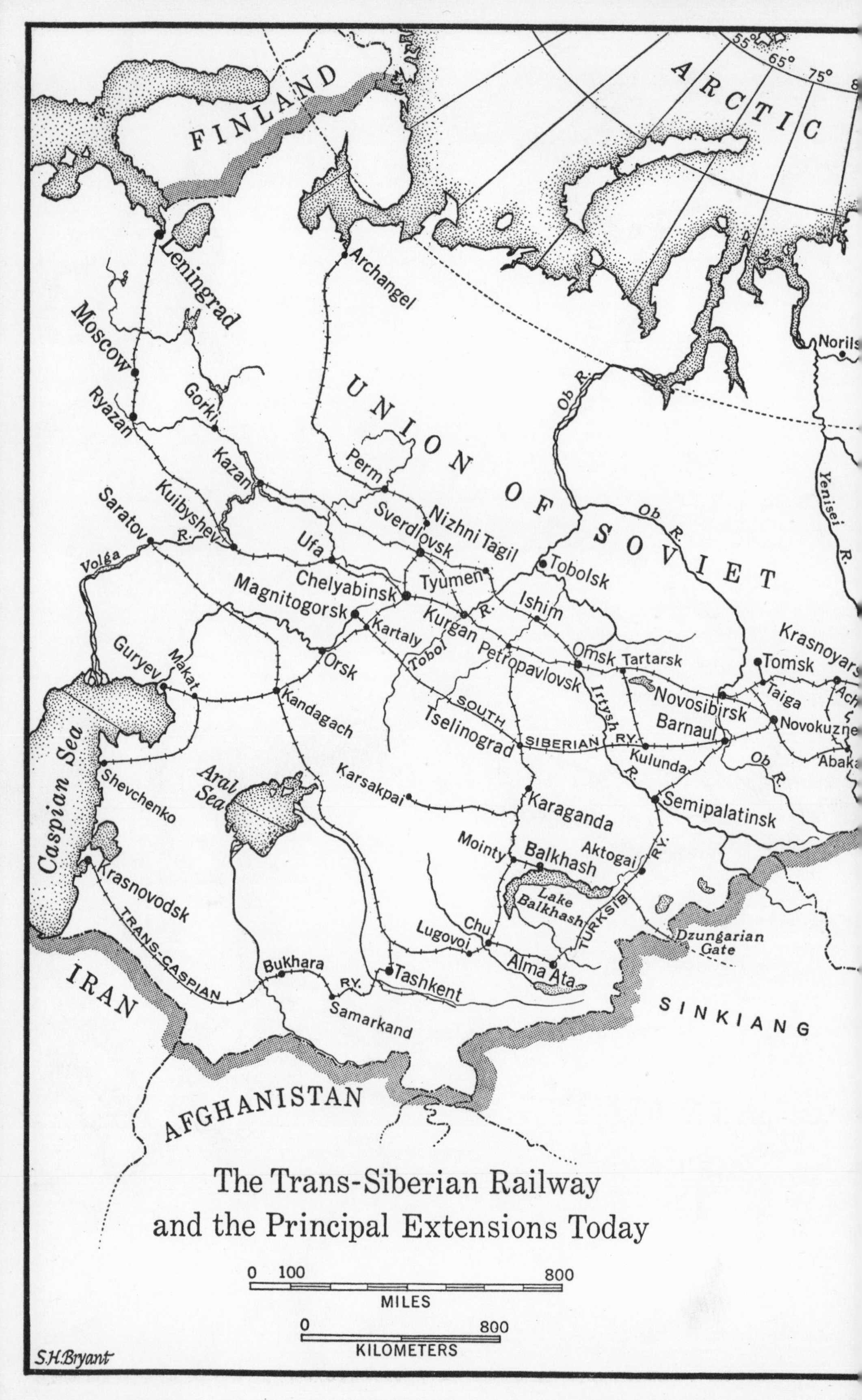

The Trans-Siberian Railway and the Principal Extensions Today